THE ATLANTA CHILD MURDERS

the Night Stalker

JACK MALLARD

ISBN: 1-4392-6337-X
ISBN-13: 9781439263372
Library of Congress Control Number: 2009910937

"Someone needed to write a book on the saga of the most-notorious killing spree in Atlanta's history, but the call was left unanswered for more than a quarter century. The wait was worth it, because the best person to pen the story finally found time in retirement. In his trademark style, Jack "Blood" Mallard, lead prosecutor in the infamous Wayne Williams' murder trial, went for the jugular in his retelling of the drama that kept Atlanta behind locked doors while investigators sought the killer of 28 children and young people ..."

Dink NeSmith, President, Community Newspapers, Inc., Athens, Georgia

———

"No one in Atlanta – or indeed around the world – will ever forget the Missing and Murdered Children's case that froze the City of Atlanta in fear as one victim after another disappeared during a two year span between 1979 - 1981. Now, twenty-five years later, the lead prosecutor, Jack Mallard, brings us the compelling inside story of the successful prosecution of Wayne Williams. Mallard delivers a 'page turner' detailing how he made his case, brought Wayne Williams to justice and brought the Atlanta murders to an end in the balance."

Doc Schneider, Chairman, Mercer University Press

Dedication

Since the trial of Wayne Bertram Williams in 1982, family, friends, acquaintances, fellow-lawyers, media persons, those interested in the Rule of Law, and others have urged me to write an accurate account of the Williams' trial so *the truth will be known.*

To those people I dedicate this book to set the record straight because of the past negative reflections upon the criminal justice system and claims of a few that the jury-trial system did not work for Williams. The many distortions and false claims previously written have motivated me to *get it right.* Thus, I have accessed the trial record and my recollections and notes from having lived the Williams' trial for its duration – and no one can claim knowing it better. Since the doubts of some would not go away, I decided I was the most logical person from within the small group of trial participants to re-live the trial of Williams so the World may read the truth of it. And, it appeared no other person was going to write a book from the files and archives of the jury trial itself.

This has been my primary motivation in writing this book. I would like to believe that the book will be of some guidance to attorneys in conducting themselves in a lengthy, complicated jury trial, and that [it] will better educate the average citizen who may have different views about the criminal justice system.

This book is also dedicated to "Jo" – but for her, there would have been no book!

Jack E. Mallard
Attorney at Law

Table of Contents

PART THREE
The Prosecution

Prologue

A City under Siege

As darkness descends upon the City, so does the serial killer – who prowls the streets looking for his prey: children and young people of the 'street.' Under the vigilant eyes of a Special Task Force – at times numbering over 100 agents – the phantom killer continues his 'cat and mouse' game with the police as the media reports the failures of authorities to protect its citizens while the killings continue for two (2) years and a body count of 30.

The backdrop is a traumatized city frozen in fear; children are afraid to go outside their homes for fear of being grabbed by the "night stalker." But the killings continued! Unusual and unorthodox police methods and tactics were used, including the use of psychics and profilers. One child reportedly said "he won't get me," but he too became a victim.

Will the unusual Y-shaped Wellman 181b fiber and dog hair found on victims' bodies be connected to a suspect?

After two years of death and despair, will the City recover its reputation for greatness?

With police sharp-shooters on the roof of the courthouse, and with eloquent and masterful displays of lawyerly talents in the courtroom involving science, crime scenes, river hydrology, forensics, and expert witnesses, a courtroom drama is played out not seen since the "Scopes Monkey Trial" of 1925. It was called "The Case of the Century."

The 'Splash' Heard Around
the World

The young rookie cop was near the water's edge on the embankment underneath the James Jackson Parkway Bridge over the Chattahoochee River.

It was dark! It was 3:00 a.m., and he had been there since 8:00 p.m. the evening before. He was tired of this boring assignment.

Except for the croaking of a bullfrog or the occasional beaver slithering into the water at river's edge it was quiet. Then, he heard a loud SPLASH!

Upon shining his flashlight in the river, he saw ripples in the water; and, as a former lifeguard, he recognized the sound of the splash as a body hitting the water.

The rookie looked 55 feet above to the concrete/steel bridge spanning the river, saw nothing in the dark, then looked back to the ripples in the water. He looked up again to the bridge. Suddenly, lights came on a vehicle on the bridge. The rookie reached for his police radio as the car moved slowly across the bridge.

The car's driver, a pudgy bespectacled black man, no doubt smiled to himself as if to say I've outsmarted the FBI and cops again as I have for two years. They'll never catch me! Ha, Ha.

In the water, the body was slowly sinking to the bottom of the river. It would stay there for days until the gases build up in the body from decomposition of the internal soft tissues, after which the body would slowly rise to the surface from its watery grave and move downstream with the current. After two days under water, the body of Nathaniel Cater 'popped up' like a balloon and moved along with the surface of the water, traversing from the northern side to the southern side of the river with the current, where it hung up on a tree limb 1.2 miles downstream from where it entered the water.

With the arrest of Wayne Bertram Williams, it happened. The 'mother' of all trials came along – the one in a lifetime – the case of which most lawyers dream of being a part of, a case in which defense attorneys and investigators volunteer their services for the notoriety and exposure through media coverage. I just happened to have been a prosecutor at the right time and place, (or wrong time/place, depending on how viewed) and to be assigned to take the 'lead' role in the preparation and prosecution of the case for the State of Georgia.

No other case comes close to the extent, length, and depth of media attention and coverage – nationally and internationally – as the investigation and prosecution of the "Missing and Murdered Children of Atlanta" episode from 1979 through the arrest in 1981, trial in early 1982, and the following appeals and controversies continuing to the present day. The only other case which comes to mind (as I read about it) in Georgia with some semblance of a 'media-frenzy' was the **Leo Frank** case in 1913.[1]

Americans traveling abroad during the investigation and later trial told me the Missing Children's case was news around the world from England, Europe, and Russia to large and small towns in middle-America, i.e., The Iola Register, Iola, Kansas, circulation about 4000.

At trial, a part-time information officer was budgeted $400 a month for assisting journalists from as far away as Germany and Britain.

An article *"Atlanta: The Evidence of Things Not Seen"* by the (late) noted author James Baldwin was published in 1981 by "Playboy," highlighting that "when a city lives so long in the shadow of terrifying violence, the crime grows greater than the deaths, the victims more numerous than the dead." Baldwin writes: "It's April and I am in St-Paul-de-Vence, France, eating breakfast and reading the American newspapers. I have been following the unprecedent[edly] publicized series of murders in Atlanta and now have an uneasy, unwilling feeling that soon I will almost certainly find myself in that city...."

It was such a case which brought the Vice President of the United States to Atlanta with a grant of $1.5 million and the support of the federal governmental agencies, including the Federal Bureau of Investigation. Psychics, psychologists, and unprecedented investigative tactics were utilized.

---

1   On April 27, 1913, the body of 13-year-old Mary Phagan was found in the basement of the Atlanta, Georgia pencil factory where she was an employee. She had a noose around her neck and had been sexually assaulted. The factory's manager, 29-year-old Leo Frank, was convicted on September 26, 1913, and sentenced to death. Though upheld on appeal to the Supreme Court, Georgia Governor John Slayton commuted the sentence to Life. The Governor was burned in effigy, received death threats, and was eventually forced to leave the state. On August 16, 1915, a group of armed men took Frank from the prison where he was incarcerated, transported him to a place near the victim's home, and there lynched him by hanging him from a tree.

The mysterious disappearance and murder of children, teenagers, and young people over a two year span traumatized the City of Atlanta and its people as it was acknowledged that a serial killer was running amuck.

After trial, *The Atlanta Journal/Constitution* called [it] **"The Case of the Century"** on March 1, 1982.

The *Fulton Daily Report* on February 27, 2002, 20 years after the verdict was announced by the jury – in a front-page headline **"Biggest Trial in World Not Dimmed by Time"** – did a comprehensive follow-up report.

In 2006 (24 years after trial), the *Fulton Daily Report* did something unprecedented in hiring its own independent fiber experts to re-investigate the forensic evidence in the case.

In 2007 (25 years after trial) DNA testing was performed on dog and human hair, and again, the media had a field day. Would it free Williams?

I have seen the bad, the ugly, and the beast! Once, I looked into the eyes of a serial killer, up close – close enough to touch him. I even cross-examined him for two days. It was billed as 'Williams vs. Mallard: a Test of Endurance.'

Was Wayne Williams guilty, or was he a scapegoat and railroaded, as some would later claim? Was Williams the serial killer who roamed Atlanta's streets at night for two years killing his victims under the watchful eyes of a Task Force with a city in lockdown? *And why?*

You be the Judge!

I retired in 2007 after 40 years of prosecuting criminals. I am now doing what people for the past 25 years have suggested I do – write about it!

The truth will be revealed as seen first-hand by the trial jury in *The Missing and Murdered Children of Atlanta and Wayne Bertram Williams case.* Never before has this true story been told by anyone who was directly involved in the day-to-day trial, or from anyone who was willing to look at the actual evidence presented to a jury of Williams' peers. There are some 'doubters' who continue to 'beat the drum' on behalf of Williams' claims that he was railroaded and framed.

As in other high profile cases, no doubt conspiratorial claims will continue in this circumstantial case supported by fiber and hair analysis, but the case has taken many turns and twists over the years since the verdict in 1982. The case still attracts unprecedented media attention.

There are many behind-the-scenes revelations and activities of interest to the reader in a complicated drama-driven criminal trial with teams of lawyers and investigators on each side. The anatomy of a major criminal trial with dozens of expert witnesses and other non-traditional witnesses and forensic trace evidence is fully exposed to view. It is of interest to lawyers and non-lawyers alike.

PART ONE
The Investigation

A Task Force is formed

July 28, 1979 – the beginning: Our roads and byways are littered with our trash; as we commute, we toss our litter – cans, bottles, cups, and trash from cars – upon the streets and into the woods. Area residents at times will collect such debris and help beautify America; others will intentionally look for unusual artifacts or collect cans or metal for the little money they may recover from the sale of such items.

Occasionally, someone will dump a body!

It was a hot, humid, mid-summer day when she was poking through heavy brush in a non-residential wooded area off Niskey Lake Road in southwest Atlanta. The woman was carrying a bag for cans she was collecting; suddenly, upon smelling an unusual odor, she spotted the partial remains of a human body in a clearing. Shocked at the sight, she dropped the bag and ran to a nearby house and called police.

When police responded, the woman pointed out her discovery – a horrific sight not many people ever witness – the partial mummified remains of a young male child. From having been in the woods for some time, it was obvious the body had been dissected and scattered by animals and insects. In the sweltering heat of July in Georgia, the remains of a body will quickly deteriorate and be subject to destruction and scattered by the elements and animals. It was not a pretty sight!

The area was an uphill grade of a two-lane asphalt road. Police and crime scene investigators cordoned off the area and began a methodical inspection and retrieval of what evidentiary matters could be found along with the body.

Investigators spread out some distance and began photographing and documenting evidence and body parts when they suddenly discovered partially rotted clothing in the brush along with *bones of a second victim's body!* Both victims were young black males. Investigator R. J. Eskew determined that one victim was eleven feet two inches from the road over the bank and was dressed in a pair of black pants. The body was face down with flies and eggs in the hair. The body appeared to be in 'fairly good shape.' A leg was caught on a vine holding the body from going further down the embankment (as tossed from above). This case was labeled number 79-1255.

The other body was 17 feet from the edge of the road down the embankment and in a badly decomposed state, especially the upper portions of the body. The victim was wearing black pants with the pockets turned out and a pair of slip-on type shoes. This case would be labeled number 79-1256.

Neither body had any identification!

Finding two bodies of small, unidentified male children so close together caused more consternation. The apparent dumping of two bodies in the same wooded area caused investigators to question the significance of such find. Was it mere coincidence or a 'dumping ground'? Were there more bodies, not yet found?

Routinely, investigators photographed and bagged the remains for removal to the morgue for further evaluation and autopsy. Investigators for the Medical Examiner in such cases where identity is unknown will immediately proceed to identify the remains using all haste – some mother is out there wondering where her child is at this moment. Reviewing missing persons' reports is a valuable source in obtaining leads to such identification. While adults might be expected to carry identification on them, children normally would not. The putrefied bodies found under such circumstances may not contain sufficient means of identification through the normal procedures: Photographs, physical appearance, or fingerprints.

At the medical examiner's office, Dr. John Feegel delayed the autopsies for three days pending an attempt to identify the bodies. He then proceeded with the examination, noting in case number 79-1256:

"While most of the bony material remains intact, a single small caliber gunshot wound is noted penetrating but appears to be rib 3 or 4 in the upper left back region." No bullet was found. Several of the teeth were missing. The mandible was brought in separate and examined – several teeth were absent. X-rays were made of the maxilla and mandible. No other injuries were noted! The cause of death was found to be by a gunshot wound of the chest.

After reviewing reports for missing children, on August 8, 1979, Investigator John Cameron transported the mother and grandmother to the Crime Laboratory and with Micro-analyst Larry Peterson present, Mrs. Almond, the victim's mother, identified the black trousers and a pair of black shoes with red "41" (from a sealed bag marked "UID-79-1256) on them as belonging to her son, **Edward H. Smith, age 14.** No dental records could be located for comparison. Mrs. Almond later called the Medical Examiner's office and accepted the clothing identification as her son. She wished for his body to be released to the funeral home. Edward was last seen at a skating rink in Southwest Atlanta near his home on July 20, 1979, eight days before he was found.

Autopsy of the victim number 79-1255 was conducted. He was wearing black pants with a black belt and white jockey-type undershorts – no shoes, socks, or shirt – with no labels in any of the garments. The external examination showed "ant-bite marks" on the upper extremities, but the lower parts were free of similar injuries – having been protected by the trousers apparently. Initial cause of death was undetermined, but was later found to have been from probable asphyxia due to strangulation. An extensive amount of dental work was noted, and a dental chart was made for possible identification should dental records be located. The body was not identified until October, 1980, when his dental records were matched to **Alfred James Evans, age 13,** who was last seen at East Lake Meadows, a public housing project, waiting to catch a bus. He was en-route to a theater on Peachtree Street. He never returned! Alfred did odd jobs including sacking groceries in stores for spending money.

As the sweltering heat of summer passed, the mother of 14 year old **Milton Harvey age 14** reported him missing on September 4, 1979, after she had sent him on an errand by bicycle. He never returned!

Milton's photograph and clothing description were furnished to police for circulation. His badly decomposed body was discovered 57 days later on November 5, 1979, in the area of Desert Drive and Redwine Road at I-285 in East Point. Children, playing in the woods off a gravel road discovered a ten-speed bicycle down an embankment some few feet from the road – then to their amazement, they saw a human skull!

Police responded, finding skeletal remains of a small male child protruding out of the trouser legs and shirt. The hands and feet were missing, likely by animals. After the scene investigation, the body was removed to the Fulton County morgue where Dr. James Metcalfe performed an autopsy on the body. The body was noted as being almost completely skeletonized and dressed in blue cut-off jeans, size 12, and white underpants. The initial cause of death was undetermined due to the lapse of time and condition of the body, with manner of death "probable homicide." No dental restorations were present. Identification was later determined by the clothing on the body.

Subsequently, Harvey would later be number three (Smith and Evans would be one and two, respectively) on the *Missing and Murdered Task Force List.*

Atlanta's Missing Persons Unit began working closely with the East Point Police Department because Milton Harvey's body was found within the City of East Point.

On Sunday, October 21, 1979, nine-year-old **Yusef Bell** went to a neighborhood grocery to purchase snuff for a lady. He never returned! Eighteen days later on November 8, 1979, his body was discovered at the (abandoned) E. P. Johnson Elementary School on Fulton and Martin Streets. A man, passing through the abandoned school which was marked by decay and overgrowth of vegetation, discovered a horrible sight and smell. In puttering through the building, he noted the putrid odor in the air. In following the smell to an uncovered crawl space in the floor, he saw the body – a young black child. The man hurried out and found a phone to call police.

Police and investigators combed through the scene for clues. The body was lying on its back, with the right hand on the abdomen area at the waist-band of his pants and with the left arm extended alongside the body. The floor was covered with what appeared to be pieces of plaster and dust. There were no drag marks around the area, and the bottoms of the victim's feet were clean. The hole in the crawl space was 33 inches by 40 inches, and the temperature of the crawl space was very cool.

A missing persons' officer identified the body as Yusef Bell who had been missing since 4:45 p.m. on October 21 from a report on file. His body was recovered about one mile from his home wearing the same recognizable brown denim shorts. The weather in October was nothing like the searing 90s in July when the parched bodies of the first boys were located in the woods.

Dr. Metcalfe declared the death a homicide due to asphyxia from manual strangulation, describing the injuries to the neck and head areas with bruising to the arms and thighs.

With Yusef's death there was a rallying cry from the parents of the victims, who were coming together in their sorrow and anger. Angry accusations were made that the City Administration didn't care what was happening to their black children. The City leaders promised a full investigation. Yusef Bell's mother, Camille, was not satisfied.

Atlanta's children, all black of the inner city, were being discovered dead after mysteriously disappearing without explanation or cause. "What are the police doing" asks Camille Bell, the mother of Yusef Bell?

The killer no doubt was reading and listening to the pulse of the public demanding the capture of the maniac who was killing Atlanta's children – but he would continue!

Atlanta has the claim of being "The City Too Busy to Hate" *but, is there someone hating Atlanta's children?* Atlanta has the "World's Busiest Airport" and homes of 'Coke,' Delta, Home Depot, UPS, and CNN. Atlanta is, and was, a vibrant, progressive city and the home-place of Dr. Martin Luther King, Jr.'s family, as well as the epicenter of the civil rights movement.

During the 1970s and 1980s, Atlanta was fast becoming a financial and economic powerhouse of the nation with tremendous growth in population at a time when people were moving south for jobs. At the same time it was fast becoming a city of majority black population, including leadership positions with the election of Maynard Jackson as Mayor and Dr. Lee P. Brown as Public Safety Commissioner. But with all the progress comes a criminal element to inflict stains upon the good things happening.

There have always been murders in Atlanta as in other large cities. Almost always, there are reasons (motives) for them individually – which allows a quick 'clear-up' with arrests. The circumstances under which these children disappeared and were found dead were especially intriguing to police and to the victims' families. Normally, motives for murder include a wide range of domestic killings, where identity of the victim and perpetrator is quickly determined and where – more than likely – the bodies are found at the scene of the crimes; other homicides may be associated with rape, burglary, robbery, murder for hire, and drive-by shootings – but none such motives appear here. These victims had nothing to steal – but their lives. They were not discovered at home, work, hospitals, or the usual places where people die; they had no means of transportation except bicycles, walking, hitchhiking, bus, etc. They were usually last seen on the street or leaving a location. The bodies were 'dumped.'

Camille Bell and other victims' mothers were pressing Mayor Jackson and Public Safety Commissioner Brown for answers, holding press conferences, and meeting with the Atlanta City Council members and other outside investigators who volunteered their time. The mothers saw a connection in the murders, and wanted action, not words.

The body of **Angel Lanier,** age 12, was discovered on March 10, 1980, six days after she disappeared from her home. Her body was discovered in the woods at Campbellton Road and Willowbrook Drive; her hands were bound with electrical tape, with a pair of panties stuffed in her mouth. She had been assaulted. This was the first female child who was later placed on the 'missing and murdered task force list' but was never believed to be part of the pattern for which the Task Force was eventually created. Her case was included on the list because of pressure to have the case investigated by the Task Force.

On March 11, 1980, **Jeffrey Mathis, age 10,** left home on an errand to a neighborhood gas station to buy cigarettes for his mother. When Jeffrey didn't return shortly thereafter, his mother sent his brothers to search for him. Jeffrey was reported missing to the Atlanta Police. Three hundred thirty nine days later on February 13, 1981, Jeffrey's body was found in the woods 30 yards off the paved roadway (Suber

Road) in Southwest Atlanta by an F.B.I. search party. No clothing was found at the scene.

The Medical Examiner, Dr. John Feegel, personally responded to the scene along with his investigator John Cameron. They found a skull lying in a wooded area partially covered by pine needles. In carefully removing the pine needles in the area, multiple other bones were recovered and transported to the morgue for examination.

Dr. Feegel requested the assistance of a dental specialist to examine the skull and teeth for comparison to other missing children: Darron Glass who disappeared on September 14, 1980, and Jeffrey Mathis, who disappeared on March 11, 1980. A great deal of work went into the examination and comparison of the condition of the teeth. Although there appeared some similarity of both missing victims with the teeth found, it was the opinion of both Dr. Feegel and the specialist that the teeth in the skull found in the woods were *not* those of the Glass child but were those of Jeffrey Mathis. The family was so advised, and they requested return of the remains. The cause of the death could not be determined from the skeletal remains, but the manner of death was listed as probable homicide in view of the circumstances surrounding the disappearance of the child and the discovery of the body.

On March 12, 1980, City police began analyzing all homicides of children for the past five years, with Deputy Chief M. G. Redding giving Commissioner Lee Brown daily progress reports.

Eric Antonio Middlebrooks, age 14, was raised in foster care since about age four. He was at home in the late hours of May 19, 1980, but after receiving a phone call, he went outside. About eight hours later his body was discovered at the rear of a lounge on Flat Shoals Road. His bicycle was lying nearby with both tires flat.

Atlanta homicide Detective R. H. (Bob) Buffington remembers this case well; he arrived at the scene finding the body displayed in a manner similar to some other victims – on its back with limbs angled to the side. Buffington described the area with garbage dumpsters near the body. In examining the body, the Converse tennis shoes on the feet of the victim were of particular interest to Buffington. A part of the rubber band around one shoe had become unglued. As a homicide detective, he was trained to notice small things ... *such as the tuft of fibers wedged in the tear in the shoes* as if becoming attached while the body was 'dragged across a carpet.' He also noticed other fibers and foreign hair on the back of the victim's head. Buffington discussed with superior officers the possible significance of being able to identify fibers as you can hair; they were not impressed. But, when he delivered the trace evidence to the Crime Laboratory, Micro-analyst Larry Peterson was impressed.

Upon transportation of the body to the medical examiner's office, Dr. Feegel began the examination and autopsy. He noted that the clothing consisted of blue swimming-type trunks, rust-colored pants, white T-shirt (soiled), black and white athletic type socks and white underwear. Dr. Feegel also found a large 'wad of pink bubble gum' in the stomach. Feegel described two irregularly shaped lacerations to the scalp and a superficial incised wound in the left upper chest. The cause of death was diagnosed as brain injuries due to blunt trauma of the head.

And the killings continued!

A few weeks later on June 9, 1980, **Christopher Richardson, age 11,** left his home where he lived with his grandparents to swim at a local recreation center pool in south DeKalb County. Like others, he didn't return home when expected. Two hundred fourteen days later on January 9, 1981, Christopher's body was discovered by a search party in woods off Redwine Road/Desert Drive and across the road from where victim Milton Harvey was found. Like some others, Christopher's body was in a mummified state.

Medical Examiner Investigator J. E. Hendrix responded to the scene on Desert Drive where he found a roadblock and about 75 officers on the street. (Search parties had been searching for days). As he approached, a crime laboratory technician and an F.B.I. agent bagged a skull and some bones. Seeing nothing further, Hendrix returned to the Medical Examiner's office whereupon a radio call came in advising a second body had been located nearby. Hendrix along with Dr. Saleh Zaki returned to the scene. About 75 yards north of the previous location, they found the skeletal remains of a human. The remains were bagged and transported to the morgue.

On Sunday, January 11, Zaki and Hendrix took the skulls from both victims to the office of Dr. Peter Mills, Chief Forensic Odontologist and consultant for the medical examiner's office where x-rays and examination of the teeth were made. Since many of the teeth were missing from the first skull found, they returned to the scene where they recovered eleven (11) teeth, some vertebrae, and other small bones. Upon returning to the Medical Examiner's office, Dr. Mills set the teeth in place in the skull and took photographs. On Monday, Investigators Hendrix and Cameron went to the home of the missing child where the family members identified the swimming trunks of Christopher Richardson. Likewise when shown a photo of the teeth in the skull, all agreed that there was similarity. They then identified the upper right lateral incisor as having the noted "chip" in the tooth. Dental records for Christopher were obtained from his dentist, and a definitive identification was made through comparison with the X-rays from the skull. Although the exact cause of death could not be determined because of the condition of the body, Dr. Zaki concluded that due to the circumstances of the disappearance and the discovery of the remains in the woods are indicative of foul play; it was his opinion that Christopher's death was a violent one, most probably homicidal.

The second body was subsequently identified as Earl Lee Terrell who was missed on July 30, 1980.

LaTonya Wilson, age 7, was abducted from her home in northwest Atlanta on June 22, 1980. She was sleeping with other children when she was taken from the home. The parents were not awakened. Her skeletal remains were recovered four months later on October 18, 1980, near her home by a search party of volunteers at Sewanee Avenue and Verbena Street NW. Initial cause of death was undetermined. She was identified through dental records and some clothing she had been wearing. LaTonya was the second and last female on the Task Force list and was placed there under the same circumstances as the other female.

Aaron Wyche, age 10, disappeared on June 23, 1980. He was last seen in the Moreland Avenue Shopping Center. His body was found under a six-lane highway bridge over two railroad tracks in DeKalb County the next day. Aaron was the first child found in DeKalb County of what would be many 'missing and murdered children' with bodies dumped in the metropolitan area of Atlanta.

Dr. Joseph Burton, DeKalb County Medical Examiner who performed the autopsy, initially believed Aaron's death was 'accidental' due to a fall from the bridge because of the immediate circumstances of his death. Dr. Burton personally went to the scene where the body was discovered at the bottom of the overpass in thick brush; broken limbs were noted above the body which was found in a face-down position.

Routinely, a postmortem autopsy was performed by Dr. Burton with a finding of "Respiratory arrest and asphyxia, secondary to injuries sustained in fall" as the cause of death. Dr. Burton told me that, based on the immediate facts, it appeared that the deceased fell straight down from the top of the bridge but that he was so concerned about the case he conferred with Dr. Saleh Zaki, Fulton County Medical Examiner; they both agreed it was a very "unusual death – bothersome." Further, Burton said that by this time 'we medical examiners were getting calls from virtually all over the world' regarding the 'cycle of death of children' in Atlanta. Burton noted in his "comment" section of the report: This represents a very interesting forensic case in which without a careful evaluation of the scene, the autopsy findings might be quite misleading.

During a subsequent meeting with authorities including Larry Peterson of the State Crime Laboratory and the comparison of trace evidence from the body of Aaron with that of other bodies of other homicides, Dr. Burton told me that 'he wanted the case placed on the Task Force list' for further investigation. Burton personally made the decision to 'call it a homicide to get him (Aaron) on the list.' Aaron's case was added to the Task Force list as a possible homicide by asphyxiation in April 1981.

Anthony Carter, age 9, was last seen playing with a relative on Sunday, July 6, 1980. As many children do during the summer, he hung out in the streets. He was reported missing at 11:35 a.m. on Monday by his parents who had last seen him outside the apartment on Cunningham Place the night before. Anthony was found by employees at the rear of a warehouse on Wells Street, SW, less than a mile from home. Police responded. The body was face down on a grassy bank near the road and was showing blisters from the hot July sun. The body was removed to the morgue for autopsy.

Dr. Zaki performed the autopsy, finding moderately advanced decomposition with marked gaseous distension and skin slippage. He was wearing clothing, except for a shirt. Zaki determined that death was due to stab wounds to the back and chest, with the manner of death being a homicide.

Some of the victims were initially thought to have been runaways or stayovers and were not immediately reported to police or added to the Task Force list until further investigation and some indication of foul play. Anthony lived near several other children who would become victims.

On July 7, 1980, the first Task Force was unofficially created consisting of one sergeant and four investigators. On July 9, 1980, the Committee to Stop Children's Murders (victims' mothers) held their first press conference pressing authorities to see a linkage between the murders.

On July 17, 1980, Commissioner Brown *officially announced* the creation of the Special Task Force of Sergeant Bolton and four investigators to supplement the normal activities of investigators. This force would evolve into "The Missing and Murdered Task Force" which would 'list' the cases they investigated as believed to be connected. The exception was the two females whose cases were never connected to the other cases, but were nevertheless added to the Task Force List for investigation.

On July 22, 1980, Atlanta Police did an analysis on all missing and runaway children reports for the past five years and requested the assistance of the FBI Behavioral Science Unit in addition to local psychiatrists. On July 23, 1980, a briefing was held with law enforcement officials from DeKalb County, Fulton County, and the City of East Point to discuss these cases. On July 24, 1980, an order was issued instructing investigators to maintain constant contact with parents of the victims.

And the murders continued!!

On July 30, 1980, **Earl Lee Terrell, age 11,** went with relatives to a local swimming pool. He left during the afternoon and was never seen alive since. His body was discovered one hundred sixty one (161) days later on January 9, 1981, in the woods at Redwine Road/Desert Drive where another victim, Christopher Richardson, was also found. The remains of both victims were removed to the morgue for autopsy. Investigator J. Hendrix visited the child's mother who identified the gold colored swimming trunks found on the body. She then was shown a photo taken of the teeth from the skull, whereupon she responded: "That's his mouth," and began to cry. Hendrix next went to Fulton High School and showed the same items to two relatives of Earl's who were with him when he was last seen at the pool. They in turn identified the swimming trunks Earl was wearing when he was reported missing. One of the relatives said the photo of the teeth "looked like his teeth." No dental records were available for comparison. However, in obtaining a picture of Earl taken in the spring of 1979, Dr. Zaki noted that it was apparent that the front upper teeth are very similar if not identical to those of the remains found in the woods.

Dr. Zaki described the remains as attached together by 'leathery, dried, decomposed skin and by ligamentous structures.' While the cause of death could not be determined, Dr. Zaki found from all the circumstances that Earl's death was a violent one, most probably homicidal. Earl Lee Terrell was placed on the Task Force list as No. 12. But the Task Force seemed no nearer to solving these murders!

On August 9, 1980, FBI Special Agent John Glover delivered all data on these cases to the FBI Behavorial Science Division (profilers).

On August 11, 1980, about 3,000 fliers with pictures of the missing children were distributed throughout metropolitan Atlanta.

On August 18, 1980, Mayor Jackson requested assistance from the Governor's Office in reference to the cases. Also, Deputy Chief Redding began personally placing telephone calls throughout the nation seeking advice and obtaining other data in reference to major case investigations.

Clifford Jones, age 13, was last seen on August 20, 1980, in the Hollywood Road and Louise Place area. His body was found by police the next morning behind a Laundromat near the trash dumpster at the rear of the building in Hollywood Plaza after a call was received from an unknown person advising that a body was on the ground near the dumpster.

Detective R. H. (Bob) Buffington recently recalled to me that he initially responded to the scene where he found the body later identified as Clifford Jones near the dumpster similar to the case of Eric Middlebrooks which he had worked three months before (also near a dumpster at the rear of a business). Buffington began inspecting the body of Jones for similar trace evidence. He did notice fibers on the back of Jones' head. **The body was not wrapped in anything,** contrary to a reported sighting by witnesses who later claimed to have seen something wrapped in plastic being carried from the Laundromat to the dumpster by the Laundromat manager.

A superior officer came to the scene, Buffington says, and instructed him to turn the case over to Detective Welcome Harris, a Task Force investigator, who then took charge of the investigation. Harris was never able to support the claim that Jones was killed in the Laundromat and dumped outside in open view behind the accused killer's workplace.[2] The bodies were being dumped in woods – now in the open behind businesses near dumpsters. The killer could have easily discarded the bodies in the dumpsters, whereby they may have ended up at the City dump and never discovered. Did the killer consider them trash – leaving them in the open to be found for the morning news media to whip up hysteria in the community that the night stalker was smarter than police who were running around but accomplishing nothing?

Chief Medical Examiner Robert Stivers conducted the autopsy. The face showed multiple petechial hemorrhages and bruises to the inside of the lips and a cut in the right lateral corner. The neck showed a discontinuous non-patterned abrasion around the circumference, more prominent in the posterior and right side, measuring 3/8 inch to ½ inch in width. The death was a homicide by ligature strangulation.

On August 21, 1980, the Task Force was expanded, placing Captain Sparks in charge, which now included four supervisors and thirteen investigators. On August 24, 1980, the Task Force Office was moved to the

---

2   Detective Harris told me he was never able to verify the information furnished regarding the Laundromat manager, Jamie Brooks. The physical evidence contradicted it; the body was not wrapped in plastic as reported; the story did not make sense – a killer leaving the body behind his workplace for the police to come ask him about? The witness, a 'retarded boy with serious mental issues,' reportedly claimed to have seen the victim murdered in the laundromat by the manager who then carried the body wrapped in plastic to the dumpster. [Would a killer murder one boy and let another boy – a witness – live to talk?] Detective Harris said that as bad as he wanted to be the one who solved the case with an arrest, Brooks was cleared. Larry Peterson from the State Crime Laboratory personally came to the crime scene and inspected the body. It was not wrapped in anything. He found fibers and dog hair on the body similar to other cases. Peterson compared fibers from the Laundromat to those found on the body – there were 'no matches.' However, after Wayne Williams' arrest in 1981, the fibers and hair from the body of Clifford Jones were compared to fibers from items in Williams' home and vehicles and revealed the following matches: The unusual Wellman green carpet fibers in Williams' bedroom, the violet acetate fibers from Williams' bedspread; and the hair matched the Williams' dog, Sheba. More-so after trial of Williams, trunk liner fibers from a rental Ford Fairmont rented by Williams (but not discovered until after trial) was matched post-trial to fibers found on Clifford Jones' body.

basement of the police headquarters. At this time the Task Force began developing a computer program in reference to this investigation.

On September 9, 1980, a meeting was scheduled in the Civic Center with all ministers in metropolitan Atlanta. The Task Force personnel began holding weekly briefings with all other units within the Bureau of Police Services in reference to this investigation. Meanwhile, Mayor Maynard Jackson requested the Governor's Office to establish a reward fund in reference to these cases.

On September 10, 1980, Metropolitan Crime Stoppers began developing a film in reference to these cases in an effort to warn the children of the dangers involved.

On September 11, 1980, the Task Force requested Dr. Larry Howard of the State Crime Laboratory to go back and re-examine all blood samples and other body chemicals in reference to this investigation.

Darron Glass, age 10, was a foster child who became missing on September 14, 1980. He was last seen in the area of Second Avenue and Glenwood Road about 5:30 p.m., Sunday. Because Darron had run away before, police did not add the case to the Task Force list until much later. Darron was never heard from since. *Darron's body has never been found; he was presumed to be a victim of the serial snatcher because of all the circumstances of the case known to police.*

On September 17, 1980, Major W. J. Taylor was (administratively) placed in charge of the Task Force. Inspector Robbie Hamrick of the Georgia Bureau of Investigation was assigned Supervisor of Investigations. Deputy Chief Redding mailed letters to all major police departments within the United States and to every Chief of Police and Sheriff in the State of Georgia in reference to these cases. The District Attorney assigned two assistant district attorneys to assist with the investigation. In addition, on September 19, 1980, the local FBI assigned two special agents to serve as liaison with the Special Task Force.

Also, in September, 1980, Task Force personnel began interviewing all previous runaway children in the same age grouping as the victims. Commissioner Brown requested assistance from the C.D.C. and the Fulton County Health Department. Psychic Dorothy Allison came to Atlanta and consulted with police, as were others with special talents. Captain Robert Robertson, Commander of Birmingham, Michigan's Task Force, was given a briefing in reference to these cases. His department in turn began offering assistance. Commissioner Brown began taping public service announcements which were broadcast throughout the City instructing the public about crime and child safety. Over 80,000 child safety brochures were distributed by the Atlanta Public School System and the Bureau's Crime Prevention Unit.

Recently, while writing this, I attended an extended family annual reunion. Debbie Allen and her daughter, Melissa, were present; they spoke to me of the 'cycle of fear and death' surrounding the murdered children in Atlanta. After some 27 years, Debbie recalled the public service warnings on TV when parents were told of the dangers of allowing their children outside after dark. Her oldest daughter, Melissa, 10 at the time, told me she vividly recalls the warnings and asking her mother what they meant. In reliving the incident, I could see the concern Melissa felt about all the children being snatched and killed, notwithstanding she lived in suburban Cobb County and seemingly safe from where the kids were being taken from the streets of Atlanta. Debbie told me she listened to the public announcements urging parents to keep their children close after dark with a warning of the time and "do you know where your children are tonight?" Debbie said this was the first time she ever felt real fear for her children who were 10, 7, and 5 at the time. She reminded me that children loved to play outside and by restricting them to the house was a deprivation of their innocence as a child – in growing up feeling safe and secure in their surroundings. Debbie responded by keeping her children close and inside after dark; she says she watched them like hawks, and was relieved with an arrest in the case.

Charles Stephens, age 12, disappeared on October 9, 1980, after leaving home – a housing project on Pryor Circle – where he lived with his mother and sister. He had been watching TV, and his mother later missed him. His body was discovered the next morning on a hillside near the Longview Mobile Park on Normanberry Drive in East Point.

Investigator R. J. Eskew met East Point Police at the scene. The body was found up the driveway about 100 feet from the street lying on grass, face up. The body was that of a young black male with no identification, clothed in blue jeans, white shorts, and no shirt; one shoe was present on the right foot – another shoe was found about 20 inches away. The body was cold and rigor was set. A small amount of dried blood was on the left side of the nose. Task Force and Crime Laboratory members appeared on the scene with a missing persons report on Charles Stephens, last seen about 4:30 p.m. the prior day. The grandfather identified the body, which was missing a T-shirt, custom-printed with the grandfather's picture. Neighbors said the victim, like other victims, was a hard worker who earned spending money by running errands and emptying garbage cans. After autopsy, Dr. Feegel found the death to be a homicide and concluded that death was caused by asphyxia due to probable suffocation – finding petechia of the heart and lungs.

On October 10, 1980, the East Point Police officially joined the Task Force. The Task Force expanded to approximately 34 people.

On October 18, 1980, citizens of metropolitan Atlanta began volunteering for weekend search parties. Latonya Wilson's body was discovered by the first weekend search party.

On October 21, 1980, the Atlanta Bureau of Police Services and the Atlanta Bureau of Fire Services jointly began door-to-door canvassing of all Atlanta residents.

On October 23, 1980, the Atlanta City Council enacted a citywide curfew for youths under 16 years of age. Within a few months, the ages of the victims would gradually become older through the teen years and into the early adult years – as if the intention of the curfew was working – children were staying inside.

On October 27, 1980, the reward fund was now over $150,000.

And the killings continued!

Aaron Jackson, age 9, and a friend of victim Aaron Wyche (victim No. 10) disappeared on November 1, 1980, from a shopping center on Moreland Avenue. His body was located on a river bank beneath a bridge in the 2800 block of Forest Park Road, SE, at the South River the following day. The body was on its back in a stretched out position and in almost direct line with the edge of the bridge and railing, as in a 'drop-straight-down' position from the bridge. There were two small spots of blood on the rock under the head. He was fully clothed with full rigor set.

Dr. Feegel performed the autopsy, finding two 1/8 inch areas of superficial scratching on the left lower aspect of the neck with other injuries to the head and lip. The manner of death was "homicide" and cause of death was asphyxia due to probable suffocation.

The Task Force list was getting longer with Aaron Jackson listed as No.16. When would it stop? Black male children were outside on the streets, running errands, playing, carrying on the activities of their young years, and were routinely disappearing at the hands of a sadistic, twisted mind of a killer. Why? If police had a motive, it would no doubt help lead to a suspect.

On November 3, 1980, ten additional investigators were assigned to the Task Force, and on November 6, 1980, the FBI officially entered the investigation. On November 7, 1980, the Task Force office was expanded and moved to its own quarters at 350 West Peachtree Street (separate from the police department) in a former automobile show-room/business.

Patrick Rogers, age 16, disappeared from his home in Thomasville Heights on November 10, 1980. Police first feared he was a runaway. His body was recovered from the Chattahoochee River at Paces Ferry Road in Cobb County 28 days later on December 8, 1980. Cause of Death: Trauma to the head.

On November 12, 1980, the Bureau of Police Services began setting up roadblocks in isolated areas. These were to be in strategic areas such as to catch the killer with a victim.

In November, 1980, the Atlanta Public School System began distributing pamphlets entitled: "Kids Don't Go With Strangers." In addition, school principals began making daily telephone calls to parents of children who were absent from school. Also, through the Safe Program, an Adult Community Patrol Program was implemented.

Commissioner Brown began meeting daily with all high officials within the Bureau to discuss this investigation. Additionally, in December, 1980, Commissioner Brown began using the computer dialing telephone system to reach citizens throughout the City in reference to these investigations.

On December 15, 1980, retired officers from the Bureau of Police Services began volunteering their time to interview all arrested persons who were processed through the city jail in reference to these cases.

Lubie Geter, age 14, left home on Dahlgreen Street in Southeast Atlanta on January 3, 1981, for the Stewart-Lakewood Shopping Center to sell car deodorizers to make a few dollars. It was a new area for his salesmanship, and he was looking forward to making some money. He never returned home! Lubie, unlike some victims, had a stable home life and family, and had not been in trouble; he was not believed to be 'street-wise' as were other victims. He did well as a freshman at Murphy High School. It is believed Lubie got caught up in the killer's net by virtue of his being on the streets doing 'odd-jobs.'

Lubie's extremely decomposed body was found on February 5, 1981, by a man collecting rabbit traps. The body was dressed only in undershorts. It was lying about 50 feet off the south side of Vandiver and Enon roads in the woods. It appeared that the body had been dragged about 10 feet and showed signs of being mutilated by animals – both feet were missing. Investigator Hendrix responded to the scene for the medical examiner; after the crime lab technician searched the body for fibers, hairs, and trace evidence, Hendrix documented and preserved the body in a sheet and disaster bag and transported it to the morgue. Later that day, Hendrix was present when family members identified the face as that of Lubie Geter. Follow-up identification was provided through fingerprints.

Dr. Robert Stivers, Chief Medical Examiner, performed the autopsy and described the fatal injury as a homicide from asphyxia, due to strangulation.

On January 5, 1981, police officers and police recruits began forming search parties and conducting searches throughout the metropolitan Atlanta area in an attempt to locate bodies of missing children. On January 9, 1981, the skeletal remains of Christopher Richardson and Earl Lee Terrell were discovered.

On January 17, 1981, Commissioner Brown ordered an executive review of all cases on a weekly basis. On January 21, 1981, an executive review in reference to these cases was held with Special Agent John Glover and other FBI agents.

On January 21, 1981, the Task Force requested from the zone commanders a list of all isolated areas and abandoned houses within their respective zones. These areas were then placed under surveillances. Every effort was being exhausted.

Terry Lorenzo Pue, age 15, was reported missing on January 22, 1981. He lived in a public housing project with ten siblings. He had no fear of the streets; he was known to be out by himself at all hours of the night. Terry had a history of run-ins with juvenile authorities and had been placed in a special education program. He was last seen alive the night of January 21, 1981, at a fast-food restaurant on Memorial Drive.

Terry's body was discovered about 7:30 a.m. on January 23, 1981, on the east side of Sigman Road in Rockdale County four miles west of the City of Conyers – some miles from his home in the Hollywood Court Apartments in Atlanta. Conyers police and Rockdale County Sheriff's officers responded to the scene which was secured to await the arrival of the State Medical Examiner and Larry Peterson of the Crime Laboratory. The body was in partial rigor; time of death was estimated to have been at 8:00 p.m. the previous evening. The body was fully clothed except for undershorts.

After a full scene-investigation, the body was removed to the morgue for autopsy by Dr. J. Byron Dawson. A full-body exam revealed, among other things, blood present in the mouth, a ligature mark around the lower neck, abrasions, hematomas, and some postmortem abrasions. Dr. Dawson described an "apparent triple ligature mark around the neck," the most superior at "9 ½ inches below the top of the head," the second beginning at "11 inches below the top of the head …" and the third (and lower) mark at "12 inches below the top of the head." Dr. Dawson recorded the exact location and description of the mark. At one location it measured "¼ inch in width" and was described as "an abrasion pattern suggestive of a braided cord." The death was determined to be a homicide by strangulation. Dr. Dawson, in finding "fingernail-like abrasions on the front of the neck" and "hemorrhage in the neck area … above the ligature mark," opined that the "subject was manually strangled before the ligature was placed around the neck."

On January 29, 1981, Sammy Davis, Jr., announced he would schedule a concert for Atlanta. All monies would go to the missing children investigations.

On January 30, 1981, a meeting was held with all metropolitan Atlanta law enforcement agencies in reference to these cases. Then, on February 2, 1981, Mayor Maynard Jackson met with Governor George Busbee to request additional assistance.

On February 3, 1981, a new procedure was implemented for handling missing person reports. Then, on February 4, 1981, City Hall computer personnel were put on a temporary assignment to assist the Task Force in developing the computer system.

Patrick Baltazar, age 11, was reported missing on February 6, 1981. He was last seen near the Omni in downtown Atlanta. Patrick lived with his father in a housing project near the Omni Hotel. He worked odd jobs for money and played the electronic games located near his home. He was reported to have no fear of asking for work or dealing with adults. He had a lot of ability in living in the streets. After he went missing, his father searched the streets for him where he was known to hang out.

His body was found by a maintenance man on February 13, 1981, in a wooded area behind Corporate Square, an office complex in DeKalb County. The body of Baltazar was dumped in DeKalb County after Chief of Police Dick Hand had publicly announced through the media that 'they' had not had any killings in DeKalb.

Dr. Joseph Burton, DeKalb County Medical Examiner, used a rope to descend the bank; he discovered the body 'face down' caught in dead limbs and frozen debris halfway down the embankment. The body was fully clothed. There was ice present on and under the body, as well as sticks frozen to the clothing. Meticulous crime scene investigations were by now being done routinely to protect any trace evidence from contamination before removal of bodies. Using a magnifying lens, Burton noted that numerous fibers and animal hairs were present on the body; he removed them at the scene. The body was then carefully rolled onto a sterile sheet, and the front of the body was similarly examined with additional trace evidence recovered. Clothing and facial features compared to photographs at the scene resulted in a presumptive identification. The body was covered with a second sterile sheet and was removed to the morgue for autopsy.

The autopsy was performed the same day. Burton noted that, while an exact time of death cannot be determined, Baltazar had been dead for longer than 72 hours; and within a reasonable degree of probability, he had been dead for most of the time that he had been missing. On examination of the neck, Burton described a ligature mark measuring four inches in length and one-fourth inch in diameter and an abrasion measuring one-half inch in diameter; the cause of death was "asphyxia due to ligature strangulation." Burton noted that from the location of the ligature marks, "the ligature was most probably applied by someone behind or off to the backside of the victim."

Dr. Burton further noted in his report that he had personally examined numerous fibers and animal hairs from the body of Baltazar with 'other cases in the other child deaths in the Atlanta area' and that 'These fibers bear a significant similarity both in their size – caliber, and color.' Burton further noted that the mechanism of death as well as the characteristics of the victim and the similarity of the trace evidence suggests that the Baltazar case might be connected with other black child deaths in the Atlanta area in the past 18 months.

On February 13, 1981, the skeletal remains of Jeffrey Mathis were discovered in south Fulton County. Also, on February 13, 1981, Commissioner Brown went to Washington, D.C., to meet with officials of the Justice Department about the cases.

On February 16, 1981, the Task Force was reorganized placing Deputy Chief Redding in command, relieving him of all other responsibilities. New efforts included the following:

On February 17, 1981, the Task Force started utilizing police officers as decoys.

On February 18, 1981, Commissioner Brown issued orders to stop all vehicles that were observed with a young black male in them. [To my knowledge, no one complained of violating anyone's civil liberties].

On February 18, 1981, police began surveillances on shopping centers in metropolitan Atlanta. But the murders would continue!

Curtis Walker, age 13, was reported missing on February 19, 1981; he was last seen at Bankhead Highway near where he lived in Bowen Homes. His body was found floating face down in the South River at Waldrop Road in DeKalb County on March 6, 1981.

Dr. Burton and Lt. Michael Shockley from the DeKalb County Medical Examiner's Office responded to the scene and took charge. DeKalb Fire and Police personnel were present and had secured the scene. The body, caught on a limb and stump debris in an "eddy" in the stream a few feet from the edge of the left bank facing downriver, was visible from the bridge. The depth of the river at this point was three to four feet deep. The back, arms, and upper buttocks were visible, reported Dr. Burton. Navigating to the location of the body via sandbars, Dr. Burton noted only the apparent tracks of the fireman who had initially gone down to view the body; no other tracks were visible in the sand. The body was found caught on a limb from a stump – folded across the limb with the legs, arms, and upper torso protruding downstream or, as Burton described, "jack knifed around the limb." The body was wearing only jockey underwear. Although some Medical Examiners are represented at the crime scenes by their investigators who perform the necessary tasks and report back, in the DeKalb County cases Dr. Burton personally responded to the scenes and was directly involved with the recovery process. Dr. Burton removed his shirt and entered the stream to ensure the protection of any remaining trace evidence from loss and contamination; he assisted in manipulating a sterile white sheet in a Stokes stretcher while maneuvering the body onto the stretcher. The stretcher was then placed in a small Department of Public Safety boat for removing the body from the river; it was then transported to the morgue for autopsy.

From an external examination of the body, Burton described, among other things, gaseous distension of certain areas of the body, areas of de-pigmentation and skin slippage secondary to decomposition, plant and insect debris, an earthworm embedded in the hair, and numerous small red wormlike organisms present on the body.

Microanalyst Larry Peterson from the State Crime Laboratory was present and assisted in the evidence collection from the body; numerous fibers and animal hairs were removed from the victim's hair and body with the use of a magnifying lens. Once this process was completed, Burton proceeded with an internal autopsy of the body.

A slow and detailed examination of the body resulted with a finding that death was caused by "asphyxia, due to probable suffocation." Dr. Burton noted that "The pattern of bruising on the body suggests that the deceased was being held down or restrained during the process of asphyxiation. This represents evidence that the deceased resisted the at-tacker." Burton further noted that the fibers from the body were similar to fibers in other related cases.

Joseph "Jo-Jo" Bell, age 15, was reported missing on March 2, 1981. Jo-Jo did odd jobs to earn spending money. He was known to joke about the 'missing children,' saying that 'no kidnapper would get him.' He was last seen at Captain Peg's Seafood on Georgia Avenue. His body was recovered from the South River at the DeKalb/Rockdale

County line 48 days later on Sunday afternoon, April 19, 1981. A man on a dirt-bike noticed the body caught up in tree limbs in the river near where other bodies had been found. The body was nude except for undershorts.

Dr. Burton responded again to the South River and, as before, found a young black male floating face down in the river. He described gaining access to the scene by walking two miles through the woods to a secluded area of the South River: *"The River was quiet, deep, and relatively gentle flowing in this area. Within several hundred feet above this site some small rapids were noted to be present. There was a large open field on the Rockdale County side of the river, slightly above the point where the body was found. The body was floating in the 'eddy' currents of a cove-like area protected by fallen trees in the river at a sharp turn south into Rockdale County."* Such was the description of an idyllic place for murder! The exposed part of the body was that of the back; jockey underwear was visible. The body was removed by boat after wrapping it in a clean sterile sheet and placing it in a disaster bag. Various areas of the body were skeletonized while other areas had been partially eaten by aquatic and wildlife. Maggots and larvae of several generations of flies were present on the body.

After being supplied dental records of a missing person, Joseph Eugene Bell, Dr. Burton made a positive identification of the body.

Microanalyst Larry Peterson was present with Dr. Burton at the autopsy proceedings. Burton told me that this autopsy took 13 hours! The body's surface was first given a careful, inch-by-inch, search for trace evidence. The scalp hair and pubic hair areas were searched with a magnifying lens for foreign items (trace evidence) which were forwarded to the Crime Laboratory for further examination and comparison.

In conducting the autopsy, Burton found that death was caused by asphyxia associated with apparent neck injury.

On March 10, 1981, Commissioner Brown held a meeting with all Chiefs and Commissioners in the metropolitan Atlanta area to develop guidelines in reference to the Task Force and, on that same day Sammy Davis, Jr., gave a concert to raise funds in support of the investigation.

Timothy Hill, age 13, and a friend of "Jo-Jo" Bell, was last seen in the area of Lawson Street and Sells Avenue on March 13, 1981. Seventeen days later, his body was located on March 30, 1981, by a boater in the Chattahoochee River near Cochran Road partially submerged in the river, some 25 feet from the bank. Medical Examiner Investigator Eskew responded to the scene in South Fulton County, south of the Campbellton Road Bridge and downstream about one-half mile. The body was lying on the bank after having been towed to shore by the boater and police. The body was dressed in shorts only. After a crime scene investigation, the body was removed to the morgue. A crime laboratory analyst was allowed to remove trace evidence before autopsy.

Dr. John Feegel performed the autopsy. In association with Dr. Peter Mills, a dental comparison was made to a dental chart of Timothy Hill, and a match was found without exception. The death was declared to be a homicide, probable asphyxia, due to probable suffocation.

Timothy was known to, or connected to, several other victims on the list. Timothy was No. 23! The list would grow!

On March 14, 1981, the Vice President of the United States (George H W Bush) visited Atlanta in reference to the investigation, which resulted in the City obtaining a one and a half million dollar ($1.5 million) grant to assist in the investigation.

Eddie Duncan, age 21, and the first adult on the list, was last seen on March 20, 1981, in the Techwood Homes area where he lived and where the citizens' Bat Patrol was active. Like others, Duncan picked up odd jobs for a little money and was known on the street. His body was recovered from the Chattahoochee River south of Highway 92 on the Douglas County side of the stream during the late evening hours of March 31, 1981, the day after the previous victim (Timothy Hill) was pulled from the river at about the same location, but on the opposite (Fulton County) side of the river.

Douglas County Sheriff's Investigators, along with the Georgia Bureau of Investigation, worked the crime scene. State Medical Examiner, Dr. J. Byron Dawson, had the body removed to the morgue for autopsy at 1:20 a.m., April 1, 1981. Dr. Dawson described a "decomposing" body clothed only in a pair of boxer-style undershorts with a torn crotch. The body showed signs of "marbling, swelling, and gaseous distention" and "some mummification." Because of the condition of the body from having been in water for some time, Dr. Dawson called the death a "homicide" with cause of death "undetermined."

It appears the killer has now found a fertile place to dump bodies – in the rivers – and especially in the Chattahoochee from east to west, contiguous to Fulton, Cobb and Douglas Counties and easily accessible by highways with bridges from Interstate 285.

Michael McIntosh, age 23, disappeared on March 25, 1981, from Milton Avenue in Atlanta. His body was found on April 20, 1981, in a brush pile beside the Chattahoochee River, three-fourths of a mile south of highway 92 by men clearing land in the area. The body had caught up in the limbs. The workers smelled an odor and investigated. Police responded. After the crime scene was completed, the body was removed to the morgue for autopsy.

Finger-skin tissue was removed and a quick identification was established through fingerprints. Dr. John Feegel determined the death to be a homicide, with cause of death a probable asphyxia, due to probable suffocation.

Michael, like many other victims, knew other task force victims.

Larry Rogers, age 20, lived with his father in an apartment in a housing complex near the Omni Hotel when he disappeared on March 30, 1981. His body was discovered ten days later on April 9 in a ground-floor abandoned apartment on Temple Street; he was lying on his back, face up, on the kitchen floor with feet and lower legs protruding through a wall partition where the sheetrock had been torn away. He was clothed in swim trunks and gym shorts. He had been strangled and had been dead for some time.

Fulton County Medical Examiner Robert R. Stivers, who conducted the autopsy, described the fatal injury to the neck organs showing "hemorrhage into the strap muscles …;" he recorded that "asphyxial signs are noted consisting of petechial hemorrhages over the heart, lungs and temporal sinuses." Dr. Stivers declared the cause of death to be "asphyxia due to strangulation."

Rogers, as the others, earned money on the streets hustling – yard work, running errands, etc. He, too, had a juvenile record. He was friendly to everyone; and, as one relative put it, he would have jumped into a car with someone to earn some money. Rogers was reported to be mentally deficient and could be taken advantage of by another.

In March, 1981, Commissioner Brown and other officials of the Bureau of Police Services conducted Town Hall Meetings to brief the communities on the ongoing investigation, and on March 31, 1981, the Task Force expanded to a total of 92 personnel. Shortly thereafter, on April 3, 1981, Commissioner Brown established a Rumor Control Center.

John Porter, age 28, was found in a vacant lot on Bender Street on Sunday, April 12, 1981. A neighbor found the body. Police and Investigator M.E. Horton, Medical Examiner's office, responded to the scene where the deceased was found lying on his back with stab wounds to the body. The neighbor reported that his dog was barking at 10 p.m. the previous night but not since. Rigor had begun to set into parts of the body. Petechial hemorrhages were noted in the lower eyelids and some discoloration to both sides of the neck. The crime scene investigation was completed, and the body was wrapped and removed to the morgue for autopsy.

Fulton County Medical Examiner Robert Stivers conducted the autopsy. The deceased weighed 123 lbs. and was dressed in a blue and white shirt, brown pants, and shoes and socks. Stivers described six (6) stab wounds to the body in ruling the death was a homicide, caused by stab wounds, chest and abdomen.

Porter had had a troubled life, having been in prison and institutions. He stayed at times with his grandmother. He did not make the task force list until after an arrest was made, and the case was reevaluated in light of other homicides by similar means and trace evidence found on the body. His body was found near where Barrett's body was located.

Jimmy Ray Payne, age 21, was reported missing April 22, 1981, after he left home on Magnolia Street, en-route to the Omni. Five days later on April 27, 1981, his body was pulled from the Chattahoochee River, 225 yards south of the I-285 Bridge.

On May 9, 1981, Mayor Jackson announced that Heavyweight Boxing Champ Muhammad Ali had donated $400,000 to raise the reward fund to one-half million dollars.

The reward fund would never be paid!

William Barrett, age 17, was last seen on May 11, 1981, in the Kirkwood area of Atlanta; his body was discovered the next day in weeds along Winthrop Drive in DeKalb County by a passing motorist who called police. Like many others, Barrett had a troubled life – having been in and out of jail. He had been released the day before he disappeared.

Who would want William Barrett dead? For that matter, who – or what type person – would want any of these victims dead? What would motivate such heinous murders?

Dr. Burton responded to the scene where the body, later identified as William Barrett, was found lying on his back with his legs turned slightly to his left side. He was fully clothed. Several fibers were present on the shoes; a ligature mark was present on the neck. Rigor mortis was fully set with the right leg elevated off of the opposite knee and fixed in this position. Several stab wounds were visible on the abdomen beneath the shirt. The body was placed in sterile sheets and removed to the morgue for autopsy. Burton and Microanalyst Larry Peterson from the Crime Laboratory conducted a careful examination for trace evidence which was forwarded along with clothing to the laboratory.

Dr. Burton proceeded with an internal autopsy finding seven injuries to the abdomen made with a sharp instrument, such as a knife; all of the wounds had the appearance of postmortem injuries (made after death) in that "there was no readily apparent hemorrhage associated with any of the wounds." Except for two, the wounds were very thin abrasions or superficial pricks of the skin. In determining the cause of death as asphyxia due to ligature strangulation, Dr. Burton described a ligature mark on the neck contiguous in the front; there was no evidence of the mark in the posterior neck area, suggesting that the ligature was applied by someone behind the deceased.

On May 19, 1981, the Special Operations Section and the Missing Persons Unit were placed under the command of the Task Force. The Task Force, *with over 100 personnel at this point*, dedicated to nothing but catching the serial killer, was fully working out of the West Peachtree Street location.

The world was watching, as the killer was obviously watching the news and responding by continuing the killings under the eyes of the largest manhunt in the state's (perhaps nation's) history – gleefully perhaps, as for two years the full force of the police, federal, state and local, were being utilized. In fact, the killer for several months had accelerated the rate of the killings. Thus far, unheard of techniques and unorthodox methods had been unable to catch the hated and feared animal who was stalking and killing children, teenagers, and *now* young adults.

Community leaders had been preaching in the pulpits, in the schools, and everywhere people congregate, to keep young people off the streets at night. Welfare and healthcare professionals were treating children because of the 'fear' generated in their lives brought about by the mysterious killer in their midst. Children were 'bed-wetting' and other side effects detrimental to the education and welfare of children were noted by health-care professionals.

Would this nightmare ever stop, they continued to ask?

Thus far, nothing had worked; all the heretofore efforts still had not produced a good suspect. Though requiring a heavy influx of resources with questionable results, the only thing not tried would be given a chance – bridge surveillances at night. Many of the victims had been recovered from rivers in the previous weeks and months. On April 3, 1981, occasional surveillance of some bridges had been started without success. On April 24, 1981, a memorandum for *Bridge Surveillance* was issued whereby certain selected highway bridges across the Chattahoochee River and other waterways would be placed under physical surveillance during the night by members of the Special Task Force and the FBI. *The specific purpose of this surveillance was to apprehend the individual(s) responsible for dumping a body off a bridge into the river.*

The procedure for such surveillance(s) was set out in detail providing for a four or five-man team, composed of one FBI Agent and three or four officers furnished by the Atlanta police. The procedure provided for officers on the ground as well as a 'chase car' at each end of the bridge concealed out of sight.

Profiling a Serial Killer

Profiling is not new – its origin goes back centuries, but it was used only sparingly until the early 1970s when the Federal Bureau of Investigation formed the Behavioral Science Unit at Quantico. Since that time, the Unit has been involved in many major cases, along with local authorities, involving serial rapists and killers. The Unit was later more appropriately called the Behavioral Analysis Unit. Two of the early members of the unit were John Douglas and Robert Ressler who interviewed and studied many convicted rapists and murderers over the years providing valuable behavioral patterns which contributed to the offender profiling program. Such profiling can be a good investigative tool to profile suspects with a behavioral pattern and assist police in solving crime.

Psychologists and psychiatrists, as well as self-made experts, psychics, and 'mind-readers' have dabbled at looking into the minds of serial killers and sex offenders in an attempt to elucidate upon the motives and mentality of those who might be expected to commit such crimes.

Criminal profiling (as distinguished from racial profiling) is an analysis of the crime, the details and manner in which the crime was committed – before, during and after – in an effort to identify the offender (or the type person suspected). An offender may leave clues through his/her method in committing the crime which tells police something of the criminal's personality or identity – or, at least limit the potential suspects. An analysis of the criminal manner, method of operation, tool, weapon, demeanor, motive, and all aspects of the crime may be helpful in solving the crime in the absence of eye-witnesses, DNA, or more practical means.

During the height of the Atlanta child murders, Jeane Dixon, Dorothy Allison, and other astrologers and psychics voluntarily offered the Task Force their assistance in the investigation. Ms. Dixon offered her opinion that the killer would continue to kill until he was caught, but that the authorities would be able to solve the murders with the arrest of a stocky built man. The police by this time with no conclusion in sight welcomed the advice of anyone because of the lack of good leads in solving the murders. Over 1000 pieces of information were received from psychics around the country.

After the fourth victim's mother, Camille Bell, could not convince the authorities that someone was killing the city's children, she 'found a sympathetic ear at the Georgia Psychological Association' reported John Currie, then President of the state association. Ms. Bell and other mothers of victims had formed the *Mothers' Committee to Stop Children's Murders.*

Currie was later quoted in the *American Psychological Association Monitor* in a 1982 Article "Tracking the Mind of a Killer" by Ian McNett, that "she (Camille Bell) was very specific about what she wanted when she called me" and "she asked for help in stopping someone from doing what he was doing"- "she said that a killer was taking the lives of young, black, male children. She wanted us to construct a profile."

Currie went on to say that while few people believed the killings were related, he felt "empathetic toward her as a psychotherapist." He said: "I was touched by her need and also a little bit overwhelmed, because one does not produce a profile by magic."

Following Ms. Bell's call, it was reported that there was a lull in the killings and nothing came of her request until the murders started recurring at an increasing tempo during spring and summer of 1980 when a pattern was being seen. Currie reportedly said that he became "distressed at the damage being done to the social and emotional climate of Atlanta" due to talk of a "race war in the city as blacks feared for the safety of their children and some people became convinced that the murderer was a white person."

As a result, local and state psychologists, including the FBI's Behavioral Science Unit, came forward to offer their support to the authorities.

An ad hoc resource committee of the state association of Currie, George Greaves and Allen Carter, offered their assistance to Public Safety Commissioner Lee Brown.

Greaves, a "diagnostician and an expert on multiple personalities and exotic mental disorders" had an interest in police work and mass murderers, and Carter, of Morehouse College, was especially interested in the mental health issues of the city's children. Dr. Carter recently confirmed to me his involvement in the work as reported by the Monitor.

The committee held its first meeting on March 18 (1981) and met with Commissioner Brown on May 14 where he presented it with an agenda.

As the murders continued, Dr. Carter confirmed that the healthcare professionals witnessed the 'emergence of a new syndrome among black children: Heightened anxiety was the common symptom, with many secondary expressions such as school phobia, fear of strangers, bed wetting, night terrors, insomnia, lack of appetite, and regressive behaviors such as thumb sucking, clinging to parents, whining and whimpering, and insisting on sleeping with parents.' Carter learned that children called the killer "the Snatcher" or "the Man." The committee report further said that "a second range of emotional disturbances affecting whole families were related to crowding" from being kept inside with families in small quarters which was unlike their usual routine of staying outside roaming neighborhoods and going about their leisure time, especially in the summer. This was contrary to their whole lifestyle and was seen to give rise to "increased tensions, fighting, sulking, withdrawal, and flight."

Dr. Carter again confirmed the report's finding that the preventive role in the mental health care effort to "keep single children off the streets; teach them always to move in pairs or groups; make sure children always carry a dime for a phone call; engage them in activities to divert their attention and help discharge their tensions; reduce the total number of children on the streets ... by supervised group activities" and by identifying the homes as safe havens to which children could flee ... *may have played some part as the pattern of victims shifted from children and teenagers to men in their 20s.*

The passage of the City curfew ordinance barring children under 16 from being on the streets at night is consistent with Dr. Carter's observation.

Dr. Greaves reportedly observed that "The Atlanta murderer was able to snatch children from the streets, in broad daylight, without being noticed ... and that the murderer was 'part of the social fabric' of the community where the murders occurred – somebody who had a right to be where he was." This indicated to Greaves that the murderer was almost certainly black and was a man. Greaves thought the killer was between 18 and 40 years old.

The Georgia Psychological Association committee came together with a profile based upon what they now knew.

"As the physical and demographic evidence began to pile up" the report said, "specific characteristics of the main culprit became clearer: He was clearly literate, media conscious, mobile, charismatic to economically-aspiring young children and teens, so knowledgeable of the particular section of Atlanta that he was likely a resident or worked there [and he was] uncommonly familiar with police routines and was most attentive to destroying physical evidence. [It] could, for that matter, *have been a policeman.*"

Profiler John Douglas, FBI Behavioral Science Unit, came to Atlanta to assist the Task Force in identifying the type person they should be expecting to find. He reviewed police files and came up with certain conclusions about the victims and a possible offender.

Douglas would later indicate that Williams fit most of the characteristics for serial killers formulated over several years in other cases; Douglas was 'prepped' for possible rebuttal testimony in the event [it] became an issue in the case at trial.

The noted African-American writer James Baldwin in *Atlanta: the Evidence of Things Not Seen* published by Playboy magazine in 1981 wrote that *"whoever was slaughtering the children saw only a black child. Furthermore, whoever was slaughtering the children was almost certainly black. There aren't that many friendly white people in black neighborhoods, they didn't go unnoticed, certainly, and black children aren't likely to jump into a white man's car – especially not as their peers, their schoolmates, are being dragged out of the river or being found dead all over town."*

The 'Splash'

05/22/1981 – 03:00 a.m. – The James Jackson Parkway Bridge & the Chattahoochee River

During the evening hours of May 21, 1981, a four-man surveillance team pursuant to written directives dealing with bridge surveillances was stationed at the Chattahoochee River and James Jackson Parkway Bridge because of recent activities of bodies having been recovered from the river. James Jackson Parkway was a two-lane highway and bridge crossing the river from northwest on the Cobb County side to southeast into Fulton County (the Atlanta side). On the northwest side is the South Cobb Drive entrance ramp to Interstate 285 (which circles the Atlanta Metro area). The stake-out was scheduled for the hours of 8:00 pm to 6:00 am.

The stakeout team of four officers consisted of FBI Agent G.G. Gilliland, Atlanta patrolman Carl Holden, Recruit R.E. Campbell, and Recruit Freddie Jacobs.

Agent Gilliland, in plain clothing, was stationed in a concealed position in a parked 'chase' car on the Cobb County side of the bridge/river intersection a few hundred yards up from the bridge, next to a small building. Holden, likewise, was stationed in a concealed position in a separate unmarked car on the Fulton County side of the bridge/river intersection parked next to the side of a liquor store, *less than 25 yards beyond the bridge.*

Recruit Jacobs was on the Atlanta side of the bridge concealed in bushes, waiting.

Recruit Campbell was *below the bridge at the river bank* on the Cobb County side, waiting … about eight feet from the water. It was a few minutes before 3:00 a.m.

Suddenly, *SPLASH!*

Recruit Campbell heard the loud splash "very similar to a body hitting the water." He had been on his high school swimming team, and as a lifeguard, knew the sound of bodies hitting the water. Using his flashlight, he saw ripples in the water where he heard the splash, but saw no body. Traffic on the bridge had been light during this time in the morning. He had not heard a vehicle stop on the bridge!

Campbell immediately looked up to the bridge directly above where the splash had been seen, but initially saw nothing in the dark, when – "all of a sudden lights appeared on the bridge and simultaneously they started moving." The vehicle began to move slowly across the bridge toward the Fulton (Atlanta) end of the bridge.

Recruit Campbell, using his radio, called to officers on the other side of the river, asking if they saw the vehicle proceeding slowly across the bridge. The car was unusually close to the southerly edge of the bridge and traveling very slow.

Recruit Jacobs, on the Atlanta side of the river, upon receiving the radio signal, leaned around the guard railing and spotted the headlights of a white Chevrolet station wagon moving slowly away from the curb.

Jacobs ducked back behind the railing as the car drove past him. *He watched the driver pull into the liquor store parking lot at the end of the bridge, turn around, and come back, returning across the bridge.*

Jacobs radioed Officer Holden and asked "Did you pick it up?" Jacobs said there had been very little traffic on the bridge at this time of morning – 20 to 25 minutes since the last vehicle; he saw no lights before seeing the station-wagon. There had been no noise from the expansion joint in the bridge when the car came onto the bridge – the car was only going 3-5 mph (for him not have heard the expansion joint).

Patrolman Holden (parked next to the side of a liquor store) witnessed the vehicle make a U-turn at the end of the bridge. Holden, dressed in plain clothes and driving an unmarked car, pulled in behind the vehicle and followed it back across the bridge toward Interstate 285 highway. FBI Agent Gilliland, stationed on the Cobb County side, fell in behind and followed until the vehicle was stopped by Holden on Interstate 285.

The driver exited the vehicle and was identified as Wayne Bertram Williams. He was dressed in a dark shirt and slacks with a baseball cap. He responded: "I know – It's about those boys, isn't it?"

A Serial Killer Emerges

Gilliland took charge, and for about 60-90 minutes Williams was questioned and the vehicle was inspected, but nothing was seized. Williams consented to agents looking in the vehicle and talking to him. [Details of this questioning hereafter appear at trial]. Williams' vehicle contained a few bags of clothing, a flashlight, a pair of gloves, and nylon cord about two feet in length.

Meanwhile, other officers were looking in the river for any signs of a body.

FBI Agent Mike McComas was further south on the river at the Fulton Industrial area. He heard the radio signal about 2:55 a.m. and arrived at the location where Williams had been stopped on I-285. A roving agent, James R. Quinby, was in the area and arrived shortly afterward.

Since a body was not found, a supervisor was contacted at home and the decision was made to permit Williams to proceed without an arrest or seizure of the vehicle.

[There was much discussion afterward, second guessing the decision as to whether Williams should have been arrested and the vehicle seized; the legality of these issues was dealt with in pre-trial motions and subsequent appeals].

Other officers were on stake-out at other locations and came to assist in throwing blocks in the river to duplicate the splash. The presence at the river would continue through the night and morning in a search for a body and further investigation to document the events of that morning. No cars were stopped at other bridge locations that night.

PART TWO
The Trial of the Century

The beginning of the end: Friday, May 22, 1981. It was a day not unlike many others as I wheeled my Plymouth Duster into the parking lot on Pryor Street in Atlanta. I walked down the street to number 136 where I walked up the steps to enter the courthouse.

I looked up and noted the engraving above the entrance to the building: FULTON COUNTY SUPERIOR COURT. Never did it cross my mind that 23 years later I would be standing on these very steps for the ceremony renaming and rededicating the courthouse, the "LEWIS R SLATON COURTHOUSE."

I took the elevator to the third floor and exited into a large lobby designated: LEWIS R. SLATON, DISTRICT ATTORNEY, ATLANTA JUDICIAL CIRCUIT, in large letters. The entire floor housed the District Attorney's Office and the Grand Jury Room. I knew this routine well. I had been making this trip for the past 20 years, the last 15 as an Assistant to the District Attorney. Only a few people would be at the office this early – usually attorneys preparing for the day's trial calendar.

I went through the lobby, turned left, and walked down the corridor to the last office in the right corner – a small office for the elected District Attorney of the largest prosecutor's office in the State; but District Attorney Slaton was not one who could be accused of ostentatious desires. Slaton's secretary was not in her outer office; I walked through.

I knew I would find Slaton in his office as usual reading the newspaper. He had no outside hobbies or activities – except going to funerals and marriages – just the office he held since 1965. He immediately began filling me in on the past night's activities at the James Jackson Parkway Bridge at the Chattahoochee River where a suspect Wayne Williams had been stopped and questioned.

As I learned of the possibility of finally solving the two-year-long siege of Atlanta and the mysterious slayings by a phantom among us, I began to reflect back upon those events ... and more. Was the nightmare over, I wondered?

To ensure that Justice is done, we have to trust our jury system and the people who make it the best in the world – not the fastest or least expensive, but still the best method of determining the guilt or innocence of a human being. To that end, "The Rule of Law" is paramount; [it] *intends* that all guilty persons are to be convicted and punished while all the innocent are acquitted. There are many safeguards in the criminal justice process as a bulwark to an innocent person being convicted, before a case reaches a verdict, as well as after a guilty verdict is handed down – *all in the interest of justice*. Those safeguards include the involvement of many persons and offices including decisions of the police or investigator who make the decision to arrest or seek a warrant, the Magistrate Judge in issuing a warrant and committing the accused or dismissing the charges, the prosecutor's decision whether to dismiss in his guided discretion upon initial receipt of charges or whether to pursue formal charges before the Grand Jury (or add new charges as the evidence may indicate), as well as that body's decision to formally 'indict' or 'no bill' the case. The Trial Prosecutor may still (after formal charges are filed) decide to dismiss after further reviewing the charges and evidence or referring the case to a diversion program (notwithstanding all the prior decisions to send the case forward to trial). The Judge may dismiss charges during motions' hearings and before trial, if appropriate. In fact, the prosecutor has absolute authority to dismiss charges for any or no reason, with or without the consent of the victim before trial, and may even do so during jury trial and before verdict (with consent of the Court) in his effort to *do justice*.

In most jurisdictions here and around the country upward of 50% of *charges initially made* are actually dismissed or adjusted downward during the foregoing periods in the prosecutor's discretion due to legal or evidentiary issues, weakness of the case, wishes of the victim, judicial economy, diversion programs, etc *(none of which may involve the innocence of the accused)* so as not to waste the resources of the government in a jury trial. After all, the prosecutor does not wish to prosecute a *loser* case, unjustifiably, or that of an innocent person. Someone must make such decisions affecting the lives of many; the law gives that authority to the elected District Attorney who mandates the law be executed through his appointed prosecutors to see that justice is carried out so far as humanly possible. After screening, roughly 80-90 per cent of (formally charged) cases plead guilty before trial. Of the remaining cases which reach the trial docket you can be sure that 99 percent of those few cases left for jury trial *are in fact guilty – though the jury will acquit a small percent of those cases.* After a conviction by a jury, the Judge may grant a motion for a new trial. Finally, appeals from the conviction may be taken by the accused through the State and (possibly) Federal Courts – for decades and lifetimes of some of the participants. Of course, the advent of dioxyribonuclecicacid (DNA) testing to clear one's good name may be available. Despite all the foregoing efforts in discretionary screening, *it is a fact that a number of innocent, but convicted, inmates have been set free through the advent of DNA testing in the past two decades – in many cases at the urging and cooperation of the prosecutor.* Thus, a prosecutor's duty, above all else, is to get it right! All of the foregoing is done in the effort to obtain justice! *It is those few cases (compared to the whole) of the innocent but convicted, which rightfully gets magnified globally – not the few cases which are guilty, but acquitted!*

Early in my career I prosecuted a felony case which went so far as reaching the jury deliberation stage when I was approached by the defendant's attorney who asked whether my original offer of a certain sentence on a negotiated guilty plea was available. I indicated it was. The Judge was notified and agreed to accept the negotiated disposition and sentence as presented by counsel. The jury was notified to cease deliberation (while the Judge accepted the defendant's guilty plea and pronounced the sentence). The jury was then called in and told they were dismissed with the thanks of the Court, whereupon the foreman said they had decided on a verdict of "not guilty" (but had not announced it). Of course, the defendant had waived his right to a jury verdict by his guilty plea, had been found guilty by the Court based upon his admission of guilt and could not avail himself of the jury verdict. He was guilty although I had not convinced 12 jurors of that fact. *Justice was done. A guilty person did not evade his punishment.*

On another occasion, after a jury convicted a man of burglary and was sentenced to a prison term, I was not satisfied. The defense presented a viable alibi, I thought (but the jury did not). At least, I had lingering doubts about the case after hearing the defense witnesses. I asked the detective to re-investigate the alibi presented at trial. (The defendant's own actions lent credence to his arrest, perhaps shielding the real perpetrators initially). Some time later, the investigator presented his report which verified the alibi, along with evidence to charge two others with the offense. I went to the sentencing Judge and requested that a new trial be granted. The Court so granted the new trial, whereupon I immediately dismissed the charge. *The convicted defendant went free. Justice was done!*

Mistakes have been made! Where human beings are involved, perfection may escape us. But we must rely on some system of justice, or people will rely upon the law of the jungle – not the land – and survival of the fittest.

The *splash at the river* was later referred to as the break in the case police had been looking for over the past two years and was known as *the splash heard around the world* because of the media event which continued. Now, the forces of the District Attorney's Office along with police and laboratory experts would be in the eye of the storm! Since we had a suspect, I knew we would now be directly involved with police and crime laboratory personnel in obtaining search warrants and such to concentrate the focus of the investigation.

Nathaniel Cater, age 28, was last reported seen during the afternoon of May 21, 1981, on Luckie Street, downtown Atlanta. His body was pulled from the Chattahoochee River, 250 yards south of I-285, and north of Bolton Road on May 24, 1981, 1.2 miles downstream from the James Jackson Parkway Bridge where Wayne Williams had been stopped and questioned two days before. Investigator Horton responded to the river at 12:35 p.m. on May 24 where he observed a nude body later identified as Cater. Boaters had found the body and called police.

After a crime scene investigation was completed, the body was placed in a sheet and a disaster bag for transmittal to the morgue. Cater was the largest of the victims, weighing 146 lbs. He died of asphyxia due to strangulation, as reported by Fulton Medical Examiner Robert Stivers.

Interrogation at Williams' Home – 05/22/81 –

After questioning Williams at the 'bridge scene,' FBI Agents McGrath and Benesh went to his home where he lived with his school-teacher parents. They questioned Williams further about the preceding night. Williams signed a waiver of counsel and agreed to be interviewed further. Details of this interview which was helpful in furthering the investigation was later revealed at trial as to his version of being in the area of the bridge/river at that time so far from his home in the morning hours.

With the body of Nathaniel Cater having been recovered two days after the 'splash,' the Task Force and Crime Laboratory personnel went into full mode of determining if Cater could be associated with the task force victims and Williams (as a suspect) through trace evidence from his (Cater's) body.

Will we be able to associate Cater's body with the 'splash' heard two (2) days earlier at 03:00 a.m. with Williams on the bridge? Other bridges in the area on that night had no such activity – thus, the place of entry of Cater's body to the river? Could we also show that victim Jimmy Ray Payne's body entered the river a month earlier from the same location floating downstream until it hung up on a tree? Could we exclude other possible sites of the entry of Cater's body to the river? These would be matters for further investigation.

Interrogation and Polygraph by FBI – 06/03/81 –

FBI agents located Williams at a phone booth during the afternoon of June 3, 1981, and requested that he come to headquarters to try to clear up some of the discrepancies in his statements.

Williams again waived his Miranda rights to be questioned at FBI headquarters by Agents Mathews and McGrath and to be administered a polygraph examination by Agent Richard Rackleff. The conclusion of the polygraph examination (which is not legally admissible in court except by agreement of the defendant and was not admitted at the trial) was that Williams showed deception to the relative questions as to whether he had killed anyone and specifically to the question: "Did you cause the death of Nathaniel Cater that night?" He flunked the test!

Williams, in his interview with Mathews and McGrath, again discussed his activities of the previous evening and morning of the bridge incident, denying ever having any contact with any of the "missing and murdered children." His interviews would again be helpful to the further investigation, trial, and cross-examination of Williams at trial.

Searches of Williams' Home and Automobile – 06/03/81 –

At about 5:00 p.m. on June 3, 1981, agents and crime laboratory employees descended upon 1817 Penelope Road with search warrants for Williams' Chevrolet station-wagon and home where he lived with his parents, Homer and Faye Williams.

The search warrant was issued by Superior Court Judge John S. Langford, based upon an 18-page typewritten factual affidavit signed by Deputy Chief of Police Morris G. Redding, on June 3, 1981. The warrant sought evidence connected to, or property of victims, trace evidence (fibers and dog hair), weapons, photographs, etc.

The affidavit of probable cause detailed the two-year-long investigation conducted by law officers into the deaths of 28 black victims in the Atlanta metropolitan area.

The facts cited in the affidavit include reference to the Task Force records of the murders of 19 victims: **Yusef Bell, Aaron Wyche,**

Anthony Carter, Earl Lee Terrell, Clifford Jones, Charles Stephens, Aaron Jackson, Patrick Rogers, Lubie Geter, Terry Pue, Patrick Baltazar, Curtis Walker, Joseph Bell, Timothy L. Hill, Eddie Lamar Duncan, Larry Eugene Rogers, Michael McIntosh, Jimmy Ray Payne and William Barrett, and the facts of their becoming missing and subsequently discovered with similar fibers and dog hair on their bodies; further that their deaths were due to various causes, including manual strangulation, asphyxiation, stab wounds, blunt trauma to the head, or unknown;

The facts further cited the surveillance at the Chattahoochee River on May 22, 1981, where Williams was in the possession of the vehicle to be searched in which officers observed certain named items in the vehicle.

The further interrogations of Williams were cited along with his implausible reasons for being at the river. It was further cited that Williams had a 14 year old German shepherd dog which rides in the back of the station-wagon.

The warrant further cited that Cater died of asphyxiation, and that his body was totally nude when it was found; further that on May 27, 1981, the crime laboratory found that dog hairs found attached to his body hair were similar to the hair of a German Shepherd dog; further that the dog hair on Cater was similar to the dog hair found on other victims; further, that certain light yellow fibers found on Cater were also found on certain other victims.

It was further alleged that since December, 1980, eight (8) young black males were found dead in the metro Atlanta Rivers, seven of which were nude or partially clothed – six died from asphyxiation. It was further alleged that Williams admitted that the vehicle to be searched was one he had unrestricted use of, that he used for business purposes, and that his business is the location of talented black persons for commercial purposes. Further, that Williams furnished a copy of what he indicated was a flyer that he hands out for the purpose of locating clients. The handout stated:

The affidavit for search warrant ended with a recitation of a physical surveillance of Williams which began on May 29, 1981, and continuing until the day prior to the warrant was requested on June 3, 1981, alleging that Williams had been watched with his showing erratic behavior of leaving his home in his vehicle, arriving at certain locations, staying momentarily, then returning; driving around the block several times through his neighborhood, hesitating at green lights, driving down streets, stopping, and doubling back, driving from home through neighborhood, returned home, stopped and idled the car for two minutes, then drove away, and finally on June 2 at 4:30 p.m., Williams drove by FBI Agent John Palmer, smiled, and waved.

Mr. Homer Williams met agents at the door where he was presented the warrant to search.

A preliminary survey of the residence determined that the home was a red brick one-story single family dwelling with white trim, with a driveway running along the east side of the house. The interior of the east side of the house consisted of a living room, dining room, den, and bedroom for the parents. Behind their bedroom was a combination bedroom-utility room; about middle way of the house on the west side was a bedroom which their son, Wayne, used. Behind his bedroom was another room on the west side designed as a storage-office room, and behind this room on the west side at the end of the house was another room used as an office. Behind the kitchen and the den was a storage room and an inside porch. At the north end of the house on the east side of the storage room and office was a covered porch area. Two bathrooms were located in the middle of the house. Wayne had a private entry for his side of the house.

Investigators did a thorough search, taking hours, by removing samples of carpet, fibers from items in the house and vehicle, vacuum sweepings, dog hairs from 'Sheba,' Wayne's German Shepherd dog, miscellaneous papers, documents, photographs, and a slapjack found in the ceiling. Of course, the items observed in Williams' car at the river/bridge on the morning hours of May 22 were no where to be found.

On June 22, 1981, a second search warrant was issued based upon the previous affidavit, and twelve (12) new paragraphs describing the June 3 search were appended to the initial 157 paragraphs. The additional information stated that fibers recovered in the first search were determined by scientific tests to be "microscopically identical" to fibers found on the bodies of 16 of the Task Force victims, and requested that another search be allowed to gather evidence to corroborate the results of those tests.

Testing was a continuing effort to match "questioned" fibers from bodies of victims against "known" fibers from Williams' surroundings, as well as against any other persons of interest, suspects or not. This slow, tedious, time-consuming work in the crime laboratory by scientists was to continue until, during, and even after trial and verdict – accumulating additional evidence against Williams.

Williams' News Conference – 06/04/81 –

It was perhaps unprecedented for a criminal suspect (who has been questioned by federal and state agents, had his home and vehicle searched and flunked a polygraph) to call a news conference – but then, Williams had the daily media attention of a 'rock star' since his identification in the case. He was hounded at his home by reporters from around the country who invaded his privacy with cameras pointing at his every move including his peeking around the curtains in his home, while stomping on his grass, following him as he left home – all this and more, but Williams decided to *call a news conference* on the day following the FBI interrogation and polygraph of June 3.

Thank you again Wayne, for giving us more information, lies, and contradictions we can use against you at trial.

Of course, the press conference was covered and recorded by news reporters, from whom I would (later) before trial subpoena the recordings for use at trial.

Some of the issues and questions put to Williams by reporters were as follows:

Question: Why are you doing this?

Answer: Well, ... the reason that I'm doing this is because there are a lot of circumstances surrounding the events of the past few hours, and uh – as you are well aware, no charges were placed against me, and I was released, and there are a lot of things that went on that I feel you people and the public should know, and specific-wise, I'm saying somebody engaged in the line of work that I'm engaged in, some kind of things can be personally detrimental to somebody and I just want to get the air cleared once and for all.

Regarding the incident at the river at 03:00 a.m., 5/22/81 -

Question: What were you doing out near the Chattahoochee and what did you drop in the river?

Answer: Okay. Let me take the first question. On that morning, I was in Cobb County. Uh – the company that I'm working with is a music production company and we're doing a series of interviews, and one of the persons who wanted to interview with our company called up and gave this address and all and told us that we could reach her at that address. The interview was set for 7 o'clock that Friday morning, and I was out in the area anyway making some pickups. I had to go to a local nightclub to pick up a tape recorder, and uh – make a couple of other errands, so I was in the area and I just decided to see if I could try and find the address that she gave me, since it was at 7 o'clock in the morning, and I was out. The second part of your question – what was dropped in the river, nothing.

Further, in response to this river incident, he said: Yea – according to their records, it was 2:52 a.m. on that Friday morning. Yes I was stopped by them at that time, yes.

Question: What did they ask you?

Answer: They didn't ask me – well, I'll relate the series of events, what happened. I was leaving the scene, I was on I-285 just about to cross over into the Fulton County side and – the two unmarked cars came up and uh – flashed the lights, so I pulled over. They got out of the car hollering "Don't move. FBI. Put your hands on top of the car. Let me see some identification, and after that they said, "Do you mind – Well, before that, they said, what did you have in the car? Who was that you threw off the bridge? Do you mind if we look in the car? And I told them I didn't mind if they looked in the car because I didn't have anything to hide …. A couple more agents came to the scene. They didn't ask that many questions until after, I guess one of the supervisors … came on the scene….

Williams acknowledged that he voluntarily talked to police at the bridge, and later at the FBI office where he signed a waiver.

Williams said the FBI accused him of murdering Cater, and twenty-something Others and "it's time for the charade to end" in their attempt to gain a confession from him.

Question: Did they ever call you a suspect? Did they ever use the word suspect?

Answer: *"They – they did it stronger than suspect. They – they openly said, 'you killed Nathaniel Cater, and you know it, and you're lying to us.' They said that . . . ."*

Obviously, Williams slipped up with saying that the FBI accused him during the Bridge interview of having killed Cater; *at that time, the FBI had no idea who the victim was until the body of Cater was pulled from the river two days later and identified.*

Again later in the interview, when pressed about being in the adjoining Cobb County looking for a mysterious female at 2:52 a.m., Williams gave a rambling account of his actions of that a.m., saying "I left the house I guess about 1 o'clock that morning. I had been on the telephone all night on a conference call talking about some business with the group and all. I left the house about 1 o'clock. My first stop was down to a local nightclub in Atlanta to pick up a tape recorder that a friend had borrowed uh – to tape some tapes on from a studio session. I left the nightclub on my way back home, but I decided well since I had this 7 o'clock interview and I had no idea as to where the heck this place was, and I didn't know at the time that the woman had given some false information to me. In other words, the address that she gave uh – was correct, but the apartment number and the telephone number were not correct. And I went up there trying to find the address that she gave me, and uh – I guess I was up there – well, I guess it took maybe about 30 minutes or 40 minutes to get there. I stayed there maybe about another 20 and about the same time to come back, and on my way southbound on South Cobb Drive was the first time that I crossed over the bridge, because I had stopped previously uh – to pick up some boxes . . . and I stopped to put some boxes in the car just to bring back.

"I used the telephone once at a gas station there. I crossed the bridge, and as I was crossing the bridge, I think the reason they'd interested in it, when I crossed it I stopped on the other side of the bridge because I was trying to find the sheet of paper I had the number written on before I got to the telephone. I stopped maybe about ten or fifteen seconds, went to the telephone at the Starvin' Marvin Station. After I went to the telephone at the (station) I got an answer on one of the numbers that I called and they just said, well 'she's not here,' and slammed down the phone and I decided to go home. That's when I crossed the bridge the second time, and I saw the FBI agents had already come out of hiding. (Sighs)."

In pressing Williams further, a reporter asks –

Question: And your appointment was at 7, but that gives you about three or four more hours, what were you planning to do in all that intervening time that you were . . . .

Answer: Go back home and get some sleep, because that's where I was headed when they stopped me.

Question: How were you gonna find the address in the dark? Is that what you were doing?

Answer: Well, I had a street guide in the car. I'm saying, I had a general idea as to where the address was, but the directions that she gave were pretty vague. All she gave was an apartment complex and a building number and a street, and that was all. She was just somebody we were ... considering to be auditioned and interviewed, that's all...I wasn't gonna visit her. I was just going to find the address . . . . I couldn't get through on the telephone; there was some discrepancy as uh . . . when the telephone call was taken, I did not take the call. One of my workers took it, and they are not sure of the exact number that she gave 'em . . . .

Question: It does seem rather strange ... As you can see, why would you be up there at that time of the morning looking for an address.

Answer: Yeah. Sure. What I'm saying, I don't have any problems with them stopping me about that, not at all, because I'd consider it strange myself, somebody being out there.

Further, Williams denied knowing any of the Task Force victims being investigated – children, adults, associates or families.

Williams stated his company is a registered artist development company and he was a performing arts manager who's job is to take some entertainers, say basically from the street, polishing 'em up, get 'em professional and try and shop a record deal for them – and that he had a young group that they'd been putting together since 1977 called Gemini.

He further said he made a trip to Los Angeles, California, and talked with a producer out there, Wade Marcus, who worked on Jackson Five Projects, the Silvers and a 'bunch of 'em,' and he had gotten some agreements and commitments from them to produce a group from Atlanta, and what we set out to do was try and form this particular group ... by holding interviews ... it just so happened that's a male vocal group where the youngest one is 12 and the oldest one is 16.

When asked why he thought the police are interested in him, Williams responded: "Mainly because the events that happened on the bridge, but I don't think they really got interested until after they put the trail on me, and they have followed me all over town, and I'm saying, I'll be honest with you, I know a lot of people in this – in Atlanta, and they've seen me going in a lot of places, and that was some young people or some young-looking people, and with the investigation, I'd assume they'd say, 'Well, we wanna know who this guy is and whose talking to him and why.' I'm saying – I don't have any problems with that."

Williams, further, in explaining the motivation of police to embarrass him, said ... "In the tails and all they had done, they (FBI agents) put a tail on me starting last week, I made 'em probably in the first hour or two, and uh – in the process of tailing me, a couple of guys apparently weren't very good drivers, and I caused 'em to have a minor accident, ..." and further that: "No. They didn't hit mine. They hit one of their own." [Rear-ended]! "Yeah. They're FBI agents. That's correct. And I mean the tail was not obvious."

Further questioning by reporters indicated that Williams did own a German Shepherd dog, but he refused to give the dog's name.

Williams admitted taking a polygraph by the FBI, saying "the agent went over all the questions and answers, and the charts and everything with me, and the first chart, I was upset, it's natural – he says. I'm saying the first chart had a lot of little ups and downs on it, naturally now, and I'll have a copy of those charts by this afternoon."

Asked if he ever wanted to see a lawyer, Williams responded, "No I didn't," and that he had signed a Waiver to talk to them.

The most revealing information about Williams and his attitude about the victims were shown in his answer to a reporter's question:

Question: A lot of people have their own theories about uh who may be responsible for the murders that have happened … what is your opinion of whose doing this, what kind of person is doing this, and why?

Answer: "Well, I'm gonna be honest with you. At this point, it's – from what I read and everything about what you all are doing, I really don't have any – firm opinions except to say that it just looks like to me you may have a bunch of – just a bunch of murders out here. I mean, some of 'em might be connected, some of 'em might be connected, but just from what I see, it just seems like uh – a bunch of homicides because just being honest about the situation, I've worked with kids a while, and some of these kids are in places they don't have no business being at certain times of the day and night. Some of 'em don't have no kind of home supervision, and they're just running around in the streets wild, and I'm saying, when you're doing that, that's not giving anybody a license to kill, but you're opening yourself up for all kinds of things. That's my opinion on it. I just feel that some of these parents just need to tighten up and get strict on the kids."

Williams was questioned about a prior incident he reportedly had in 1978 or 1979, where a report of a vehicle which was wrecked, had emergency lights and equipment. Williams claimed that was a bunch of lies they told. [Williams had been charged with impersonating police].

This lengthy question and answer news conference turned out to be a valuable piece of information, along with all the prior police interviews, to evaluate this person who claimed to be a 'successful talent scout.' It would be useful at trial in revealing the 'real Wayne Williams.'

Formation of a Prosecution Team –

Once everything kept pointing toward Williams as the serial killer who was being 'unmasked' day by day through follow-up investigation of his activities for the past two years, as well as the scientific investigations being conducted by the crime laboratory personnel and other special projects, I knew the ultimate decision to charge Williams was days or weeks away.

I also knew District Attorney Slaton would be depending upon me in leading the prosecution since he had many times before called upon me in high profile or sensitive cases which needed special attention.

A few years before, Slaton sent me into Court to prosecute the case of subornation of false swearing and conspiring to defraud the City of Atlanta by a 'sitting' County Commissioner. I was up against two prominent attorneys who contended it was a 'political prosecution.' During the trial, the Commissioner would be in his offices or in regular commission meetings in the courthouse building when not in the courtroom for the trial. During closing argument – in response to the defense's argument that this was a political prosecution – I pulled my paycheck (what little it was) from my coat pocket and told the jury that I had just that morning received my pay for the month and guess who's signature was on the check – yes, the signature of the defendant (County Commissioner) on trial. The jury's verdict affirmed it was not a political prosecution.

During the 1970s, I was prosecuting murder cases routinely since Atlanta during this period was in the top tier of Capital cities with skyrocketing murder rates – at times designated as the 'Murder Capital of the World.'

In one such murder trial, I was questioning on direct examination a woman I called to the stand to establish that she had heard the shot and called the police to the apartment building. Trying not to lead the witness, I asked: Would you tell the jury if you heard anything unusual [about 1:00 a.m.] the morning you called the police? [A question is not leading where the inquiry is of a single fact and does not suggest the desired answer – a simple "yes" or "no" would be appropriate and not suggestive; had I asked if she heard a 'gunshot' rather than 'anything unusual' would make it leading].

With a quizzical look and shake of the head, she said:

Nooo!

Again trying not to suggest the desired answer, I vented my legal wisdom:

Ma'am, my question is – did anything unusual occur the morning hours in question?

The witness: "No, not that I recall."

Now, concerned that the witness was backing up on me, I made no effort to refrain from leading her, and I tried again:

Please listen carefully, did you or did you not hear a gunshot, and call the police?

Her happy response: Oh, yeah, a gunshot – but that's not 'unusual' in my neighborhood!

When the Judge, Jury, and spectators stopped laughing, we continued the trial.

District Attorney Slaton called me into the office, and indicated he wished me to 'put the case together' and take the lead – that we would be presenting a case to the grand jury in the near future. We discussed a trial team which would include me, himself, and Gordon Miller who had been coordinating the police investigation with our office. Joe Drolet, though not in the "trial division," was added to the team at my request. His assignment as head of our "appellate division" would allow him to support us with legal research in dealing with any unusual legal issues which might occur and to have a bird's eye view of the trial. This would be helpful in an eventual appeal of the conviction as I was confident of such a conviction – *if we were successful in getting the full case before the jury.*

Slaton agreed, and this would be the trial team – or, so I believed at the time. On the eve of trial a new member, Wally Speed, would be added for reasons initially unforeseen, but soon to be known.

I was relieved of all my other responsibilities and case-load to work exclusively on the Williams case. My first task would be to 'see what

we had' in the way of reports. Although I was heretofore familiar generally with the police investigation, the office did not have an 'investigative file' – as prosecutors are routinely sent a file by the police detective
at some time after a case is cleared by arrest. The normal case file may
consist of a single folder or several folders.

However, all the rules were different in this case. We did not have
one agency or detective working the case – we had a multitude of agencies and hundreds of investigators over a period of two years who had
contributed to the case in some way: FBI and other federal agencies;
Georgia Bureau of Investigation; Atlanta Police Bureau; and county
and city police agencies within the surrounding metropolitan Atlanta
area.

Thus, I personally went over to the Task Force headquarters to see
what files were available. Upon entering the large office, I asked for the
files and was directed to the far wall of file cabinets (14 – 4-drawer file
cabinets) and was told 'there you have it.' For the following weeks and
months, I would be found there sifting through the file cabinets for files
needed for the case. After the case was indicted, I would find the trial
Judge and his law clerks there as well, going through the same files for
reports which were considered exculpatory (or helpful) to Williams and
his lawyers.

Arrest and Committal Hearing – 06/23/1981 –

Williams was arrested on June 21, 1981, on a single count of the
murder of 27 year old Nathaniel Cater – the last victim pulled from the
Chattahoochee River two days after Williams was stopped at the river.
[This was not unusual to secure a warrant on a single charge, although
others would be considered, in order to allow time for further investigation and review before presenting to the grand jury].

In the courtroom of State Court Magistrate Albert Thompson on
June 23, 1981, there was a three hour committal (or probable cause)
hearing for Williams for the murder of *Nathaniel Cater*. An estimated
crowd of over 200 people attended the hearing.

As six marshals stood behind Williams and fifteen others stood
around the room, Defense Attorneys Mary Welcome and Tony Axam
represented him at the hearing as the State presented evidence in support

of the single murder charge by calling witnesses in support of two main points: (1) Microscopic fiber and dog-hair evidence that was removed from Cater's body as compared to dog-hair and fibers found in searches of Williams home, automobile, and from Williams' dog; and (2) the "river incident" of early morning hours on May 22 when a loud splash was heard at the river.

Microanalyst Larry Peterson from the State Crime Lab testified that a comparison of the hairs and fibers recovered in the search of Williams' home and car bore *"no significant microscopic differences"* to those removed from Cater's hair. Using tweezers, he said he picked dog hairs and about a dozen textile-type fibers and took a sample of Cater's hair from Cater's body at the morgue; the sample revealed a dozen more fibers during later testing. Of the two dozen fibers, one bore "no significant difference" to the fibers taken from the green carpet in Williams' bedroom. A second fiber bore "no significant microscopic difference" from violet fibers found in Williams' violet and green bedspread, and two to three fibers bore "no significant microscopic differences" to fibers taken from the carpet during a "vacuum sweep" of Williams station wagon. The three to four dog hairs found in Cater's hair were similar to those found on Williams' dog.

Officers Holden and Jacobs testified to Williams being on the bridge and to the activities of the early hours of May 22.

Medical Examiner Investigator J. T. Cameron testified that a body dumped into the river would first sink and after decomposition produced gases within the body, it would then rise within two to three days later and move downstream with the current. This was consistent with Cater's body being in the river for two days before recovery.

The Defense then called two (state) witnesses, Medical Examiner Robert Stivers and Officer Jacobs (obviously to gain some discovery). They were no help to the Defense.

After presentation of the evidence Magistrate Thompson ordered the case bound over to the Superior Court for trial after finding that 'probable cause' existed.

Afterward, District Attorney Slaton announced he would seek an indictment from the grand jury within 30 days. Defense Attorney Mary Welcome told reporters the case was very, very weak and predicted the Grand Jury would not indict Williams.

Williams' Bond Hearing – 07/14/1981 –

Williams requested and was given a bond hearing before Superior Court Judge Sam Phillips McKenzie, on July 14, 1981.

At the bond hearing, the defense called Wayne's mother, Faye Williams, who testified in part that Wayne was 23 years old and that he went to Douglass High School, he had never been convicted of a crime, and they never had problems with him. He lived at home with them. They were members of a local church, where Wayne was christened and served as an Altar Boy. She testified that she and her husband would see to it that Wayne follows any court orders if granted bail, etc. On cross-examination, Slaton asked the witness if Wayne, shortly before his arrest, had made a trip to see Julius Alexander at the Fulton County Airport, and whether there was some talk about Wayne and his father taking a trip to South America. Mrs. Williams responded that it came from a news reporter who was staked out in front of the house and that Wayne went to see about riding with Julius in the air – as he does quite often; he just wanted to ride in the airplane – to circle the city with Julius.

It was further discovered that most of Wayne's earnings came from the parents, jobs he assists his Daddy with; she further testified that Wayne has been working with youth, trying to locate talent and trying to get people to help in recording groups to put out records ... and that Wayne was negotiating with a record company.

Wayne Williams took the stand! His attorney went through a litany of the usual tidbits of his not intimidating witnesses, fleeing or interfering with the administration of justice, (the legal foundation for bond) and asked Williams about his financial plans involved with the "Gemini Project." Williams explained that the Gemini Project was presented to "Motown and Capital Records;" that they have been working on it since 1976; that he is self-employed; and that he has received about $10-12,000 dollars in the past year or so; that eight other people were dependent financially on it; and that he and his parents had their house mortgaged and $80,000 personal money sunk in it. Williams said they negotiated record contracts with two record companies, and if that's not dealt with this summer, (they) could lose over $150,000 as well as investments from other people. He testified if released on bond, he would better be able to assist his lawyers and help in preparation of the case.

Wow, I thought, it will be great when we disprove all this stuff at trial.

On cross-examination, Williams admitted driving to Police Commissioner Brown's house while under surveillance and parking in front, blowing the horn; further, that he again drove by Brown's home, as well as the Mayor's house, and that he had received a copy of charges for some traffic offenses. When asked if he left the premises hidden in the trunk of a car with his father driving, he admitted only being in the front floorboard of his father's car – trying to tie a shoe. Williams continued to enjoy the feisty exchange with Slaton regarding whether he was trying to elude the police who were there to protect him – having been requested to do so by his parents. Wayne said he could identify an unmarked police car.

Both sides argued the law. Other motions were argued including Williams' motion to appear and testify before the Grand Jury when and if the case was presented.

Williams lost his motion for bail and remained in custody pending indictment and trial.

It was later learned that Williams' 'record deals' testimony came as a surprise to his lawyers, and it was quickly denied by the record companies. One lawyer reportedly familiar with the defense recounted that Williams' explanation afterwards was: "He said he forgot where he was."

I can't believe the strategy of the defense allowing Williams to speak to the press, to the police, or to respond in proceedings every chance he got. Williams gave interviews to authorities on several occasions, a polygraph, a news conference, a bail hearing, and a jail interview he gave to "Us" Magazine published on October 13, 1981. Attorneys are usually reluctant to allow their clients to be interviewed or of 'running their mouth' to the media or others, for fear they might say something that will come back to haunt them at trial. This will happen with Williams' comments which were used to prove him a habitual liar at trial. However, we know that some clients and families cannot be 'managed' by the attorney and will insist upon how the case is to be defended. I later learned this to be true with Williams.

It was obvious that Williams was a 'loose cannon' and would testify at trial – I would be ready for that. Also, it was indicated from feedback we received from those around Williams and the media that Williams and his family were making decisions about the defense, including testifying before the grand jury (heretofore unheard of by prosecutors).

The Charging Strategy

What to Charge –

This case was different than any I had ever seen or knew about, not only in length of investigation but also in complexity of facts and legal issues. I knew this case would be in the appellate courts for decades after any conviction because of its notoriety and complexity. I knew also it would continue to draw the attention of the media around the world, and with it lawyers who would attach their names to the case on behalf of Williams so long as he was in life. This has turned out to be true so far!

Ninety-Nine percent of cases are easily charged. In the normal murder case, you simply present a proposed indictment to the Grand Jury along with the investigating officer who would narrate the facts as found by the persons involved in the investigation. Hearsay is admissible. The Grand Jury would either indict by returning a "true bill" (finding sufficient evidence to send the case for trial) or refuse to indict by returning a "no bill." This case was different because it was not an easy decision as to the formality of charging, the evaluation of approximately 28 cases (not including the two female victims, whom we never thought should have been on the task force list) as to whether there was sufficient evidence to proceed to trial. Secondarily, I would consider the evidence which would be admissible in the case, and for which cases it would be relevant, and by categorizing the evidence to show that Williams was the type person who could have committed the murders – reasons for doing it (motives), and who had the opportunity and the means of committing the murders. It was obviously a circumstantial case; and while the State was not required to present a motive for the killings, a jury needs to hear, and expects to hear, why someone would commit such horrendous crimes. Thus, a motive was imperative – and, we had plenty of evidence showing motive.

Evaluation of this case revealed to me that police at the river on May 22 had identified the serial killer, Wayne Bertram Williams, who had been haunting Atlanta and its residents for two years. And, further, I believed a jury would convict if we were able to present the evidence to the jury, as I envisioned it, of perhaps as many as 25 or so cases on the Task Force List of Missing and Murdered children, teenagers, and young adults, who were connected together and to Williams. I evaluated the evidence as being very strong for conviction! There was just too much evidence pointing to and identifying Williams to be the serial killer of Atlanta for him to be able to 'explain it away.' A jury would convict, I had no doubt. But I mused – did we have sufficient evidence from a legal viewpoint to sustain a conviction upon appeal on the Cater case, or others, or all of them? Which cases should we formally charge by indictment?

I give great credit to my humble experience as a criminal investigator in the District Attorney's Office for several years while I attended night Law School in the mid 1960s in being able to recognize and quickly assemble a trial plan – something not forthcoming in the classroom. As an Investigator you learn how to interview witnesses, secure evidence, and assist the prosecutor in planning a case; I had been tested in the field many times in many ways!!

One case which came directly to the District Attorney's office for investigation involved hundreds of complaints from citizens all over the State and beyond – that three associated money order companies headquartered in Atlanta had been issuing money orders which were bouncing. Search warrants were issued for the company offices in Atlanta and another for the top official's home in an affluent residential area of Atlanta. The Investigation Unit of the District Attorneys Office was divided into two teams, with one team simultaneously striking the offices while the Chief, another Investigator and I went to the home of the company president, for execution of the warrants.

About nightfall, we arrived in the driveway of the home. The Chief told me to go to the rear of the home while he and the other Investigator went to the front door and made entry. I was to make sure no one left by the rear until the place was secure for searching. Although we were 'packing' (armed), there was no trouble expected; this was a great neighborhood with beautiful homes, and only the wife was expected to be there at the time.

As I rounded the rear corner of the home – the carport entry was from the rear – I peered into the darkness of the carport. To my great surprise, I heard a low growl; then I saw a large brown German shepherd dog coming at me at full speed. I vividly recall the dog taking a bouncing leap – mouth open with fangs showing!!

The shot was deafening to my ears!

The dog instantly stopped in front of me, then turned and ran across the yard – never to return.

I smelled the smoke and gunpowder! Then, I saw I was holding the smoking gun in my right hand at waist level. I realized I had instinctively drawn and fired my 38 caliber Smith & Wesson from the hip without aiming and without considered resolve to do so. It was a reflex – the danger had obviously triggered my brain to send a signal to my hand and trigger finger to act under the circumstances, though this was the first and last time I would be put into a self-defense situation.

Clint Eastwood would have been envious!

Suddenly, I realized that my associates would be concerned that I had shot someone or someone had shot me. At that time, the Chief rounded the corner, excited, and … I was still holding the smoking gun. I waved him off, saying: "It's OK, a large German shepherd attacked me; I ran it off by firing my gun." The Chief instructed me to come on into the house – that the wife was home – and we would await arrival of the truck for the file cabinets.

I joined the others in the living room where I was introduced to the wife. We sat around a coffee table in the living room for a few minutes – just small talk between us. Suddenly, the wife's little Chihuahua dog (about 12 inches tall) entered the living room, ran up to me aggressively while barking ferociously at my feet; I looked across the coffee table at the Chief. He looked at me, back down to the dog, then back to me in puzzlement, as I quickly responded: "No. No. It was a large – gesturing to my waist – tall German shepherd."

We completed the job and left. I later learned the dog was a trained German shepherd guard dog. The principals of the case including the President would later be convicted of this massive fraud.

As for me, I never lived down the rumor around the office that I shot a Chihuahua dog that attacked me during the execution of a search warrant.

From a review of the investigative files, I knew there were no 'smoking guns' such as fingerprints, confessions, or eye-witnesses to Williams killing anyone. Some cases were stronger than others. DNA testing was not available at the time. The presence of dog hair and fibers on bodies of 23 victims were enough to connect the victims to Williams' home where he lived (with his parents) and to his dog and automobile(s). But, how strong would identification through trace evidence be? Trace evidence had never before – anywhere – been used to such an extent upon which to base a conviction, rather than in support of other evidence. Now we were reversing that proposition by using other evidence to support the scientific trace evidence. Certainly, such evidence was not the same as fingerprints, but was overwhelming from a comparison of questioned hair and fiber to known samples from Williams' surroundings. [At the time of charging, we did not have all of the expert evidence and work completed, as well as many support witnesses who were still being found and interviewed]. We had a great amount of supportive circumstantial evidence. We had witnesses who saw Williams with various victims shortly before they went missing, contrary to Williams' assertions to police and via his press conference that he knew none of them. We could prove Williams to be a recidivist liar; and there was supporting evidence that he had the opportunity and motive to carry out a long string of such horrible crimes and thus would probably lead a jury to convict on some if not all of the cases. Of course, his presence and actions at the bridge/river were damning evidence he would be unable to counter in a lifetime. And, it was important that *a jury would not like Wayne Williams!*

Could the prosecution prove that Williams murdered any of the victims, in that he did, 'unlawfully and with malice aforethought, either express or implied, cause the death of another human being.' The State of Georgia would have to prove Williams guilty; there is no burden on a defendant to testify or prove anything, and the burden upon the State would be to prove guilt beyond a reasonable doubt – not beyond all doubt.

Of course, a conviction could rest upon direct or circumstantial evidence, either or both. The Judge would thus instruct the jury in pertinent part: "Direct evidence is evidence which points immediately to the question at issue. Evidence may also be used to prove a fact by inference. This is referred to as circumstantial evidence. Circumstantial evidence is the proof of facts or circumstances, by direct evidence, from which you may infer other related or connected facts which are reasonable and justified in the light of your experience. To warrant a conviction on circumstantial evidence, the proven facts must not only be consistent with the theory of guilt, but must exclude every other reasonable theory other than the guilt of the accused."

Thus, each crime charged must independently be proven under this burden upon the State. The prosecutor may present whatever charges he feels are justified by the evidence, though the arrest and the Magistrate's findings only involved the one murder charge for which the police had sought the warrant at the District Attorney's behest. We decided to look at each one of the murders – just as a jury would have to do – and then evaluate them accordingly.

In doing so, we immediately seized upon the 'trial plan' which would give the State a better chance to prosecute a case which would be upheld on an appeal after conviction – **from a legal insufficiency of the evidence 'attack.'**

The evidence supporting a conviction is insufficient if no rational trier of fact (jury) could have found the essential elements of the crime beyond a reasonable doubt!

My theory of the prosecution and trial plan would be built around the morning hours of May 22, 1981, at the Chattahoochee River and James Jackson Parkway Bridge incident, **where we have the presence of Wayne Bertram Williams,** under immediate circumstances that he, without more, 'looks guilty,' and his explanation for being there at that time was bizarre and would be disproved. We would build the case around Williams and exclude anyone but him by showing that Cater was literally holding hands with Williams just hours before the splash was heard at the river. Thus, the murder of the last of the victims, Nathaniel Cater, whose body was taken from the river two days after the 'splash' in my view would be upheld from a legal view of the evidence – and, the case for which a Magistrate had found probable cause.

Next, the murder of Jimmy Ray Payne could be tied to the same location in that his body was 'fished' from the river in the same area downstream of the same bridge on April 27, 1981 – one month before that of Cater. Testimony at trial would show that Payne's body must have entered the river at the same place as Cater – the James Jackson Parkway Bridge – thus traversing downstream to the same location. There was also a witness who had seen Williams and Payne near the river about the time of Payne's disappearance.

Rather than overcharging and taking the chance of other cases being 'insufficient in law' to sustain a conviction, we decided to present the Cater and Payne cases to the grand jury for formal charging. We further selected some of the remaining cases to use as 'Similar Transactions' to show a pattern – so the jury would see the 'big picture,' the whole investigation – from which the jury could consider those cases for a specific reason relevant to the offenses on trial, such as to prove identity, bent of mind, knowledge, intent, course of conduct, etc.

I knew that a single conviction for murder would bring a life sentence (since the state was not pursuing the death penalty), [3] and that whether one or twenty life sentences was imposed really made little if any difference from a view of his being paroled. I knew then (as we have seen since that time) that the parole board reviews the entire case investigation and all facts known in evaluating a case for parole. And, while the board must review those eligible for parole consideration – then seven years – Williams would never be paroled in my view; there is 'no right to parole,' only the opportunity to be considered. For one under a "valid Life Sentence," the only door out of prison is by way of a grant of parole by the State Parole Board (in Georgia). After all, a human being can only serve 'one life sentence.' [In 1982 in Georgia, there was no life without parole sentence – only death or life].

---

3   The only technical legal aggravator which would possibly qualify the case for the death penalty would have been the 'multiple murder' aggravator, and prosecutors prefer having two or more 'statutory aggravating circumstances' as set out in the Georgia death penalty scheme (Official Code of Georgia 17-10-30) when asking for death. Also, I knew District Attorney Slaton would not have approved seeking the death penalty, especially in a circumstantial case. Likewise, I would not have recommended it inasmuch as the chances of a jury imposing death would not have been good.

We selected ten of the best remaining cases (arbitrarily selected that representative number from the stronger cases on the list) to proffer to the Court and jury at trial as 'pattern cases.' I could just as easily have selected others. I have never before, or after, seen the extent of use of that high number of uncharged similar or pattern cases in a prosecution – that is, presenting to the jury ten uncharged murders upon a trial of two charged murders; however, there was and is authority to use similar uncharged crimes in cases where you can show similarities or connections between cases such as we had here. Likewise, I had never before seen such a case involving some twenty-eight unsolved, connected, murders under these circumstances, obviously committed by a serial killer. In my mind, the ten similar cases and the two charged murders would sufficiently show a pattern during the two-year span which would identify Williams as a serial killer.

The question will be, and has been asked many times, why not prosecute those ten similar cases if we could use them in such a way? The answer is quite simple: The burden of proof in showing guilt of charged offenses is 'beyond a reasonable doubt,' while the burden of proof was much less in proving a similar transaction. At that time, the State had only to show 'some evidence existed,' less than 'beyond a reasonable doubt' to justify presentation of a similar transaction. In later authority on this issue, the Georgia Supreme Court held that the burden was by a 'preponderance of evidence' [4] – which is enough to tip the scales for admission. We could satisfy the burden of proof as to the similar cases sufficiently in light of the different standard of proof. I knew at the time there would be people who would second guess this decision, but the decision on charging is left to the prosecutor – not the police, public, or victim families. We know the outcome of this decision to charge as we did – but, we'll never know the outcome had we charged differently.

The Grand Jury –

The Fulton County Grand Jury on July 17, 1981, upon being presented the facts, returned a two count indictment against Wayne Bertram Williams, in that he did in pertinent part, Count one, commit "Murder" … on April 22, 1981, did unlawfully and with malice aforethought, cause the

---

4   Freeman v. State, 268 Ga. 185 (4) (1997); 486 SE2d 348.

death of Jimmy Ray Payne, a human being, by asphyxiating him with objects and by means which are to the grand jurors unknown; and further in Count two, commit "Murder" ... on May 22, 1981, did unlawfully and with malice aforethought, cause the death of Nathaniel Cater, a human being, by strangling and asphyxiating him with objects and by means which are to the grand jurors unknown. "Objects and means" of the homicide are unnecessary to a charge of murder and need not be alleged or proven, but reveals the State cannot declare the exact mechanism of death.

Of course, I was assuming the trial judge would permit the state to present the additional ten uncharged murders to show a pattern. We had researched the issue and knew there was authority to do so. I also knew the Judge was a student of the law and would follow the law if we could show similarities or connections between the cases.

I was confident of our position on the matter. Had I not been, we could have formally indicted the other cases. But had we done so, would the weaker cases infect the stronger cases? Also, I knew the cases not charged would be potential for charging later if there was additional evidence forthcoming in the future – but to charge and lose those cases, the State would never be able to prosecute after an acquittal.

Homer and Faye Williams appeared at the Grand jury proceeding and wanted to testify. This was very unusual, but we decided we would lose nothing by permitting it. Both Homer Williams and Faye Williams appeared before the Grand Jury. This proved helpful later at trial in cross-examination. As Mrs. Williams completed her Grand Jury testimony, she turned and told the jurors *"just remember, I'm a mother and he's my only son."*

Pre-Trial Motions and Activities

Arraignment, Motions and Pleas –

Soon after Indictment, Wayne Bertram Williams, through his attorneys, entered his not guilty plea to the two count indictment. This was routine, which was followed by the Court scheduling many motions filed by the defense from mundane administrative requests, discovery of state's evidence, to a change of venue for the trial.

There were never any efforts on either side for a negotiated guilty plea or a disposition without trial as both sides, I believe, knew from the start this would have to be a jury trial, since there was too much at stake and no room for give and take or compromise was available.

On October 5, 1981 (the initial scheduled trial date) Joe Drolet and I – with defense attorneys – met with Judge Clarence Cooper in chambers away from the press to discuss scheduling and other issues not completed so the trial could again be scheduled, perhaps the first of the year. The Judge, after agreeing with the Defense to examine voluminous prosecution and police files for any information that supports Williams' claim of innocence – that is, what we call any exculpatory evidence – ordered the case delayed so he could review the police files on all 28 cases of slain young blacks which were investigated by the Special Task Force. [The Judge did in fact review and disclose any evidence found favorable to defendant from the Task Force files and filed an order to that effect on November 10, 1981, listing the files reviewed. This was a matter contested by all the lawyers representing Williams at trial, after conviction, and through the appellate courts that exculpatory evidence was denied *from the task force files*].

The 9:00 a.m. meeting in the Judge's chambers was interrupted by a bomb threat by a male caller that a bomb had been set to go off between 9:00 a.m. and 2:00 p.m. in the Superior Court building. We were moved into another room and the courtroom was searched with nothing found. Judge Cooper ordered the trial to begin with jury selection on December 28, 1981.

The Role of the Media –

On December 3, 1981, the Judge issued an Order regarding press coverage of the trial with guidelines on "Fair Trial – Free Press." The order provided seating arrangements, weapons detector screening, credentials and press passes, court schedule, etc. The front row of seats was reserved for "sketch artists," while a separate pressroom was being provided for overflow press persons with a direct video link; all would be issued badges with access to the courtroom and/or the pressroom. The order listed 54 reporters and media outlets (television, radio, and newspapers) who thus far had requested access to the trial, including six (6) artists for national networks.

The Judge's decision to deny photographs of jurors was based upon guidelines made with the assistance of a Free Press/Fair Trial Advisory Committee headed by Senior U.S. District Judge Newell Edenfield. Judge Cooper also asked the news media not to publish the names or addresses of jurors, but occupations, race, and sex of jurors were allowed.

Cameras in the Courtroom: In August of 1981, the Atlanta Press Club, representing the Atlanta media, filed a formal request with the Court requesting that cameras be allowed in the courtroom during the trial. A hearing was scheduled by Judge Cooper, who announced that he personally would introduce testimony by mental health experts during such hearing on whether the trial should be televised, explaining that over the past several months many people had shown concern for the mental health of all Atlantans and especially the children. He said: "I want to be sure that no psychological harm might be done if this trial is televised." At a hearing on August 21, the parties and witnesses addressed the court on this issue, including Dr. Lloyd Baccus, Director of the West Fulton Mental Health Center and Senior Consultant for Psychiatry and Law Services at Grady Memorial Hospital. He testified to the deleterious effects of such public proceedings upon the community, especially children who had lived with this nightmare for so long. The Judge denied the motion for live cameras in the courtroom.

The power of the media – newspapers, magazines, radio, and the electronic media – is immense, as is the responsibility of the prosecutor. I see the difference as the media tends to inform the public (publish the news) while the prosecutor must do the utmost to see justice served in a fair-trial venue. In that respect, the atmosphere in the courtroom must be seen as fitting to resemble a solemn setting for the Judge, Attorneys, and Witnesses to be candid and responsive to the solemnity of the occasion for which they are in a courtroom of law, *not a theatre*. Light humor should be distinguished from theatrics – the former is OK. It is nothing unusual for an incident in the courtroom to cause a ripple of laughter or chuckle from someone – including the Judge; it keeps down boredom, maybe even preventing a juror falling asleep in the jury box. A fair and balanced jury, not affected by undue theatrics or outside influences, is necessary for the administration of justice.

Therefore, the confrontation (between the media and attorneys) at times is friendly but necessary. Over the years, the Court has had to deal with this issue of whether the public will be able to see the drama of a courtroom trial through the eyes of a live camera placed in the courtroom by news organizations. I won't go into the legal controversy litigated for years – the questions are too many and the answers few – but prior to the Williams' trial, I don't recall a single jury trial in Georgia with live cameras in the courtroom. Both defense attorneys and prosecutors routinely objected, and the Courts sustained the objections. This was a joint position taken by both adversaries in a criminal trial – one of few in which both agreed – and in which both believed it was necessary for a fair trial. The defense wanted to shield the defendant from the exposure of cameras in the courtroom by raising a myriad of objections including the effect of cameras on witnesses. I was especially concerned that some Attorneys and even Witnesses and Judges (yes, Judges) would 'play' to the 'camera' in the courtroom, knowing the community (or world) was watching them. However, I knew this was not Judge Cooper's character; I had been assigned to his courtroom for the preceding year he had been a Superior Court Judge, and I knew his courtroom was administered with the necessary decorum of a solemn institution. I believe, at the time of this writing, one good example has been the *O.J. Simpson trial* in California with some participants acting for the camera. But, I have seen it occasionally over the 40 years I have been a prosecutor. Further, one of my special reasons over the years (for keeping live cameras out of the courtroom) was in the cases of certain witnesses (informant/witnesses who had concern for their safety if their face was broadcast, and children or females in sexual offense cases). So both the defense and prosecution for their own reasons routinely objected to live cameras in the courtroom.

Since 1982, the media has been proactive in testing the waters, legally, and won. After the Williams' trial, cameras in the courtroom became the norm in high profile cases. Defendants would continue to object as well as some prosecutors. The burden for keeping cameras out of the courtroom was a tough sell to Judges, who in balancing the interests of the public to know … against that of a fair trial … would rule in favor of exposure except in special circumstances where exclusion of the public and press was necessary, i.e., vulgar language, phases of sex offense testimony involving youthful victims, pre-trial hearings where the participants agreed to a closed hearing to protect the fair-trial rights of a defendant, dealing with confidential government information, witness's safety concerns, and so forth.

Over the years since the Williams' trial, I gradually moderated my view on the policy of objecting to the cameras ... as I recognized the essential role the media had in informing the public of what was going on in their courthouses, including trials of major cases in which great interest was placed and which made it impossible for some who wanted to view the trial but were unable to do so – as in the Williams' case, where the courtroom was limited to those having access who lined up early and was able to get a seat; some would return for days hoping to be seated. I spoke to several friends who told me they tried for days to gain access to parts of the trial but were unable to do so. Also, had the public had access (through the TV camera) to the evidence, especially the witnesses' testimony and the many color photographs and postures of the fiber evidence, there would have been more confidence, perhaps, in the jury's verdict and less suspicion about the comparison and identification of fibers. I also found that where there was a legitimate concern of a witness to be exposed to public view through cameras in the courtroom, Judges would balance those concerns of the fair-trial issue. Further, I came to respect the interest of the press in informing the public, in that it served a useful purpose in the purification of proceedings under the watchful eyes of the public which serves to enhance the public confidence of jury verdicts and Court proceedings.

'Gag' Order: On August 27, 1981, Judge Cooper on his own motion after weighing and considering the impact of pretrial publicity on the case and in order to safeguard Williams' constitutional rights to a fair and impartial trial, issued a three page 'gag order' upon all attorneys, both prosecution and defense witnesses, court personnel, law enforcement personnel, and others to refrain from the release of any extra judicial statements for dissemination by any means of public communication, relating to any matters having to do with the Williams' case.

Motion to Dismiss; Excessive Pretrial Publicity: On October 1, 1981, defense counsel filed a motion to dismiss the charges against Williams claiming that since he was stopped at the river and questioned, there had been excessive local, state, national and international pretrial publicity which had tainted the fundamental fairness of any prosecution.

In this three page motion, supported by a 16-page brief, the defense cited many instances in support of their motion (but not attributed to the prosecution). Paragraph 12 of their motion claims that "**Defense counsel has in no way instigated or solicited any type of publicity pertaining to this case.**"

What???

On October 13, 1981, the prosecution team filed a "RESPONSE TO MOTION TO DISMISS …" attaching a stack of about 30 newspaper articles, magazine interviews and press releases attributed to the defense team and Williams, and rebutting the defense's contention that they had not instigated or solicited any of the publicity. In fact, the Defense had been busy seeking out media attention. In an article in *The New York Times,* June 5, 1981, Williams was quoted extensively, adding that "I still think I'm a prime suspect." He had also told reporters at his home that he had undergone intense "interrogation" and that he "had been given three polygraph or lie-detector tests," and was told that "all of my answers were deceptive." Other examples include an article by *The Atlanta Journal,* August 12, 1981, titled "WILLIAMS' LETTER READ ON RADIO: 'Joe, I never killed anyone.'" The letter had been sent by Williams to a Sports Announcer for Station WAOK and broadcast with Williams' claims of innocence and declaration "it will be proven shortly."

Additional interviews included the following: Interviews of Williams from the county jail by *Us Magazine* and published on October 13, and October 27, 1981; Article in *Atlanta Constitution,* September 24, 1981, titled: "Williams Claims He's 'Scapegoat,' Ridicules Police In Magazine Story;" Article in *The Albany Herald,* August 16, 1981, entitled: "Killer Is Still Loose, Williams' Lawyer Says;" Article in *Atlanta Journal,* July 15, 1981, entitled: "Williams gets offers for book, film rights;" Article in *The Atlanta Journal,* September 24, 1981, entitled: "Magazine: Williams lawyer set up interview" – (Us Magazine); Article in *Atlanta*

Journal, September 25, 1981, entitled: "Williams fund drive in works;" Article in *Atlanta Journal/Constitution,* dated October 3, 1981, entitled: "Williams Defense Raps Judge, Prosecutor," wherein the defense claims the prosecutor was attempting to try Williams by "ambush ...," and "The criminal process will not be exorcised by Slaton's Manifesto." And, other communications of like nature were provided indicating the Defense had caused and instigated much of the pre-trial publicity, contrary to their own motion to dismiss because of the intense publicity.

In an article, "Magazine: Williams lawyer set up interview" in the *Atlanta Journal* on September 24, 1981, recited that Defense Attorney Welcome had arranged for her client to be interviewed by Us Magazine at the Fulton County Jail, and personally escorted a reporter into the jail for the interview. The magazine also paid Williams' father $350 for processing ten photographs he took for the article. The Sheriff, Leroy Stynchcombe, responded: "We have not allowed him to have any interviews with any of the media since he's been in our jail. We absolutely have not," and indicated he was investigating the circumstances of how the reporter gained admission.

The Motion to dismiss the charges because of pretrial publicity was denied by Judge Cooper.

Judge Clarence Cooper scheduled and heard pre-trial motions in September and October. Forty-two defense motions had been filed. One of the critical motions involved a motion to suppress evidence taken from the search of Williams' home and automobile on two occasions, pursuant to two search warrants, contending that the warrants were deficient in several technical aspects. Had Williams won this motion, the evidence from those locations, including testimony about the fiber and hair matches would have been in jeopardy.

Williams lost – the warrants were legally issued.

"Gag" Order; Violation; Contempt of Court: In early December, Judge Cooper cited Attorneys Binder (Binder replaced Axam) and Mary Welcome for contempt of court for allegedly violating provisions of the gag order he had previously issued on August 27, 1981. Cooper charged in the contempt petition filed with the clerk's office that Binder and Welcome repeatedly violated his prohibition against "making comments to the media on the merits of the case or the merits or demerits of any motion."

Cooper indicated that he had met with prosecution and defense attorneys on November 19 "to discuss, among other things, articles which appeared in both Atlanta newspapers which quoted a Dr. (Michael Brad) Bayless, a psychologist from Arizona who had examined the defendant in response to a request by defense counsel." At that meeting, defense attorneys said that they would make sure the contents of the gag order were made clear to their witnesses.

Cooper further charged that two weeks later however, articles appeared in both papers about a pathologist hired by the defense to examine the autopsy reports on the two men Williams is accused of killing, in direct violation of the court's order. [This pathologist from New York later appeared and testified for Williams at trial].

Judge Cooper ordered the defense attorneys to be prepared to answer the contempt charges after Williams' trial but warned that if the violations continue, a hearing to answer the charges could come sooner than the end of the trial.

Despite all of the foregoing and the defense motion to dismiss charges because of pre-trial publicity, an article **"Did Mary Welcome defy Williams case gag rule?"** appeared in the *Atlanta Journal* on December 16, 1981, claiming that Welcome granted an interview that had been published in the December issue of *Hip magazine*; she maintained in that interview that her client is innocent of charges and complaining of how the case had been handled. Ms. Welcome, upon being asked by the reporter about such interview, responded that she believed the interview was before the gag order, and Judge Cooper indicated that he would have to investigate. Obviously, this good Judge was thinking of the consequences of imposing sanctions for contempt against Williams' attorneys (before trial) in light of causing more publicity on the eve of trial. The Judge evidently considered the effect of such action upon their status in being ready for trial as scheduled – thus, the Court in delaying such action until after the trial was good judicial restraint.

Another pre-trial conference was held on December 14, 1981, to handle many housekeeping type issues that may come up during trial, as well as court schedule, stipulations, etc.

As anyone can see, there are more time consuming details and pro-cedures in pre-trial activities than in the actual trial.

The Participants

As expected, the local newspapers came out with a spread on the eve of trial, identifying the parties and lawyers. Such was the case on December 28, 1981 (the day jury selection began), by *The Atlanta Journal and the Atlanta Constitution* wherein the Judge and the Attorneys for both sides were matched up. The Judge, **Clarence Cooper**, was a former Assistant District Attorney in the office and at age 39 was sworn in as the youngest judge of the Atlanta Judicial Circuit. He came to the case highly commended by local lawyers and by those who knew him, as one who would see to a fair trial. Judge Cooper was also closely connected to Defense Attorney Mary Welcome, who was formerly a City Solicitor when he (the Judge) was an Atlanta Municipal Court judge; she would appear before him in such capacity. Judge Cooper and I were associates in the prosecutor's office at the same time, and I knew him to have come to his position in life by hard work, education, and perseverance; and no one would be claiming that he was anybody's pawn – he would be seen as following the law to the best of his ability.

For defendant Williams, the paper identified a long list of attorneys and private investigators to be involved in Williams' defense, including **Mary Welcome,** who had been on the case from the beginning. She was identified as the daughter of a surgeon and the first black woman state senator in Maryland. She was a City of Atlanta Solicitor who got her reputation in her smut-fighting days as "Wild Mary" Welcome, and who had been "alternately described as inexperienced and publicity-hungry, or talented and high-principled." After Ms. Welcome had a falling out with original co-counsel **Tony Axam** just before trial, he was dismissed from the case; she then brought in veteran Mississippi trial lawyer **Alvin Binder** to replace Axam. Binder had been characterized in Mississippi "as mean as a yard dog, with a mind like a steel trap and a personality unafraid to take on the political powers." He had won an acquittal in a big case through his cross-examination of a star witness.

The prosecution team actually breathed a 'sigh of relief' upon the release of Axam, whom we considered to have been very effective in the courtroom and who would have given us a hard time at trial. As it turned out Binder, and Jim Kitchens who would later join the defense team, were the best lawyers for the defense and did an excellent job. They would, with the support of a vast team of attorneys and investigators, put up a spirited defense of Williams presenting 66 witnesses of their own.

Others reportedly on the defense team included **Clifton O. Bailey,** who obtained his law degree from Woodrow Wilson College of Law at night; **Harold Spence**, a young attorney from Rutgers University law School; **Bobby DeLaughter**, a partner in Binder's law firm in Jackson, Mississippi; **Gail Anderson**, a graduate of Howard University Law School; and **Jim Kitchens**, a former prosecutor and friend of Binder's from Mississippi, who was passing through town during the trial and decided to join the defense team for the trial duration. He turned out to give the defense a big boost with his entry, showing a good knowledge of the law and trial strategy. Others assisting the defense included several private investigators: **Kenneth McLeod,** who was also a lawyer; **Bud Myers,** a Jackson, Mississippi native, who reportedly likes to project the image of a real-life James Bond: tough, secretive, and smart. Two other investigators had been hired back in the summer, **Sam Walker** of Atlanta and **Will Northrop** of Phoenix, Arizona. Others would later join the defense team. Most all claimed to be in the case because of "Wayne's innocence."

Therefore, it cannot be claimed that Williams was not represented by sufficient counsel and investigators, advisors, and consultants – they were falling over themselves to be involved in the case. None were court-appointed, but were hired and paid by the Williams family, or they volunteered their services.

The public was told that **District Attorney Lewis Slaton** would be involved in the prosecution, though he had not been involved in a major case since the murder of Mrs. Martin Luther King, Sr. at the Ebenezer Baptist Church in 1974. It was further reported he had been criticized, particularly by federal authorities, in the weeks just prior to Williams' arrest for not moving fast enough to put the suspect in jail. I know we refused to be hurried by outside influences to rush the case (to indictment and judgment) on anyone's timeline but our own. I personally suggested to District Attorney Slaton that we needed more time to prepare and allow the crime laboratory to do their work. I knew no one, including the federal officials or the Governor, was going to dictate how we would be prosecuting the case or when. Slaton was lauded as a great administrator of the District Attorney's Office and would not be dictated to about how he runs the office. He was politically safe in the office – no one ever contested his office so long as he held it – 31 years.

The newspaper spread was flattering to all the participants, defense and prosecutors, pointing out that prosecutor **Joe Drolet** was noted in the prosecutor's office in handling appeals and would be on hand during the trial to argue the fine points of law. **Gordon Miller,** having monitored the investigation with the Task Force, was experienced in handling major white collar crimes. Further, the paper stated that **Jack Mallard** who was "considered by Atlanta defense attorneys to be the top trial lawyer in the office" had been "expected to play a leading role in the trial, but a recent illness in his family (will) apparently reduce the role he plays." It was reported that **Wallace Speed**, another prosecutor in the office, had joined the team to get familiar with the case and assist during the trial depending upon Mallard's presence.

"A recent illness" was putting it mildly. Actually, my dear wonderful wife, Jo, had six to twelve months to live (the Doctor reported) with inoperable pancreatic cancer; this became known a few days before jury selection. I didn't show up in court on the week of jury selection, having called and left a message that I didn't know when, or if, I would be back to work. I was still in a daze and didn't want to think about the case.

For the past year, Jo had been complaining of abdominal pain and had seen a dozen or so different doctors, been tested repeatedly, and nothing was found. She was even referred to a psychiatrist to see if it was all in her head – that bounced back to medical without a blink.

Then suddenly, Jo's pain took us to Piedmont Hospital ER where her Doctor met us and did exploratory surgery. After surgery she was sent to her room with the Doctor calling us together for further consultation.

It's all like a blur, but yet something you can't forget. Here I have our two kids, Jack Jr. (Eddie), age 14, and Anne Marie, age 11, in the room waiting for the pronouncement that Jo would hopefully receive a prescription and would be released to go home and recuperate. The Doctor, who had become close to the family over several years, and a couple nurses were present. Jo was propped up in bed, smiling and reassuring as always that everything would be fine when the Doctor announced that she had pancreatic cancer which had spread to other parts of the body and was inoperable ... that she had about six (6) months to live, maybe 12. He explained that all the tests did not find (it) because this particular cancer was hard to detect because of its location.

I was hearing, but not believing what I was hearing – this couldn't be true - Jo was only 41 – she hadn't lived long enough. The ceiling began to spin, and I fell to the floor in the corner of the room as a nurse came over to administer something. I tried to tell her I was alright and got up to see that the kids were having a hard time of it while Jo was the calmest one in the room – trying to reassure us and even the nurses that she would be fine. The Doctor couldn't take it and left the room – he either never returned, or I just don't remember seeing him again that day.

Most of us have gone through such incidents, or will, involving a family member if we live long enough. You are helpless, absolutely helpless, and dependent upon the professional medical care workers to make things right – but, sometimes to no avail.

I have no memory of when we left the hospital or arrived home, but I have plenty memory of Jo dealing with death in the near future, and her main concern was what would happen to me and the kids. I managed to call the office and left the message, since the biggest trial of the century which affected so many people was about to begin jury selection. I knew how complicated and detailed the case would be, since I took the lead role in putting the case together for trial, had prepared a trial plan, etc. The District Attorney and other members of the staff were depending upon me – not to mention the general public who deserves the very best effort from the office. A continuance of the trial was not an option. Hundreds of witnesses were under subpoena to be called. I knew we had a trial team – that everything did not depend upon me – but, I also realized that I had more experience (with several hundred major jury trials) than all other members of the team combined, perhaps several times over. The other prosecutors, however, could and would be able to carry on as the professionals they were, and thus I reasoned my priority was at home.

But, after a couple of days, Jo asked me why I was not at the office. I told her they could handle it without me and that I couldn't go back to work leaving her. Jo got in my face, telling me I was going back to work – that they needed me, and I was not going to stay home to "baby-sit" her and that she could manage since she would be out of bed in another day or so. She said that the neighbors who had been helpful would be there for her. I protested, but she kept working on me, explaining that there was nothing she couldn't do for herself and that the neighbors had agreed with her... saying that they would be looking out for her; they, too, expected me to be in the courtroom. Finally, Jo said that her sister was coming to stay with her for a while, and that I would be in the way.

We lived in Roswell, an Atlanta suburb, and had the very best neighbors anyone could ever have. They always looked after each other when there was a need, and Jo was in and out of their homes as they were with her. Everyone loved Jo as the sweetest, most unselfish person who was always there for anyone with a problem.

By the end of the week, Jo had blown away all the reasons why I should stay at home, insisting that too much was invested in my job and my responsibilities to our children; that it was left up to me to raise our children. Besides, she said she was now feeling better and expected that she would be able to attend some of the trial; this would help her by keeping her interested in following the case at trial. Further, we could hire a housekeeper/cook. She had all the answers, I thought. She wanted us to go on a cruise after the trial was completed. I capitulated as always. I would go back, but only after the jury had been selected which would be after the first of the year, in early January.

I couldn't believe this was happening – that I had to make such a decision. I just wanted to go to bed at night, and wake up as if it was a nightmare. I didn't want to leave Jo at home for a minute; she was the bravest person I ever knew. She dealt with her short future with a smile on her face and spent all the time possible with Eddie and Anne.

I remember Jo telling them not to be angry with her for leaving them; that she didn't want to leave them.

I wanted answers! I wanted to know why, why, why? Why would God want to take the best? Why couldn't doctors do more? Why couldn't it have happened to a bad person? I had met, and known, plenty of bad people in my career – those who were nothing but leeches upon society – who had done no good – those who only took and never gave back. Why Jo, with two children who needed their mother? Why not me? She was a better person than I. I had many questions, but no answers.

I met Jo by chance. My roommate at the time, a friend from my home town, and I rented a place in Atlanta. We considered ourselves confirmed bachelors. In the summer of 1961 – it was a Saturday – my friend brought a female friend of his by where we lived; his friend had another female as a 'tag-along.' I was introduced to Joaline (Jo) Jones. And then it happened without warning! As our eyes met when I looked down – she was petite – I was drowning! She had big eyes and a smile that would 'disarm a robber.' We both knew something was going on. I was in love for the second time in my life!

The first time was in High School, but it was not to be. I had no time … and my priority was to get through school and get away from the farm life where I grew up as one of eight children – four boys and four girls. That is not said as a 'put-down.' My family was, and still is, immensely close; we siblings have never had a serious argument between us as adults – not even in 'divvying up' the estate after death of our parents. We remain to this day unbelievably close. At that time, I thought obtaining a High School Diploma and a dollar an hour clerical job would be a success story – although I did have grandiose ideas about what could be if I handled it right. But the hardships were common to most rural people following the Great Depression into the 1930s as there was little work outside farming; there were no manufacturing plants except in the large cities until the economy was shaking off the depression in the late 1930s as the country began a buildup for WWII when the United States became the breadbasket for the World. Life then became better for the farmer. Even during the Depression with long 'soup lines' in the big cities, we could grow our food on the farm. We always had plenty to eat.

My siblings and I – to this day – reminiscence, happily, about our 'early years' on the farm together; none of us would have had it differently. We recognize and appreciate those years and the teachings of our parents about God, Country, Family, and hard-work as being the foundation upon which our lives would be built (which has served us well to this day). I just wanted the opportunity to remove myself from the hard-work on the farm with visions of a better life. Never did I foresee that one day I would be stepping around mutilated bodies at gory crime scenes, or that my exploits in the courtroom would be recognized nationally from the prosecution of some of the most sensational and landmark murder trials in the State and Country.

Shortly after arrival, Jo announced she was walking up the street a block away to a drug store. I volunteered to walk with her. *As we traversed the short distance in public – it was midday – it seemed natural ... our hands locked. Unbelievable! This doesn't happen – to me! The sun was shining – the birds were singing. As we walked, people on the streets looked our way ... and it wasn't me they were looking at...*
We entered the drugstore and had an ice cream. Jo noticed a 'run' in her stocking. I noticed 'high-heeled spikes' on a beautifully shaped foot. Ladies commonly wore 'spikes' in those days – today I would probably have noticed 'running-shoes.' Jo went to the rack and found a pair of stockings; she then went to the cashier. Without thinking, I whipped out my billfold and insisted on paying the bill. Was this proper protocol, I wondered – paying for a stranger's stockings. I didn't care! I wanted to take care of her.
We were married a few months later. She was 20; I was 26. It was the beginning of a beautiful life together – for the following 21 years.

The Jury Selection

Jury selection began on December 28, 1981. I kept current on what was happening during the jury selection. The previous week I learned that an estimate on the cost of the Williams trial would be slightly over $100,000, a pittance by today's cost for a similar trial. This would be the most expensive judicial proceeding ever to occur in a Fulton County courtroom, according to county administrators. The cost would include the expense of paying sheriff's deputies in protecting the courtroom, the prosecutors, and the jurors who would be sequestered throughout the trial at a hotel. It also included the costs of the judge and his staff, and the *cost of* accommodating the 51 press organizations planning to cover the high-publicity trial. Some 15 sheriff's deputies would be assigned fulltime to guard the courtroom and to stand guard on the roof of the court building while Williams was to be transferred from a sheriff's car to the building. They would also keep watch on the special reporter's rooms housing a closed-circuit TV system to insure that the proceedings were not taped or photographed. Metal detectors which had never been used at court before were installed. Other costs associated with the case were for a part-time information officer who would earn $400 a month while assisting journalists from as far away as Germany and Britain. The Court issued guidelines on the conduct of the trial.

The media was saturating the community daily with a revival of the past two years of investigation. The long quest was over with Williams going on trial for two of the 28 black Atlantans, most of them children, whose deaths over two years aroused worldwide concern and prompted an unparalleled police investigation.

And yet, the defense, who had before trial filed a Motion for a Change of Venue from Fulton County (Atlanta), had reserved that motion, was now telling the Judge they did not wish to invoke the motion. Notwithstanding all the publicity at trial, the defense still did not want a change of venue, but wanted it tried in (Atlanta) Fulton County. After the motion was filed we prosecutors had discussed whether we would fight it or not – and decided we would not object to moving the trial. We believed there was plenty of reason to change the venue because of all the publicity; at the same time we believed we would find more 'prosecution-minded jurors' outside metro-Atlanta. I also felt the Defense would want to stay in Atlanta because they might find more favorable jurors, and because Williams and his family were lifelong residents where his parents were retired school-teachers. I predicted the Defense would not ask the Judge for a change of venue.

I was right!

Jury selection was beginning with juror notices having gone out for some 900 residents, with 500 to appear the first three days for questioning and completion of questionnaires. This was a mammoth undertaking in an effort to find a pool of 60 qualified jurors from which a jury of 12 trial and 4 alternates would serve (jurors who could be fair in spite of the overwhelming media attention to the case). Never before had anyone experienced such a jury selection in Georgia!!

A jury of nine women and three men, eight black and four white jurors, were selected; the jury was predominantly young, black and female. Under the law at that time, the defense was allowed twice the number of peremptory strikes (excusals), 12 to only 6 for the state (in non-death penalty cases) – thus enabling the defense to get a more favorable jury from that view. The only white man was an ex-Detroit police officer who was surprised and disappointed. As I write this, I spoke to one of the jurors – by chance – and though now 90 years of age, she vividly recalls the case and the hardships jurors must endure by being sequestered in a hotel for weeks away from home. She tried to get excused, but Judge Cooper rejected her request; she says it was all she could think of at the time and be truthful – that she had cats which needed her attention. She was able to get her brother to care for the cats.

Judge Cooper instructed the chosen 12 plus 4 alternates that they would have until 3:00 pm that day to pack luggage for a trial expected to last from six to 10 weeks. They would be taken to an undisclosed hotel where they would spend their nights until the trial was concluded.

Finally, a trial would now be underway with sharp-shooters on the roof of the buildings, and people in long lines would daily enter by the main entrance of the courthouse after waiting for hours to get a glimpse of justice at work; they would after going through the metal detectors, wait to be transported by only one of the three elevators which emptied onto the fourth floor for the trial in Courtroom No. 404 of Fulton Superior Court. **The Criminal Justice System was at work in bringing the biggest criminal trial to the State of Georgia.**

PART
THREE
The Prosecution

The Opening Statements

January 6, 1982 – The end was finally beginning. A trial is America's best and surest way of dealing with the truth; 12 good and true citizens would decide Williams' fate. There were plenty of investigators and lawyers in this case to present both sides of the issue fairly to a citizens' jury such that it would take a unanimous vote of all jurors to render a verdict that all could live with – that is 12 out of 12 votes for a guilty verdict; otherwise, it would be not guilty or a 'hung' jury.

Being the elected District Attorney, Slaton decided he would make the opening statement to the jury for the State (as was expected of him), with Al Binder doing the same for Williams.

We had discussed with Slaton whether he would make a lengthy detailed opening or give a brief summary with a 'broad brush.' There are two views among attorneys about this with most believing there should be a detailed lengthy opening to persuade the jury from the beginning of your view of the case. I like this view as a general rule. After discussing the pros and cons, Slaton decided to go the other route and use a broad brush which was fine and made sense in this detailed, lengthy case. This would deny the defense our trial strategy and prevent an upfront preview of our presentation of the evidence in advance of testimony. Jurors would have no outline to go by, but could be like 'investigators' as the case unfolds in their presence.

Slaton's opening lasted only about ten minutes; he invited the jury to join him in assembling a jigsaw puzzle; he had decided the jury would be more alert if they didn't know what was coming, making the jury 'like investigators.' Slaton said that at the conclusion, there will be enough pieces of the puzzle that they would be able to see the picture, (like building a house brick by brick). Slaton presented an excellent, though short, summary for the jury which appeared to be well received by the jury.

Binder to the contrary, took about 35 minutes painting a picture of Williams as being a free spirit with proud parents behind him; that he had been an Altar Boy and Cub Scout, and that "when he was three years old his father bought him a Lionel train." He said: "The theory of our case is that you don't get a killer from a boy [that] was raised the way this one was." Williams, he said, had played softball, basketball, badminton, and tennis.

I was hearing in opening statement by Williams' attorney that they are putting his "good character" into evidence in the trial. I was somewhat surprised. In a criminal trial, the *prosecution* cannot bring into the trial a defendant's "bad character" unless the defendant first introduces his 'good character' – then the state may counter with 'bad character.' However, "good character" puts a defendant in a positive light, and a jury wants to hear about the person on trial.

The defense is playing right into our hands. By bringing up what we refer to as 'good boy stuff' about the accused, now the prosecution can find and present anything to the contrary which would show *bad boy stuff.* Much bad stuff was later presented. Most of the so called 'bad stuff' would have come in for other reasons as well, such as the similar transactions and evidence tending to show motive, intent, etc. Of course, some defendants and families insist on directing the attorneys in trial strategy, such as playing up their good deeds. But if you do, you need to weigh those things against what the prosecution may be able to do in rebuttal, such as stripping him clean for the jury to see just what type character he really has. I knew the Williams' family and friends would need to testify in his behalf in an effort to raise a reasonable doubt of his guilt. Would the 'good' outweigh the 'bad?' I knew a great deal of the 'good' stuff was years before as a youngster and teenager.

Binder continued by warning the jury that victim Payne had attempted suicide twice and that victim Cater "drank excessively ... and sold his blood and body for money."

I knew that the Defense would attack our victims since they came from the 'street,' but this just proved what our evidence would show, that the profile of the victims was a similarity that bound them all together to show motive and a pattern – that a serial killer was killing 'poor black street victims.' Williams had a negative animus (to put it lightly) toward 'street kids' of his race.

Further, Binder told the jury the White House had an interest in the Atlanta child killing cases and referred to a "midnight meeting" about the case at the Governor's Mansion shortly before Williams' arrest. Vice-President George Bush came to Atlanta and met with the state high officials in 1981 to offer federal support and financial assistance.

Judge Cooper looked to the State to proceed with our evidence!

We were ready with witnesses, exhibits, and props. We brought in certain courtroom props, including huge aerial photographs and a 12' scale model of the bridge and river intersection at James Jackson Parkway to illustrate the testimony of witnesses, since it would play a major role in the State's case.

The bridge model was placed prominently in the courtroom in front of the jury-box rail. Witnesses would be allowed to step down from the witness box and point to the relevant locations on the scale model as they testified. The 12-foot area model was one of two of the largest and most elaborate exhibits ever built by the FBI Special Projects Division (along with the one constructed in the Kennedy assassination) and cost something in the range of $25,000 (as I recall). The exhibit represented the area of the bridge and river as it was staked out by the task force. It showed the bridge/river intersection with trees, foliage, and little men and cars, as well as a white station wagon on the bridge representing the Williams' vehicle.

Logically, our trial plan would start off with proving the corpus delicti of count one of the indictment, the recovery of *Jimmy Ray Payne's* body on April 22, 1981, and events leading up to that time; next the formation of the Task Force and events of the morning of May 22, 1981, after which the body of *Nathaniel Cater* was recovered from the river, such as to satisfy the corpus delicti of count two of the indictment. Then, we would present the trace evidence connecting those two cases to Williams and request the court for permission to introduce the ten

similar murders, after which we would present other evidence applicable to all twelve of the cases.

Proving the Charged Murders

Jimmy Ray Payne – victim – Count No. 1, Murder

Jessie Clyde Arnold testified that he was a truck driver for Weaver
Transportation for about 20 years, and that about 3:30 – 4:15 p.m., on
April 27, 1981, he was fishing on the Chattahoochee by the I-285 overpass. His wife was with him. They were on the Cobb County side of
the river. He was asked:

"Did anything happen that day that attracted your attention while
you were fishing?"

"Yes, it did. I had just caught a small fish. I turned around to take
that off, and I was getting ready to bait my hook, and this body floated
by." "At first it didn't dawn on me, and I kind of jerked my head around
and took a good look. I noticed that it was clad in red shorts. Right
away from the reports I had heard, I thought that it was the Payne boy."
[Jimmy Ray Payne].

"Where was the body when you saw it in the river?"

"It was just before going under 285 (I-285), and it was floating basically down the middle." [Floating in mid-stream; this eye-witness testimony will become important in the river hydrology investigation].

"Up the river from 285?"

"Yes."

"What type of current did the river have at that particular place at
that particular time?"

"I would say it was relatively slow."

"All right, Sir. After you observed the body, what did you do
next?"

"Well, it scared me so bad, the first thing I did, I called out to my
wife, and I ran over to where she was and asked her if she was afraid
to stay down there while I ran and called the police. And she said she
wasn't. At that time, I ran up to the car, got in and drove to ... I can't
even think of the name of the place now, this ... they sell everything.

It's right there at Bankhead and River Road. And that was the closest place I could use a phone. So I called then."

The witness said they waited for the police.

On cross-examination, the witness explained where he first saw the body in the middle of the stream up-river of the 285 bridge, and he watched it as it floated downstream. He said:

"I watched it while it went all the way under the bridge and down to this area to where I couldn't see it any more." [The body floated underneath the I-285 Bridge].

Mark Stanley Arnold, an apartment painter, and a friend were on the Chattahoochee fishing on April 27, 1981 at the same time as the preceding witness. Arnold and his friend were located about one-fourth mile south of the I-285 bridge fishing from the bank while the previous witness, Jessie Clyde Arnold (no relation) was just above the I-285 Bridge, fishing from the bank beside the overpass.

"And did you see anything that day unusual?"

"Yes, Sir."

"How long had you been there?"

"Right at an hour, maybe an hour and a half."

The witness said he and his friend were on the bank on the Cobb County side of the river. He was asked:

"What did you see?"

"Well, it was a young man. He was floating down the river."

"Where were you in relation to 285?"

"Well, I was right down, just right at, I believe, a quarter of a mile down the river from 285."

The witness was asked to point out on the aerial photograph the location of the 285 bridge where he was fishing and where the body was when he saw it. He said while his friend went to call the police, he watched the body …

"It was floating down the river right along in here (indicating). And then it just floated on down, and it got caught up in some trees which was laying across the river (on the Fulton County side), not actually across, just on the river."

The witness actually saw the body float downstream until it got caught up in the trees. He showed the police where the body was located. The rescue squad brought a small boat to the river and the body was removed.

This is a photograph of a body (red shorts) in river.

Agent James Hallman, Georgia Bureau of Investigation, testified he was at the Special Homicide Task Force when he received a call to a location on the Cobb County side of the Chattahoochee River during the late evening of April 27, 1981. He arrived at the west side of the river just off Highway 78, Bankhead Highway. He went down to the bank of the river; and looking across the river to the east side or Fulton County side of the river, he saw what appeared to be a body floating in the water face down, close to the bank on the east or Fulton County side.

Hallman testified the river is the dividing line between the two counties at that location. A Cobb County rescue unit with a small motorboat hooked the body with a rope and pulled it back across to the Cobb County side where they removed the body from the water.

"Was there a reason for not removing it on the Fulton County side?"

"Yes Sir. Just the terrain was such that it wouldn't be feasible for us to get down to it."

The body was placed on a sheet, then into a disaster bag – protecting any trace evidence – then into a carrying basket. The body on the stretcher was then walked out through the woods to an ambulance.

Hallman identified the location where the body was recovered on a large aerial map, State's Exhibit No. 500, and photographs were taken looking north towards the I-285 Bridge. Photographs were also taken of Payne's body in the river before being moved and of his right hand showing a mole or scar on the little finger (which fit a description given for the victim). Hallman testified he requested fingerprints of the body be taken at the morgue to verify identity. The witness identified the shorts worn by Payne which had been removed at the morgue and brought to the court for trial.

On cross-examination, Binder elicited that the body was secured with a hemp rope around the body, holding it close to the boat as they brought it across the river, and that the men touched the body as they lifted it out of the river. The witness further affirmed that he helped remove the body from the river and watched the others wrap the sheet around the body. He believed Larry Peterson from the Crime Lab was present. The witness said they had a missing report on Payne before the body was found.

Ruby Jones, Payne's mother, testified that she lived in Decatur and was employed as a Security Guard. She identified a photograph of her son, Jimmy Ray Payne. She also identified the wart on his right hand, little finger. She described her son as about 5'3" and weighed 130 lbs. She said that Payne lived with his girlfriend and sister and was unemployed. She said he was just out of jail; he had no car and no driving license. He was the product of a broken home and was last seen on April 21, 1981, at her daughter's apartment. She testified:

"He left me there. And he was to return. He asked me to wait for him."

"Where was he going?"

"He left going to the Omni."

"To the Omni. And how was he dressed?"

"He had on a gray and black jacket, red pants, white tennises."

"Was he in good health when he left?"

"Yes, he was."

"Do you know whether or not your son ever went swimming?"

"Yeah, he goes swimming. He had went swimming to Parks and things like that."

"What about in a river?"

"No."

[The Chattahoochee at this location is perhaps 15 miles from downtown Atlanta and Payne had no car].

Noteworthy, the *prosecution* is eliciting un-flattering testimony about the deceased victim – something I don't recall ever before, or after this case; *but, this goes to show the killer was targeting those victims who apparently had nothing to give, but their lives – not even their reputation. So, the motive will become clear.*

Ms. Welcome, on cross-examination, asked Mrs. Jones if she knew that Payne had attempted suicide while in a state institution for young offenders because she had not visited him. Nearing tears, she didn't recall such a suicide attempt.

Kathleen Turner, Payne's girlfriend of about six years, testified that on April 21 Payne walked her to the MARTA Train Station at Ashby Street. He had on a grey and black jacket, red pants, and white tennis shoes. She identified the shorts Payne was wearing when his body was recovered. She said she and Payne had never been to the Chattahoochee River.

Hardy Mallory, Identification Bureau, Atlanta Police for eight years, identified the body as Jimmy Ray Payne, by taking fingerprints and comparing those with the known prints of Payne obtained in 1976 when he had been arrested. The witness had rolled Payne's prints at the time of the prior arrest.

Mr. A. B. Dean, age 80, was called by me, knowing he would be subject to vigorous attack; but I thought the jury should hear from him. I knew his hearing and sight may be brought into question. Starting off, I asked him:

"Are you hard of hearing?"

"How's that?" – came back at me.

He proceeded to tell the jury that on April 22 (1981) he saw two men he later learned to be Williams and the deceased, Jimmy Ray Payne, standing by a taxi cab on Highway 78 near the Jackson Parkway bridge about one mile from the Chattahoochee River. On the opposite side of the street, he saw a white station wagon parked.

Upon cross-examination, Binder was able to confuse the elderly gentleman by getting him to misidentify Durwood Myers, a defense investigator, as the man who went to the witness' house to interview him some time in the past, thereby calling his eyesight and hearing into question.

But, I later called a witness who testified she had been sitting outside the courtroom with the elderly witness before he was called to testify, when the defense investigator Myers had walked up to Mr. Dean and said: "Don't you remember me? I was at your house a couple of months ago." Mr. Dean did not respond.

Dr. Saleh Zaki, Fulton County Medical Examiner testified that he performed the autopsy on Jimmy Ray Payne.

The body of Payne was received at the morgue covered in a white sheet within the body bag. Larry Peterson from the Crime Laboratory first did his examination, removing any trace evidence from the body. Then fingerprints were taken for identification and photographs were made, after which Dr. Zaki began his tedious and slow external and internal examination of the body. The red shorts were removed from the body and maintained as evidence. Then Zaki gave Mr. Peterson hair from the victim's scalp and from the pubic region, along with the white sheet the body was wrapped in for examination and retrieval of any foreign trace evidence.

Dr. Zaki noted that the body was in a decomposing state and distended with air; the body had a lot of air, discoloration of the body, and the smell of decomposition. The body had obviously been in water for some time. He said "the skin was tight like a balloon ... with a lot of air inside." Zaki further described "skin slippage in areas which we do see, and some abrasion. Most of them were apparently post-mortem." "He also had a mark in and around the neck area ... which was around two inches." The witness also described bruising to the leg area, the chin area, the mouth and lip.

Zaki then proceeded to his internal examination of the body. He described: "... two small portions of whitish gum-like material. This gum was on one of the teeth. He had cavities in the teeth and one of the lower teeth, molars here on the lower right side was kind of filled with this gum, and corresponding smaller portion was in one of the upper teeth, too." [Interestingly, testimony at trial showed that gum wrappers were found in Williams' trash can when the house was searched].

Zaki further noted air in the tissues and in the chest cavity; in the airways, there was some decomposition fluid. **There was no mud or water in the airway, nor in the stomach (eliminating drowning).** Further examination confirmed the bruising earlier described: one bruise over the forehead in the center of the forehead and two smaller ones over the right parts of the eyebrow.

Zaki testified death was caused by "asphyxia" (undetermined method) and was a homicide. He testified he estimated the body was in water for approximately five days, give or take one to two days.

Asphyxia is a condition caused by insufficient intake of oxygen which sometimes results from many sources including depriving the lungs of oxygen by compressing the trachea, blocking off the jugular veins carrying blood to the heart, or compressing the arteries on the side of the neck that carry blood to the brain. Typically, manual strangulation (usually by hands, arms or ligature around the neck) is determined by an examination of the throat and neck area for signs of trauma to the larynx and hyoid bone. If the body is not too deteriorated, a ligature mark or bruising around the neck is quite often seen. Also, ruptured capillaries (petechial hemorrhage) may be found in the eyes or around the face area where manual strangulation is present.

Zaki's findings of injuries to the neck area and face and the absence of mud or water in the stomach, as well as the circumstances from the investigation in general, was more than sufficient to make a determination as to the cause of death due to homicide, especially in the absence of anything to suggest death by natural causes, accident, or suicide.

Zaki came under intense cross-examination from Binder. Zaki had initially issued a death certificate on June 16, 1981, when he listed the manner of death as "undetermined," but later on August 6, 1981, he had amended the death certificate listing the manner of death as "homicide." Zaki said he could not rule out accidental drowning, but all the circumstances of Payne's death pointed to homicide. Under further direct examination by me, Zaki explained that the appearance of five other young black murder victims in the rivers since March and the fact that Payne did not frequent the Chattahoochee area, made him conclude that Payne's death was not due to accidentally drowning.

The Defense at trial and over the years since seems to think there is, and was, something sinister and illegal about a medical examiner changing the death certificate to reflect his opinion after further information was learned. Defense attorneys were very agitated and critical about it as though they had never known of such to happen. Amending a death certificate is not unusual, especially in 'cold' cases.

I was well aware that the defense would attack the testimony of the medical examiners as to the cause of death because of the condition of some of the bodies when recovered, i.e., being in water several days, some having been found in woods weeks and months afterwards (some mummified) where the bodies were in such bad condition that identification and the cause of death could not be readily determined. In such cases, a medical examiner at times will indicate "undetermined" or give other reasons so as not to over-reach with conclusions as to a homicide. You can always amend or re-issue a death certificate to update further investigation.

Contrary to popular belief, it is not required, in order to prosecute, that a Medical Examiner should agree with the prosecution as to the death being a homicide – assuming there is other proof of such, including testimony of lay witnesses or experts. The Judge will instruct the jury that the jury will determine the weight and credit, if any, to be given the witnesses, including an expert. The State has to prove the cause of death by some means to the satisfaction of the jury – the jury is not bound by the testimony of the medical examiner or any witness.

[I have successfully prosecuted murder cases many times after a change in the cause of death, including my two most recent cases before retirement, the cases having originally been determined to be death by natural causes but later changed – one after six years – to "Homicide" by ingestion of Ethylene Glycol (Anti-freeze); both trials ended with convictions].

Usually in such situations, medical examiners will initially look at the immediate autopsied body and circumstances known at that time; but upon broadening their investigation, they will learn more facts which cause them to be more specific of the cause and manner of death. Some cases do not make it easy to determine the cause of death as it would in cases of gunshots or stab wounds, for example. 'Cold cases' are revived years later when further evidence (including cause of death) surfaces.

While a Pathologist will determine cause of death from an autopsy or tests in a laboratory setting (generally, due to natural deaths at home or in the hospital), a Forensic Pathologist is one who, by further education and training, is qualified to expand the investigation beyond the hospital or laboratory. A State-appointed Medical Examiner is such a Forensic Investigator and will appear at scenes where bodies are found, either in person or by their investigators – before the body is removed – and will investigate the circumstances, including the interview of witnesses, family members, and police. His investigation becomes a part of the Medical Examiner's report and contributes to the findings as to the cause of death and manner of death – how the deceased came to his death.

Dr. Zaki was such a licensed forensic pathologist with eight years with the Fulton County Medical Examiner's Office at that time, and he testified to his experience going back to Cairo, Egypt, in 1959; he had conducted about 3500 autopsies. He was well qualified to give his opinion as to the cause of death of the deceased at the time of trial, based upon his autopsy findings plus the outside investigation of the circumstances as determined from his investigator and police.

Dr. Lee Brown, Public Safety Commissioner. I called Dr. Brown to acquaint the jury with the establishment of the Task Force, how and why it was established. Dr. Brown was responsible for creating the task force and took an oversight position of its activities. In an effort to apprehend the person in the act, one of the strategies was to assign police officers on stakeout at the bridges on the rivers in the area after the killer began dumping bodies in rivers. He said at some point in time the Task Force was staking out up to 24 locations on the Chattahoochee. I asked him:

"Did you have the manpower to do that?"

"Well, the Atlanta Police Bureau in itself would not have had the adequate manpower because we still had to provide the police services to the City. But through the combined efforts of the law enforcement agencies in the area with the assistance from the Federal Bureau of Investigation, we did put together the teams that allowed us to do so." There were 11 different organizations that were involved in the Task Force. The Task Force was started in July 1980, and as the workload increased, the resources assigned to the Task Force increased. I asked:

"Did there come a time that the Recruit School was affected by the stakeout?"

"Yes Sir. We did stop some of the recruit classes for the purpose of using that manpower to be part of the stakeout team."

The stakeouts were started the first part of April, 1981, but were shifted from location to location depending on circumstances.

I asked him if anything happened about February 11, 1981, regarding the fiber connections.

"Yes," Brown responded. "On that date was a front-page article in *The Atlanta Constitution* indicating there were fibers found" on bodies of several victims.

Cross-examination would attempt to show that police were watching all the bridges and would have seen something if Payne's body had been dumped on the day he was missed as testified.

At one time, the cross-examination of Dr. Brown became testy and sarcastic by Defense Counsel Binder, when a sharp exchange between them stunned all of us at the State's table (and later, was the talk of the day). Binder was questioning Brown about some empty police booths through the city – whether he had instituted them. Brown had asked Binder several times to repeat his question. Binder, apparently annoyed, said,

"You can understand English, can't you?"

After a few moments – we could have heard a pin drop in the court-room – Dr. Brown, who was obviously well-educated and well-versed in the English language, responded:

"I have for some years."

Robert Campbell, Atlanta Police Recruit was about eight feet from the water under the James Jackson Parkway Bridge on May 22 when he heard a 'loud splash' as he testified concerning the vehicle's appearance on the bridge. He insisted he had seen the car 'stopped' on the bridge after seeing the splash in the water – he had not seen or heard the car come onto or initially stop on the bridge.

He said he used his flashlight to follow the ripples from the bank to their center at a point just below the bridge. He said:

"I looked up, I looked down, looked up again and I was about to look down again when I saw (car) lights come on right there above where the splash originated."

"Then what did you see?" I asked.

"The car went on across the bridge very slowly," he responded.

Campbell testified he had been a certified lifeguard for three years before joining the police.

Responding to the suggestion by Binder on cross-examination that the splash was probably a beaver, he insisted the splash was much larger than beavers and resembled a body hitting the water.

He said:

"I can tell the difference between a body falling in the water and a beaver." "A Beaver diving for fish goes ka-thump, a double noise. A body hitting the water makes a single noise, except if your' doing a jackknife."

"Did you dive in the water after this body?" asked Binder.

"Nooo, sir," Campbell responded.

"Did you use your lifeguard training to save this person?"

"No sir."

"I see."

Campbell: "I thought about it. But I didn't know the depth … I wasn't sure about animals and snakes. I wasn't about to jump in that water."

"Was it difficult to stay awake?"

"Not on this bridge, it wasn't."

"Why?"

"Frankly, I was very uncomfortable with all the noises and the animals. I didn't want any of them to get to me."

"Did you see beaver?"

"I saw many beavers."

In ending his cross, Binder asked:

"Officer Campbell, do you drink beer?"

Campbell responded that he drank beer twice a week.

"You have a problem, don't you?"

"No sir."

"Isn't it a fact that you were concerned that you were becoming an alcoholic?"

"No, Sir."

"And that is the truth, so help you God?"

"Yes Sir."

Campbell explained that he had heard no noise from the expansion joint in the bridge. He hadn't heard anything prior to the splash for more than 10 minutes, and when they later dropped cinder blocks and parts of a wall into the river, the last one was comparable to the splash. Further, when they did a re-enactment he couldn't hear the expansion joint with a vehicle going under 10 mph.

Freddie Jacobs, Atlanta Police Recruit, testified. I went through the details of that night's activities and his location on the Atlanta side of the bridge in the bushes by the rail when he received the call from Campbell. He saw the station wagon close to the rail, as it came across the bridge from a parked position moving very slowly. The vehicle turned around after crossing the bridge and came back across the bridge and was stopped by police at I-285.

He was cross-examined vigorously by defense counsel, Ms. Welcome, in her attempt to cross him up on his facts. She asked him about when he had become a sworn police officer, pointing out that he was a recruit who had received no formal training at the time he was assigned to stakeout and asked him:

"Isn't it a fact that you were told you could share in the reward because you were a civilian?"

"Nobody ever talked to me about any reward," responded Jacobs.

Ms. Welcome wasn't deterred in her effort to corner the witness in further exchanges:

"Isn't it true that you testified (last year) that he radioed he had heard a loud splash, Mr. Campbell?"

"My name is Jacobs" responded the witness.

Welcome: "I'm sorry, I have a bad habit of calling people the wrong names," "I called (task force commander Morris) Redding, Otis Redding once," said Ms. Welcome in apologizing to the witness.

Welcome: "Does your memory improve with time?"

Jacobs: "It improves all the time."

Jacobs testified he had talked with her private detectives in November.

Welcome: "And this is December?" she asked.

Jacobs: "No, this is January" responded Jacobs to laughter from courtroom spectators.

Ms. Welcome tried to prove by the witness that he tried to read a book during the boring hours on stakeout. Jacobs responded that the stakeout had occurred in the dark, making it impossible to read at 3:00 a.m.

Then in a loud accusing voice, Ms. Welcome said to Jacobs:

"Isn't it true that at least 10 different times you radioed that you heard ghosts out there?"

Jacobs: "No, it's not true. I don't believe in ghosts," he replied.

Finally, Ms. Welcome made a point:

"You never saw Wayne Williams stop on that bridge, did you?"

Jacobs: I never saw a car stop," he responded.

Afterwards, Ms. Welcome's role in the trial diminished as Binder's increased. As Kitchens came into the case, his role supplanted that formerly held by Ms. Welcome, as he and Binder did most of the cross-examination of state's witnesses and presentation of the defense case. There would be another 118 state witnesses called before Ms. Welcome again cross-examined a witness, so reported Patrick Yack of *The Florida Times-Union/Jacksonville Journal* on February 7, 1982.

I called to the stand **Officer Carl Holden** who testified that he was hidden in trees near a liquor store on the Atlanta side of the river in an unmarked Ford Grenada and witnessed Williams' station wagon make a U-turn in the parking lot and return across the bridge. From his position, he could see the bridge guard rail. He heard the radio transmission between the two recruits regarding the car on the bridge.

The witness testified that Williams *did not* make a phone call from a phone booth at the liquor store or at Starvin Marvin's (four-tenths mile down the road) nor pick up boxes to help his parents pack, as he had stated at his June 4 news conference and in statements to the FBI. Further, there were no other cars on the bridge during this interval. The witness followed the vehicle, and along with Agent Gilliland, used his blue light to stop the vehicle. Neither could he hear the expansion joint in the bridge if a car was crossing the bridge at below 5 mph, he testified.

On cross-examination, Al Binder elicited from the witness that when they returned to the bridge, they found no blood or skin on the bridge guard rail.

FBI Special Agent Greg Gilliland. I questioned the witness about the stakeout and subsequent inconsistencies in the statements of Williams regarding his appearance on the bridge. Gilliland heard the radio transmissions from his location and assisted Officer Holden in stopping the vehicle. The first response from Williams was: *I know, this is about those boys, isn't it?*

The witness testified that Williams said he was in the area trying to locate a Cheryl Johnson's phone number 934-7766, who lived at Apt. F, Spanish Trace Apartments, in the vicinity of S. Cobb Drive, Smyrna (Cobb County); he planned to return later that day to talk with her about an entertainment job with Nova Entertainment Corporation of which he was Vice-President. Williams voluntarily responded to questioning about his conduct in the area, denying he stopped or threw anything in the river but said other vehicles were on the bridge when he was. (Gilleland had recorded 25 of the 32 allegations Williams stated were found to be lies).

FBI Agent Mike McComas. This witness, who was further south on the river when the stop of Williams was made, arrived some time later and questioned Williams as well. He testified he interviewed Williams in the car and that he had on a black baseball cap. Williams told him that he was trying to contact "two sisters by the names of Cheryl and Barbara Johnson" at the Spanish Trace Apartments (their apartment) so he would know where to go to interview them later that morning about a singing engagement; further, that the interview was set for 9:30 – 10:00 a.m., and he had tried the telephone number, but it was a bad number.

McComas further testified he saw a pair of suede-type gloves and a flashlight in the front seat, and a 24-inch-long braided nylon cord on the hump in the rear floor of Williams' car, as well as lots of dog hair. Williams said he had an old German shepherd dog and the dog had previously ridden in the station-wagon. [Fibers from the glove and Williams' dog hair would later be connected to victims].

Officer T. C. Cook testified he threw three successively heavier cinder blocks and concrete wall from the bridge into the water below in an attempt to duplicate the splash Officer Campbell heard below: 60 lbs; 100 lbs; then about 130 lbs; the last set being close to the splash heard by Campbell. [Cater weighed about 140 lbs].

Major W. W. Holley testified, in part, that his men were not drunk or sleeping during their stakeouts at the bridges as suggested by Defense Counsel Al Binder. Further, he testified that the surveillance of the bridges across the rivers did not begin until April 26, five days after Payne was last seen – that only a roving surveillance of the bridges was conducted from April 3 to April 26, and that no recruits were under the bridges during that period. (Thus, no police would have been under the bridge when Payne's body was dumped into the river in April).

Officer Gene Nichols, Identification Unit, Atlanta Police, testified about the measurements taken at the bridge; it was 55 feet from the rail to the water; four feet one inch from roadway to rail top; two feet ten inches from little sidewalk to rail top; the little sidewalk (cat walk) on the bridge is one foot two and one-half inches wide. The witness found four (4) pay phones at the Exxon Station. [Defendant did not need to cross bridge to look for a phone to use – he drove right by them on the Cobb County side of the river]. Testimony of the height of the rail and access thereto would indicate how easy it was to lift a body from the tail-gate of the station-wagon and drop it over the rail into the river.

Sgt. Henry Bolton testified there were only ten vehicles like Williams' 1970 Chevrolet Concourse in the Atlanta area. He obtained one to demonstrate Williams' vehicle on the bridge. The sidewalk on that side of the bridge was very narrow so that a vehicle could get very close to the bridge rail. The walkway was only one foot and two and one-half inches wide and it was only two feet ten inches from the sidewalk to the top of the rail. The vehicle tailgate was twenty four inches above the road; the tailgate to the bridge rail top was thirty-one inches; the bridge was one-tenth mile long, and the liquor store to Starvin Marvin's store was four-tenths mile down the road from the bridge. Photographs of the vehicle on the bridge were taken for illustration to the jury.

FBI Agent William (Bill) McGrath testified he went with FBI Agent John Benesh to Williams' home on May 22, 1981, at 10:30 a.m. (after the river incident) where they were given a third version of the events of the night of May 21. Williams waived his Miranda rights and was interviewed. In substance, the witness testified that they went over Williams' version of the prior two days' events. Williams said he spoke with a Cheryl Johnson on May 20, 1981, during the afternoon at about 2:00 – 3:00 p.m.; that she provided him with the following address/ phone number: 2300 Benson Road, Marietta Drive, Marietta, Georgia, telephone: 934-7766.

Williams said that his mother took a message on Thursday, May 21, 1981, when Cheryl Johnson called again. Williams said the appointment was at 6:30 a.m., May 22, 1981, with regard to an interview concerning her acting in a local commercial – the commercial was to be taped on May 22 at 10:00 a.m.

Williams related that on Thursday evening, May 21, he went to the Sans Souci Club on West Peachtree to see Wilbur Jordan and talked to a female at the door who said that Jordan was not there. He was to pick up a tape recorder from Jordan which he had loaned to him. Williams told the witness he then went to Cobb County (Smyrna) in an attempt to find Cheryl Johnson's address.

Williams said he had called the number, but it was busy; he called again with no answer. He picked up boxes and crossed the bridge. He saw three cars on the bridge; he then pulled in by the liquor store, checked the phone number and then went down Bolton Road to Starvin Marvin's where he called again. He was told "There's nobody here by that name." He picked up boxes, went back over the bridge, and was stopped.

Agent McGrath again interviewed Williams on June 3, 1981, at the F.B.I. office. On this occasion, Williams again gave varying accounts of his activities on May 21.

Williams gave five varying accounts of his activities (including his later press conference). There is a saying that: If you tell the truth, there is no fear of contradicting yourself – you repeat the event from memory, rather than trying to remember what you last said about it.

F.B.I. Agent **Richard Rackleff** received still different information when he polygraphed Williams on June 3, 1981, and talked with Williams about the conversation with a Cheryl Johnson. Williams told Rackleff that he had an appointment with Cheryl Johnson for 7:00 a.m., but he had never personally spoken to her. He said she had called and left a message.

Wilber "Gino" Jordan, of the Sans Souci Club, testified that he thought Williams was a police officer. He said he returned the cassette player to Williams on Friday evening – before 11:00 pm; that Mrs. Smith was working the door at the Sans Souci, and that no other lady works the door. [This witness, as did others, thought Williams was the police].

Annie B. Smith testified that she was the female who 'worked the door' at the Sans Souci on Friday, Saturday, and Monday since 1967 and that no other females work the door. She did not work on Thursday and Williams could not have spoken to her.

Sgt. Henry Bolton was recalled and testified that there were telephones visible, starting at Benson Pool Road (the alleged address of his contact, Cheryl Johnson) – 25 phones before you get to the bridge. [Williams had stated he was looking for a phone to call the number he had been given and made the call after crossing the bridge – by his version – passing all the phone booths before crossing the river. In 1981, it was common knowledge there were banks of public phone booths all up and down highways and at businesses near the roadway for use by travelers – this was before the advent of cell phones].

Various witnesses testified that the phone number given by Williams, 934-7766, could not have answered as he claimed. The number was inactive; the number rolled over to a recording and could not have been a personal number.

Apartment managers from various apartments on Benson Poole Road in Smyrna and Spanish Trace Apartments testified that there was no person and address resembling that claimed by Williams.

A Purolator Company witness testified there were no company trucks in the area of the Jackson Parkway Bridge on the evening in question, disputing Williams' claim he saw Purolator trucks on the bridge.

A witness testified that "Schlitz" did not sponsor a basketball team in contradiction of Williams' claim that he was playing for such a team on the evening in question; and on the evening of May 21, 1981, there was no men's basketball at the Ben Hill Recreation Center – it was ladies' exercise night, which disputed Williams' claim that on the evening of May 21, he was there.

Nathaniel Cater – victim – Count No. 2 - Murder

Alan Maddox, a toolmaker, testified he was canoeing on the Chattahoochee River with a friend on Sunday, May 24, 1981, going downstream. They had been canoeing on the river from 9:30 a.m. until about 10:40 a.m. when they found the body later identified as Nathaniel Cater. They were paddling on the Cobb County side when Maddox saw the body over his left shoulder on the Fulton (Atlanta) County side.

Maddox: "I told Tom, the friend with me, that it looked to me to be a body, but I couldn't identify it. There was no, no legs or arms exposed."

Slaton: "Exposed?"

Maddox: "Right. It was just the trunk, the bent trunk part of the body. So I said, let's go check it out. So we checked it out and I got quite close to it, and I was able to look down and see the hair. So then I paddled upstream where I tried to flag somebody down to call the police. I flagged a truck driver down. It was a pickup truck. And he was … he called Cobb County and they came immediately."

After the Cobb police arrived, Maddox paddled a Lieutenant down to where the body was found. The witness estimates it was a hundred fifty, two hundred yards downstream of the I-285 Bridge but on the Fulton County side. Maddox described the area where the body was located as having a lot of overhanging trees and growth. He described an opening in the trees where the light was shining on the body which reflected the light. The body was caught in an eddy behind a big log, close to the bank.

The witness identified photographs showing the area, including the I-285 highway. Maddox described the body as looking "scarred — swelled-up blistered places."

On cross-examination, Mr. Binder asked the witness if he had ever seen anything like that in his life, whereupon Maddox replied, "overseas, but I was prepared for it there; I wasn't here."

Maddox described the day as "sweltering hot – over a hundred degrees." He testified he had been canoeing all his life. He was led back through much of his testimony on direct and added that after dropping the officer off, he gave the police his information and he and his friend continued on their way.

Lt. R. F. Brown, Cobb County Police, testified he received the dispatch and proceeded to the river and met Mr. Alan Maddox who told him what he had found. Maddox paddled Brown across the river to the body. No one touched the body. Brown called for Atlanta Police to respond since the body was on the Fulton County side of the river. Several members of the Atlanta Task Force soon arrived along with Major Redding, who took over the responsibility of removing the body.

Detective Frank McClure, Atlanta Police, testified he helped retrieve the body. He used surgical gloves and put the body on a sheet into a disaster bag. The body was about 200 yards downstream from Interstate Highway 285 and 100 yards up from where Payne's body was found one month earlier. The body was one and two-tenths miles downstream of the James Jackson Parkway Bridge.

Willard Ford, Identification Bureau, Fulton County Police, testified he fingerprinted the body and identified Nathaniel Cater with his known prints on file. Ford had gone to the Chattahoochee River with others where the body had been discovered. He took photographs and assisted in removing the body from the river which turned out to be a major undertaking. The river bank was about thirty feet high and steep. Several officers managed to remove the body up the embankment after wrapping it with a white sheet to safeguard any trace evidence and with use of ropes lifted the body from the embankment. The body was taken to the morgue, where Larry Peterson from the Crime Laboratory completed the work of removing the trace evidence before he (Ford) further examined the fingers of Cater for purposes of obtaining fingerprints. However, due to the condition of the body from having been in the River, it was necessary for Ford to cut the skin from the fingers. Ford then went to the Atlanta Police Identification Bureau where he cleaned up the skin, then placing Cater's finger skins on his own fingers, he rolled the prints. Obtaining legible prints, he then classified the prints and compared them to those on file for "Nathaniel Cater," thereby verifying the identity of the body.

Ford believed, as did other officers, that the 'serial killer' was someone who 'fit into the community,' who was able to come and go *without suspicion* or appearing out of place – the city had been in lockdown by patrols and a curfew for some months.

Dr. Robert Stivers, Chief Medical Examiner, Fulton County, testified to his qualifications as a forensic pathologist since 1971 and before. He had done about 6000 autopsies. I had him to describe the duties of a pathologist who deals with diseases versus a forensic pathologist, such as a medical examiner, whose duty is to determine the cause and manner of death. A forensic pathologist or medical examiner has specific training over that of a traditional pathologist in the investigation of cause and manner of death.

Dr. Stivers allowed Larry Peterson from the State Crime Laboratory to go over the body for trace evidence after he (Stivers) opened the bag containing the body of Nathaniel Cater. Willard Ford was allowed to obtain the fingerprints after which the autopsy was performed. They were working on the body for about six hours. Stivers explained that the autopsy of the body was just one part of his investigation – perhaps twenty-five percent, and that other investigation is necessary to enable him to arrive at his conclusions about how the decedent met his death. There was no water in the lungs. Once a body is in water, decomposition sets in from bacteria in the intestinal tract and other body cavities, he explained, and the body becomes buoyant; but it takes a period of time. The body at the bottom of the river will become slightly buoyant and will rise slightly; move along; and finally there is enough gas to bring the body to the surface.

Cater had hemorrhage in the neck area and there were asphyxial signs in the chest cavity and the head. Also noted were signs of injury in the neck muscles (hemorrhage on the sides of the voice box and behind it) into the anterior vertebral column. There was indication of upward force which could come from a choke hold formed with a broad, soft surface such as a forearm – like in the crook of your arm. Dr. Stivers said if a person is grabbed from the rear, the person would probably grab the assailant's arms and try to tear them away. [This would explain subsequent testimony that witnesses had seen Williams with scratches on his face and arms]. Stivers submitted blood samples to the Crime Laboratory and specimens to the FBI laboratory. The alcohol content in Cater's blood was .13 grams percent.

Asphyxia, Stivers explained, is a cutting off of the oxygen, which cuts off blood to the heart (strangulation); it is like fainting – it's a very quick way of passing out. He said that asphyxia in Fulton County was a rare form of homicide – zero to 3 per year – back to 1963.

Dr. Stivers, on cross-examination, explained that the time of death was an educated guess only and that the body in his opinion had been in water from 2-5 days. The eyes were still present and they will begin to decompose right away along with loss of nails and skin slippage. The lungs and heart were unremarkable, and no water was found in the sinuses, stomach, or airways. He responded that a body hitting the water from 50 feet wouldn't harm the body. He said that two of his investigators were at the river when the body was found.

On cross-examination when asked: "Do you know with absolute certainty what happened," he replied: "No."

The vigorous cross-examination tried to show that Cater had been in the water longer than the prosecution contended, in an effort to prove that Cater must have been in the river before May 22 when Williams was on the bridge. [The following witnesses would prove that Cater was alive on May 21, consistent with Dr. Stivers' testimony and with the State's contention that Williams introduced Cater's body to the river when the splash was heard only hours after he was seen alive in Atlanta].

Ms. Vicki Snipes, American Plasma Inc. This witness, a licensed practical nurse who had seen Cater at the blood bank many times, identified Nathaniel Cater (the last victim whose body was pulled from the Chattahoochee on May 24, 1981) as a frequent customer who sold his blood many times in late 1980 and early 1981. He tried in March, but there was protein in his urine, so he was refused. She last saw Cater on May 21, 1981, between 10:00 – 11:00 a.m. when his protein was checked and found to be too high – so he was rejected. The last time he gave blood had been January 30, 1981. The records confirmed this history of Cater.

Lyle Nichols, Desk Clerk, Falcon Hotel. This witness testified that he last saw Cater on May 21, 1981, at 3:00 – 3:30 p.m. on Luckie Street one-half block from the hotel. He said that Cater had no vehicle and he drank and hung out at the "Cameo" and "Silver Dollar" (downtown) bars. He testified that Cater couldn't hold his liquor, and sometimes hotel employees would help him upstairs to his second floor room. He paid about $4.00 a night to stay there. [The intent is to chronicle the victim's last day and time alive, the closest time to his being missed and found dead. Who was the last person to see the victim alive?]

Robert I. Henry. This witness, a credible 37-year-old who worked for a north-side nursery, devastated the defense when he identified Williams in the company of the victim, Nathaniel Cater, just hours before Williams was on the bridge in the morning hours of May 22, 1981.

In a low-key voice and quiet demeanor, Mr. Henry testified that he saw "Silky" Cater about 9:15 p.m. on May 21, 1981 (the State contends that Cater's body was thrown from the bridge less than six (6) hours later just before 3:00 a.m.). Henry said that was his night 'off work' and he was going down Forsyth Street to eat at the Huddle House. He saw "Silky" and three others coming from the Rialto Theater – the two in front were Silky and Williams who were holding hands; the other two were dressed like women, but they appeared to be men. Mr. Henry knew Silky (Cater) from the time when they both worked at a labor pool, and that caused him to stop Cater to inquire about the possibility of a job. Henry identified Williams as the person who continued to hold hands with Cater as he greeted Cater with a hand slap and a "What's happening?"

At the testimony that Williams and Cater were holding hands hours before Cater would be dead, whispering and murmurs were heard through the courtroom, but Williams showed no reaction or emotion.

When I called this witness to the stand, he was objected to by the defense, claiming they had not received sufficient notice. However, Judge Cooper promptly overruled the objection as I pointed out that this witness was unknown until during the trial. The witness did not voluntarily come forward, and we had just discovered him this week and promptly notified the Defense.

Mr. Henry acknowledged that he did not come forward voluntarily, saying "I didn't want to get involved," and that he was in court because the "detective found me and they subpoenaed me to come down here." This gave the witness credibility as a reluctant witness and shook the defense.

On cross-examination, Mr. Henry admitted that "I been in jail a lot of times" for minor stuff but nothing that ever earned him more than three or four days in jail. Binder pressed him that he must have discussed the case with his boss and fellow workers at the north-side nursery where he worked. Henry answered: "People up there are not too concerned with what blacks do to one another in Atlanta."

Margaret Carter. This witness placed Williams in the company of Nathaniel Cater less than a week before he was last seen alive. Ms. Carter, who lived on Verbena St, Atlanta, said she saw Williams and Cater sitting at a picnic table in the park next to her apartment complex on a Friday of the week before Cater was discovered dead. She had known Cater for four to five years as Cater had once dated her niece, "Slim." Ms. Carter explained that at the time she did not know Williams but later saw him on television.

I asked her: "Who was it that you saw?"
She replied: "Wayne Williams."
"Where had you seen him?"
"Sitting in the park on that bench with Nathaniel Cater."
I asked if she was sure; she replied: "I'm sure."
"Is there any question in your mind?"
"No," she responded as to her identification.

When asked if she could identify the man with Cater if she saw him in the courtroom, she responded:

"He's sitting between the lady and the man, in blue," identifying Williams sitting between his lawyers, Welcome and Binder. Williams showed no reaction; he had been taking copious notes.

The witness further testified that Williams had his feet resting on the picnic bench; he was wearing gray trousers, a gray long-sleeved shirt, glasses, and had a medium-length afro. *She also saw a station wagon and a German shepherd nearby.*

She was vigorously cross-examined by Binder showing that she had been interviewed by as many as ten investigators, including two working for the Williams' defense team; she also thought the station wagon was light blue and that the dog was 'frisky.' She would not agree with Binder, however, that the dog was "young." [Williams' station-wagon was white and the dog was 14 years old].

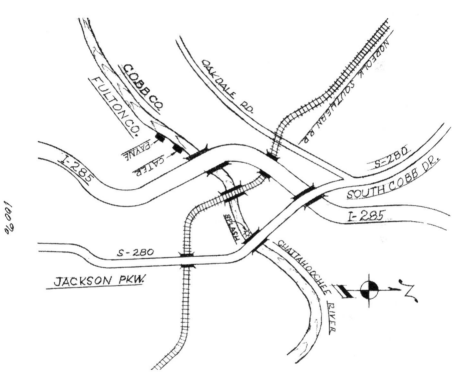

Drawing of bridge/river intersection

Image of Bridge/Welcome Fulton County sign

Image of Bridge/River Splash

Blue car on bridge, close to rail

Blue car on bridge;tailgate down; man with ruler

River/Bridge scenes

RiverScenes

Red boat at river with 4 men

Aerial view of river; Cater's & Payne's body located

Hydrology and the Chattahoochee River

Hydrology is **"the scientific study of the properties, distribution, and effects of water on the earth's surface . . ."** [*American Heritage Dictionary,* 2nd College Ed.].

The State, which had the complete support of the federal government from the White House down, requested the assistance of the U.S. Army Corps of Engineers in determining, if possible, the water flow and current of the Chattahoochee River in the area from which the bodies of Cater and Payne were found and 1.2 miles upstream from that point to the Jackson Parkway Bridge. This was to account for a body having traversed from north of midstream to the south side of the river where it lodged on a tree limb. Since the sides and banks of the river were dense with jungle-like heavy growth which would make it improbable for anyone to reach it carrying a body, it would be important to determine if we could eliminate any points of access except the bridges manned by guards on the night of May 21-22, 1981.

We wanted to be able to support our theory through expert testimony, photographs, and evidence that not only Cater's body went into the river at the place where the splash was heard, but also that of Payne's body a month earlier (since the bodies ended up on the opposite side of the river 1.2 miles downstream from the James Jackson Parkway Bridge). Was there a current in the river which could cause that to happen? We knew there must be since witnesses watched Payne's body traverse downstream from the middle of the stream to the south side of the river and lodge on a tree.

As in other scientific investigations, we wanted the very best and experienced witness we could find to lend credence in this endeavor. We found this person in **Benjamin L. Kittle**, Chief of the Hydraulic Section in the Engineering Division, South Atlantic Division, Army Corp of Engineers. Kittle held a Bachelor of Civil Engineering Degree from Georgia Tech (some will say the top engineering school in the country), a Master of Science Degree from Georgia Tech in Civil Engineering with a Hydraulics and Fluid Mechanics Option. He was a Registered Professional Engineer and a Civil Engineer, a Registered Land Surveyor, a Fellow of the American Society of Civil Engineers, a member of SIGMA XI which is devoted to Research and Science; and he had 30 years experience as a Civil Engineer (27 years were in Hydraulic Engineering).

Kittle's experience included civil works and military construction, navigation channels, harbors, hydraulic structures such as dams, navigation locks and similar works. He had received a special commendation for a technical paper he co-authored for the International Conference for Water and Peace. Kittle was also responsible for the overall water design of the Tennessee Tom Bigby, the largest project (dollar-wise) under construction by the Corps of Engineers. We wanted to be sure the defense could not top our expert in Hydrology, as we had endeavored to do in the other scientific fields.

Kittle identified State's Exhibit 525 as a report of which he was the principal author, entitled Technical Service Report for the City of Atlanta, Special Hydrologic Conditions in the Chattahoochee River at Atlanta, Georgia, dated July 1981.

The witness also identified State's Exhibit 526 as a second report of which he was the author, identified as Velocity Measurements in the River Reach from South Cobb Drive Bridge (James Jackson Parkway) to 900 feet downstream of the I-285 Bridge, Chattahoochee River, dated December, 1981. The witness explained that the "Bridge" is known as the South Cobb Drive Bridge on the northwest (or Cobb County) side, and as the James Jackson Parkway on the opposite (Atlanta) side.

Kittle explained what he and the people under his general supervision did in support of his reports: "We picked eleven what we call cross sections on the river where we measured the velocity and the depth at which the velocity measurement was made. And we made what is known as a velocity cross section. We had eleven of those beginning at the upstream edge of the Jackson Parkway Bridge extending down the river to the approximate location where Mr. Payne's body was found (marking the cross sections on the map)."

He explained the velocity study: "We utilized the personnel of the United States Geological Survey whose job it is to do this type of work. That's the thing they do. We had five crews on the river and one on the bridge. One gentleman walked back and forth and this bridge was marked off. They had painted marks so he knew where he was. He would drop a machine that had a sounding weight which is a large piece of lead (which) looked like a submarine about that long (indicating) … dropped that into the water. About six inches before it, he had what is known as a price current meter. A current meter has a little propeller thing on it, and the velocity of the water would cause that propeller to turn, and that generates an electric current. He wears an ear set and uses a stop watch. By counting the number of clicks that the electricity makes as that propeller goes around, he can go to a table and determine what the velocity of the water is at that point. These instruments are calibrated by the National Bureau Standards in the Hydraulic Laboratory in Washington.

"So what he did, he started at one end and came to the first station where he was going to take a velocity measurement. He has a board and has a reel on it that reels this steel wire out. There's a dial that is a counter. It tells him how far … the depth.

"So he lowers the sounding weight until it touches bottom. And when it touches bottom, the operator through experience can sense this. The cable goes slack, and he can tell fairly precisely where the bottom is. He sets the dial, his gauge, to that elevation, and then he pulls, cranks up the weight until it just leaves the water surface or just touches. That gives him the total depth of the water at that station.

"He then made three measurements of velocity at a depth of two-tenths the total distance from the bottom. That is, he took two-tenths of the total depth of the water and he made a measurement there. This dial tells him where that is automatically. Then he pulled the weight up, and he would take another measurement at sixth-tenths of the total distance, six-tenths from the bottom of the total depth of the water, and then he made a third measurement at eight-tenths from the bottom.

"He would move then to the next section, and we repeated that process. He did this all day long, starting at about 8:00 in the morning until 5:00 or 6:00 in the afternoon.

"The other sections were taken by personnel in boats. What they did. They got on the station and they stretched a steel cable across the river. This cable had little beads on it which indicated the distance across the river. They also put pieces of cloth on it so that they could tell exactly where they were.

"Then both of them would set up on one of the stations, and he would measure the depths and the velocities. He would proceed all the way across the river and start back again. This was done ... one crew, one boat, had two sections. He'd go from here to here and back again (indicating), similarly for the entire reach of the river, making these velocity measurements."

Based upon the measurements and calculations, Kittle then testified to the behavior of the water and current from the James Jackson Parkway Bridge down to the Last Cross Section:

"Well, in general terms, the velocities are what we would term as un-uniform velocity. That is, the velocity is generally greater at the center of the river; as you go towards the bank, the velocity gets less and less, and that's caused by the friction of the bank. As you go down, the greatest velocity is near the top. As you go down towards the bottom, the velocity, of course, at the bottom is theoretically zero.

"So where you would have, for example, a velocity of two or two and a half feet per second near the top, when you got down to a foot or so off the bottom, the velocity had decreased to about one half foot per second."

As the water is moving downstream, he explained:

"When the water comes under the bridge, it has ... its coming in this direction which is a fairly straight reach. It's a very mild bend. There are two piers under the bridge as I remember. And those piers have the effect of straightening the flow as it comes through it. When you progress down the river in a straight reach, the velocity stays ... the maximum velocity is at the center of the channel; the lesser velocity on the side.

"As you come around the bend, and I would term this as a mild bend, the water having ... a volume of water moving down the river has mass and it has velocity; and that's momentum, mass times velocity. It does not want to make the turn. It tends to go straight ahead. So you would find, then, that your higher velocity would be on this shore as you come to a bend.

"Now, as the water makes the bend and comes down further, it is reflected off of this bank (indicating). And many times, not always, but many times it would bounce back onto the other shore, be reflected."

Indicating on the aerial map, the witness refers to the large trees projecting maybe 50 feet over the riverbank along the shore. He was asked his opinion of how the river would affect a body that was in the water floating or submerged:

"I would expect it to tend towards this bank (indicating). But because it's a mild curve and the velocities were two and a half feet per second, something like that, and it's a mild curve, I would say that the probability is that it would pass that bend because it's rather mild. It would probably tend to this shore, but would eventually make the turn and come on out and get into the current again.

"When it gets to the southern ... it is the Southern Railroad Bridge, I believe, we had very confused velocity patterns at this bridge. You notice this little square right here is a pier (indicating) from a former bridge. And this is a very massive structure. And there's also two piers under the existing bridge. When you come under, the water passes under that bridge, it comes through at a very high velocity because it's constricted. But then when it gets downstream of these piers, an eddy forms, like a whirlpool.

"And actually we did measure what we call negative velocities; that is, the water ran in an upstream direction in this eddy or pool due to the piers. But the velocity on either side was very high.

"I think that, assuming that a body did not hang up in front of the piers that it would pass readily through that opening because of the higher velocity. There's a possibility that after it passed under the bridge, it could have been caught in this eddy motion and could have remained there for some time. I think it would have eventually moved out. It would have been caught up in the velocity and the current and moved.

"When you come on downstream, we have another relatively mild bend. You would expect the momentum of the water to carry the higher velocity to the North shore, the North bank. In my opinion, the bend is so mild that I think that an object could have passed the bend and moved downstream. When, assuming it reaches this point, it's a straight reach, and there's really no reason at all in this area for an object not to remain in midstream in the fastest current and go on down.

"We did find in the cross section here that the velocities tended ... must have been something to do with this bridge ... the velocities were a little bit higher on this side. But then on the last section here, we found that the higher velocities tended towards the South shore (Atlanta side) *which is consistent with where Mr. Payne's body was found."*

[Kittle's testimony was supported by previous eye-witness accounts of fishermen on the river, who witnessed Payne's body upstream of the

I-285 Bridge and then passing under it and downstream to where the body caught up on a tree].

The witness explained that his reference to 'piers' were what some refer to as 'pylons,' that support the bridge.

Kittle further discussed the use of U. S. Geological Survey Stage Recorders (gauges), which automatically – once an hour – records the elevation of the water at that location; that is, they have correlated the flow of the river with the elevation of the river at that point, so they can tell the discharge in the river, how much water was flowing when the water was at a certain elevation – so we have a continuous record of elevations and discharges.

Kittle was asked whether he recreated the conditions in the river that existed at approximately 3:00 a.m., on May 22, 1981:

"Yes, Sir, we did. I felt that in order for any measurements that we made to have validity, we had to have approximately the same flow conditions.

"Now, the flow in the river at the Jackson Parkway Bridge is controlled by several factors, the principal factor being the discharge from Morgan Falls Dam which is upstream about ten miles.

"Of course, that's influenced by whatever water is released from Buford Dam. But the control, assuming that Buford Dam doesn't overwhelm this small Morgan Falls structure, the control is Morgan Falls. It can also be influenced by the flow in the river ... at this point it could be influenced by rainfall downstream of Morgan Falls Dam to this point. . . . It could be influenced by ground water seepage. . . . It can also be influenced by releases from a sewage treatment plant which is upstream. It can be influenced by the intake and release of cooling water at the Georgia Power Company plant, McDonough steam generating plant.

"The quantity of water taken, used in cooling, is a small quantity compared to what comes down the river. The sewage treatment discharges, that stays fairly constant from day to day. That doesn't vary. We were in a relatively dry period during this time. . . . so the seepage of ground water is minimal. So we concluded that if we could get the Georgia Power Company to reproduce the same generation pattern at Morgan Falls Dam, that is, release the same amount of water in the same sequence for a similar period that they had done on the 21st and 22nd of

May, that we would, in fact, have the same conditions in the river as far as depth and discharge. And that's what we did.

"Georgia Power Company and Buford Dam, by pre-agreement on the 21st of May, started to go through the same generation pattern. They have records of this, though know what they discharged. . . . And our test was done on the 28th of September. When the day was over and we had the hydrograph … A hydrograph is a curve showing the stage of the river versus time, that is, if the water level is increasing as the day goes on, you'll have a curve that goes up. If the water level decreases, it goes down. We call that a hydrograph.

"In comparing the hydrograph for the 22nd of May from about 2:00 on until about 6:00, we found with the hydrograph that we obtained on the 28th of September when we made our test, we found that the water level in the river was an inch and one quarter higher than it was on the 22nd of May. So our test was very, very close. We were within an inch of what the water level was in May. So from that we concluded that we had, in fact, recreated as far as was humanly possible the conditions of the river on the 22nd of May."

On cross-examination, Kittle testified that he was first contacted on May 26, 1981, after the body of Cater was recovered two days before. He had received a call from Major W. J. Taylor of the Task Force and later met with Investigator Frank McClure, who briefed him.

Kittle affirmed that he told the authorities what he reported, that is, that the movements of both submerged and floating objects placed in a flowing river are influenced by many variables – that such objects are affected by cross section, topographic bends in the river, debris, structures, hydraulic friction, and that the prediction of the trace of a moving object in a natural channel is a problem, that in the absence of detailed data, can be approached only on the basis of experience and engineering judgment. He further reported that the final conclusions can be no more than the best judgment of the members of the study team.

Kittle was questioned about the effect of temperature on 'drag,' which would have been no measurable increase with the temperatures in question. He was asked about the decomposition and the formation of gases in a deceased body being inhibited by cool water and speeded up by warmer water (according to medical authorities).

Binder questioned the witness about his conclusion that the body could have been placed in the water at five places (from the first report), but he later narrowed it down to two. The first five places being: The Highway 280 (Jackson Parkway) Bridge, the Southern Railway Bridge, the I-285 bridge, the access river road, and the place where it was found (from the July 1981 report). The second report in December, 1981, narrowed the locations to two places: *The Highway 280 (James Jackson Parkway), or near the I-285 Bridge.* The witness testified he had walked down the railroad track and went down the river in a boat for access points. He spent a day in the area and drove down a short road to a launching ramp that goes into the river.

Binder: "And it looks like you could even launch a boat from it?"

Kittle: "If you could get the chain unlocked."

Binder: "You saw a chain there?"

Kittle: "Yes, Sir."

[The State introduced photographs and testimony of the launching ramp showing the gates locked].

Binder questioned Kittle about the second report having been changed to reflect the places omitted due to information of witnesses having seen the body of Payne in the river upstream of the I-285 Bridge (to delete the possibility that Payne's body was placed in the river downstream of where it was seen in the water).

Kittle was asked whether he had contacted Mr. David Dingle, a member of Kittle's team, and tried to get him to agree with the change. Kittle related that Dingle was sent a copy of the report.

Binder: "After you made the change, did you try to get him to agree to it, too?"

Kittle: "I went out and discussed it with him, yes, sir."

Binder: "And he refused, didn't he?"

Kittle: No, Sir; He agreed to it."

[Dingle would later be called by the defense].

On re-direct examination, Miller questioned Kittle regarding the elimination of the access points:

"We felt that the possibility of it coming off the Southern Railroad Bridge was very remote because it's very difficult to get up on this bridge. You have to climb a very steep hill to get up on the track, and then you have to walk the ties. There's no walkway there.

"We felt that I-285 Bridge was so heavily traveled that it's unlikely anyone would stop there and throw something off the railing." [Six-lane Interstate Highway].

[Of course, the boat ramp was closed and locked, which therefore leaves only the Highway 280 Bridge (Jackson Parkway), a narrow two lane road, in a somewhat isolated part of the area and river as the obvious place to stop and dump a body].

Detective Frank McClure testified as to the location where Cater's body was found one and two tenths miles downstream from the Jackson Parkway Bridge. He also testified regarding the points of access to the river (including the 'boat ramp' which had a chain lock) on the night in question; all were eliminated except the James Jackson Parkway Bridge. He identified photographs of the river on both sides up and down the river, showing rough terrain and not being accessible by vehicle. At the request of the Task Force, the FBI had flown an airplane over and down the Chattahoochee River corridor taking aerial photographs which were greatly enlarged and brought into the courtroom for illustration for the jury to see first hand the possible points of access, where the bodies were located, and the bridges over the river.

The hydrology tests and aerial photography would be an indication of the extent to which the Prosecution would go (having all needed resources) in securing evidence to answer any question the jury might have, hopefully ensuring a quick and easy verdict by the jury.

It was Tuesday mid-afternoon, and the judge was forced to call a halt to the proceedings early. Weather reports had been warning citizens that a heavy blast of freezing rain and snow was moving in from the west, but the Judge kept pushing the case along until he finally recessed the trial for the day. It was too late to beat it out of town!

Wednesday's court session was called off when the snowstorm made it impossible for people involved to reach the courthouse; although the Judge had recessed the trial at 3:13 p.m. on Tuesday in order to avoid travel problems, the jurors did not arrive at their College Park hotel near the airport until after 11:00 p.m. Some workers from the courthouse were unable to get home. I personally started home but only got a few blocks; I then returned to the courthouse where a police vehicle with chains started out with me but the hordes of travelers by now were blocking all the roads. Abandoned vehicles were everywhere! We were forced to return to the courthouse when the officer said he would be unable to get me to Roswell where I lived. District Attorney Slaton and I were forced to stay in the office overnight (we had two couches). We managed to get home on Wednesday. It was later found that some of the lawyers made it home after delays of up to eight hours.

It was likewise reported by The Detroit News that "the storm forced a recess in the trial of Wayne Williams ..." and that "Governor George Busbee had declared a state of emergency in Atlanta, which was immobilized by six inches of snow. He sent 230 National Guardsmen to aid stranded motorists and help clear out thousands of abandoned cars." I had never personally seen anything like it, only on TV up North. I recall [it] as the worst storm to strike Atlanta during my memory, paralyzing a city of a million people.

Robert McMichael, Investigator, District Attorne'ys Office. This witness was called to the stand to identify and introduce a tape recording of an interview at the county jail between Williams and District Attorney Lewis Slaton *at Williams' request* on July 10, 1981, and in the presence of his lawyer, Mary Welcome. (The interview came after Williams' arrest but before his indictment by the Grand Jury). McMichael testified that each of the questions and answers were subjected to Mr. Williams and Ms. Welcome before they were recorded.

An objection was made by lead defense attorney Al Binder before the witness was allowed to testify, whereupon the jury was excused and a recess was taken. The jury would never hear the recording of that conversation.

When court resumed almost an hour later, Slaton withdrew the witness in view of the ruling by the Court that certain parts of the interview would be deleted. This just confirms what we had been seeing about Williams from day one. He believed he was smarter and could 'out-talk' anyone, i.e. the FBI, the polygraph, the bond hearing, the public news conference, the grand jury, and now Slaton. Williams was in charge, including running his defense. Although Williams had Ms. Welcome present at the jail, at times objecting to certain questions, Williams insisted on answering the questions by Slaton. But, since the Judge would not allow the entire interview over Binder's objection, Slaton saw no reason to present a portion of it.

Dan Keever, WAGA-Channel 5 TV News. This witness was called by me to lay the foundation for admission of a taped news conference at Williams' home at 7:00 a.m. on June 4, 1981 (the day after his FBI polygraph and search at his home).

Keever played a 35-minute tape recording of this conference for the jury wherein Williams made many statements regarding his activities at the bridge incident, the FBI interviews, a disclaimer of knowing any of the victims, and other statements indicating many conflicts between what he claims happened and what the authorities reported.

Upon Williams' objection and a ruling by the court, the tape recording was altered to delete certain references in Williams' conversations and his answers to newsmen about whether he was homosexual and referencing his statements about his polygraph and failure to pass, matters which would not be heard by the jury.

Although the State presented its testimony as to the fiber connections between Williams and the two charged offenses at this point in the trial (as the Court required), I will discuss that evidence later in summary with the overall fiber evidence in all 12 cases.

After the prosecution completed presentation of evidence concerning the two charged murders of Payne and Cater, a motion to allow the State to present ten 'similar transactions' was made. The Judge excused the jury and heard arguments from both sides. It was Friday, January 22, 1982.

Joe Drolet informed the judge that we wished to present the ten named similar cases; and like the two charged cases, there would be evidence connecting Williams to them in a like manner: dog hair, fibers, and eye-witnesses. Also, there would be blood recovered from Williams' vehicle which would connect Williams to two of those victims. Further, the circumstantial evidence would show "a pattern so obvious it caught the attention of virtually the entire Western World." Common details of the similar cases were proffered for the Court's consideration.

Binder vehemently argued to the contrary, that nothing so far has shown "anything in a criminal manner," and "you know you can take all the fibers in the world and dress 'em up in all these fancy exhibits, but they're still circumstantial evidence." He argued that to allow the other cases would be highly prejudicial and would result in a mistrial.

Doesn't Binder get it, I thought. Of course, the scientific testimony and other evidence presented is circumstantial evidence – but, there is nothing wrong with circumstantial evidence. All evidence is either "Direct" or "Circumstantial," and a verdict can be supported by either or both, as the trial court will instruct the jury. The question is whether there is sufficient evidence to satisfy the jury beyond a reasonable doubt.

The judge announced he would study the State's motion, excused the jury for the week-end, and said he would announce his ruling by Monday morning. I felt confident the Judge would agree with us.

The trial resumed on Monday after Judge Cooper ruled in favor of admission of the similar cases. Judge Cooper said he would instruct the jury as to the law applicable to the similar cases before each 'similar case' was begun; in substance the jury must decide for themselves whether the deaths form a pattern and whether prosecutors prove that the defendant committed the murders. The prosecutors would tell the Judge when we were to begin each 'similar case' whereupon he would then so instruct the jury as follows:

Ladies and Gentlemen of the jury, the district attorney contends that independent offenses have been committed by the defendant. The defendant is not charged in the indictment with these offenses. You are to consider any evidence with regard to independent offenses solely and only under the provision of the law which allows independent offenses to be admitted. This evidence is being admitted for the sole purpose of showing plan, scheme, pattern, bent of mind, and identity, if any, to the extent that it bears upon the crimes charged in the indictment. The question as to whether the evidence does or does not show plan, scheme, pattern, bent of mind, and identity is a fact question for you and you alone to resolve. If you do not determine identity or intent in the commission of the offense charged or similar transaction, then you are to disregard any evidence of independent offenses. Ladies and Gentlemen of the jury, I further charge you that you are not to permit this evidence to bias you against the defendant, but are to consider this evidence for the sole purpose for which I have previously charged.

The Judge was not required to repeat this instruction to the jury ten times – at the beginning of each similar case – but did so in an abundance of caution.

It was never a mystery as to whether the similar cases should be admitted by the court so far as we prosecutors were concerned. The law was clearly in our favor, and upon a factual consideration of each of the cases, there was no doubt as to the 'pattern.' The Defense and their supporters consistently contend there was "no pattern" and "the causes of death were different in some cases." The law doesn't require each victim to have been murdered by the same weapon, means or manner, or be a duplicate of each other factually for there to be a 'pattern.' Quite often in using similar crimes, there will be dissimilar facts, but a logical connection between the cases. If we waited for there to be two cases with no differences than the names and dates, there would never be a pattern or similar case shown. These cases not only showed connections (dog hair and fibers), but also an obvious pattern of crimes which fit a profile of the victims. *The killer was targeting poor black street victims.* The law hasn't changed over the years, and it remains the same today as it was before and after the Williams' case.

[An appeal of the Williams' conviction to the Georgia Supreme Court[5] would uphold the trial court's decision in permitting these similar transactions, in citing the rule of law and an analysis of the profiles of each case as presented during the trial. The Court:

The test for admissibility in Georgia is that the independent crimes must be similar or logically connected to the crime for which the accused is on trial. (Cit.). The comparative profile illustrates the necessary similarities and logical connections. [Emphasis added]. (The court in a lengthy profile of each case, then cited the similarities and logical connections between all ten cases with the two cases on trial)].

Witnesses and the similar cases were not presented at trial in the exact order in which I will deal with them hereinafter in the order they occurred and later placed on the Task Force List.

Proving Ten Similar Uncharged Murders

Alfred Evans – Pattern Case No. 1

Alfred Evans, age 13, No. 2 on the Task Force List, was the first to be presented. Evans, who lived in the East Lake Meadows public-housing project in southeast Atlanta, was last seen on July 25, 1979; his decomposing body was discovered on July 28 in the 1700 block of Niskey Lake Road area, about one mile from its intersection with Campbellton Road, a four-lane highway in Atlanta.

Although it was not used as a similar case, the body of Edward H. Smith, age 14, and the first victim on the "list" was found the same day – a short distance away from Evans. [The ten selected pattern cases were only a 'representative' number of all].

---

5   Wayne Bertram Williams v. The State (of Georgia), 251 Georgia Reports 749 (4), 312 S.E.2d 40 (1983).

A next-door neighbor testified that Evans hadn't been seen since he disappeared. Evans rode the bus, had no access to a car, and did odd jobs in the East Lake Meadows housing project; he kept late hours.

Detective G. M. Lloyd preserved the crime scene down an embankment and used surgical gloves and a sheet for the body. Evans had no shirt, shoes, or socks on the body, and was clothed only in slacks. The body appeared to have been dumped there as it was laying face down about eleven feet off the road on a steep decline.

Dr. John Feegel, a board certified forensic pathologist, conducted the autopsy, indicating there was no indication of disease; that the cause of death was asphyxiation, probable strangulation. He explained that strangulation can be easily done without marks, especially if "you are in my confidence" (unexpectedly attacked) or unaware of the danger.

Evans' body was not identified for some time because his mother would not accept the fact that it was he, despite the fact he fit the description including scars and clothing. A picture matched the victim's description. Finally, an examination of his teeth compared with his dental records confirmed the identification.

Eric Middlebrooks – Pattern Case No. 2

Eric Middlebrooks, age 14, was victim No. 7 on the Task Force list. He was last seen on May 18, 1980, and discovered dead on May 19, 1980.

Since he was about four years old, Eric lived with a guardian on Howell Drive in Atlanta where he liked to hang out and watch TV. He used his bicycle for transportation, ran errands, and did odd jobs for people in the neighborhood.

Eric's half-brother, **Kerry Middlebrooks**, had spent several years in the Marines and worked as a security guard at a local hotel. Kerry regretted he hadn't been able to see Eric as much as he wished. After Eric's death, Kerry joined the Atlanta Police force. Eric did whatever odd jobs he could to make money; he was out on the streets at night a great deal of time.

Officer R. H. Buffington recovered Eric's body behind a Flat Shoals Road business near I-20 highway. He had injuries to his body. His torso was in a contorted position with his shoulders off the ground, with the appearance of having been dumped at that location. His bicycle was nearby, appearing to have been thrown to the ground. Buffington recovered a 'tuft' of fibers from Eric's shoe [wedged in a break in the shoe band). He explained that if Eric had walked to that location, it would have dislodged or crushed the fibers on the shoe (suggesting a dumped body).

Eric had last been seen at 10:00 p.m. the night before. His home was over a mile away. No apparent motive was observed, but it did not appear to be robbery. [Another victim, John Porter, was discovered about a mile from I-20 on April 12, 1981].

Dr. John Feegel, who performed the autopsy on Alfred Evans, also autopsied Middlebrooks. Trauma to the head was the cause of death, which could have been caused by a "slapjack." He had two cuts or lacerations on the right side of the head that had caused significant external bleeding as well as internal hemorrhaging under the scalp. There was also a stab wound on the right upper arm and a superficial stab wound in the left upper chest area. Dr. Feegel concluded that the death was homicidal and was probably caused by blows to the head by some kind of blunt instrument. Finding a pool of blood near the body, he believed Middlebrooks died where he was found; but he could have been hit with a blunt instrument elsewhere and then dumped where the body was found. [A slapjack was recovered from the attic of the Williams' home when it was searched by the FBI in June, 1981]. The body could have been dumped unconscious. *Bubble gum was found in the stomach.*

Charles Stephens – Pattern Case No. 3

Stephens, age 12, and victim No. 15 on the Task Force list, was last seen October 9, 1980, at 4:00 p.m., and his body was found the next day. He was last seen leaving his public housing project home on Pryor Circle wearing a T-shirt with a picture of his grandfather. His body was recovered off Norman Berry Drive, East Point, near the rear entrance to a mobile home park, with the body laid out on a grassy knoll near a local trailer park. He was about five (5) miles from home. There were no signs of a struggle, and no motive could be established for the killing. The body was clothed only in blue jeans and one tennis shoe, missing his T-shirt, a belt, and one shoe.

Officer Sonny Lowery, East Point Police, discovered the body on October 10, 1980, and secured the area until Larry Peterson of the GBI Crime Lab could come out and work the crime scene to secure any trace evidence. Stephens' head, chest, and stomach were covered with fibers.

Stephens was described as always eager to do odd jobs for spending money, i.e. running errands and emptying garbage cans so he could buy candy and cookies. A neighbor said he hung out in the streets a lot and visited the stores on Pryor Road.

His grandfather identified Stephens' body, saying he was from a broken home and a product of public housing. Stephens was a sixth grader at Perkerson Elementary School; he was a quiet child. He loved to draw and watch TV. He apparently left home about 8:00 p.m. and was never seen again – except by the 'killer.'

Dr. John Feegel, Medical Examiner, conducted the autopsy on this victim as he had the two preceding cases. He found no diseased organs for which death could be attributed. He did find petechial hemorrhages of the heart and lungs. His opinion as to cause of death was Asphyxia – probable suffocation.

Lubie Geter – Pattern Case No. 4

Lubie Geter, age 14, and victim No. 18 on the Task Force list was reported missing on January 3, 1981. He left home on Saturday morning to sell car deodorizers at the Stewart-Lakewood Mall. His decomposed body, clothed only in undershorts, was found in a wooded area about 70 feet off Vandiver Road in South Fulton County on February 5, 1981, by a local citizen looking for illegal rabbit traps. Fulton Police Detective George Coleman responded to the scene on Vandiver Road off Campbellton and Enon roads.

Geter's family missed him when he didn't call. He had never run away from home and had never been in trouble, according to his parents. He was a freshman at Murphy High School and close to his sister. He had worked at a carwash and sold car deodorizers supplied by a fellow employee. His uncle described him as being industrious in doing jobs such as washing cars and cutting grass to make extra money. He later identified the body.

[From the apparent familial background of this victim, it appears Lubie just got caught up in the killer's 'net' by his 'street activities,' odd jobs, and a killer who was looking for kids on the street].

A witness and brother, **Franklin Jordan,** took Lubie and his friend, Eric Conway, to the Big Star at Stewart-Lakewood shopping center on Friday, January 2, 1981. He never saw Lubie again.

Eric Conway, age 16, and friend of Lubie's, said Lubie's brother took them to the Big Star Grocery at Stewart-Lakewood on that Friday where Lubie got out – he never saw him again. Lubie had a box of deodorizers.

Another witness, **Ruth Warren**, had driven to Atlanta to take her mother shopping. She testified they first went to a Kroger grocery on Stewart Avenue about a block from the Big Star Grocery; she said that a boy, whom she identified as Lubie Geter, approached her in front of the Kroger at about 1:30 p.m. and asked her if she wanted to buy an air freshener.

From the Kroger Store she and her mother went to the Royal Mattress Company next to the Stewart-Lakewood Shopping Center, then to her mother's home to put away the groceries, and then back to the Mattress Company, arriving around 3:00 p.m. She testified that her mother picked out a mattress and that when she went outside to open her van door so the mattress could be loaded, she saw, about 20 feet from her, a black man and boy talking. The boy was Lubie, and she identified the man he was talking to as Wayne Williams (in the courtroom). Lubie, she said, had a box in his hand and said: "I'd like to go with you, but I've got to sell these." The witness identified Williams and said he had two (2) scratches on his face (a fact to become important later), and was wearing a red baseball-type cap. (A similar cap was in Williams' home when it was searched). The car that the man and boy were walking towards looked similar to her Ford station-wagon.

Ms. Warren, a middle-aged woman from Rockdale County, later helped a police sketch artist prepare a composite sketch for use in the investigation; the sketch showed a resemblance to Williams.

A 13-year-old girl testified she had a date with Lubie for Sunday, January 4, 1981. She tried to call him on Saturday but he was missing.

Geter's mother took the stand as a 'quieted courtroom' waited and listened as she haltingly confirmed that the deceased was her son. She explained that Lubie was just trying to sell car deodorizers for a little money. As I removed a bright blue T-shirt from a plastic bag and asked if she recognized it, she was filled with emotion as she identified it as belonging to Lubie.

[An FBI witness, Robert Swabe, would later testify to having found the T-shirt some ten feet from the pavement with blue jeans and shoes found nearby, about three-fourths mile from the scene].

Willard Ford, fingerprint technician, went to the scene where Geter's body was discovered. It was in bad shape from exposure to the elements and animals in the woods. He rolled the fingerprints, and finding no criminal record on file from which to compare, went to Geter's home. Geter's mother provided Ford with the child's school books and an attaché case from which he dusted for prints. Ford was able to recover prints from the items which matched those from Geter's fingers. The body was that of Lubie Geter.

Dr. Robert Stivers, Medical Examiner, did the autopsy on Lubie Geter. A visual identification of Geter was done by family members. Agents from the Crime Laboratory were at the crime scene and at the morgue. Stivers described the trauma to the neck, hemorrhage in the brain and voice box, in determining the cause of death as asphyxia by strangulation. The victim weighed 103 pounds.

Cross-examination of Stivers by Binder elicited that Stivers had given an interview to the American Medical Association, published the past spring, indicating that there was no apparent pattern among the cases being investigated by the Task Force. He was giving that opinion based on only the different causes of death which included asphyxiation, i.e. by manual strangulation, chokehold strangulation, ligature strangulation, and suffocation. This seemingly undercut the State's position of a pattern.

However, legally, a pattern is not shown just by a method of homicide but by all the circumstances connecting the cases together. The cause of death alone, in my view, is very seldom enough to show a 'pattern' (except to prove one element of the homicide – that those cases were caused by the same method), unless by chance the cause of death was so unique as to leave the killer's identification through their 'handiwork', i.e. homicide by Ethylene Glycol (anti-freeze) as in the case of Lynn Turner versus the State (2004 and 2007) (the very first such homicides by anti-freeze in Georgia).

On redirect examination, I asked Stivers to discuss his statistical research regarding the cause of death by "asphyxiation" in Fulton County. He responded that asphyxia was very uncommon; that he had only a few such deaths in the past several years. He said there was no more than one case per year from 1975 to 1979 (none in 1978), but there were six victims in 1980 between ages two and sixteen years who died from asphyxiation and six again in 1981 (during the time the serial killer was at work). I then brought to Stivers' attention that since the AMA article was published there were 10 deaths by asphyxiation placed on the Task Force list of which he was familiar. He further testified that since Williams arrest there had not been a single strangulation death where the body was found in a river or beside a roadway in the Atlanta area.

I called **Darryl Davis,** a 15-year-old juvenile, as a witness – but more than a witness in the Lubie Geter incident. Darryl dropped a 'bomb' in the courtroom with the first suggestion that Williams was homosexual and thus would point to a motive in the cases – which the court had ruled admissible.

Darryl said that in August, 1980, he was on Stewart Avenue. A man he identified in Court as Wayne Williams asked if he would like a job. Darryl explained that he was 'stealing paper out of the machine' and 'selling papers' (newspapers).

Mallard: He asked you if you wanted a job?

Darryl: "Yes, Sir."

What kind of job?

"Washing cars."

And what did you say?

"I said yes, sir."

And what did he do and what did you do then?

"He drove down to a car wash down between the streets."

Darryl explained that after getting in the car with the same subject that he later saw with Lubie Geter, the man asked him about his family members, the ages of his brothers and sisters, and whether he played a musical instrument. I asked:

What did you tell him?

"I told him yes, sir, you know."

What did you tell him you played?

"Drums."

… What else did he say?

"Then he asked me if I had any money. I said no, sir. Then he felt down my pocket. He wasn't really feeling of my pocket; he was feeling of my penis. And he gave me $2, and he drove down to Pickfair Street."

All right. What was around there?

"Woods. That's all. Woods."

All right. What did he do then?

"Felt of my penis."

Did he stop or was he driving?

"He was stopped."

All right. Was there any houses right around there?

"No. No houses on Pickfair."

What else did he say and do?

"Then he drove to Valley Village – Village Apartments over there, you know, where dump places, woods, high bushes and stuff. And then he started feeling my penis. He got me to take my penis out. Then he said he had to go to the trunk for something."

Let me ask you this. Before he did that, did he ask you any – if you had any kind of sex with boys?

"Oh, yeah, he asked me that."

What did he say about that?

"He asked me, does you have any sex with boys, you know. Have you ever had."

All right. Go ahead. What – you said he got out of the car and was going to do what?

"Then he said he was going to the trunk to get something."

Did you see where he went?

"No. When he went to the trunk, I jumped out and ran."

Where did you go?

"I went straight to Village Apartments and hid."

I asked: Now, the man that rode you out there and fondled you as you indicated and gave you $2, is that the same man you've identified in Court here, Wayne Williams?

"Yes, Sir."

Is there any doubt in your mind?

"No doubts."

This witness also testified he saw victim Lubie Geter get into Williams' vehicle at the Stewart-Lakewood Shopping Center on a weekend in early January, 1981, on a Saturday, supporting other witnesses' testimony. He knew Geter from seeing him around.

Darryl testified he was working at the Carpet Place "throwing away paper and wood over the wall" when he saw the youngster identified as Lubie Geter get into a vehicle driven by the person in Court he now knows as Wayne Williams.

I asked: You were on the deck?

"Right. And I seen Lubie Geter get in the car with him" (indicating Wayne Williams).

Now, you say you didn't know his name at that time. Did you later learn his name was Wayne Williams?

"I learned his name from the paper."

The witness described the vehicle they drove off in as a white and black-top vehicle.

Darryl further testified he saw Williams at the funeral for another victim, Terry Pue, age 15, in late January 1981; he did not know Pue, but he and other classmates at a school for juvenile offenders were asked by a school counselor (Brandon Southern) to volunteer to be pallbearers. He said he pointed Williams out to a classmate, Erik Thompson, as the man who grabbed him in August 1980.

Question: And was Mr. Southern at Terry Pue's funeral?

Answer: "Yeah, he was there. He was supposed to be helping out Terry's funeral, to tote his casket. Most of the children there were poor."

Do you know Eric Thompson?

"Yes, Sir."

Was he at Terry Pue's funeral?

"Yeah, he was there. I pointed out Wayne Williams to him."

Did you see Wayne Williams at the funeral?

"Yes, Sir."

And did you see Wayne Williams leave after the funeral?

"Yes, Sir."

How did he leave?

"In a white car – station wagon."

And did you point him (Wayne Williams) out at that time to Eric Thompson?

"I pointed him out in Church."

In his usual forceful fashion, Mr. Binder attacked this 15 year old witness on cross-examination.

After going through preliminaries on talking to law officers about the case, Binder asked:

How many times have you been arrested for Stealing?

Mr. Mallard: Your Honor, I object to that, the record itself would be the highest and best evidence.

At that time, the Judge had counsel approach the bench to argue the legal issue out of the hearing of the jury, whereupon after about 10 pages of discussion and argument the Court ruled in favor of my objection that Defense Counsel could not impeach the witness in the manner he was attempting to do – but the Judge said he would research the issue further later, and if he was wrong he would allow the defense to recall the witness for that purpose. I did not object to counsel going into Darryl's testimony which came out on direct that Darryl at the time of the incident was 'stealing and selling newspapers.' Opposing counsel may thoroughly cross examine the testimony given on direct, but cannot impeach a witness by asking how many times the witness has been arrested or convicted of a crime.

In a further attempt by Binder, he asked:

Now, you just told us that you were stealing newspapers. Just being honest and frank, do you steal quite often?

Darryl: "I don't want to answer that question."

After further objection to Binder's cross on the issue, Judge Cooper ruled that the witness had invoked his right against self-incrimination, thereby stopping further cross except what the witness admitted on direct.

Binder further questioned Darryl about the time he saw Geter get into the vehicle, the details, description of the car, and his identification of Williams and the Geter boy. When asked about the boy (Geter),

But you couldn't see his face?

"Yeah, I seen his face when he was going toward the car."

All right. Did he have anything with him?

"Yeah. He had perfume stuff, perfume stuff to go in the car." [One question too many; remember, the victim was at the shopping center selling his car deodorizers, according to his family. This gives the witness credibility].

Binder: Don't you hustle for money?

Darryl: "I kind of like one thing."

What do you like?

"I just do my job, to tell you the truth."

They told you to say that on the witness stand, to tell the truth?

"That's right. And I'm telling the truth, anyway." [I try to always remember to tell the witnesses that if asked, that I told them to 'tell the truth.']

Binder again tried to attack the witness in that he had missed school days monitored by Court Services and Mr. Brandon Southern:

Question: And have you missed much school?

Answer: "I miss a lot of days."

You do. Last year did you miss a lot of school (1981)?

"Yeah, for one reason. I was scared to come outside."

You were scared? What were you scared of?

"Because the killing was going on."

Binder again visited the identification of Williams as being the person the witness saw drive away with Lubie Geter in early 1981:

All right. But you do remember the man you saw in that car never got out of the car, did he? That's a fact, ain't it?

Darryl: "I remember the face. I can't forget his face."

You can't forget it?

"No."

Did they tell you something good would happen to you if you'd remember his face?

"No. I remember the face, and I wake up in dreams at night and think about his face."

You do?

"Right. It make me sick."

Binder's cross tried to trip up the witness about what he told the defense investigator and details of Williams' size; the witness withstood harsh questioning. Binder strongly suggested that the witness knew a mysterious Amp Wiley who the witness said he did not know, but did know his girl-friend.

Binder: Have you ever gone with some folks to do what we know as homosexual acts?

Darryl: "No, I ain't had no sex with no boy."

Erik Thomson would later testify and confirm Darryl's account that he was at Pue's funeral when Darryl pulled him aside and said "There's the man that grabbed me." Thompson saw Williams in a station wagon; he had seen Williams before but didn't know his name at the time. Thompson was cross-examined by Binder:

"You gay?" Binder asked.

"No," responded Thompson

"You sure?"

"What kind of a question is that?"

At this time, Judge Cooper told Binder to move along.

Terry Lorenzo Pue – Pattern Case No. 5

Terry Pue, age 15 and No. 19 on the Task Force list, was last seen on January 22, 1981. His body was recovered on Sigman Road and I-20 in Rockdale County the next day, January 23, 1981, about one-half mile from Interstate 20 about two feet off the pavement. Officer Hunter with the Conyers Police helped seal off the area.

A neighbor had seen Pue on January 22, 1981, at between 4:30 – 5:00 p.m. in College Park at a hamburger restaurant on Memorial Drive in southeast Atlanta.

Witness **Charmaine Kendrick** testified she saw Pue with Williams about a week before she learned of his death. Kendrick worked at a Church's Fried Chicken, and occasionally Pue would come by the store to sell odd items. Late one afternoon, Pue came by the store and tried to sell her a water gun; when she asked him where he got it, he said that he worked for a man. Pue then left, walked over to a green station wagon, and talked to a man sitting in a car that Pue had identified as the man for whom he worked. The witness identified this man as Wayne Williams, the defendant on trial. (Several witnesses have identified the station wagon as "green" or "white;" police say it could have been confused as either).

Officer H.B. Starr, Conyers Police (formerly with Rockdale Sheriff), set up a perimeter around Pue's body. He saw Wayne Williams with camera equipment: black bag, large lens on the camera. Williams identified himself, saying he was a free-lance photographer, and offered to make photographs of the area for the police. It was 9:30 to 10:00 a.m. Police have their own crime scene units. (Williams did do free-lance photography).

[Darryl Davis (juvenile) earlier testified he saw Williams at Pue's funeral in late January].

Family and neighbors revealed that Pue was a street-wise youth who lived with some of his ten siblings in a Hollywood Courts public-housing project. He was out on the streets at night traveling all over the city. He did odd jobs and hung out at the Omni game rooms. He used the bus to get around. [Several references have now been made to the Omni Hotel area where Williams had flyers handed out and where some victims had visited or hung out]. Pue had a lengthy juvenile record and was placed in special-education in 1980. He knew Lubie Geter (another victim) while at the state facility for delinquent boys.

Dr. Byron Dawson, Assistant Director of the Georgia State Crime Laboratory, conducted the autopsy. He went to the scene where the body was found on Sigman Road. Larry Peterson from the Crime Lab was also there to see first hand that all trace evidence was collected. The victim was described as being 'laid-out.'

Dr. Dawson described the victim having three separate ligature marks with voice box damage and traumatic injury under the scalp. Pue died of asphyxia, definitely by ligature, and possibly manual strangulation (from having a cord or ligature-like instrument wrapped around his neck three times). The body was clothed except for his underwear which was missing.

Patrick Baltazar – Pattern Case No. 6

Baltazar, age 12, and No. 20 on the Task Force list, was last seen on February 6, 1981. His body was found seven days later on February 13, 1981, in a wooded area behind Corporate Square, an office complex in DeKalb County close to I-85, by a maintenance man.

Officer B. W. Humble, DeKalb County Police, reported that Baltazar was found 17-20 feet down an embankment from the curb. He preserved the scene. The victim was reported to have roamed the area of Foundy Street and the Omni; he walked or used the bus. The body appeared to have been dumped at that location. Baltazar was from a broken family, his mother living in Louisiana and the father living in the Atlanta area.

Baltazar lived in a one-room apartment in a housing complex near the Omni Hotel where he was known to hang out and play electronic games. He worked the streets for odd jobs and was good at it. It was said that he would do anything to make money, and he kept late hours. He also worked as a dishwasher, according to friends and family.

This was the first 'declared-homicide' victim who had been discovered in DeKalb County (which adjoins Fulton County with a part of the City of Atlanta inside DeKalb County). Then Police Chief Dick Hand of DeKalb County (now Chief Assistant District Attorney, Dougherty County) and Detective Gene Moss (now Lt. Col, Dep. Chief, Enforcement Division, Forsyth County Sheriff's Office) were both on the scene. Since Chief Hand had several officers on the Task Force, he was aware that the Crime Laboratory had been finding trace evidence on the bodies; Medical Examiner Joseph Burton was on the scene. There was a slow and methodical crime scene investigation with the removal of the body by ensuring there was no contamination of the body and evidence. It was obvious to Detective Moss that this would be one of the victims who would fit the profile of the missing and murdered children of Atlanta. Baltazar appeared to have been killed elsewhere and dumped in the rear of this office complex; the mysterious disappearance with no apparent motive was evident.

Another interesting thing was noted – the killer appeared to be responding to publicity. A few days before Baltazar was found, Chief Hand had stated to a reporter that they (DeKalb County) had not had any victims found in their county. [6] This response by Chief Hand was later publicized in the newspaper. (The killer had now left DeKalb County a body). Similarly, the month before (January) there was a false report of a body being found on Sigman Road in adjoining Rockdale County; but when it was publicized that no body was found, the police did in fact respond a few days later to a body being discovered on Sigman Road on January 23, 1981 – the body of *Terry Pue, Pattern Case No. 5.*

---

6   However, 10 year old Aaron Wyche whose body was found on June 24, 1980, was subsequently upgraded to possible homicide by asphyxiation and added to the list.

Dr. Joseph Burton, Medical Examiner, did the autopsy. He described a windbreaker pulled down and gym shorts over underwear. He found ligature marks on the neck, with hemorrhages in the eyes and lungs. Cause of death was asphyxia due to ligature strangulation.

Joseph Bell – Pattern Case No. 7

Joseph "JoJo" Bell, age 15, and No. 22 on the Task Force list, was last seen on March 2, 1981, at Capt. Peg's Seafood on Georgia Avenue. His body was not recovered until April 19, 1981, when it was discovered hung up on a dead tree in the South River at DeKalb/Rockdale County line where the bodies of two other victims were found.

"JoJo" did odd jobs and had told people that *no kid snatcher was going to get him.* He reportedly wouldn't be *eager to jump in nobody's car.* JoJo lived on Lawson Street in West End with his mother and eight other family members; he played basketball in area schools in Mechanicsville and Adamsville.

Dr. Joseph Burton, Medical Examiner, testified that when he arrived at the scene he found JoJo Bell in the South River face down wearing jockey shorts. He put the body in a sterile sheet and had it removed from the river. He said the water in the river was cool. The body was removed to the morgue for autopsy.

The body was in a fairly advanced state of decomposition, evidenced by partial skeletonization of the skull, hands, feet, and chest; by distention of the abdomen; and by several generations of flies and maggots present on the body. Because of decomposition, he estimated that Bell would have been dead since the early part of March 1981. (The victim was last seen on March 2).

Burton found evidence of ante-mortem hemorrhaging behind the Adam's apple and in the high part of the neck, just in front of the spine. There was no water in the sinuses or airways. Based on these findings, Burton eliminated natural death or drowning and opines that death was by asphyxia due to some kind of manipulation of the neck area. Al Binder, on cross-examination, could not shake Burton on his crime scene handling of the body and conceded he (Burton) did a good job of preserving the evidence.

A witness, **John Laster**, testified he had met Wayne Williams at his grandmother's house. He said that he and Bell had auditioned before Williams.

Witness **Lugene Laster**, 21, (brother of John Laster) testified that in November of 1980 he saw Williams talking to John at his grandmother's house. Also, about the first of March, 1981, he was playing basketball with Bell at an elementary school; when Bell left and began walking down the street that ran beside the court, he saw Bell stop, talk to, and then get into the car with a man driving an old white or sky blue station wagon. The witness identified the man as Wayne Williams who was driving the station wagon; later that night Bell's brother came to his home asking if anyone had seen Bell.

A witness, **Kent Hindsman**, age 24, a songwriter, said he had seen the 'flyer' left at a record store and called Williams. The call resulted in their meeting on December 8, 1980, at a studio. When Hindsman returned to the studio about one week later, he met Joseph Bell. After the session, Williams drove Hindsman and Bell home in a white station wagon. Hindsman at one time brought up the subject of the missing children with Williams; he was told by Williams that they "ought to keep their damn asses at home." On another occasion, Williams passed him a note (through Carla Bailey) at the studio which read, "I could be a president, I could be a mayor, or I could even be a killer." They laughed. Hindsman further testified that Williams liked to go "stargazing" at the Omni, where he passed out flyers. Williams told him he knew karate, he had a black belt, and the first time he met him –*he was in law enforcement.*

Larry Rogers – Pattern Case No. 8

Larry Rogers, age 20, and No. 25 on the Task Force list was last seen on March 30, 1981, at West Lake and Ezra Church Road and his body was recovered on April 9, 1981, in an abandoned ground floor apartment on Temple Street in Northwest Atlanta. The body was clad only in blue shorts. Footprints found near the body resembled the pattern on shoes found during the search of Williams' bedroom.

A neighbor testified Rogers lived with foster parents and did odd jobs in earning cash from cutting grass, running errands, and cleaning gutters; he played in the neighborhood with young children at parks and schools in the area. He was well liked and friendly. Rogers hung around the corner grocery store. He was slightly retarded. He had no vehicle; he rode his bicycle or a bus.

Identification Technician **Willard Ford** went to the scene where the body of Rogers was found. He took photographs and rolled the finger-prints. Rogers had a juvenile record and was identified through his fin-gerprints. Ford would years later receive a copy of a news article from a French newspaper with byline "Atlanta: le cauchemar continue" (the nightmare continues) regarding the missing and murdered children of Atlanta, with a photograph capturing Ford and others in the removal of the body to an ambulance.

Officer Milton Jones sealed the area off until Larry Peterson from the Crime Lab arrived. Simpson Road is nearby the scene.

I called a witness, **Tilman Baynham,** who went by **"Cool Breeze,"** who knew Rogers. He was on Simpson Road when he saw Rogers – three times with Williams – on a day before Rogers disappeared. I knew this witness was not one we found to be of high character and intelli-gence but – like our victims – some of their acquaintances and friends were going to be the 'poor and downtrodden from the street.'

Immediately there was an objection by Binder because the witness had been put under hypnosis to attempt to learn more from him. After a lengthy hearing outside the jury's presence, the Judge agreed with the State that the testimony did not involve any enhanced facts and the de-fense would be able to cross-examine the witness.

Mallard: Mr. Baynham, did you know Larry Rogers before his death?

Baynham: "All right. Now, I want to know which one is Larry Rogers. The names get me mixed up. I want to know."

I knew the problem. I would need to handle him delicately. The witness told the Court that Larry Rogers was the one with a burn on his face. I was allowed to show the witness a photograph of Rogers (show-ing the burn).

Mallard: Mr. Baynham, what was it you said about his face?

Baynham: "I was speaking of his face, Larry Rogers. I been know-ing him for about a year, a year and a half."

On direct examination, the witness testified he had known Rogers one and one-half years, and that he saw him three times on a day shortly before he disappeared.

The first time was about 9:30 a.m. at a fast food place on Simpson Street. He said Rogers approached him and asked for a 'joint' or "herb" so that he and a friend could get high.

Cool Breeze: "So he said, I want a joint. That's what he was saying, you know. So I say, you ain't never asked me for a joint. I ain't got no joint. So he said, but, I – I got a dollar. Said, me and my friend over there, you know."

Cool Breeze further testified that Rogers pointed out his friend sitting in a 'fast-looking' car. The witness couldn't say what color the car was, but it was like a Firebird or a Dodge.

"So then he say, me and my friend want to get high. Said, that's my buddy, that's my buddy, I know him, I know him. So I said, man, you ain't trying to bust me, is you? He said, no, no, no. You know. So I said, come on, I take you down here, I know somebody got some marijuana. I said, you don't want nothing but one joint? I don't call it a joint, I call it a herb. He said, I get the dollar. So he got the dollar (from the guy in the fast car). So when he got the dollar, I said, come on. So I took him and we went to white folks. And the white folk gave him the joint. And he came back and said, thanks, man, thanks, man. He kept on." [Rogers left].

I asked: Where did he go after that?

Cool Breeze: "He walked back up by the car. I looked at the car good, the tag and everything. I thought he was trying to bust me because he looked clean-cut and everything, you know." [The man in the fast car looked 'clean-cut].

"Cool Breeze" identified Williams in the courtroom as Rogers' friend in the car. The witness said he saw Rogers and Williams a second time that day between 1:00 – 3:00 p.m. At that time he said Williams and Rogers were in a car which was stopped at a traffic light at the corner of West Lake and Simpson Streets; the witness was at a gas station getting cigarettes and gas. He said that Williams was driving and Rogers waved at him. The third time the witness saw Williams and Rogers was between 6:00 – 7:30 p.m. the same day in the area. The witness next saw Williams on TV.

The witness was confused by cross-examination and evoked some laughter as Al Binder had a field day with him. This uneducated witness didn't stand a chance against a polished, yet abrasive, defense attorney.

Binder: You say your name is, Cool Breeze?

Cool Breeze: "That's what they call me. That's my nickname."

I'm Al Binder. How are you today?

"I'm from Florida."

Binder questioned the witness about his many jobs: Cook, Quick Checks, M and M, Walgreens, Sheritons, Rountables, Busters, Short Order Cook.

Where do you live now?

"I live with a young lady now."

You do?

"Yeah. Another Young Lady."

Well, we won't go into that.

The Court: Thank You.

I had decided I would not object to cross-examination on the witness's background since the jury would believe the worst ... in any event.

Binder: You like to smoke dope; makes you feel good, don't it?

Answer: "It's better than worrying."

Sure is. Did you smoke any before you came up here today? A little bit?

"Herb? I had coffee and herb."

"Had a little coffee and had a little herb. You put that old herb in your mouth and take a puff and it makes you feel good, doesn't it?"

"I wish I had 27 hundred thousand."

Right on, Brother. [Responded Binder].

Binder: Now, let me tell you, when you say all this, you didn't tell anyone, did you?

Cool Breeze: "I didn't come forward because I thought that they wouldn't believe me because I have had crimes before."

You've had crimes before?

"Every time you get arrested it's a crime, isn't it?" [Why object, everyone's having fun]. Binder continues to question him about his crimes; but his crimes aren't as bad as I would have thought, i.e., Gambling; Driving without a License; and Drugs for which he had served only a matter of months and had been to a hospital to kick the

habit. Binder asked if he had smoked any herb before he was hypno-
tized. Cool Breeze:

"I been smoking herbs 23 years, and I'm 35."

Despite the efforts to impeach the witness on his character, the witness stood his ground on his identification of Williams with Rogers just
before Rogers' disappearance. Binder questioned him about seeing
Williams on TV.

Cool Breeze: "That's when I saw him with Larry Rogers in the
car, and I said, that's the same one that was with him on T.V. I told my
wife."

Witness **Nellie Trammel,** a grandmother, who had known Rogers
since he was about five years old testified that she last saw Rogers on
Monday, March 30,1981, and that on Thursday she heard on the news
that he had been missing. She testified she was driving home about
noon, when a green station wagon with Williams and Rogers in it, cut
in front of her and came to a stop beside her. She spoke to Rogers, who
was slumped over, but he didn't say anything. She said Williams was
driving. The witness then drove home. She said she had seen Williams
ten days earlier in another section of town taking pictures of a confrontation between police and the Techwood Homes "Bat Patrol."[7] He was
in a white station wagon that day. She thought he was a camera man.
She further testified she saw Williams at Rogers' funeral. She withstood
a ferocious cross-examination.

Dr. Robert Stivers, Chief Medical Examiner, described a thin scratch
line on Rogers' neck, blood and hemorrhage around the voice box, and
cracked bones in the neck. Also, hemorrhage was found over the temporal bone (right side of head). There was no disease found. Death was
due to asphyxia by strangulation, possibly by a chokehold. Stivers said
the body was five foot two inches long and weighed 130 pounds.

John Porter – Pattern Case No. 9

John Porter, age 28 and number No. 30 on the Task Force list (it
was last added to the list), was reported missing. His body was found

7   The Bat Patrol was a citizens' group who organized at the height of the missing children
episode whose members armed themselves with baseball bats to provide security in Techwood
Homes housing project. Several leaders of the group were arrested on charges of carrying weapons without permits. *Atlanta Constitution*, 1/29/82.

on April 12, 1981, in a vacant lot on Bender Street about one mile from I-20 near Capitol Avenue in downtown Atlanta; he had been apparently dumped at that location with feet on the sidewalk – fully clothed. He had been stabbed several times in the chest.

[Victim Barrett's body was later found with similar stab wounds although he was also strangled]. Porter's body was found just four blocks from where Anthony Carter, another victim, was found, and Porter – like many of the adult victims – was small in size and youthful in appearance.

Officer R. H. Buffington testified that Porter's body was recovered with six stab wounds, but there were only two (2) perforations in the shirt he was wearing, indicating that the shirt was partially off when the stabbing occurred. Buffington said there was no blood at the scene, indicating that Porter had been stabbed at another location and dumped by the road. The victim lived in an abandoned apartment on Capitol Avenue; he was unemployed. He had no vehicle and was just released from Georgia Regional Hospital. No obvious motive for the murder appeared. The body was identified through fingerprints.

Dr. Robert Stivers, Medical Examiner did the autopsy and reported the size of Porter being 5 feet 10 inches and weighing 123 pounds. Upon examination of the body, Stivers described six stab wounds to the chest and abdomen, all of which were approximately 2 to 2 ½ inches deep. Death was caused by stab wounds to the chest and abdomen. He further said that there were no marks or hemorrhaging around the neck area. No disease was found which would have contributed to death.

William Barrett – Pattern Case No. 10

William Barrett, age 17 and No. 28 on the Task Force list was reported missing on May 11, 1981, (ten days before the last victim Nathaniel Cater was missed). Barrett's body was discovered just off Winthrop Road within 100 feet of I-20 on May 12, 1981, by a passing motorist who saw it in the weeds.

Officer Banks responded and found the body 50-75 feet from I-20, and secured the area. The body showed signs of being stabbed and strangled by ligature and dumped by the roadway.

Barrett was always in trouble with the law and had been put in a State foster home. He had been released from a Youth Development Center on March 10, 1981, and was to report the next day.

James Barrett, the victim's cousin, said "Billy" had no regular job and no automobile; he rode his bicycle or bus for transportation. The witness testified that Barrett had come by in 1980 or early 1981, and that he had just gotten out of juvenile home. Billy was with a 'friend' whom the witness identified as Williams. James gave Billy $10.00. **Mary Harris,** James Barrett's mother, witnessed the incident and identified Williams as well.

The identifications were attacked because they came after Williams had been identified on television as a suspect. However, these witnesses appeared credible and had absolutely no motive to lie or frame anyone. This is somewhat natural for persons who later become witnesses to events of which they testify; they will view people or suspects on TV or in public and recognize them from some period in the past – especially where there is an event associated with the person.

Dr. Joseph Burton, Medical Examiner, conducted the autopsy, fixing the cause of death as asphyxiation due to ligature strangulation. Burton found ligature marks around the neck and hemorrhages within the neck and on the eyes, heart, and lungs.

Burton identified two (2) post-mortem (after death) stab wounds in the abdomen and five (5) other "pricks" with a knife which had some symmetry to them, and suggested a type of marking of the body or a type of ritual associated with the body. There were only two (2) holes in the shirt. He also described a one-inch laceration on Barrett's scalp, which had caused some bleeding beneath the scalp, and which he felt had occurred when the body was tossed to the ground. Dr. Burton opined that Barrett had not been killed where his body was found but had been dumped there after death. Burton further testified that the victim's stab wounds resemble those suffered by two other slaying victims, Porter and Middlebrooks.

Burton testified the 'attacker' could have scratches on the arms and face. (See later testimony that Williams had scratches on his arms on certain occasions).

Williams Seen with Victims

Contrary to Williams' statements to the FBI, the public statement he gave at his news conference and later at his own trial that he knew none of the task force victims, many witnesses testified that Williams was seen with various victims in the case shortly before their disappearance and death. This was crucial evidence of Williams' guilt in light of his denials. Had he admitted he *did* know and was in contact with such victims *but in an innocent way*, the testimony would not have been as damaging. The United States District Court for the Northern District of Georgia, Atlanta Division, in a federal habeas corpus by Williams would later cite to the record of such testimonials.

Victim - Jimmy Ray Payne: Mr. A.B. Dean (age 80) testified that he saw Williams with victim Payne near the Jackson Parkway Bridge about the time he went missing. Payne's body was recovered in the river on April 27, 1981.

Victim - Nathaniel Cater: Margaret Carter testified she saw Williams sitting on a park bench with Cater about a week before Cater's body was found and that there was a German shepherd dog with them. Williams did have such a dog at that time. James Thompson Jr. testified he once met a man named "Nathaniel" at the Williams home, and that he had given the police the name of Nathaniel Cater. Witness Robert I. Henry also testified he saw Nathaniel Cater (known to him as "Silky") holding hands with Williams on the very evening before Cater's body was pulled from the river.

Victim - Lubie Geter: Darryl Davis testified he saw Lubie Geter get in a car with Williams the first weekend in January (1981) at the Stewart-Lakewood shopping center; likewise, Ms. Ruth Warren, who was there shopping, saw a man she identified as Williams (who had 'two scratches on his face') with the boy she identified as Lubie Geter (whom she had seen earlier trying to sell her an air freshener).

Victim - Terry Pue: Charmaine Kendrick testified she worked at the Church's Fried Chicken where she regularly saw Terry Pue. She said she last saw the victim the last time he was reportedly seen alive talking to a man in a station wagon whom she identified as Williams. Darryl Davis testified he saw Williams at Pue's funeral.

Victim - Jo Jo Bell: Witness Kent Hindsman testified he knew Williams through the music business and that he met victim Jo Jo Bell at the Atlanta Studio when Williams was there. The witness further related that Williams gave victim Bell, Carla Bailey, and he (Hindsman) a ride home on that day. John Laster testified he knew victim Bell and that Bell and Williams knew each other. Victim Bell had told John Laster that he had an audition with Williams. Further, Mr. Lugene Laster (John Laster's brother) testified that he had seen John Laster talking to Williams. Lugene Laster further testified that he had seen Jo Jo Bell get into a station wagon with Williams.

Victim - Larry Rogers: Tilman Baynham, nicknamed 'Cool Breeze,' testified he saw Larry Rogers with Williams shortly before it was reported that Rogers was missing. Baynham identified Williams in a car while Rogers had solicited a marijuana cigarette for himself and his friend. Ms. Nellie Trammell testified she saw Rogers in the car driven by Williams on the day Rogers became missing.

Victim - William Barrett: Victim Barrett's aunt, Mary Harris, testified that her nephew, Billy, (William Barrett) or her son, James Barrett, had brought Williams to her home. James Barrett testified that he had seen Williams at the Harris home with Billy (William Barrett).

The Trace Evidence: Fibers and Hair

Our environment is filled with fibrous items and materials, including clothing, carpet, blankets, and such – most of which are manufactured in the textile industry. Through the manufacturing process, textile materials and the individual fibers they are composed of develop their own particular identity; that is, their own color, size, shape, and composition.

During the Task Force investigation, micro-analyst Larry Peterson of the Georgia Bureau of Investigation Crime Laboratory had been comparing hair and fibers from Task Force victims to determine if a common source could be established. He doesn't know just when he started noticing them; it was just that they kept appearing from an examination of the bodies of unsolved homicides of black males who had mysteriously disappeared and were later discovered with no apparent motive for the deaths. Sometime during the fall of 1980, three common materials were identified which linked several Task Force victims: Green carpet, violet acetate, and dog hair. Once he continued seeing them on different bodies, he began to associate them together and look for them on other bodies.

This was not the first time that crime laboratory scientists had seen or analyzed fibers in the investigation of criminal activity. Nor was it the first time that prosecutors used fiber or hair as evidence in a criminal prosecution; but it was and is the first time of which I am aware that such trace evidence was used in more than a minor role – such as in rape cases where the rapist left a body hair on the victim, or perhaps fibers found on a victim from a car or item associated with the perpetrator, where they merely supported other evidence in leading to a conviction. In such cases, it was always important that the victim did not know or have prior contact with the perpetrator, so that there would be no reason for the trace evidence to connect the two.

Likewise, it was important that Williams had always maintained that he knew none of the victims. Therefore, there was no reason for victims to have trace evidence from his surroundings on their bodies. Had Williams claimed the victims were in his surroundings such as to get hair/fibers on them, the importance of this evidence would have been diminished somewhat. Worth noting, the large numbers and location of items recovered, i.e. in their hair or loose on their body, would indicate a very recent transfer of trace evidence.

A micro-analyst is a scientist who deals with minute bits of material; and in examining bodies he is looking for small transferred material, be it hair, fiber, glass, paint, or soil, which may lead to where the body has been or to a connection to a perpetrator. He finds trace evidence so small that a microscope may be necessary to do an examination. While additional instrumentation may be required for further testing, the microscope is the primary instrument for trace evidence examination. In short, micro-analysis refers to the chemical identification and analysis of extremely small quantities of matter.

The number of Task Force bodies was piling up, as were the searches of suspect vehicles and homes developed by the investigation. Peterson was working long hours in his office at the laboratory trying to put the pieces together – studying and examining the foreign items on the bodies in an effort to solve the puzzle.

Finally, he saw the connection between some of the 'task force' bodies. It was the trace evidence he was finding – those unusual fibers and dog hair. During his prior work involving fibers, he had not seen such a tri-lobal-shaped carpet fiber. He told Task Force officials of his findings; initially, they were dubious. He continued to do his meticulous and tedious job in the lab while the Task Force investigators continued their efforts in the field. The process involved examining the clothing and body of the victims for foreign fibers and hair (or other matter not belonging to that item or person) by using tweezers and cataloguing them for further reference.

As part of the investigation, efforts were made to eliminate other potential sources for those fibers, such as the victims' own residences. Fiber and hair samples had been collected from other suspects or persons of interest who had been investigated and eliminated. Peterson could never find another source for the trace evidence from the bodies of the victims before Williams came along.

The break came for Peterson when he learned of Williams being at the bridge on May 22 and of subsequent searches of his vehicle and home on June 3. Peterson collected fiber samples from the Williams' home during this search and took them to the laboratory for an initial examination. He immediately went to work, and during this late-night examination on June 3 – *he knew he had a match.* There was no doubt in his mind. He reported his discovery to Task Force officials that night.

By sheer coincidence, Crime Laboratory and Task Force officials had located some of the best fiber experts in North America, who had been scheduled to come to the Georgia Crime laboratory to review the examinations done by Peterson. This was scheduled to impress upon a skeptical Task Force the importance of cases linked by the dog hair and fibers. During the weekend of June 13-14, 1981, over a dozen forensic scientists agreed to examine the questioned fibers recovered from many of the victims. Little did laboratory and investigative personnel know that apparent matching sources – not just victim samples – would be available for comparison! *It was unanimous that Peterson had it right!!!*

At trial, we would use the three foremost fiber and hair experts in North America in presenting the evidence and testimony to the jury: Micro-analyst Larry Peterson, Georgia Crime Laboratory; and two highly experienced outside experts, Dr. Harold A. Deadman, Special Agent, Microscopic Analysis Unit of the Federal Bureau of Investigation, and Barry Gaudette, a scientist from the Royal Canadian Mounted Police Laboratory, in Ottawa, Canada. The defense would not be able to obtain higher qualified experts.

We knew it would be necessary to present the testimony of the experts to 'lay' persons on the jury so that they could understand; and in doing so we needed to educate the jurors on how fibers are different and how they are made. It was imperative that the jurors 'see the difference' for themselves. Thus, charts and slide presentations and the like would be necessary. Gordon Miller worked with the experts in this regard.

Deadman and Gaudette came to Atlanta and worked directly with Peterson in preparing the trace evidence in the case of the century utilizing scientific means to connect 12 murder cases so that a jury of lay people could understand what they were being told. This apparently worked, judging by the later deliberation period by the jury. The experts worked on the case until and into trial – and even during and after trial Peterson was still following up on further leads and examinations as well as other cases connected to Williams by sifting through hundreds of fibers. The case against Williams, even after trial, became stronger. The case had been scheduled for trial on the 'fast track.'

Williams, of course, had lived in the home with his parents during the preceding two-year investigation, but the known fiber samples came directly from Wayne Williams' immediate surroundings – his room and contents. The station wagon he was driving was only one of the many vehicles he (or his family) owned or used during that span. Since the prosecution was presenting a total of 12 murder cases from the two-year span, it was necessary to have the Task Force investigators locate every vehicle Williams or his family used during that time period (for comparison of the carpet fiber from the vehicle he was using at the time a particular victim was missed). This was an enormous task; but with the unlimited resources made available by the President of the United States, Ronald Reagan, and Vice President George Bush, the FBI was only glad to respond. As any state prosecutor will affirm, this type of cooperation by the federal authorities was unprecedented.

Witnesses testified at trial as to the location of vehicles, proof of ownership or rental, and the seizure of the carpet samples and debris from those cars.

The Williams' Automobiles –

Richard Ernest of the State Crime Laboratory, and **Special Agent Dale Morea,** a member of the FBI, had searched and vacuumed Williams' 1970 Chevrolet station wagon which he used at the time of his arrest and by his own admission had exclusive use of before that time. The methodical search was conducted at the FBI garage on June 3, 1981, and lasted eight (8) hours. A vacuum sweeper with a special filter was utilized to conduct the removal of debris from the front and rear seats and the cargo area. Three cartons of vacuum sweepings from those areas were obtained along with a white throw rug from the cargo area. The search yielded thousands of fibers, hairs, and other debris which needed to be examined in the laboratory. Also collected were samples of carpet from the floorboard areas.

Vehicles, some of which had been rented and found out of state, were located and samples taken from the carpets and turned over to the crime laboratory. Also, mileage was determined since from investigation through witnesses, it was learned that Williams had been roaming the streets of Atlanta at night – so far as we could tell, nightly – and his high mileage nearing 100,000 miles (from various vehicles) annually supported that information.

1970 Chevrolet Station Wagon. This faded, white-in-color vehicle which was being primarily used by Wayne Williams (and processed by authorities on June 3, 1981) was obtained by his father, Homer Williams, in October 1980 from his brother-in-law. Carpet fibers from this vehicle will match fibers on William Barrett (missing 5/11/81); Jimmy R. Payne (missed 4/22/81); John H. Porter (missed 4/12/81); Patrick Baltazar (missed 2/06/81); Lubie Geter (missed 1/03/81); also, fibers from a gray glove found in this station wagon glove compartment matched two of the same victims: Barrett and Baltazar. Quite significant also, fibers found in debris from the vacuuming of the station wagon revealed matches to several victims missed during the time Williams had this vehicle: Nathaniel Cater; William Barrett; Jimmy

R. Payne; John H. Porter; Larry Rogers; Joseph Bell; and Patrick Baltazar. And more, white polyester fibers found in the debris in the station wagon cargo area contained fibers matched to Patrick Baltazar, Terry Pue, and Charles Stephens, all missed during the period Williams had this vehicle.

1979 Ford LTD. This burgundy-in-color vehicle was purchased by Homer Williams on May 15, 1979, from Hub Ford. This vehicle was found in Eastaboga, Alabama, and taken to the Georgia State Crime Laboratory on August 28, 1981. Fibers from the trunk liner matched fibers on Charles Stephens (missed 10/9/80)[8] and Eric Middlebrooks (missed 5/19/80 – 4 days after the vehicle was purchased).

1978 Plymouth Fury. This light blue vehicle was purchased by Wayne Williams on May 24, 1978, at Bob Maddox Chrysler Plymouth. When purchased, it had less than 100 miles on it. When repossessed on December 31, 1979, the mileage was 60,000 – it had been driven about

---

8   At trial, Homer Williams testified that the 1979 Ford LTD was not in the family's possession when Charles Stephens was missed, that the car had been returned in August, 1980; they
were driving rental cars at the time due to the LTD being in and out of the dealership for repairs.
After trial, and because the defense had only one valid issue regarding the vehicles and the fibers
there-from, Peterson decided to follow up in an effort to see if there was any validity to the 1979
Ford LTD not being the contributor of the trunk liner fibers. Peterson conferred with Prosecutor Joe Drolet in locating the rental agreements for the Ford vehicles Williams had possession
of during the period Stephens and several other victims went missing. The Georgia Bureau of
Investigation then tracked down three Ford Fairmont rental cars Williams used in 1980, including the one when Stephens was missed. Peterson examined samples from each of three (3) 1980
Ford Fairmont vehicles rented to the Williams family from July to September, 1980, for short
periods of time. One 1980 Ford Fairmont (white) was rented on 9/11/80; Stephens went missing
on 10/9/80, with the vehicle being returned on 10/13/80 (this vehicle was located in Valdosta,
GA). Results: fibers from the vehicle trunk liners and interior carpet matched those found
on Stephens – validating the prior results, though from a different Ford vehicle. The match
results for the 1980 Ford Fairmont were stronger than the previous comparison with the 1979
Ford LTD. This follow-up investigation revealed, as well, that two other 1980 Ford Fairmonts
produced evidence connecting Williams to two other Task Force victims, not used at trial, i.e.
Earl Terrell, and Clifford Jones. The corresponding matches of the three rental vehicles were
as follows: (1) 1980 Ford Fairmont (brown) rented 7/30/80; Earl Terrell was missed 7/30/80.
Three brown carpet fibers and 25 trunk fibers were found on Terrell. This vehicle was returned
on 8/6/80. (2) The 1980 Ford Fairmont (yellow) was first rented on 8/8/80, returned on 8/12/80
but re-rented the same day. Clifford Jones went missing on 8/20/80. 25 beige carpet fibers and
30 trunk liner fibers from Jones matched the interior carpet and trunk liner from this vehicle.
This vehicle was returned on 9/11/80. These findings from the rental cars (not previously located) just reinforced other strong trace evidence of dog hair and various fibers from the victims'
bodies to Williams' habitat. [Homer Williams' testimony at trial led to further investigation
(after trial) which turned up the three rental cars, connecting Wayne Williams to two additional
victims].

59,900 miles during this 19-month period that Williams owned it, an average of about 3,000 miles per month. After this car was repossessed, it was resold and went through seven (7) owners; and on August 6, 1981, Larry Peterson, from the Crime Laboratory, processed the vehicle at the owner's home. This vehicle was equipped with police emergency equipment including a whip (aerial), siren, scanner, four-channel radio, and blue lights. Fibers from the trunk liner matched fibers on Alfred Evans (missed 7/25/79).

1975 Plymouth Fury. This silver-gray vehicle was purchased by Homer and Wayne Williams on September 1, 1977, from the Atlanta Police Department. It was sold by Williams on July 2, 1980. Larry Peterson processed the vehicle at the owner's home on August 13, 1981. [Williams was known by witnesses to drive police vehicles with police equipment which caused them to believe he was the police].

1976 Plymouth Fury. This brown vehicle was purchased on April 13, 1976, by Faye Williams from Kelly Chrysler Plymouth and was repossessed on June 1, 1979. This vehicle was processed although it was repossessed before the death of the first victim Edward H. Smith was reported. It was not involved in any of the reported victims.

1979 Fairmont Station Wagon (Rental). Homer Williams rented this vehicle on February 11, 1981 – it was driven 104 miles before being returned. The dates did not correspond with any of the victims being missed.

1979 Ford Pinto (Rental). Homer Williams rented this vehicle on May 12, 1979, and returned it on May 14, 1979. The dates did not correspond with any of the victims being missed.

1979 Ford Fairmont (Rental). Homer Williams rented this vehicle on February 25, 1980, and returned it on February 26, 1980. The dates did not correspond with any of the victims being missed.

Contrary to what may be thought of mass production, the carpet in Williams' 1970 Chevrolet station wagon was uncommon since similar carpet was last installed by the car's manufacturer in 1973 – a blend of rayon and nylon fibers. Likewise, in Williams' 1979 Ford, the trunk liner contained un-dyed manmade fibers that had black adhesive material on the surface and had not normally been seen by crime lab personnel.

The Original Source of the Carpet Fibers

It was a major investigation to determine the source of the unusual carpet fiber found in Williams' home carpet. This fiber's tri-lobal (Y) shape being unique was helpful in tracing its origination. With photomicrographs, Investigators and the Federal Bureau of Investigation personnel met with manufacturers and contacts within the fiber industry. Textile industry contacts all agreed that this was an unusual shaped fiber and was consistent with being a carpet fiber. After Williams was found to be a suspect, the Wellman Company was determined to have manufactured that particular Wellman 181b fiber in limited quantity (which was pure luck, making it easier to trace to a distributor). Customer lists for the 181b were contacted (some were out of business) to determine who made the carpet from the Wellman fibers.

Once the origination source of the fibers was determined, it was important to follow the trail to a distributor if possible and to determine how much carpet was manufactured and distributed in the Atlanta area – whether it flooded the market or was in a limited supply.

The Wellman Company customers who had purchased this fiber were located and interviewed. It was learned that the West Point Pepperell Company of nearby Dalton, Georgia, a major carpet manufacturer, had turned their purchases of this fiber into floor carpet.

Prior to trial, that's as far as the investigation was able to go in tracing the fiber. Since we could prove by expert testimony and examination of Williams' 'known' carpet fiber sample that it was the same as the questioned fiber from the bodies of the victims, it was unnecessary that we make the link between the manufacturer/distributor and the carpet that was actually installed in the Williams' home. We had been unable to locate the actual sale and installation link of the carpet after it left West Point Pepperell.

This would leave an opening for the defense to attack during the trial through testimony of Williams' parents, who contended they installed the carpet in the home in 1968 – prior to 1971, the year West Point Pepperell claimed the fiber was purchased.

In order to educate the jurors, witnesses were called at trial to explain how fibers are made and distributed.

A Senior Technical Specialist from DuPont's Textile Fibers Department, **Dr. Herbert Pratt**, and an expert on the manufacture of fibers, was allowed to give the jury a lecture on fibers, how they are made and identified by their color, size, shape, as well as chemical composition. He had 30 years experience with DuPont, the nation's largest synthetic fiber producer. Dr. Pratt said that 75 percent of fibers sold in 1981 were manmade.

The witness explained there was 10 billion pounds of fiber produced each year, and it is manufactured by forcing polymer (molten chemicals) through "spinnerettes." The witness described the processes that bind the molecules of the fibers together and noted the various identifiable factors such as absorbency, durability, and dye-ability. Each dye varies chemically and can be identified by means of a microspectrophotometer. The shape of the spinnerette (likened to a gun barrel) determines the distinctive shape and dimensions of the fiber as it is forced through the spinnerette opening.

Dr. Pratt showed the jury how fibers could be "tailor-made" for specific uses and how different shapes, cross-sections, crimps, staples and dyes made such fibers patentable.

FBI agents delivered samples of carpet fibers from the Williams' home to Dr. Pratt for analysis. He identified the state's exhibit of the tri-lobal cross-sectional shape of the green fiber from Williams home carpet as very unusual; he looked everywhere, and there was no other fiber producer that had it but Wellman, the "Wellman type 6,6 nylon."

Mr. Henry Poston, Director of Technical Services, Wellman Inc., Johnsonville, S.C., helped design the particular unique "nylon 6, 6 polmer" named the "Wellman 181b" fiber to circumvent the existing DuPont patents. The "18" stood for the dernier; the "1" stood for the "crimp set" in the fiber, and the "b" stood for "bright."

This unique fiber was manufactured from 1967 to 1974. *Poston knew of no one else in the world that produced a similar fiber shape.* Wellman checks all competitive producers. Wellman produced a total of only 9.7 million pounds in six years.

This unusual tri-lobal shaped fiber was sold to several companies in un-dyed condition for carpet manufacturing, including the West Point

Pepperell Carpet Company in Dalton, Georgia, during 1970-1971. No other manufacturer was found to have had a similar cross-section fiber as that particular fiber. The proprietary right of the manufacturer is zealously protected by their patents so competitors will not copy the product.

Wellman sold one-half million pounds of this fiber in six inch lengths to West Point Pepperell in 1970 and another 371,000 pounds in 1971 – a very small amount by textile standards.

Mr. Gene Baggett, West Point Pepperell Company, testified. West Point Pepperell, of Dalton, Georgia, purchased the fiber which was made into carpet and later distributed in the Atlanta area (as well as ten southeastern states).

The West Point plant was contacted by investigators who confirmed that they had manufactured a line of carpet called "Luxaire," which had the same construction as that of the Williams' carpet; it was confirmed visually and by lab examination. One of the colors of the Luxaire carpet was the same as that in the Williams' home, the "English Olive" color.

The Luxaire line was manufactured during the period 1970 through 1975, but the particular "Wellman 181b fiber" for the "Luxaire" line was only manufactured for the year 1970-1971, thus making the fibers in Williams' carpet 'more rare' because of its limited one year production. The "Luxaire" line was made in 16 different colors.

Carpet sales of all the West Point "Luxaire" carpet that might have had the Wellman fiber in it (including all colors) totaled 54,000 square yards in 1971 and 125,000 square yards in 1972. The totals for the color "English Olive" in Region "C" which took in ten states, in both "Luxaire" and "Dreamer" (a different line) carpet styles for 1971 and 1972 combined was 16,397 square yards – thus, establishing the limited supply of carpet like that in the Williams' home in the Atlanta area. Further, most of those sales were commercial, not residential. Assuming approximately twenty yards per room, this was enough carpet for 820 individual rooms of carpet. In the Atlanta area alone there were in excess of 638,992 housing units.

Now that the jury hopefully understood how fibers were manufactured and distributed, we then moved the trial to focus on comparing the questioned fibers from the bodies to the known fibers from Williams' surroundings.

Presenting the Fibers and Hair Evidence

[At trial, the Judge required the State to present the fiber evidence for the two charged murders before entering into the other ten murders; however, I am summarizing all the trace evidence as to all twelve murders at the same time].

The state's three experts, **Peterson, Deadman,**[9] and **Gaudette**, would all conclude from an examination of the fibers from the victims in the 12 cases as compared to Williams' surroundings, that

"It would be virtually impossible for the combinations of fibers to have come from a source other than that associated with Williams."

This was strong testimony! Would the jury understand it? The jury would need to know how a fiber can be identified.

Fibers are those miniature pliable filaments which are made into yarn and knitted or woven into carpet or fabrics. As the fibers transfer from one place and item to another through contact, they may be so small as to be hardly visible. In the laboratory, they can be easily examined through the standard microscope, as well as sophisticated instruments such as the electron microscope and the microspectrophotometer. *Micro-analysts can compare the diameters, size, and shape of fibers as well as the chemical composition.*

In presenting the testimony to the jury through the witnesses, it was necessary to have charts prepared and mounted on poster-boards for each of the twelve murders, utilizing enlarged color photographs showing the more important fibers magnified 200 to 400 times so the jury can see the differences in color, shape, size, and even imperfections in the fiber. The prominent fiber comparisons were the Wellman tri-lobal green bedroom carpet, the violet and green acetate from the bedspread, a yellow blanket (found under Williams bed on the first search), and the carpet fibers from the automobiles. Other important fiber sources included rugs, bedspread, a glove, and a leather jacket. Less important

---

9   Deadman would later write an article published in the May 1984 issue of FBI Law Enforcement Bulletin, "Fiber Evidence and the Wayne Williams Trial (Conclusion)": To any experienced forensic fiber examiner, the fiber evidence linking Williams to the murder victims was overwhelming.

were common cotton fibers; the dog hair was concluded to be consistent with hair from Williams' dog, Sheba (DNA was not available).

A poster-board with *color photographs* was prepared for each of the twelve cases showing enlarged fiber comparisons for illustration purposes for the jury to actually examine and see the identifying characteristics. I regret the inability of the publisher to include *color images* of these exhibits due to the size of this book.

Microanalyst Larry Peterson, Georgia Bureau of Investigation Crime Laboratory, testified to the procedure of removing the trace evidence from the bodies (clothing and body hair) with tweezers and mounting them on glass slides for examination under a microscope; they were then magnified and photographed for display charts showing the many fiber comparisons for each victim. He explained that there were less fibers found on victims who had been stripped and dumped in rivers, while more fibers were recovered from other victims who were clothed and found on land.

Peterson testified as to his findings from an examination of the fiber and hair evidence from the bodies as compared to Williams' automobiles and home environment, including the bedspread, carpet, blanket and other items associated therein including a glove from the station-wagon in arriving at his conclusions. He said he had never before seen anything like the unusual Y-shaped tri-lobal fiber which was traced to the Wellman Company until he examined the carpeting in Wayne Williams' home. *Peterson also agrees with the other State experts that the two hairs removed from Patrick Baltazar's body were microscopically similar to samples taken of Wayne Williams' head hair and could have come from the same source.*

During about two hours of cross-examination, Peterson was asked if there could have been a transference of fibers from officers at the scene and from the materials (including ropes) used to recover bodies; he explained that he examined the ropes used in recovering the bodies, and river water for mud and vegetable fibers were examined at a later date.

He said there could have been several hundred fibers recovered from Payne's body and dozens from Cater's. (More would be expected on Payne who was wearing briefs while Cater was naked).

Peterson found fibers from these victims matched Williams' bedroom carpet, bedspread, and a blanket in his bedroom; he also said there were no significant differences in the microscopic characteristics or the optical properties when he compared the trace evidence to other items in Williams car and home, i.e. (a) a blue acrylic fiber from Payne's body with a blue bathmat found in a carport, (b) a blue-green rayon fiber from Payne's body with carpet from his station wagon, (c) a blue rayon fiber from Payne's body with fibers in vacuum sweepings from the house and car, (d) a green polypropelene fiber from Cater's body to green carpet squares in Williams storage room, and (e) a partially melted yellow-green nylon fiber from Cater found in the rear floorboard of Williams' station wagon.

Binder pressed Peterson about the comparisons to the station wagon carpet and found that Peterson had determined that only 620 of the 2.3 million vehicles in metro Atlanta (.026%) have the same type of carpet as in Williams' station wagon. The prosecution had not elicited that on direct examination, knowing that Binder would probably stumble into it.

Peterson had also tested fibers from homes of victims and suspects for elimination purposes.

When Binder brought up green cotton fibers that had not been brought up by the prosecution, Peterson answered that he could not offer any opinion on the significance of the green cotton fibers in the material of Williams' bedspread because cotton fibers are more common.

Binder inquired if Peterson agreed with the 'transfer principle' that fibers will transfer from one to the other. When Peterson agreed with it, Binder inquired if anything of Payne's had been found in the searches of Williams' house or car. Another trap left for the defense. Peterson replied that "I found a red cotton fiber with the same characteristics as Mr. Payne's (red) undershorts" in the Williams' car – and again urged the caution that cotton fibers were more common. When asked about Cater, Peterson said that Cater was nude when recovered and there was nothing to use as a basis for comparison with Williams.

Harold Deadman, the FBI agent with a doctorate in organic chemistry, was called following Peterson's testimony. Deadman had testified as an expert in fiber comparison in Federal Courts and the Courts of approximately 25 States. He testified to the work done in all twelve cases before the Court. He, too, agreed with the 'exchange principle,' noting that foreign fibers found on a body usually reflect the environment that person was in shortly before or after his death; further, that the fibers found on the under-shorts of Payne and the head and pubic hair of Cater would indicate the fiber transfer took place while they were undressed.

Deadman testified extensively on the various tests and comparisons which can be made in determining the nature and significance of fiber associations. He explained that fibers are distinctive and can be compared on structure, appearance, color, diameter, coarseness, cross-section, processing, inclusions, airspaces, delustering agents used, surface characteristics, surface debris, and damage. He also indicated how various tests could distinguish between two fibers by comparing their optical properties (light passes through them). Among these techniques are birefringence, dichroism, fluorescence (how much the fiber lights up under different lights) and absorption spectroscopy.

Deadman did separate tests on victims Payne and Cater at the FBI laboratory at Quantico with identical findings to those of Larry Peterson. He found some 50 yellow rayon fibers on Payne's cotton shorts. In testing three of those he found no significant difference from the yellow blanket at Williams home. Of about 60 violet acetate fibers on the shorts, he found they had the same composition as the Williams' bedspread; likewise, for the Wellman carpet fibers found on Payne's shorts. Similar links were made between two violet acetate fibers and one yellow rayon fiber found in Cater's head hair to Williams' bedspread and blanket.

Deadman explained that the Williams' bedspread had a *very unusual* combination of acetate and cotton fibers. He further displayed charts from the 10 similar murders and explained how fibers from each victim matched up with the Williams' carpet, bedspread, the yellow blanket (which became missing after the first search of the Williams' home and before the second search), blue throw rug, bathroom toilet cover, and interior of vehicles Williams drove during the time frame.

The witness also tested **two human hairs found inside the shirt of victim Patrick Baltazar which exhibited the same microscopic characteristics as the head hair of the defendant, Wayne Williams.**

Deadman said he reviewed the comparisons of known and questioned fibers conducted by Peterson and was in agreement with the conclusions. Deadman had calculated the chances of randomly finding carpet in Atlanta similar to that in Williams' bedroom and found it would be no greater than about 1 – in 8000, and that only involved the one item from Williams surroundings (carpet). Deadman agreed that fiber comparisons are not like fingerprints, but as indicated in the FBI manual – only circumstantial evidence. He also had never seen a fiber like the Wellman 181b, nylon 6, 6 fiber. When asked if he had compared the fibers with the victims or suspects, he said he had spent six hours examining fibers in Nathaniel Cater's hotel room. He also examined samples of fibers from the homes of victims and from the Omni.

Barry Gaudette, Scientific Adviser to the Royal Canadian Mounted Police and a foremost expert in North America on microscopic analysis of hair and fibers, was invited to Atlanta to assist in the preparation of the State's case against Williams and to lend his credence and testimony for the jury's consideration. He said that most fiber cases since the 1930s involve man-made fibers, such as nylon, and that of the 18 classes of fibers they differ in chemical composition, including glass, acrylic and polyester. He explained that by using advances in technology, experts can now compare sizes, diameter, chemical composition, and varying 'roundness' allowing manufacturers to identify their fibers. Gaudette reviewed the work of Deadman and Peterson and agreed with their methodology and conclusions. He did cross-sections analysis on the two hairs found on victim Baltazar and concluded they were consistent with Williams' head hair.

In summary, *the experts would conclude that "more than 28 different fiber types, along with the dog hairs, were used to link up to 19 objects from Williams' environment to one or more of the victims.* Of the more than 28 fiber types from Williams' environment, 14 of these originated from a rug or carpet. The combination of more than 28 different fiber types would not be considered so significant if they were primarily common fiber types. In fact, the light green cotton fiber is the only more common fiber type of the 28 fiber types examined. This cotton fiber was blended with acetate fibers in Williams' bedspread. Light green cotton fibers removed from many victims were not considered or compared unless they were physically intermingled with violet acetate fibers which were consistent with originating from the bedspread. It should be noted that a combination of cotton and acetate fibers blended together in a single textile material, as in the bedspread, is in itself uncommon." [10]

Williams was strongly linked to all the victims except Joseph Bell, a 'river victim' who was in the South River for 31 days before being recovered wearing only his under-shorts and thus would not be expected to retain a large number of hair/fibers, if any.

As expected, the nine victims apparently dumped near streets and highways partially, or fully, clothed contained more trace evidence than those recovered from the water.

What made the power of the fiber connections so strong were the many sources of different fibers from Williams' automobiles and home environment consistently matching fibers from various victims. Also, it is of major interest that the three automobiles Williams had access to during the period the victims were missed, corresponded with dates the victims were missed. As Williams moved from one car to another, the fiber comparisons would likewise change to match the new vehicle to the new victim.

Literally dozens of charts and several hundred photographs were made for illustration purposes. We wanted the jury to "see" what the experts saw through the microscope. Educational charts showing the different classifications of textile fibers, Williams' environment, objects in Williams' environment, and the comparison charts of items from Williams' environment were utilized.

An illustration chart for each of the 12 victims were prepared showing the fibers from the victim on the left side of the chart versus the known fiber samples from items in Williams' home and automobile on the right side of the chart which allowed the jury to see some of the prominent fibers in living color. The size of the fibers had been magnified several hundred times the original size and photographed so that the fibers could be seen by the naked eye for easy comparison.

---

10   Ibid.

Transference of Fibers – "Exchange Principle"

A courtroom drama was presented for the jury as it was shown that there is a scientific theory of an exchange of fibers from one person to another or with an item when there is a contact between the two – there is a mutual exchange or transfer of fibers from one to the other.

A demonstration was shown by Gaudette who presented a sweater and carpet square dyed with material which causes the fibers to shine when subjected to an ultraviolet light. Prosecutor Gordon Miller rubbed the sweater on his jacket, and the lights were turned off in the courtroom causing his jacket to glow with fibers transferred from the sweater. The material was dyed to show that those particular fibers would transfer from that item to another item, Miller's jacket.

The same transference was shown again when the carpet square was placed on the floor. Miller laid down on it, got up, and when the lights were turned out, again the fibers (now on the jacket) glowed in the dark.

The importance of this exchange principle should not be lost as "studies[11] conducted in England indicate that transferred fibers are usually lost rapidly as people go about their daily routine. Therefore, the foreign fibers present on a person are most often from *recent* surroundings. ... Accordingly, the victims' bodies ... are not only associated with Williams, but are apparently associated with Williams shortly before or after their deaths." Once hair or fibers become intertwined or 'matted' in body hair (pubic or head hair) you would expect those to be harder to lose.

The Bleaching Effect of the River Fibers

An interesting aspect of the examination of the fibers from the victims recovered from the river to fibers from Williams carpet was the color intensity. Fibers from Payne and Cater (the two charged offenses) which had been in river water for several days appeared to have been bleached.

---

11   Ibid.

Thus, by subjecting known fibers from Williams' home to the same environment as the river victims – small amounts of Chattahoochee River water in containers – it was learned that the same bleaching effect was noted. This was especially true with Williams' bedroom carpet and bedspread from his room.

Corresponding fibers from victims found on land did not show such bleaching effect.

Trace Evidence Identified from each Body –

Varied items of trace evidence (fibers and hair) from the bodies of victims were compared to known samples from Williams' home and automobiles driven during the relevant time period involved. The length of time before the bodies were discovered and whether a body was stripped and dumped in a river were conditions affecting the number of items of evidence found on the bodies.

Fiber and hair associations between the bodies of the victims and Williams would be hard to comprehend and appreciate without a review of the many sources, as found from the evidence at trial by the Supreme Court of Georgia's analysis in its decision, hereinbefore cited and now detailed hereafter:

Jimmy Ray Payne (Count 1 – Murder Victim):
Seven (7) fiber and hair associations between Williams and Payne were identified:
- Pale violet acetate fibers consistent with fibers present in Williams' bedspread, except that they were lighter in color (bleaching effect of river water);
- Green fibers similar to Williams' bedroom carpet, but they were also lighter in color (bleaching effect of river water);
- Blue-green or blue-gray rayon fibers consistent with fibers comprising the carpet of Williams' white station wagon;
- Light yellow fibers consistent with the fibers composing the yellow blanket found in Williams' bedroom except they were also lighter in color (bleaching effect of river water);
- Blue fiber consistent with fibers from a throw rug in Williams' bathroom;

- o Blue fiber consistent with blue fibers found in various fibrous debris removed from the Williams' home; and
- o Approximately seven animal hairs which could have originated from Williams' German Shepherd dog.

Nathaniel Cater (Count 2 – Murder Victim) –

Associations of fiber and hair between Williams and Cater were identified as follows:

- o Violet colored fibers having the same characteristics as fibers in Williams' bedspread;
- o Yellow fibers from Cater's hair were consistent with the properties of the fibers in a blanket found under Williams' bed;
- o A melted nylon fiber compared to fibers recovered from vacuum sweepings taken from Williams' station wagon;
- o A green fiber taken from Cater's pubic hair had the same microscopic characteristics as carpet squares in Williams' workroom;
- o A green fiber from Cater's head hair had similar characteristics and properties as Williams' bedroom carpet sample, and
- o Animal hair recovered from Cater was consistent with the characteristics of the hair of Williams' dog.

Alfred Evans (Similar Case No. 1) –

Associations of fiber and hair between Williams and Evans were identified as follows:

- o Two violent acetate fibers removed from Evans exhibited the same microscopic and optical properties as violet acetate fibers removed from the bedspread of Williams;
- o A fiber removed from Evans exhibited the same microscopic and optical properties as the Wellman fibers present in the carpet in Williams' bedroom;
- o Six polypropylene fibers found on Evans could have originated from the trunk liner of Williams' 1978 Plymouth Fury; and
- o Animal hairs removed from Evans could have originated from Williams' dog.

Eric Middlebrooks (Similar Case No. 2) –

Associations of fiber and hair between Williams and Middlebrooks were identified as follows:

- o   Four (4) violet acetate fibers removed from Middlebrooks were consistent with having originated from Williams' bedspread;
- o   Thirty-two (32) red nylon fibers that were wound in a clump on one of Middlebrooks' shoes could have originated from the interior carpet of the 1979 Ford LTD (this was the 'tuft' of fibers the officer at the scene noted in the victim's shoe);
- o   Two (2) white acrylic and two (2) secondary acetate fibers found on Middlebrooks could have originated from the trunk liner of the 1979 Ford;
- o   One yellow nylon fiber found on Middlebrooks could have originated from either the toilet cover in the Williams home or from the same source (not identified) that produced the loose yellow nylon fibers found in the debris vacuumed from the 1970 Chevrolet station wagon; and
- o   One animal hair removed from Middlebrooks could have originated from the Williams' dog.

Charles Stephens (Similar Case No. 3) –

Associations of fiber and hair between Williams and Stephens were identified as follows:

- o   Thirty-five (35) violet acetate and a number of green cotton fibers found on Stephens could have originated from the bed-spread found on Williams' bed;
- o   Three (3) yellow nylon fibers removed from Stephens could have originated from the carpet found in Williams' bedroom;
- o   Two (2) polypropylene fibers found on Stephens could have originated from the room in the back of the Williams' home that is adjacent to Williams' bedroom;
- o   About thirty (30) un-dyed synthetic and about twenty (20) secondary acetate fibers recovered from Stephens were con-

sistent with having originated from the trunk liner of the 1979 Ford LTD;

o Nine (9) blue rayon fibers found on Stephens were similar to blue rayon fibers, the source of which was unknown, found in debris vacuumed from the 1970 station wagon, debris removed from the sweeper found in the Williams' home, and debris removed from the bedspread found in Williams' bedroom;

o One (1) yellow nylon fiber taken from Stephens could have originated from the toilet cover found in the Williams' home, or from the same source, which was unknown, that produced the yellow nylon fibers found on some of Williams' clothing in the debris removed from the 1970 station wagon;

o Five (5) coarse white polyester fibers removed from Stephens could have originated from the same source, which was unknown, that produced the white polyester fibers removed from a white rug found in Williams' 1970 station wagon; and

o Approximately seventeen (17) animal hairs found on Stephens could have originated from Williams' dog.

Note: The transference of fibers is shown through vacuum debris from two different vehicles, the station wagon and the Ford LTD; both vehicles were accessible during the same period that Stephens was missing, indicating that trace evidence may be transferred from items to vehicles, and reverse or cross-transferred, as persons or items make contact as they move around.

Lubie Geter (Similar Case No. 4) –

Associations of fiber and hair between Williams and Geter were identified as follows:

o Several violet acetate fibers found on Geter were consistent with having originated from the bedspread found in Williams' bedroom;

- ○ Five yellow nylon carpet fibers removed from Geter had the same characteristics as the fibers present in the carpet located in Williams' bedroom;
- ○ One yellow acrylic fiber discovered on Geter could have originated from a carpet found in the kitchen of the Williams' home;
- ○ A green rayon fiber found on Geter could have originated from the carpet of Williams' 1970 station wagon; and
- ○ Ten animal hairs removed from Geter could have come from Williams' dog.

Terry Pue (Similar Case No. 5) –

Associations of fiber and hair between Williams and Pue were identified as follows:

- ○ Over 100 violet acetate and a number of green cotton fibers found on Pue were all consistent with having originated from the bedspread found in Williams' bedroom;
- ○ Three (3) yellow nylon fibers found on Pue could have originated from the carpet located in Williams' bedroom;
- ○ Two (2) pale green polypropylene fibers removed from Pue could have originated from the carpet located in the room in the back of the Williams' home that is adjacent to Williams' bedroom;
- ○ One coarse white polyester fiber recovered from Pue had the same properties as white polyester fibers, the source which was unknown, vacuumed from the rug and interior of Williams' 1970 station wagon; and
- ○ Approximately 17 animal hairs found on Pue could have originated from the Williams' dog.

Patrick Baltazar (Similar Case No. 6) – [12]

Associations of fiber and hair between Williams and Baltazar were identified as follows:

---

[12] Another example of the State's experts' conservative calls, when deciding whether to include trace evidence for trial, is the Baltazar case, where only two out of three of the experts agreed there was a match. A pubic hair found on Baltazar's body was *not used at trial* where FBI agent Deadman and Georgia Crime Lab expert Peterson matched the pubic hair to Williams, but the Canadian expert, Gaudette, gave the comparison an "inconclusive."

o   Violet acetate and green cotton fibers removed from Baltazar
    were consistent with having originated from Williams'
    bedspread;

o   Seven (7) yellow nylon Wellman-type fibers that were re-
    moved from Baltazar exhibited the same characteristics and
    properties as fibers present in the carpet located in Williams'
    bedroom;

o   Four (4) yellow rayon fibers removed from Baltazar's jacket
    could have come from the yellow blanket found in Williams'
    bedroom;

o   Four (4) rayon fibers found on Baltazar, because of deteriora-
    tion, ranged from green to yellow in color, could have origi-
    nated from the carpet of Williams' station wagon;

o   Two (2) woolen fibers and one rayon fiber found on Baltazar
    exhibited the same characteristics as woolen and rayon fi-
    bers taken from the cloth waistband of Williams' leather
    jacket;

o   Thirteen (13) gray acrylic fibers removed from the T-shirt,
    jacket, and shirt of Baltazar could have originated from
    the gray glove that was found in the glove compartment of
    Williams' 1970 station wagon;

o   A light yellow nylon fiber; a coarse white polyester fiber, and
    a pigmented polypropylene fiber had the same properties as
    fibers present in the debris vacuumed from the 1970 station
    wagon, and could have originated from the same sources,
    which were unknown, that produced the fibers discovered in
    the debris;

o   Approximately twenty (20) animal hairs found on the
    clothing of Baltazar could have come from the Williams'
    dog; and

o   Two (2) scalp hairs (several fragments) removed from Baltazar
    were *inconsistent* with Baltazar's own scalp hair, but were
    consistent with scalp hairs taken from Williams and could
    have originated from Williams. [Check the post-conviction
    DNA testing on these hairs 25 years later in 2007 – DNA tests
    implicates Williams].

Joseph Bell (Similar Case No. 7) –

Associations of fiber and hair between Williams and Bell were identified as follows:

- o   Five (5) blue rayon fibers found on Bell were similar to rayon
      fibers recovered from debris collected from the 1970 station
      wagon and from debris collected from Williams' bedspread;
- o   Two (2) pale violet acetate fibers found on Bell were consis-
      tent with the fibers present in the bedspread of Williams, with
      the exception that they were lighter, attributed to exposure to
      river water.

[The small number of trace evidence is attributed to the body only being
clothed in underwear, and having been in the South River for 48 days].

Larry Rogers (Similar Case No. 8) –

Associations of fiber and hair between Williams and Rogers were
identified as follows:

- o   Thirteen (13) violet acetate fibers removed from Rogers were
      consistent with the violet acetate fibers taken from the bed-
      spread of Williams;
- o   Three (3) yellowish-green nylon fibers removed from Rogers
      were similar to the Wellman fibers found in Williams' bed-
      room carpet;
- o   Eight (8) yellow rayon fibers discovered on Rogers could
      have originated from the yellow blanket found in Williams'
      bedroom;
- o   One yellow-brown to green fiber taken from Rogers could
      have come from the carpet of the 1970 station wagon;
- o   Two (2) secondary acetate fibers removed from Rogers' shorts
      could have originated from the bedspread found in Williams'
      garage;
- o   A light yellow nylon fiber removed from the head hair of
      Rogers exhibited the same characteristics as yellow nylon fi-
      bers removed from the toilet cover in Williams' home, from
      the sweepings made of the 1970 station wagon, and from sev-
      eral items of clothing of Williams.
- o   Animal hairs found on Rogers could have originated from
      Williams' dog.

John Porter (Similar Case No. 9) –

Association of fiber and hair between Williams and Porter were identified as follows:

- o   Violet acetate and green cotton fibers found on Porter could have originated from the bedspread of Williams;
- o   One yellow-green nylon fiber removed from the sheet used to carry Porter exhibited the same characteristics as the Wellman fibers from Williams' bedroom carpet;
- o   Three yellow rayon fibers removed from Porter matched the yellow rayon fibers removed from the blanket found in Williams' bedroom;
- o   Several green rayon fibers removed from Porter could have originated from the carpet of the 1970 station wagon;
- o   Two secondary acetate fibers removed from Porter could have originated from the bedspread found in the carport of the Williams' home;
- o   A blue rayon fiber found on Porter could have come from the same source, which was unknown that produced the blue rayon fibers found in the debris removed from the 1970 station wagon and in the debris removed from the vacuum cleaner found in Williams' home.
- o   Approximately seven (7) animal hairs removed from Porter were consistent with having originated from the Williams' dog.

William Barrett (Similar Case No. 10) –

Associations of fiber and hair between Williams and Barrett were identified as follows:

- o   Many violet acetate and green cotton fibers removed from Barrett could have originated from Williams' bedspread;
- o   Five (5) yellow-green nylon fibers recovered from Barrett could have originated from Williams' bedroom carpet;
- o   Seven (7) yellow rayon fibers removed from Barrett could have originated from the blanket found under Williams' bed;
- o   A blue rayon fiber recovered from Barrett had the same characteristics as blue rayon fibers recovered from the debris removed from the station wagon, from the Regina Sweeper, and from Williams' bedspread;

- o Approximately thirty (30) acrylic fibers recovered from Barrett could have originated from the glove recovered from the glove compartment of Williams' 1970 station wagon;
- o Three (3) fibers removed from Barrett could have originated from the carpet of the 1970 station wagon; and
- o Approximately thirteen animal hairs recovered from Barrett could have come from Williams' dog.

NAME OF VICTIM	VIOLET AND GREEN BEDSPREAD WILLIAMS BEDROOM	GREEN CARPET WILLIAMS BEDROOM	DOG HAIRS WILLIAMS' DOG	YELLOW BLANKET WILLIAMS BEDROOM	BLUE RAYON FIBERS DEBRIS FROM WILLIAMS' HOME	TRUNK LINER 1978 PLYMOUTH	CARPET 1979 FORD	CARPET 1970 CHEVROLET	ADDITIONAL ITEMS FROM WILLIAMS' HOME, AUTOMOBILES OR PERSON
Alfred Evans	X	X	X		X				
Eric Middlebrooks	X		X			X			YELLOW NYLON — FORD TRUNK LINER
Charles Stephens	X	X	X		X				YELLOW NYLON — BACKROOM CARPET — WHITE POLYESTER — FORD TRUNK LINER
Lubie Geter	X	X	X					X	KITCHEN CARPET
Terry Pue	X	X	X						WHITE POLYESTER — BACKROOM CARPET
Patrick Baltazar	X	X	X	X				X	YELLOW NYLON — WHITE POLYESTER — HEAD HAIR — GLOVE — JACKET — PIGMENTED POLYPROPYLENE
Joseph Bell	X			X					
Larry Rogers	X	X	X	X				X	YELLOW NYLON — PORCH BEDSPREAD
John Porter	X	X	X	X	X			X	PORCH BEDSPREAD
Jimmy Payne	X	X	X	X	X			X	BLUE THROW RUG
William Barrett	X	X	X	X	X			X	GLOVE
Nathaniel Cater	X	X	X	X					BACKROOM CARPET — YELLOW-GREEN SYNTHETIC

Summary fiber chart

Other Evidence

The Blood in Williams' Vehicle –

Only two of the victims, William Barrett and John Porter, were stabbed during the time Williams operated the 1970 Chevrolet station wagon. Barrett died from asphyxiation but also suffered several stab wounds; Porter died from stab wounds.

Blood was found in Williams' 1970 Chevrolet station wagon when it was searched.

DNA testing was not available in 1982; however, conventional serological analysis and identification of certain enzymes, proteins, and antigens present in the blood was done routinely in the State Laboratory.

Crime Laboratory Serologist Connie Pickens tested a sample of Porter's blood, identifying it of the type "B"; Serologist Linda Tillman tested Barrett's blood and verified it to be type "A."

- Porter's blood type was "B" with blood enzyme type PGM-1
- Barrett's blood type was "A" with blood enzyme type PGM-1

Serologist Tillman tested Williams' blood for comparison purposes and found it to be of type "O" – inconsistent with the blood found in his station wagon.

- Williams' blood type was "O."

Ms. Tillman also performed tests on the blood found in Williams' vehicle after his arrest. Testing of the 'questioned' blood stains from the station wagon was done from the cut-out piece of the rear seat where the blood spot was found; it soaked through the stitching holes binding the seat panels into the canvas underlining. The blood area was designated as in areas A, B, C and D. The type = International Blood Group:

- Area A blood =Blood type "A" with PGM1 enzyme (Barrett)
- Area B blood = Blood type "A" with phosphoglucomutase (PGM) type 1 enzyme (Barrett)
- Area C blood = Blood type "B" with PGM1 enzyme (Porter)

Thus, the only two victims who were stabbed during the time Williams had the 1970 Chevrolet station wagon left their blood sample in Williams' car.

Serologist John Weagle testified that type "B" with PGM1 (Porter) would involve about seven percent of the population, while type "A" with PGM-1 (Barrett) would involve about 24 percent of the population – that is, they shared with that percentage of the population their genetic marker found in the sample.

Weagle testified that the blood found in the station wagon was no more than eight (8) weeks old. Barrett's body was recovered May 12, 1981, while Porter's body was found a month earlier on April 12, 1981 – both within the eight (8) week time-frame of the search of the vehicle.

Was it coincidence that the only two victims' blood types who were stabbed – having different blood types and different from the car's operator – just happened to have been found in the very vehicle Williams operated during the period that both victims were murdered? I think not, and had DNA testing been available at the time there would have been further proof incriminating Williams. But, why was there not a request by Williams for DNA testing until 2007? More later!

Williams Suffered Scratch Marks –

Four (4) witnesses testified that Williams had scratch marks on his body during the period of the murders in Atlanta.

Dr. Joseph Burton, Medical Examiner, testified that such described marks were consistent with injuries left by a person struggling to free himself from a person choking him from behind.

Kathy Andrews, operator of Atlanta Studios in Atlanta, knew Williams because he used her studio. She testified that during late 1980-1981 Williams was in the studio when she noticed severe scratches on his arm from the elbow to the wrist, both arms, and Williams explained: *I fell.*

On one occasion, Keith Andrews, co-operator with his wife of Atlanta Studios, testified he saw Williams with scratches on the arm, possibly both arms.

Witness Anthony Barber, a member of the Gemini music group that Williams was associated with, testified that he remembered seeing some scratches on the right side of Williams' face and on his right arm. He also noticed that Williams' vehicle, a Plymouth, had a radio and lights (as in police equipment).

A 14-year-old youth, Dennis Bentley, testified that Williams auditioned him, afterwards saying: *You made it.* Dennis testified that Williams came to his house on one occasion when he (Dennis) saw scratches on Williams – he believed on the right arm, like someone grabbed him and he had a band aid on the thumb. When asked how he got the scratches, Williams said *a dog bit him.* Dennis said he asked Williams how it happened, and he wouldn't answer. When news about the missing kids came on the radio, Williams would change the station. Dennis told Williams he was going out of town, and Williams replied that the last person who said that was one whose funeral he (Williams) attended. (Williams was seen at some of the victims' funerals, although he denied it). Under cross-examination, the witness said that once when riding together while police had Williams under surveillance, Williams kept looking in the rearview mirror thinking police were following and said: "They ain't gonna catch me – I wrote the book."

Under re-direct examination, I elicited that the witness remembered seeing a blanket in Williams' station wagon. (Fibers removed from six victims matched fibers in a yellow blanket found under Williams' bed).

At trial, Williams denied ever having scratches as testified by the witnesses. He did say "I got one (scratch) when I was cooking in the kitchen and got some grease burns, and some I got when I fell when I was trying to get to the telephone."

Evidence of Motives –

Although the prosecution is not required to prove a motive for the murder existed since it is not an element of the offense, still if there is evidence suggestive of a motive it would be admissible for the jury to hear such evidence as relevant in showing such person has a reason (bent of mind) to commit the crime(s). Thus, in almost every murder prosecution there will be evidence presented as to one or more motives as inculpating the accused in the crime. Evidence of a motive is admissible even though it may tend to reflect unfavorably upon the defendant's character before the jury. A prosecutor may advance any theory as to motive which is not absolutely inconsistent with the facts. The Trial Court will normally weigh the prejudicial effect of such testimony, and upon finding the evidence is probative as to the reason offered, the testimony may be admitted for consideration of the jury.

I informed Judge Cooper that the State would be offering several witnesses' testimony of Williams' negative attitude towards his own race as showing motive and 'bent of mind.' The Defense vehemently objected to such evidence, especially racial slurs. Judge Cooper ruled that the State would be permitted to present such testimony tending to show a motive, but the witnesses would not be permitted to recite 'racial slurs' Williams made about fellow blacks – the "n" word was out (several witnesses would have testified that Williams referred to black kids hanging out on the streets by that slur).

Williams' Attitude and Contempt toward lower class black children; Racial Cleansing; Homosexuality; Physical Ability; Opportunity –

There was much evidence presented against Williams reflecting upon his 'bent of mind' and 'motive' in these murders establishing that he considered these victims below his class status, and they 'dragged down' his race. Williams, himself, was of a middle-class family where he grew up with school-teacher parents.

Earlier during the trial, witnesses testified to incidents suggesting that Williams' was 'gay' and that victims 'ought to keep their damn asses at home.' Now, a series of witnesses would buttress this position of the State as to Williams' motives in the case. Williams, of course, would later deny each witness's testimony.

Several teen-age youngsters testified to Williams' activities and attitude about low-class black kids, police, sex, talent, and stardom. A 15-year-old, **Darryl Davis,** earlier testified that Williams had picked him up on Stewart Avenue with the offer of a car-washing job, took him to a remote street, and fondled him, after which Williams got out to go to the trunk. Darryl took the opportunity to jump from the car and hid. [Darryl, himself, was murdered in 1984 when he was found dead of a gunshot wound to the back – not believed to have been related to the trial or his having testified].

Jerry, age 16, said Williams called him in February, 1981 about interviewing for a music group and came over. Williams said he did not want anyone over 21 years of age and asked if he lived with both of his parents. They discussed the group; Williams wanted him to meet another "producer" on Simpson Road in the project, Willie Hunter. Williams just showed up one night with Willie – he wanted to "catch me in everyday life." Willie, he said, started out the door when he saw my brother, Claudell, in a deputy's uniform, saying you never told me that (about my brother). The witness never saw Williams again.

Andrew, age 16, a tenth-grader who lived with his grandmother, said he met Williams when he was 13 years old at the game room in West End. He was with two other teenagers. They would ride around, go to movies, the Omni, Rialto, Baronet, and Coronet – they would see Bruce Lee movies; Williams would pay. He was seeing Williams almost every day. Williams always picked him up at West End Mall. Williams offered him $20 to perform oral sex. Williams was in a Skylark (Buick). (Homer and Wayne Williams previously owned a 1968 Buick Skylark).

Witness **"Billy,"** a musician and songwriter employed at a studio Williams used said Williams called him in the middle of the night, saying "pack your bags you're on your way to stardom." He saw Williams in a police-type car with radio and lights; he saw him two or three times a week at the Omni. This witness never saw Williams with a female date but saw him with young men a lot. He says Wayne was all "B/S."

James, age 17, testified he lived in South Carolina. Williams came to see him along with Sheldon Kemp in June 1979. James, his parents, and a friend came to Atlanta where they met Williams' parents. They went to the studio but never did make a tape. Afterwards, Williams called him at school in January 1981 and said he had something he (James) would be interested in. Williams sent him a round-trip bus ticket. Williams took James to someone he claimed was a psychiatrist, who asked about sex and girlfriends. He wanted to know if I would go upstairs. Williams later took him out to a bridge and drove over it real slow. Williams slowed down a little bit and looked at me but didn't stop, testified James. Williams took him to the Omni. The witness says he met a guy named "Nathaniel" at Williams' house. Nathaniel was a light-skinned adult with hair combed down the middle.

Joe testified that he was a recording artist; it was arranged for him to go to Williams' home to have his picture made. He was picked up in a light green station wagon. Williams wanted him to dress sexy – open his shirt. Williams and his friend, Willie Hunter, inquired whether Joe's parents were living. At Williams' home, Joe had to change clothes when he got there. When he went into the bathroom, he found children's clothes on the floor. Joe corroborates another witness who described Williams' station wagon as a light green color. Most described it as white, but police say it was an off-cream color which is sometimes mistaken for light green.

An 18-year-old youth, **Grady Summerour,** testified that he was on International Boulevard near the Omni when Williams circled him by car, stopped, and gave him $20 to pass out pamphlets.

I then called **Denise Marlin** who worked for Southern Ambulance to the stand. She knew Williams from his hanging around the office and running calls with them (ambulance chasing). She testified to his driving an old police car with radio scanners in it. I then inquired about Williams' having referred to his own race in a derogatory way when Binder objected. In excusing the jury, the Judge then heard a proffer of what she would say ... that he referred to his own race by the "N" word. I informed the Court that other witnesses would likewise testify to Williams having referred to poor street blacks in a derogatory manner.

Binder: Your Honor, this is remote as a diesel train in a mule territory. This is nothing but a bunch of junk.

I argued it was not a bunch of 'junk' but it would become clear from this and other witnesses testimony that Williams had a certain 'bent of mind' or 'state of mind' toward a certain group of his own race which was admissible to show motive. It being 4:30 in the afternoon, the Judge recessed the trial until the next day when he would rule on the objection.

The next morning as expected, the evidence would be forthcoming for the jury to consider. The law was clear! I recalled Ms. Marlin to the stand.

Mallard: Mrs. Marlin, when we recessed yesterday, I believe my last question dealt with a certain attitude displayed by Wayne Williams against a segment of the black race. What was your answer, whether he had or had not?

Marlin: Yes, Sir, he had.

Mallard: And what particular segment of the black race was that directed toward?

Marlin: The low income, low class, street blacks.

On cross-examination Binder elicited that she and Williams got along without any problems; that she did not dislike Williams, and that Williams would appear at accident and fire scenes.

Mr. Nicholas Marlin, Operator of Southern Ambulance and husband of Denise Marlin, testified. I asked him how he came to know Williams. He testified his relationship went back several years when Williams came around the office and would appear at accident scenes and so forth. He too testified about the old police vehicle with scanner and a green emergency light.

The witness testified to an incident at the office when he witnessed some 'horseplay' and 'wrestling' between Williams and another person. To show that Williams was not the weakling that the defense had tried to portray to the jury, I asked:

From what you witnessed, would you say that Mr. Williams is a weakling or is he strong?

"He holds his own very well."

I then asked him about an incident with 'mace' at the office. He testified that there was an incident of horseplay with people getting maced. He said he walked in at the end of it and Williams sprayed him with mace – all in jest and horseplay.

I then asked the witness:

From having known him during this period, can you say whether or not he ever exhibited any derogatory attitude toward any segment of his race?

His response: "Yes, Sir."

And what particular segment, if any?

"… I noticed that he would make comments about his own race that you usually don't find somebody of their own race saying . . . I would consider it derogatory."

Defense Counsel Jim Kitchens on cross-examination elicited that the mace burned but did not put him to sleep or make him helpless to defend himself.

Another witness, **Bobby Toland,** a driver at Southern Ambulance, testified to Williams' attitude toward his own race. Toland said he knew

Williams over a period of time during which he hung out there when Williams covered fires and accidents. Williams appeared "angry" and somewhat ashamed of blacks who were poor, claiming "they were not putting their best foot forward." The conversation occurred when Toland was a passenger in Williams' car, and Williams had asked him **had he ever considered how many (blacks) could be eliminated by killing one (black) child.** Williams had figures on how many children would be reproduced by one male child. Toland also rode with Williams in a 1978 Plymouth which looked like a police car; it had a flashing green light and siren.

A defense contention was that Williams, who was short at 5 feet 7inches and pudgy, was not strong enough to have lifted Cater or Payne over the bridge railing into the river. [Payne weighed 130 pounds; Cater 146 pounds]. Toland testified that in playful wrestling with Williams around the ambulance company office, Williams showed that he was above average strength for a man his size. Toland, who was 6 feet 2 inches and 292 pounds, indicated that Williams gave a good account of himself physically. Williams told Toland he knew karate. [The contention that Williams knew karate was vigorously denied and defended by Williams but was again proven upon cross-examination of a defense witness, Norris Keith Knox, when he was called by the Defense later in the trial]. The State would contend that Williams could have easily lifted a man the size of either victim – he was stoutly built and heavy with good arms and legs size. The jury could easily, from their viewpoint, make that decision.

[Toland, in late 1982 after the trial, was killed in an accident when his motorcycle struck a truck in Alabama].

Eustis Blakely, a Decatur jewelry store owner and friend of Williams, testified that Williams and the Blakelys had become friends in 1980 through a mutual interest in recruiting and promoting young black musical talent. Blakely said he and his wife, Sharon, would see Williams at their store on occasion and discuss the talent business. Willie Hunter was with Williams at times. Blakely said that Williams once picked up a bulky jewelry storage case, weighing 70 to 100 pounds. Williams tried to impress Blakely with his resume when Blakely asked what he did for a living as he didn't show a steady job. Williams claimed to have been a member of the Air Force Reserve and to have flown F-4 fighter jets on weekends at Dobbins Air Force Base. Blakely, a former Air Force Officer who had wanted to fly the F-4 but couldn't because he wore glasses, knew Williams was lying inasmuch as his eyesight would disqualify him as a pilot. Williams had always worn glasses. Blakely, an articulate witness and well dressed in a suit and tie, found humor in Williams' lies he told. Blakely had flown in the rear seat of F-4s and realized that Williams had some knowledge of the aircraft cockpit. Williams, who once built his own tiny radio station in his home, was trying to impress a young black male (Aaron) on electronics; but Blakely, who was an electrical engineer, said of Williams: "He had very good surface knowledge, but not much depth." When pressed, Williams got flushed, hyperventilated, and said "I'll bet I know more about anatomy than you do!" Blakely said he conceded that point to Williams. Williams thought we (the Blakelys) should live in Southwest Atlanta (upscale area). Blakely said Williams showed contempt for poor, lower income black kids calling them "street grunchos."

There comes a time in every case for the prosecution that you realize you are in a good place to finalize the 'case-in-chief,' that your case looks good to go to the jury, and that you need to 'rest your case' with a 'bang' or with a great witness, or by making a good point with the jury – rest on a high note!! I believed I had planned it well by holding who I thought would be the best witness to end our case, Sharon Blakely, the wife of Eustis Blakely to follow his testimony.

Ms. Sharon Blakely testified, as her husband did, that they became friends with Williams over a period of time when he was recruiting teenagers for his group in 1980. Other than operating their jewelry store, the Blakelys were managing some kids in a talent show. It came to her attention that Williams had called one of her youngsters, Aaron, several times in an effort to have him meet with Williams to audition without Mrs. Blakely knowing about it. Ms. Blakely didn't want to deprive the youngster of an opportunity and took him to Williams' house for a singing audition; Williams became upset when the child was too shy to sing. Williams still wanted to put the youngster in his Gemini group, and was taking Aaron to the Studio without her knowledge. She put a stop to it.

On one occasion, she said, Williams was watching a little boy in a grocery store. Williams said he wanted to "record him" and suggested she hear the boy sing in her shop; she told Williams the boy said he couldn't sing – to leave him alone. The boy later asked Mrs. Blakely to tell Wayne he didn't want to 'record' and he was not going to the studio.

She said Williams' resume was strange. Her husband responded that no one could go from sweeping the floor in a radio station to being the President of it in one year.

Mrs. Blakely asked Williams to help move a jewelry display case in the store. Instead he moved them out of the way and with one arm moved it; it was heavy and bulky.

Ms. Blakely said that, on one occasion when Williams came to the store, he had passed some 'street child.' Williams started pacing, making comments about "Decatur Street" kids – "they need to be off the street." She told him that those street kids would beat him up. Williams replied that "he wasn't worried, that you can press against a person's neck and they'd be out (unconscious) within seconds;" and he demonstrated how to do it by placing his hands on his throat. She further said he referred to street kids as "gruncheons."

After the incident at the bridge was widely reported, Ms. Blakely said they were discussing the music business when she told Williams she wasn't going to talk shop when people were asking questions, and she asked him why he was on the bridge.

He said he was 'throwing garbage off the bridge.'

But, why of all bridges the Chattahoochee … when you know that people are being killed, she asked?

So he said, well, 'the Investigators had gotten a tip, that's how they knew I was going to be on the bridge in the first place.'

Ms. Blakely testified she was very close to Williams and that they talked often; but she was feeling very bad. She said to Williams to just give her a reason why he was on the bridge. He said don't worry about it because he was going to sue. He was going to get rich because he was going to sue the News Media and stuff and he'd get money.

The witness testified Williams, being a Gemini, was a dual person.

I asked her based on how well she knew Williams if he had any particular hatred toward any particular segment of his race. She replied: Just the poor kids. She testified that Williams said poor kids had no initiative. Ms. Blakely explained that while Williams disliked poor street kids, he liked to associate with middle-class children, as he considered himself (although he was in his 20s).

Ms. Blakely testified that Williams called her after the bridge incident and after the FBI had questioned her about him. She said that she told Williams:

You're playing a game; before you get hurt, will you confess?

I can't answer that, Williams told her.

She told Williams: This game's got to stop sometime. If they get enough evidence on you, will you confess before you get hurt?

His reply: "Yes."

I turned her over to Binder for his usual thorough, sifting and probing cross-examination.

Binder went through the usual 'nit-picking' of her testimony without any great revelations from her past associations with Williams. She didn't know what "gruncheon" meant except it had always been used describing "poor street kids." She denied having any feeling of anger or lack of friendship to Williams.

Binder: Do you like him?

Blakely: I told you about using the word like. All right. I respect – I like Wayne. I'm going to be honest. I really do like him. I don't like what's happening, but I really do like him . . . I don't think that people understand that Wayne is weird and he has a split personality. I'm not a Psychiatrist, so I can't break it up.

Then, the boner!

Binder immediately went for the question that I later learned Williams had insisted he ask her:

Are you trying to intimate to the jury that you think Wayne Williams killed somebody? Is that what you're trying to tell this jury?

The room was so quiet you could hear a pin drop to the floor. No one moved, or spoke for it seemed an eternity. I couldn't believe I was hearing what was asked. I'm sure every lawyer in the courtroom was expecting an objection from me. I could have objected that the answer would be calling for a conclusion and 'invading the province of the jury' but I sat in my seat, unbelieving what I had heard as did the whole courtroom.

Seconds ticked off the clock!   The witness sat there – you could see the wheels turning in her head; what would she say, everyone thought?

There is a standard of thought among lawyers that you don't ask a question of which you don't know the answer – if the answer could hurt your case. I subscribe to it for the most part, especially if it is a 'killer' of a question – that is, if it goes to the heart of an issue at trial, and to have it backfire could cause you to lose the case.

This situation could be interpreted similar to the *O.J. Simpson trial* in Los Angeles where the prosecutor had asked Simpson to try on the gloves connected to the crime scene. There the prosecution had asked the performance of an act to which they obviously didn't know the answer: Would the gloves fit Simpson's hand? Well, the world knows the answer, and it put in motion the defense closing argument: **If they (gloves) don't fit, you must acquit. We know the answer to that riddle.**

Here I had personally interviewed the witness and knew her thoughts about Williams, and I believed she thought he was guilty – but would she say it? I was willing to hear her answer, so I waited along with others for the response. I had nothing to lose from her answer. The defense had a great deal to lose!

Then the witness replied after a long hesitation: Do you actually want me to say?

By the long hesitation and her response, I believe Al Binder got concerned, and he quickly re-worded the question:

"Why certainly, Madam, because if you feel that way, tell them. That's what you're here to do. Do you know that he's killed anybody?"

"You know I don't," she replied.

Probably feeling good he wiggled out of that, he quickly said "Thank you" and sat down. I arose for further re-direct examination.

I would return to the 'well' for more – since Binder brought it up. I thought Binder would object to the question (by me) as being improper (though it was his question), but he obviously thought she wouldn't hurt Williams.

After the Court Reporter read back the exact question she was first asked by Binder (if she was implying Williams killed someone), she replied after a short delay:

"Yes, I do. I really feel that Wayne Williams did kill somebody, and I'm sorry."

What a way to end it!

Now is the time to 'rest our case' with this witness' testimony ringing in the jurors' ears overnight, since there is usually a break after the State completes its case, for any motions and issues to be taken up with the Court (out of the presence of the jury).

The State of Georgia Completes its Case

It was 3:58 p.m., Thursday, February 4, 1982, after the State of Georgia presented its case-in-chief, that District Attorney Slaton announced to Judge Cooper that we were resting our case.

As expected, Defense Counsel Alvin Binder asked for a directed verdict of not guilty on the two murder charges. As expected, Judge Clarence Cooper quickly denied the motion, indicating that he had researched it in advance.

In summary, the State has now produced evidence of the homicide of 12 victims, who were murdered over a period of this two-year span – all victims having mysteriously disappeared without an obvious motive, none having their own transportation, their bodies being discovered some distance from their homes or habitat; but, someone was able to gain the confidence of the victims to entice them into a car during times when the city was mobilized to catch the killer. Was this person someone with ties to law enforcement, or even a police officer? Now, we knew the answer to that question. Wayne Williams was such a person who exuded authority with his ability to pass as a police officer, according to many witnesses and to his prior arrest for impersonating police. Williams' free-lancing activities, roaming the streets at night gave him access to teenagers, and therefore he had the opportunity to murder. Williams was always around boys younger than he, and his photography and talent scout business ventures never paid off financially but was good "bait." The State showed through testimony that Williams was strong for his size against bigger men at the Southern Ambulance where he was able to show his strength, and he certainly had the ability to lift the body of Cater or Payne from the station wagon tailgate which drops down and allows one to move a body over to the railing of the bridge. Testimony indicated that the vehicle was close to the railing. Photographs and testimony of a similar vehicle with the tailgate down, taken with the vehicle on the bridge near the rail indicated how easy it would have been to simply lift the body out and over the rail.

Several witnesses saw scratches on Williams' arms whereby he gave conflicting accounts of how he got them. Williams was seen with victims before their death.

Many witnesses testified to Williams' motives towards these victims, his contempt for low-class street victims, his sexual overtures to children, and his thoughts and math concerning the restriction of birth rates of poor blacks resulting from their death – ethnic cleansing.

Of course, last but not less important was the enormity of the trace evidence connecting all 12 victims to Williams, as well as the blood in his vehicle matching two of the similar transaction victims.

In contrast to the contentions of the defense that 'there was no pattern or similarity' shown, all the victims mysteriously disappeared without the hint of a motive, they were all small, young (changing due to circumstances), and poor who hung out on the streets, most from broken homes who did 'odd jobs' for money. Their bodies were dumped long distances from home. They were vulnerable to a person they believed to be in authority. Williams' statement to a witness (and another who will testify in rebuttal by the state) that he dropped 'trash' off the bridge was so telling. This is exactly what he considered these victims to be.

Another strong inference of guilt of Williams arises from the testimony of the medical examiners that they had not been seeing other bodies of profiled victims with those strange dog hair and fibers since the May 24, 1981, recovery of Cater's body from the river.

We still had witnesses we could have called who would testify to matters that would be more effective if we hold them for rebuttal to be called after the defense rests. However, we take the chance of losing that testimony if the defense rests without putting up witnesses as there would be nothing to rebut – but we are willing to make that gamble; this is pure tactical strategy!

Now, what will the Defense do? We had no witness list or statements of witnesses they may call – nothing, except that the police had interviewed some persons which the Defense would be expected to call to the stand, thinking such witnesses would help them more than the State. Also, in Georgia (at that time), the defense would be entitled to the closing argument, the last word to the jury which most defense attorneys treasure if they put up no evidence except for the defendant's testimony.

PART
FOUR
The Defense

The Defense Evidence

The Defense called two (2) witnesses from the True Light Baptist Church, located across the street from Williams' home, in an attempt to prove that Ms. Nellie Trammel was never at the church. Obviously, this elderly, believable witness hurt the Defense when she identified Williams with victim Larry Rogers in a car the day he disappeared. She had previously seen Williams going in and out of his house as she left a church service nearby.

But, what did the Defense prove? One witness didn't know Ms. Trammel, but he might know her if he saw her; the other witness said he knew Ms. Trammel and that she was not a regular member but could have visited the church. He didn't know if she was there on the day in question.

The defense witness verified that one can see the Williams' home from the church parking lot – giving credibility to Ms. Trammel's testimony.

That's the problem with calling peripheral witnesses who contribute very little to your case while giving the other side the opportunity to elicit testimony harmful to your case on cross-examination. This continued to be the case throughout the Defense's presentation of witnesses. The defense witnesses were favorable to Williams in many respects, but many helped the prosecution as much or more than they hurt us.

Next, the Defense called to the stand a disgruntled former Atlanta Police Recruit, **Kenneth Lawson**, who had worked on the bridge stakeouts and at the Task Force office. Lawson had been given an option of being fired or resigning by the Atlanta Police.

Under questioning by defense counsel Jim Kitchens, Lawson said he had worked on the Children's Task Force as a recruit from January to July of 1981. He testified he answered the phones and did reports on incoming calls at the Task Force, as well as working a bridge detail. He said he knew the two recruits, Campbell and Jacobs, who testified for the State.

Lawson claimed that he and other recruits at times would communicate by radio, and that he heard 'ghost stories' while on stakeout at the river; on one occasion the swat team was called down after Jacobs reported he saw someone standing by the river's edge throwing a body into the river. After investigating he said he had only seen a ghost. Lawson also said that ghost stories and beer drinking while on stakeout "was a joke among all the recruits for a while" at the Police Academy.

Lawson further testified that he knew Nellie Trammell. He claims Ms. Trammel called and came by the Task Force office all the time, saying:

"We were under the impression it was from speaking with her on the phone and her coming to the task force that she was a psychic or she had visions."

Kitchens: "How did you first become aware of her existence?"

Lawson: "Every time a body would be found, she would call or come down to the Task Force to make reports on things that she had envisioned."

Lawson testified Ms. Trammell would bring her knitting bag and sit in the front room at the Task Force and do her knitting. [Sounds strange for the Task Force to allow a psychic to hang out and knit. The Defense is doing everything possible to attack the credibility of this elderly woman, Nellie Trammell, a credible witness for the State who had identified Williams with victim Larry Rogers].

Lawson seemed to have an answer for everything the Defense wanted. When asked about the fog on the river he testified:

Kitchens: "When that fog would be down on the river, as you just alluded to, sir, did you ever try to shine a light down in it and see the water?"

Lawson: "It's impossible."

"Why?"

"Fog reflects the light."

"When you would attempt to shine a flashlight or some other kind of light down in the water, could you see the ripples on the water when the fog was there?"

"Very seldom could I even see the water," responded Lawson.

[Surely the jury could see through the 'fog' this witness was spewing; if you couldn't see the water with a light – zero visibility – what good were stakeouts, and how did the recruit find his way to the river's edge 55 feet below the bridge?]

Defense counsel asked his witness if he had completed the recruit program. Lawson responded that "I was at the time having marital difficulties, and Major Davis gave me an option to either resign or to quit or to be fired." He said he resigned. He went on to blame his marital difficulties on his having worked long hours.

Prosecutor Miller took Lawson on cross-examination.

Lawson testified that on May 22, 1981, he was stationed on the bridge detail at Bankhead Highway (I-285 Bridge) and that Campbell and Jacobs were at the Jackson Parkway Bridge. He said he reported to work at the usual time, 8:30 to 9:00 p.m. When questioned further about working on the May 21 regular shift, he said he was pretty positive. He was then confronted by Miller with the duty roster for the night of May 21, 1981, where there were no hours logged in for him on that day. He then tried to explain it with "because of the time that we spent on the bridges, seven days a week, sometimes ten – ten and a half hours a night, the team leaders would sometimes ... we would mark comp days and the days were not actually accounted for payroll-wise because we were drawing time and a half for overtime. So it was like a vacation day. And the time sheets that the team leaders kept weren't actual accounts of the time, sir." He later said he could not account for that night.

Miller: "If you got comp time for time that you weren't there, then it would be reflected on the sheet, wouldn't it?"

Lawson: "No, Sir; not to the pay. It was a system that I don't think any of the recruits understood, Sir."

Lawson further asserted that he had personally taken several calls from Ms. Trammell and that he made tip sheets on probably two; then he stopped making them on psychics.

Miller asked him if Ms. Trammell's calls to the Task Force would be among the 187,000 telephone calls the office received and recorded, to which he agreed.

Lawson testified he now worked part-time for his brother-in-law in heating and air-conditioning work and that he lived in a mobile home park. When asked, he testified the East Point Police came out to his place only one time (domestic complaint). He was then shown a letter he wrote to Chief George Napper about the domestic incident wherein he referred to the incident saying "The second time they came out there —," Lawson explains it that "Well, they never left — they sat there until we dispersed." Lawson further said the East Point Officer lied in the report as to the reason the police was called, and as to his telling them he was a seven-year veteran of the Atlanta Police assigned to the Task Force. Lawson said "That also is a lie, Sir."

Lawson re-affirmed that Ms. Trammell would come to the Task Force office and would usually ask for Officer Pollock or Banda and that she sat right beside Pollock's desk and gave reports.

Miller: Mr. Lawson, why did you leave these various police departments that you were employed by? [He was employed by four different agencies for short stints]. Lawson attributed most of his problems with the various agencies as being political in nature.

When asked, Lawson testified that he only went to the Defense with his having worked down at the Task Force "about two weeks into the trial."

It was obvious that Lawson was having his 'day in the sun' by attacking the two recruits, Jacobs and Campbell, who saw Williams' car on the bridge.

[The four stake-out team members were in place where they testified they were, and it would have been ludicrous for them (recruits) to tell other recruits who were not there that they had been committing unforgivable misconduct in a highly sensitive investigation with a senior Atlanta officer and an FBI agent with them on the stake-out].

Lawson claimed he saw Ms. Trammel at the Task Force at least five (5) times although it was later shown she was never there until June 30,

1981, (after Lawson left), and she was not on the call list of 187,000 telephone calls to the office. (It will later be shown in rebuttal by the State who that mysterious person was who visited the office).

After making two unsolicited telephone calls Friday night to a radio talk show, Homer and Faye Williams (Wayne's parents) were cited by Judge Cooper on Monday for violation of his gag order. Judge Cooper indicated that the calls were brought to his attention by the defendant's attorneys. Mrs. Williams had called WGST and told the talk show host that *"My home is not the scene of a murder, and I know that."* Mr. Homer Williams later called the station suggesting that the prosecutors had enticed young boys to testify against Wayne for reward money and were putting words in their mouths.

Dr. Daniel Stowens, an upstate New York hospital pathologist with a specialty in pediatrics, took the stand for the defense. He was supposed to deliver a blow to the State's proof of the cause of death of the victims, in opposition to our expert *forensic pathologists.* After listening to his qualifications as Al Binder navigated him through lengthy and fertile testimony of his education, training, experience and writings, I began to think he was the best thing for the medical field since aspirin was discovered. Stowens identified a thick textbook he had published which he said was in use throughout the world in its 2nd edition. He estimated during 40 years he had performed or consulted on some 90,000 autopsies. After a thorough recitation of his experience, including his having received a gold medal about 1955 from the American Society of Clinical Pathology for his work while at the Armed Forces Institute of Pathology dealing with "sudden unexpected death in infancy," or "Sudden Infant Death Syndrome" (SIDS), he was 'submitted' as an expert in his field (of pathology) by defense counsel Binder.

Prosecutor Miller took the witness on cross-examination. Once an expert witness in a given field testifies on direct as to his qualifications, the other side is given an opportunity to cross-examine on the witness' qualifications to render such opinion before inquiry into such testimony is permitted. However, the qualification of an expert is pretty much a perfunctory matter since most anyone with a degree or training in a particular field will be allowed to give expert testimony by the Court.

Normally the witness is (obviously) qualified and cross is waived, allowing the testimony to continue. At times, further examination is conducted to probe into the expert's background, hoping to reveal some weakness.

Miller inquired as to how many of the 90,000 or so autopsies he had been involved in did he *personally* perform.

Stowens: "Oh, at least several thousand. It gets a little hard to separate when you're in a teaching situation and you're supervising residents and they sort of do half and you do half; ... But doing it myself, certainly, oh, at least 4,000."

When asked how many were stabbings, he responded there were a number – whether a hundred or two hundred – but a lot. Of death by criminal strangulations, he recounted probably 25 or 30; of death by blunt trauma to the head, he guessed 25 or 30.

As to the number of autopsies performed in 1981 other than natural deaths, he said he had done about 40 or 50; in 1980, about the same – maybe more; in 1979, a few more; in 1978, "probably a few more." What started off as 90,000 has dwindled down to minor numbers as having to do with criminal cases. In later cross-examination, I would be coming back to his past experience.

Miller indicated no objection to the witness' qualifications as an expert, and Judge Cooper allowed the testimony to continue by Binder on direct examination.

It was soon seen that Stowens agreed with very little of the conclusions of the State's medical examiners in the two cases for which Williams *was on trial and thus subject to lose his freedom* and somewhat in disagreement in the other cases. He was asked by Binder to assume each and every factual finding on Jimmy Ray Payne's autopsy report other than the cause of death, and whether he had an opinion as to the cause of death of Payne from a review of the reports and the slides. His answer:

"I have – I'd have to say no, I don't know the cause of death."

He went on to explain that all he found were negatives: No evidence of trauma, stab wounds or blunt instrument or fractures. He guessed the most logical inference ... was drowning.

Binder: "In your opinion, how old is that body or from time of death to the time it was found?"

"I would say, especially from the appearance of the eyes which are beginning to bulge out of the head, that usually occurs somewhere around four or five days. I'd say five days seems reasonable." [Payne was last seen and missed on April 21, 1981 and his body was recovered on April 27, 1981 in the river].

As to Nathaniel Cater, the witness was again asked to assume all factual findings other than the cause of death in the autopsy report and to give his opinion on the cause of death. His response:

"Again, I must answer that I don't find enough solid information in the autopsy report to be able to arrive at that conclusion."

As to whether in his opinion Cater's death was the result of a homicide or any criminal agency:

"There is no indication of any criminal activity at all."

Further: "As I mentioned in Payne's case, the eyes begin to protrude from the body at about five days ..." "In Cater's case, this protrusion had gone so far and decomposition of the eyes was so advanced that I would say that it had to be at least a week and probably longer."

[What? He was most helpful to the Defense with this. Factually, Cater was last seen alive on May 21, 1981, by several persons including an acquaintance who saw him holding hands with Williams; his body was pulled from the river three days later on May 24, 1981].

Stowens went on to say that he believed that Cater died of causes unknown.

Binder: "Now, if I told you that Nathaniel Cater's body was recovered on the 24th day of May of this past year and our (the State's) witnesses testified that they saw this individual alive on the 21st day of May, what would your opinion then be?"

Stowens: "Well, there are only two possibilities. Either the eyewitnesses are mistaken or this body is not Nathaniel Cater." [Cater was identified through fingerprints and physical identification].

When asked to give his best judgment as to the time of death of Cater, Stowens responded:

"From the degree of decomposition of the body, the fact, especially, that the eyes are gone, I'd say that it had to be dead for a week, which would make it the 17th, and probably a little bit longer."

The Court took a recess, sent the jury out and took a matter up concerning a juror in chambers and on the record:

Judge Cooper brought to the attention of the attorneys that a juror had a problem, and as a result he had sworn in (City Court) Judge Kaplan (well known as a medic who was at scenes of injuries, shootings, etc., on occasions to administer to those in need – sometimes police officers) as a Bailiff in the case, "and that he is to have contact with the jurors as other bailiffs who have been sworn-in in connection with this case."

Judge Cooper explained that a juror was sick and unable to see her doctor today, and that Judge Kaplan would transmit the juror to Grady (hospital) when the court recesses at 4:30, if there was no objection.

No one objected. Al Binder responded that "we trust him explicitly. His reputation speaks for itself."

Binder questioned Stowens about the cause of death in the ten similar cases. As to Porter, the witness agreed that the cause of death was multiple stab wounds; as to Baltazar, the witness agreed with Dr. Burton as to death by asphyxia due to ligature strangulation; as to Barrett, the witness agreed that the cause of death was asphyxia due to ligature strangulation; as to Joseph Bell, the witness disagreed with the medical examiner, saying he would attribute death as "unknown"; as to Pue, the witness agreed that it was a homicidal death due to ligature strangulation; as to Middlebrooks, the witness agreed with the cause of death due to blunt trauma to the head; as to Geter, the witness agreed the cause of death was asphyxia due to strangulation; as to Stephens, the witness would not agree that death was due to asphyxia by suffocation, saying he would classify as "undetermined;" as to Larry Rogers, the witness agreed with the medical examiner as to asphyxia due to strangulation; and, as to Evans, the witness disagreed with the diagnosis of probable strangulation. Of course, Williams was not on trial for those deaths of which Stowens agreed with the state's experts as to the cause of death.

It was late Friday. The Court recessed the trial for the week so the juror could be transported to the hospital to return on Monday for resumption of the trial.

This is good! This would give us time to make some calls to New York over the weekend to check out this expert witness. We knew little about him until he took the stand. Perhaps some inquiries would give us ammunition for cross-examination. Parties putting up experts don't like to leave their expert 'hanging over' a weekend for cross-examination as this has turned out, but his direct examination was lengthy and coming on a Friday.

Another surprise – it now appears I will be doing the cross-examination rather than Gordon Miller, who started it with the witness' qualifications.

After Friday's court session, District Attorney Slaton said he wanted me to take over the cross of this witness, saying I had a better connection with the jury and would be more effective since they saw me more consistently (on my feet) during the trial. I didn't like it (taking a witness away from another prosecutor in mid-stream), and suggested he (Slaton) would have to break it to Miller. Besides, I was working nights and weekends at home preparing for upcoming witnesses including the Williams' family.... We had a great team and a 'fit' for each person on the team. Slaton broke it to Miller who took it probably with relief, giving me the file.

Recessing the trial on Friday for the week-end provided me an opportunity during the interval to read some of his book on autopsies which the defense had introduced into evidence (this was a mistake since it provided much of the ammunition for the cross examination and indicated his past in dealing with 'crib deaths' of babies with no forensic homicide background). We talked to certain officials in New York from the prosecutor's office and the medical community where he lived, worked, and testified in New York, and I learned he was not such a 'stellar' expert as he was touted as being.

Stowens had for the most part dealt with pathology in a clinical setting in a hospital (looking at slides under a microscope regarding natural deaths and diseases) and not as a forensic investigator in murder cases.

At resumption of the trial on Monday, the Court took up an unusual matter with the lawyers and parties, the question of conjugal visits for the jurors who were kept sequestered at a hotel. It seems that the jurors who had been sequestered nights and weekends at a hotel for weeks, though not revolting yet – had serious concerns!!!

Williams, his attorneys, and the State's attorneys, all agreed that those married jurors would be permitted to invite their spouses to visit with them at the hotel overnight on certain weekend dates.

Judge Cooper met with the jurors with permission of the parties to take care of their concerns as far as possible. He informed them they would be allowed to have their spouses visit with them beginning at 6:00 p.m. Saturday to 3:00 p.m. Sunday. The unmarried jurors would be able to invite a friend, business associate, or whomever they wanted to visit them during that day, explaining "now, of course, there is a law, a statute that prohibits fornication. Nobody is going to supervise what you do during this time period. It's up to you to utilize that time in the way you feel necessary." The Judge further explained that kids could not visit, and only spouses could visit the juror's room. The Judge apologized for the widespread dissatisfaction and explained that the bailiffs were to report to him any problems the jurors were having that were not being addressed by the bailiffs. He said he would address any concerns and see that activities were being provided (when not in court). Judge Cooper further emphasized the importance of the jurors' conduct about violating any of his orders while sequestered. One juror who was engaged to be married inquired whether the trial would be over by April 4 saying that, if it was not, the Judge was going to have to marry them. [No request regarding a honeymoon was made].

The Jury was brought in, and the trial resumed with Dr. Stowens being further examined on direct by Al Binder for the defense.

Binder: "Doctor, on any chance heretofore, have you had a chance to talk to Doctor Stivers (State's Medical Examiner) about his autopsy (of Cater)?"

Stowens: "Yes, I have."

Stowens went on to explain that he had called Dr. Stivers about the autopsy on Cater, and testified "I said, do you have anything else on Cater?" And he (Stivers) said: "Cater? What do you want that for?" So I said, "Well, I've been asked to review that case and your secretary couldn't find anything." He (Stivers) said: "Cater, they're not going to use that, are they? And he said, No, I don't have anything else. There weren't (sic) anything to do. The body was decomposed. I didn't take any sections."

Binder turned the witness over for cross. I got up to cross whereupon Binder asked to take a matter up with the Court at the bench. He objected to my taking over the cross since Miller earlier had the pleasure. I expected the objection.

I pointed out that Miller had done the cross on the witness' qualifications only; and this was a different phase, and I was requesting deviation from the rule. Judge Cooper took a 15-minute recess, came back and announced he would permit the cross examination by me (and would issue a written order permitting the same for both sides).

In completing the direct examination, the Defense ended on a high note by questioning the credibility of the Prosecution in 'indicting Williams on the Cater case' from an alleged telephone conversation the witness had with the medical examiner, Stivers. When that happens, I like to immediately start off with removing that 'high note' if I can – while it is fresh in the jurors' minds – thus 'bursting their bubble' (as in piercing a balloon). If I can do that, the jurors will question the remainder of the witness' testimony.

Mallard: "Doctor, I'd like to first go back to that last hearsay statement alleged to have been made by Doctor Stivers. I believe you said that Stivers told you something to the effect, quote, they're not going to use that, are they?"

Stowens: "Yes."

"Meaning the Cater case?"

"Yes."

"When did you have this conversation with Doctor Stivers?"

"It was, if I can remember the dates, it was the day after, either the next day or the day after that that I returned to New York after visiting Atlanta."

"Well, when were you here?"

"It was about the beginning of December. I don't remember the exact date."

"Of 1981, about the beginning of December. And it would have been after that time that you talked to Stivers and he said that; is that correct?"

"That's correct."

"Did you know that your employer, Mr. Williams, was indicted on Cater's death in July, July 17, four months before you say Stivers told you that?" [The Medical Examiner who performed the autopsy on Cater would not be questioning whether the prosecution was going to use that case four months after that case was in fact indicted, and especially in light of that case having been the only case for which Williams was initially arrested pursuant to a criminal warrant and had a probable cause hearing].

Cross-examination of this witness was going to be aggressive and revealing in light of his testimony in direct opposition to our evidence. On direct, he testified that he was shocked and incensed to learn that Williams was indicted in the Payne and Cater cases, in which he found no evidence of foul play – that Payne may have drowned and that Cater died of unknown causes and had been dead at least a week when found in the river. He said he could not rule out that they may have died of many things, including leukemia or pneumonia. I jumped on him for suggesting Payne may have drowned after being found in a rough river many miles from his habitat "swimming" in April. Payne had no transportation and had no water in his lungs.

I asked him where he got the information about Cater's eyes with which he determined the time of death, since the eyes were not visible in the photographs which I showed him. Then I asked if he got the information from the autopsy report which he said he had read. He said:

"I'd have to check and see."

I suggested: "Yes, I wish you would. Find it in the autopsy report. I'll wait."

After reviewing the report, he responded:

"No, it's not in the autopsy report." He could furnish no basis for that conclusion he had made about the time frame and the condition of the eyes.

Nearing the end of the cross, I again came back to his conclusion about the time of death:

"Doctor, now, you said earlier, I believe Friday it was, that if witnesses said that Mr. Cater was alive three days prior to his death they either must be mistaken or that was not the body of Mr. Cater?"

"I said that."

"Now, would your opinion be the same if you knew, one, that blood bank records and a witness there who knew him said he was there on the twenty-first of May; number two, another witness who knew him, the manager of the Falcon Hotel, saw him on the same day, May 21; number three, that a third witness who knew him personally puts him holding hands with the defendant at the Rialto Theater the same day later that night, which was six hours before the bridge incident; four, that Cater has never been seen alive since; and five, that his body was identified by fingerprints on both hands." Now, the question was, if you knew that, would your opinion be the same?

"My opinion is still that that body has been dead seven days."

"Doctor...are you as sure of that opinion as you are of everything else you've flown down here from New York to tell us?"

"I'm more sure of that than of a lot of them."

[Now, the jury wouldn't believe anything he testifies to under oath].

I elicited that the witness had never seen or performed any examination of the victims' bodies and did no investigation but reading the autopsy reports of the State's medical examiners. I emphasized his experience as a hospital pathologist versus many forensic pathologists who had thousands of testimonials in murder cases in their background, but he had read their reports and came up with conclusions contrary to theirs based upon his interpretation from their reports. I elicited that 'most of the cases' he handled were hospital deaths due to disease.

Stowens had earlier discussed his time in the Coroner's Office in Louisville, Kentucky, for which he claimed experience as a Forensic Pathologist. I asked him if Doctor Greathouse was there; he couldn't remember. [A call to Louisville that morning before Court would be helpful].

"You were there about 61 and 65?"

"Yes."

"And is it not true Doctor that you asked to be put on the staff there to finish research on S.I.D.S., in other words, Sudden Infant Deaths?"

"That's only half true. I agreed to be a Deputy Coroner in order to have access to those after they asked me inasmuch as there were so many it was getting to be a problem."

"Well, now, if Doctor Greathouse has said today that you asked to be put on for that reason and that you did no autopsies whatever; would he be wrong?"

"No other autopsies."

"No autopsies," I responded.

"Yes". . . .

"How many, and who were they on?" I insisted.

"I think your question is – you must realize it's impossible –"

THE COURT: Excuse me. Just indicate that you don't recall if you don't recall.

"I don't recall." [The Judge gave him an easy way out].

I elicited the witness was not a member of the American Academy of Forensic Sciences or of the National Association of Medical Examiners.

Using his own text book, I challenged him to show me anything therein dealing with criminal asphyxial deaths, strangulation deaths, stabbings, drownings, collection and preservation of evidence; he could not. [Although he had been critical of the State's experts in those areas and their opinions dealing with the same].

I had Dr. Stowens relate the time he took in performing each autopsy – about two hours – along with the time he spent reviewing the reports of each case – about 30 minutes each. Later, I elicited that he had spent about four (4) years on each book and many months on articles he had written. If he was present at, or performed 90,000 autopsies, I wouldn't even try to determine what he did with all his spare time.

Earlier in his testimony to Gordon Miller he had indicated he had personally done 4000 of the 90,000 autopsies in his career, and of those he had done 40 to 50 autopsies each year from 1978 through 1981 of 'other than natural deaths.'

From having talked to officials in New York over the weekend, I went back to the 'well' on his past experience.

"How many homicide cases did you perform an autopsy on in Utica (New York) homicide cases, in 1981?"

(No response)

"Or was it any?"

"I think there was only one."

"One. Were there any in 1980?"

"I don't think so."

"I'm going to put zero." How many in 1979?"

"We don't have very much homicide in Oneida County?"

"Should I put zero on that, too?"

"It's either zero or one."

"Did you do any homicide cases in 78?"

"I remember a ligature strangulation."

Binder's temper flared at the lengthy cross-examination of his expert with him objecting that I was not addressing Stowens 'with respect.' But Binder had viciously cross-examined our medical examiners and others for weeks; that is to be expected of *expert* witnesses – they should be able to defend their positions, opinions, and professional expertise. The Judge had to get us back in focus!

I knew the time to end the cross-examination, as in a direct examination, on a high note. I was there! I had saved the 'coup de grace' (death blow) for last. I would now work it in. Stowens had been on the stand all day and was tired – I could see it.

I had a newspaper article showing Stowens had been prominently interviewed by a reporter wherein he had stated some of his views of the case. Of course, Judge Cooper had cautioned the attorneys to make sure their witnesses did not violate the 'gag order.' Thus, I knew Stowens had violated the order, but I did not know if he knew about the order. Because of defense counsel having been cited earlier for contempt for violation of the order, I assumed that Binder must have notified his witnesses.

I did not like to subpoena a reporter as a witness unless necessary; the newspaper article was hearsay and if an objection was made, I would have a problem. Strategy was necessary!

I told Stowens he had been quoted in the press several times about the case, to which he said "once that I know of."

"Well, let me show you an article appearing in the December 4, [19]81, edition of the Atlanta Constitution written by the reporters Gail Epstein and Ken Willis." "Do you recall talking to those reporters?"

"I spoke to them on the phone, yes." [Leading questions are fine on cross-examination].

"I show you what's marked State's Exhibit 723." "If you need to refresh your memory, that will be fine." "Now, Doctor, this interview you gave was after Judge Cooper had imposed a gag order on all lawyers and witnesses, wasn't it?"

"Yes."

"And you knew such an order had been imposed, didn't you?"

"Yes."

"In fact, Mr. Binder told you on several occasions not to discuss the case with the news media, didn't he?" [I was guessing about several times].

"Yes."

[Wow! I can't believe the success in the admission of willfully violating the Judge's order after several warnings from counsel].

"Now, with respect to this Constitution article, did the reporters quote you correctly when they quoted you as saying that you were looking for another reasonable cause of death such as meningitis or pneumonia?"

"I imagine so."

"Were the reporters correct when they quoted you as saying, as far as money, no one's being paid; we'll talk about money if there is any?"

"Yes."

"Were the reporters correct when they reported you as saying, quote, I approach the thing with an open mind, and one of the things I have to investigate is were these deaths really homicides; maybe they weren't homicides?"

"Yes."

"Were the reporters correct when they quoted you as saying that, quote, **Fulton County Medical Examiner Saleh Zaki seemed extremely thorough and did a very good examination?"**

"Yes." [Compare this with Binder's stinging and lengthy cross-examination and condemnation of Dr. Zaki's autopsy lapses in his work, and Stowens' contradictory and critical testimony as to Zaki's findings in the case].

"Do you know how two reporters in Atlanta would have known how to call a pathologist in a small town like Utica, New York?"

"I don't know."

"… Did you have an interview with a reporter from the Atlanta Journal named Laurie Baum?"

"There were two phone calls from Atlanta."

"You may refer to this if you need to, State's Exhibit 724. If you will, look at that and tell me if you recall talking to the young lady (presenting). Do you remember that interview?"

"Yes."

"Do you also remember an interview or an article written by one Ed Ruffing, also a reporter?"

"Yes." "Is that from the Utica paper?"

"Mr. Ruffing says in his article that the trial of Wayne Williams will receive national coverage. Did he get that information from you?"

"No."

"The national coverage was very important to you, though, wasn't it?"

"Not to me." [The jury would believe otherwise].

I like to shift focus unexpectedly. I next asked:

"You testified on Friday that you always put plastic bags on the hands and heads of deceased bodies."

"That's standard procedure, yes."

"How many crime scenes have you been to in Utica in the last three years where you've put plastic bags on the hands and heads of deceased bodies?"

"None."

Now perhaps, the jury, judge, and everyone have been able to see through this witness.

During a recess by the Court, Judge Cooper cited the witness with contempt of Court for the violation of his gag order, and indicated he would deal with it after the trial was completed. [After the trial, Judge Cooper would tell me that he had no option since I proved the contempt in his presence through the witness's own testimony. Who next would be held in contempt for violating the 'gag' order? In November, before trial, Attorneys Welcome and Binder, and later during trial the parents of Williams were cited for the same infraction].

I continued the cross. I wanted to plant the seeds for this part.

"Do you recognize the name of Richard Enders?"

"Yes."

"And he was a former District Attorney of Oneida County?"

"Yes."

"And Barry Donalty is the present D.A. Is that correct?"

"Yes."

"And who is Ted Wolff?"

"He's an Assistant D.A."

"First Assistant to the present D.A.?"

"I think he still is."

I then went on to identify a Dr. Charles Brady, the Coroner in Utica, New York, as doing almost all of the criminal autopsies in Utica.

By now, the witness knows I must have talked to these people over the weekend about him.

"Doctor, we've been talking about homicide and autopsies. Let's just get right down to it." "How many autopsies have you done in murder cases in the last ten years up there?"

(No Response).

"Was it one?"

Stowens' voice began to break, he got teary eyed, and his body shook from being kept on the stand all day under pressure. I would not like to have been in his shoes. But I had no mercy or compassion for him. He was a 'hired gun' and was held out as an expert in his field. Now, it would be for the jury as to his credibility.

He responded: "It's several. But I have to add to this. I'm 63 years old. I have forty years in Pathology. I am the Chief Senior Pathologist in the area, and I paid my dues. I've done these cases —."

I wouldn't let him off the hook! I continued....

"If Mr. Enders and Mr. Donalty who have been in office for a good number of years said that you haven't performed a single criminal autopsy except for one case in 1975 in Utica since 1958, would they be correct?"

Stowens: "It depends on what you call a criminal case. I think you have it backwards in that we are called upon to do 25 or so many coroner's cases a year. Now many of those have ended up as being criminal cases is another matter." "It's probably very true only one of them turned out to be an indictable criminal case. But the cases start with the autopsy. We determine whether, indeed, there was any criminal activity."

[One prior criminal case, and he criticizes our forensic pathologists]? The Judge takes another break. I can see he and everyone was expecting me to finish. When the Court resumes, I announce that I only have two or three additional questions.

I referred the witness to the names "Migliaccio" and "Ms. Pikey." [I had gotten this information from a prosecutor in Utica].

"You did an autopsy on Mrs. Pikey — in your county up there in 1975, didn't you?"

"Yes."

"Migliaccio was the accused, wasn't he?"

"Yes."

"And since that autopsy in 1975, have you done any autopsies in any murder cases in that county?"

"None of the Coroner's cases that we have done justified a diagnosis of murder, no." [Our information was that he bungled that case and had not been used since].

Dr. Stowens left the stand an impeached witness!

Shortly after Stowens' testimony, he was the subject of an article by Shirley Williams in his hometown newspaper, the Utica Observer Dispatch. It referenced his being back at work at the local hospital after testifying in the Williams' trial wherein he had contradicted earlier findings by Georgia medical examiners. In quoting local officials, Stowens had been involved in only one homicide since the mid-1960s in Utica, the Migliacchio case.

Mrs. Lois Evans, the mother of Alfred Evans, was called and testified for the Defense. She testified she believed her son was still alive. [Dr. Feegel, Medical Examiner, had indicated she just would not accept the fact that the body was that of her son, despite the fact that the scars matched, and that identity was proven through his dental records]. I don't understand the Defense putting the mother through this, where the identity of this victim was proven beyond doubt.

Don Wright, another former police recruit, was called by the Defense in an effort to further attack the testimony of Nellie Trammell, the grandmother, who said she saw victim Larry Rogers in a car driven by Williams. Wright testified that Mrs. Trammell was a psychic who did her knitting while hanging around the Task Force headquarters.

District Attorney Slaton took the witness on cross-examination and quickly showed that Wright must have been referring to a Mrs. Tribble, not Mrs. Trammel.

Wright was asked about instances of petty theft and marijuana smoking that he admitted to in his application for employment. He also admitted that he had received a check for $154.00 from defense attorney Welcome as reimbursement, after he had earlier denied receiving any money from the defense.

As Slaton asked Wright if he had ever stolen anything, Binder replied: Just a minute! I object and I think we should approach the bench. [Proper objection].

Slaton replied: I think I'll wait a little while till he calms down your Honor.

Under direct-examination by Ms. Welcome, the witness had identified a driver's license photo of Mrs. Trammel as the person who hung around Task Force headquarters. Slaton handed the witness a group of photos, asking him if he recognized anyone. Wright looked through the photos and picked out one as Mrs. Trammel saying "except that her hair wasn't white." Slaton had him initial the photo.

For the last question before the witness was excused, Slaton asked:

"Would it surprise you to know that the photo you picked out is of Mrs. Tribble (not Mrs. Trammel) who did hang out at the task force and whose son is a police officer?"

Surprised, Wright replied that "It's been eight or nine months, sir, since I've seen the woman."

Wright also testified that Recruit Jacobs, who spotted Williams at the bridge on May 22, 1981, once told him that he (Jacobs) saw a "ghost" at the river and was very serious about it. Slaton would point out that he resigned from the police force April 12, 1981, two weeks before the bridge stakeouts began. No reason could be given why Jacobs would have been at the river while they were working together at the Task Force headquarters.

Things weren't going good for the Defense. A reporter[13] for a newspaper picked up on it – noting that each defense witness proved to contain a weakness which prosecutors quickly exploited. We needed to be ready for the next cross-examination without knowing who the witness would be or which of us would take the witness. I had put up most of the State's witnesses as well as handled most of the cross of defense witnesses. We had to be innovative in our efforts to try to ascertain who

---

13   David B. Hilder and Hyde Post, the *Atlanta Journal and Constitution*, February 7, 1982.

would be testifying for the defense (since the State had no discovery from the defense). We had our friends and investigators outside the courtroom, and some in the media were helpful by interviews they did with the lawyers and potential witnesses. Before trial – out of necessity – we had learned the Defense had certain experts by virtue of access to State's exhibits and evidence.

David Dingle, a weather service hydrologist, testified for the Defense in an effort to convince the jury that the body of Cater would not have traversed the Chattahoochee River, as the State contends, from the James Jackson Parkway Bridge to the place where it was recovered downstream on the south bank. This witness initially worked with State's witness, Benjamin Kittle, an Army Corps of Engineers hydrologist and signed off on the preliminary report. Dingle testified he didn't feel things were dealt with squarely when Kittle later changed the report, and he (Dingle) went to work for the Defense. [Kittle actually did a second follow-up report based on additional investigation]. The second report had to do with eliminating a possible entry point for the victims' bodies to the river and thus gave the Jackson Parkway Bridge greater weight as an entry point. [The investigation and testimony at trial would reasonably eliminate all possible points downstream from the dam, including all bridges, railroad trestle, and access points to the river downstream to where the bodies were found, except for the Jackson Parkway Bridge. Kittle earlier testified that Dingle had agreed to the change in the report. The State's expert, Kittle, testified regarding his own river study by re-creating conditions of the river on May 22, 1981, thereby duplicating the hydrograph within 1.5 inches].

After going over to the Defense, Dingle had done tests in the river with oranges and plastic dummies and under conditions which were not the same as May 22.

The Prosecution objected to the tests being introduced to the jury. Dingle had done nothing to re-create the same conditions of the river as Kittle had done for a study of the currents. Dingle had no knowledge of the discharge from the dam, his tests were done in the winter, and *dummies and fruit do not re-act as dead bodies re-act in the water*. The use of oranges and floating plastic will not simulate or re-create the actions of a body in the water. Because you cannot recreate the same conditions without placing a dead body in the river, the State had decided such an experiment would have no validity and be of little use for the jury. The Judge allowed Dingle's experiment over objection.

The Defense brought two dummies they named "Ferdinand" and "Horace" into the courtroom on a stretcher for demonstration purposes. Dingle testified that "Horace" was weighted with lead and sank upon being dropped into the river – it only floated a short distance and came to rest on the river bottom. "Ferdinand," the floating dummy, stayed close to the right bank of the river and did not drift over to the left side as it floated downstream. Dingle also dumped 100 oranges into the river, none of which drifted to the left bank.

Prosecutor Wally Speed, who had joined the prosecution team just before trial and had nonetheless expertly handled several witnesses, cross-examined this witness. Speed suggested that law enforcement had dropped Dingle as a consultant after he had talked to the news media about his work.

Dingle admitted he was unaware of a portion of the hydrology study by the Corp of Engineers river expert showing a cross-section "K" pull to the left side of the river resulting in the current shift to the Fulton County side where the two bodies were found.

Further, Speed elicited that the dummy in the floating tests was on its back with arms and legs lying along the river's surface, while Cater's body was floating on its abdomen with arms and legs dangling in the water when recovered from the river.

Speed questioned whether Dingle was aware that, when first spotted by witnesses in the river, Payne's body was floating closer to the right bank (down the middle) and that the body then drifted over to the left bank (where it hung up before being pulled from the river).

Dingle wanted to disregard the eye-witness reports of the body being in the middle of the river for the purpose of his tests. Under questioning, Dingle admitted that the depth of the river, along with other factors, was not the same as it was on May 22, 1981. Dingle's river study in no way simulated the actual occurrence of a human body in the river on the date in question and was therefore misleading to the jury.

During a break with the jury out of the courtroom, Judge Cooper dealt with requests of the Defense to have the jury take a trip to the James Jackson Parkway bridge for observation, and a motion to compel the attendance under subpoena of Governor George Busbee and six other state and federal officials (and including Mayor Maynard Jackson, who was not at the meeting) to testify about a 'secret' meeting at the Governor's mansion on June 19, 1981, two days before Williams' arrest. Binder argued that the meeting was the reason that Williams was on trial – and that they pressured District Attorney Slaton to prosecute. An attorney for the officials responded by moving that the subpoenas be quashed, contending that this was a 'red herring.' Judge Cooper deferred the matter until he could hear from the Mayor's attorney.

I know enough to say that no one pressured District Attorney Slaton to indict anyone. Slaton was widely known to be above political pressure, and his integrity and support by the community allowed him the discretion to be his own boss without fear of retribution. I do know also that the political leaders of the community were supportive of Slaton. However, it would not be unusual for a prosecutor to discuss with other political leaders his timeline or intentions of going to the Grand Jury regarding a decision of such magnitude in such a case of great importance to the community, *considering the volatile 'unrest' atmosphere that existed at the time in the community.*

The State argued against enforcing the subpoenas which, according to affidavits, indicated that these officials had no personal knowledge of any evidence which would be relevant to the case and that their conversations, motives, or opinions were irrelevant to the question of Williams' guilt or innocence. These persons had nothing to do with Williams' indictment by the grand jury or the trial; and, therefore, the subpoenas were nothing but a mere 'fishing expedition' by the Defense. Judge Cooper quashed the subpoenas. (The Supreme Court of Georgia would later, on appeal, uphold the Judge's quashing of the subpoenas).

Gerald A. Hightower, a Naturalist from the National Park Service who had done botanical studies and studies of salamanders, including beavers, along the Chattahoochee headwaters, testified for the Defense.

I failed to see the need or relevance of his testimony, except that the Defense had early on cross-examined the police recruits about the possible event of the 'splash' having been caused by a beaver. The witness testified to the prevalence of wildlife including frogs, turtles, snakes, and beavers (which get up to 50-60 pounds) in the area; beavers burrow into the bank and use their tails for a paddle.

This witness' testimony is enough reason to believe that none of the victims would have gone swimming in the river and that the police recruit was not expected to jump into the river at night in an effort to find a body.

Mike Gurley, a diver for the county fire and rescue team, was called by the Defense. The State considered calling him, but his testimony would add little to the case.

Gurley testified that on May 23, 1981, the following morning after the splash, he was on a team who made an attempt to find a body in the river. They started upstream and went 35-40 feet down from the bridge, but the visibility (in the water) was zero to two feet. He was in the water for 25 minutes. No body was found. He said that in eight years he had recovered 45 bodies out of 100 attempts.

Robert Ingram, a helicopter pilot, was called by the Defense. He testified he was in the air from about 10:00 – 10:30 a.m. on May 23 while the dive team was in the water. In looking from the air he saw no body in the water.

Dr. Charles Chismholm, Williams' optometrist, testified that Williams with glasses vision was 20 x 20, but without glasses he was legally blind. [Williams, of course, wouldn't be in the Air Force Reserve flying jets either].

Several witnesses were called by the Defense in attempts to attack the identification of the witnesses who saw Williams with various victims as well as Wayne's being a 'nice fellow.' His principal and teacher testified he was an excellent student and was in the top 10 percent of his class. Others portrayed him as a serious young man who was against drugs, alcohol, smoking, and homosexuality and was just trying to help poor black children get ahead in the music industry. Other witnesses testified about Williams' career and his free-lance television camera work in which he monitored fire and police radio calls and covered homicide, traffic accidents, and fires which occurred after midnight. [This would just support the State's position that he was out nights, doing things which cause people to believe he was one of the law officers which would be seen as being in authority and thus in a position of trust].

These witnesses were a mix of favoring Williams with good character and of questioning some of the state's evidence, while cross-examination elicited unfavorable testimony towards Williams in many respects, including some having seen Williams with scratches on his arms.

One defense witness testified that Williams' father had a great interest in his son, noting that he spent a great deal of money on Wayne's low-power radio station in the home as a teenager which drove the family into bankruptcy in 1976.

Other witnesses were called to show that Williams did not make sexual overtures to them, that he made no derogatory remarks about race, and that he was seen with females. It was almost comical to see the extent to which the defense was fighting the testimony which indicated Williams was gay and his attitude about street kids. Their effort fell flat!

Other testimony established that Williams had a female friend with whom he associated in his work, and that Williams got his money from his parents – he had no salaried job or income that could be identified.

One witness testified that the note (testified to by Mr. Hindsman and reading "I could be a president, I could be a mayor or I could be a killer") did not contain the word "killer" and was not written by Williams but by another young man who wanted to audition with Williams. She didn't know who wrote it. On cross-examination, I asked the witness:

To your knowledge, Wayne never made a cent from this talent scout business?

Her response: I refuse to answer that.

On further questioning the witness, I presented her signed statement she gave to the police on June 11, 1981, which was in direct contradiction of her testimony at trial in several respects. While she acknowledged she made the statement, she said: *It was wrong.* She did admit to previously saying that Williams was "mysterious and fascinating" and "by virtue of the astronomical sign of his ... he was a strong, very strong-minded person, nonconformist."

One witness, who was called to testify that Williams disliked homosexuals, was asked by me on cross-examination about vehicles he drove. The witness mentioned a green station wagon as one car she had seen Williams drive but later changed it to a white vehicle when she noted my interest.

The Defense called Captain Haney of the Arson Squad to testify that Williams appeared at fire scenes and took pictures. Williams was at 18 fires in 1979, but he never worked for the fire department – they take their own photos.

The Jury visits the bridge. On Saturday, February 13, 1982, Judge Cooper provided the jury with a bridge visit over the objection of Prosecutor Joe Drolet. He argued that the State had brought the bridge to the jury via a scale model of the river/bridge and warned of a logistics nightmare as well as creating chances of a mistrial. He argued that the visit would need to take place at 3:00 a.m. with the bridge being blocked off to keep reporters and curious spectators away. The Judge overruled the objection. Roadblocks were used to keep cars and people not a part of the court entourage away. The Sheriff's Office transported the jury on a school bus to the bridge where the jury was permitted to exit the bus, stand around a few minutes, get back on the bus, and be returned to the courthouse. The lawyers went there separately, stood around, chatted, and returned. Everyone saw the bridge and river if they wanted to do so. There was no discourse or communication with jurors about the area or case while outside the courtroom.

Dr. Maurice Rogoff, an Israeli Pathologist, was (apparently) spontaneously hired and brought in to testify after the Defense's other pathologist, Dr. Stowens, did so bad on cross-examination. Rogoff studied in England with extensive work in Kenya and Israel. He had performed thousands of autopsies on soldiers during the Israeli-Arab war. [It didn't surprise me that this witness may not understand that autopsying dead soldiers killed by military armament as opposed to the manner of deaths of victims in this case might take special training as a State Medical Examiner].

Rogoff basically supported Stowens' testimony about the cause of death of Cater and Payne, contending that he couldn't exclude drowning in Cater's case but had 'no opinion' as to the cause of death; with Payne, he noted enormous swelling to the face, lips, blisters, and he could not exclude drowning.

Rogoff suggested that Cater's body should not have surfaced for four to five days, but he had never consulted with the medical examiners in these cases and was unaware of the water temperature in the river among other things.

Rogoff agreed with written materials which he brought to court which indicated that a body would decompose, as Cater's had, in only two to three days if the water temperature was 68 to 77 degrees (consistent with the river temperature and with our position).

The jury appeared tired of hearing the same stuff they had heard from Stowens, which I thought they had already discounted. The trial was over, I thought, insofar as the question of whether the victims were murdered or had died 'natural' deaths. The Defense had not presented any reasonable theories about the deaths of these 12 victims, which would be contrary to the State's contention that they were murdered. There was no reasonable showing of drowning, accident, suicide, or a natural death – only homicides could reasonably be accepted as the cause of death by reasonable people.

Anthony Cater, brother of Nathaniel Cater, was called by the defense – for what reason I'll never know, except to show that the victim was intoxicated most of the time. The witness said you could take advantage of him (Nathaniel) when he was drunk. Meaning, *he would make an easy victim for Williams.* The witness said he last talked to Nathaniel a couple days before his birthday on May 20, 1981.

John Henley was apparently called by Ms. Welcome to impeach a state's witness, (Robert) Bobby Henry, who had testified he saw Williams and Cater holding hands in front of the Rialto Theatre hours before the bridge incident. But when questioned about Mr. Henry's reliability, the witness responded that (Bobby) was reliable!! This upset Mrs. Welcome immensely – she was visibly shaken. Ms. Welcome then tried to impeach her witness without success.

Gwen, a female friend and business associate of Williams for 11 years, said she saw him about every day. She claims she had a relationship with Williams but admitted she told the FBI that Williams had no girlfriends. She had not visited Williams in jail since his arrest, saying Williams' parents suggested it.

An organizer of the Techwood Homes "Bat Patrol" was called as a defense witness by Ms. Welcome. He testified he had not seen Williams at the press conference in which Techwood residents announced the formation of the group on March 20 (contrary to a State's witness who had testified that Williams was in the housing project that day carrying cameras).

On cross-examination, I asked the witness several questions about how many people were present at the press conference and whether there were "thousands of spectators" in the area. After many objections by Ms. Welcome with the Judge overruling them, the Judge finally stopped her arguments by telling her "Have a seat, Ms. Welcome."

I asked the witness a few other questions whereupon he suddenly refused to answer further questions, and pushed the microphone away, saying: *I decline to answer any more questions under the Fifth Amendment.*

Ms. Welcome then rose to question him further when Judge Cooper stopped her saying that her witness had refused to answer any more questions.

Ms. Welcome later attempted to elicit a witness' opinion of Williams, and I objected. She attempted to reword the same question several times whereupon objections were sustained. On the fourth try, the Judge was shaking his head and laughter was heard. She gave up and decided to sit down.

The Defense called a young man, "Mike," who attempted to show one of Williams' success stories in the entertainment business in another young man, "Keith." But when "Keith" testified later he said he was the Assistant Café Manager for a local hotel.

Many other witnesses were called and were unsuccessful in penetrating the case the prosecution had so far made; but the Defense was far from over, as I expected the Williams family and experts to keep coming.

I looked back into the courtroom (something I very seldom ever do since I try to shut out the entire world except what I am doing in court) where I saw I had a cheering section with my smiling wife, Jo, and some neighbors in court with her. She had not forewarned me she was coming to court that day. During the break, I let them know how proud I was to see everyone in court, and Jo was looking especially great that day.

The next day, February 17, 1982, I would read a nice article in the *Roswell Neighbor* newspaper by staff writer, Merri Ann Mohr. Ms. Mohr had interviewed Jo and others at court (which Jo forgot to tell me). Ms. Mohr quoted friends and neighbors as referring to me as a "soft-spoken, gentle family man," while my associates in the office referred to me as "Blood" Mallard because of my 'going for the jugular.' Prosecutor Scott Childress said, in his opinion, I was the number one trial man, that I had trained many, including him, of the prosecutors in the office. Jo told Ms. Mohr that I was going to resign from the case to be with her, but she said: "I just put my foot down. I said I didn't want him to sit and hold my hand. Anyway, I felt like they really needed Jack in court."

Jo went on to say that "people from most every county in the state are praying for me" and "I think the chemotherapy is working and the prayer is what is making it work."

The nickname "Blood" had stuck with me since the mid-1970s (and to this day) as a prosecutor. It originated from a murder case where I had entered into evidence some especially gory crime scene photographs (which I normally do in murder cases). The public defender, in his closing argument to the jury, said that I must like to view bloody photographs – and referred to me as "Blood" Mallard – suggesting to the jury that I 'probably had some hung on my walls at home.' I didn't bother to object (I try never to object in closing argument unless counsel perverts the evidence) but merely waited for my chance to reply in closing.

Over the years since, the news media in cases I have prosecuted often repeat the nickname and have kept it alive. At times it would involve a cross-examination or some other feat not related to gory photographs. In one article in *The Atlanta Constitution,* January 9, 1979, "ACCUSED OF DOGNAPPING" *Dropped Charge Just Makes Him Angrier,* related that I had dismissed a charge against a defendant arrested for "dognapping" where the accused was angry with me for dropping the charge; he was insisting upon a jury trial to 'prove his innocence.' From further investigation I knew that it would have been a waste of court time and funds to proceed as I had learned that the accused had found the dog in question running around cars in a parking lot after the dog jumped from the owner's car as she left the lot; the accused took the dog home after making inquiries in stores of a lost dog. He later checked advertisements of lost dogs, etc. He cared for the dog over the weekend; a police officer came to his house, took him to jail and recovered the dog. In dismissing the charge over objection of the defendant, a public defender was quoted as saying "We call him 'Blood' Mallard, because he always goes for the jugular." The defense attorneys claimed that I was a veteran (prosecutor) who very seldom ever dismisses a case and that I said "[it] was just a real 'dog' of a case."

One Saturday morning just after the Williams' trial was over, Jo and I were at the breakfast table when the phone rang. The caller inquired if I was Jack Mallard, who was involved in the prosecution of Williams. He asked: What is your nickname? I almost hung up, but he quickly said that he was a law student (in a well-known northern law school) and that there had been a question on a test as to the nickname of the prosecutor in the Williams' case. When I quit laughing, I said: Well, if you thought enough of it to call long distance, I suppose I should tell you: "Blood." He said he had not remembered it from the media accounts.

Insofar as utilizing color photographs of crime scenes, a prosecutor would be remiss in not bringing the very best and most reliable evidence to the jury for their review in proving a fact. Crime scenes, especially those involving personal injuries and homicide investigations, are documented by CSI personnel for later preparation and trial. One of the most basic and essential devices used is the camera; it misses nothing within the eye of the camera. The camera creates a permanent record of the scene, which is more reliable than the memory of a witness; the photograph will stand up against a cross-examination attack.

In retrials of cases decades later, the photograph loses none of its memory – as a witness is prone to do. Thus, it makes sense why police take so many photographs, and why prosecutors use them in court – to bring the crime scene to the jury.

I recall one homicide from knife wounds where the body was discovered in the doorway of a business; photographs showed the wounds and the bloody trail down the steps, across the sidewalk, and into the street. From testimony by the Medical Examiner that the heart will pump blood so long as the victim is alive, told the jury that the victim had come to a 'slow death.' There is a saying that a photograph conveys a vision better than 1000 words.

I have a rule for the CSI personnel to photograph anything that will, or will not, move; the prosecutor will decide later whether it would be admissible. The camera will follow the body into the morgue where photographs are made as the autopsy is being conducted. After all, post-autopsy photographs – thought gory – may become admissible where it may be shown to prove a 'necessary fact' which became apparent only because of the autopsy, i.e. bullet tract or location, trajectory of wound, cause of death, etc.

In the Williams' case, several hundred photographs were important in bringing to the courtroom a live rendition of each of the 12 scenes where bodies were found, vehicles searched, bridges and miles of river corridor, removal of bodies, fibers, charts, etc.

I have known of cases where jurors noticed something so small in photographs which was important to them, but was overlooked by the lawyers. Photographs are easily admitted in Court if relative to proving a material fact; you just provide testimony that the photograph accurately portrays the scenes depicted therein, and convince the Judge of the relevancy to the case.

Thus, to the objection of proffering 'bloody and gory photographs' to the jury, I respond: **Murder is gory, and that was the work of the accused!**

The Defense called **Marla Lawson**, a police sketch artist, who did drawings for the police. She had prepared about 50 composites for the Task Force, most of which were based on descriptions from psychics. She said only the composite by Ruth Warren (who saw Williams with victim Geter) looked like Williams. She said various drawings done by her came from all sorts of people and from visions, etc. She didn't know if any have anything to do with the case.

Another defense witness said he had once asked Homer why he spent so much money on his teen-age son Wayne's low-power radio station (which drove the family into bankruptcy in 1976). Homer replied he would do anything to keep his son "off the street." On cross examination, the witness said that Williams had a police Plymouth vehicle, a brownish station wagon and other police cars at various times.

The Defense called **Norris Keith Knox,** a former neighbor of Williams, who was called apparently to discount many of the State's contentions, including that a State's witness, Nellie Trammel, could have seen victim Patrick Rogers slumped over in Williams' vehicle about noon on March 30, 1981. Keith testified he visited Williams at his house on March 30, 1981 – that he arrived there at 2-3 or 4 p.m.

and was there until 6-7 p.m. (Although, this alibi would be at least two hours after the State's witness saw Williams with the victim). Keith said he remembered the occasion as being the day that President Reagan was shot and wounded. Keith said he never heard Williams express any ill will for low class people and that he saw nothing to indicate Williams was gay. Kitchens asked the witness if he saw any bodies in the house or smelled anything unusual. Obviously, the answer was "no."

On cross-examination, I elicited that when he lived next door to the Williams' home, there was an electrified wire running along the top of the Williams' backyard fence. He didn't know if Williams was gay; he never knew Williams to date a girl. He referred to a friend of Williams, Willie, as strange – feminine – who made him uneasy; and Willie wanted to go "swashbuckling." The witness also said that once Williams said he knew karate (something the Defense had been trying to disprove following another witness' testimony). The witness worked at Williams' radio station as a teenager. The witness further recounted that in late May (after the bridge incident), Williams was removing boxes and items from his back office or storage area.

I questioned the witness of his recollection of the date of March 30, 1981, as being the day he was at the Williams residence:

"Now, before testifying this morning, when before today was the time that someone referred you to that date?"

"March 30, before I took the stand today?"

"Yes. Who discussed that date with you before you took the stand?"

"I would say, well, a few minutes ago before I came in."

Without a diary or some recording of the details, it's hard to pinpoint an event to a date almost a year before.

The Defense called **Mr. Mark Oviatt,** an acoustics engineer, to testify to a 'noise test' conducted on the metal expansion joint at the Jackson Parkway Bridge.

It appears the Defense has 'one-upped' us on experts. We never believed there was an issue of whether Recruit Robert Campbell should have heard the expansion joint when Williams came onto the bridge; after all, our contention is that Williams was coming to a stop on the bridge as his vehicle entered upon that very end of the bridge. This effort just reinforces my contention that Williams enjoyed the very best defense a team of lawyers and investigators could provide.

Since the State was objecting to this experiment, the Court sent the jury out while the Defense presented a foundation or showing for admissibility of the evidence. Mr. Binder questioned the witness regarding his background and the test performed.

Oviatt had a B.S. degree in applied physics from Georgia Tech and was employed in the field of sound and noise and noise control. He testified to his background and writings in the field, of which I had no quarrel. My objection was that such an experiment would be worthless unless they could simulate the conditions and even then the true question is not what one *should* hear, but what if anything did the recruit *actually hear.* And, Recruit Campbell never said he heard the car run over the expansion joint – to the contrary, he did not. His testimony was consistent that he first heard a splash and then saw the car on the bridge.

Oviatt testified that his test was conducted Friday, just the day before he was testifying (Saturday), and that they used the Williams' station wagon which Williams had been driving on May 22, 1981. He was using a Bruell and Kjaer, type 2215 sound level meter with an associated microphone. He and his associates and one of the defense attorneys conducted the test. The equipment was set up under the bridge to capture the sound of the vehicle traveling over the expansion joint of the bridge at different speeds. The witness was operating the equipment underneath the bridge next to the piling which was next to the expansion joint.

Binder went through the motions of the associates on the bridge in driving the vehicle at different speeds across the joint varying from 4 to 27 miles an hour and of the measurements of the sound under the bridge (which allegedly would be what the police recruit should have heard).

I took the witness on cross-examination. I elicited that he was not a Civil, Structural or Metallurgical Engineer, and he did not know the temperature at the bridge on May 22, 1981, nor did he know the flow or noise of the river. He acknowledged there would be some noise, and the higher level of the river resulting from flash floods would make a difference; but he didn't know if that was the situation on May 22 or prior to the test being run. Likewise, he didn't know the condition of the expansion joint on either occurrence, whether the same joint was in place or whether there was dirt and debris in it. He testified he was on the Cobb County side of the river with the machine in front of him on a tripod. The microphone was directed upwards. I asked him:

"Really, what it comes down to, isn't it, that what you recorded was the ability of the machine to record the decibels?"

"Correct," he answered.

"Of course, you're not familiar with the hearing ability of Bob Campbell, are you?"

"No, I am not."

Then I summed up that water noise, foliage, temperature, and dirt and debris in the joint ... all these things could affect the noise level at that time.

"So really, what you did was record, as I indicated, the hearing ability of that machine?"

"Yes sir."

"Had you done this experiment before?"

"Not this precise experiment, no."

Mr. Binder submitted the witness as an expert and the test as being scientific. He argued the law dealing with admissibility of recordings as being accurately identified and not having been tampered with, which was not really the issue here.

Joe Drolet, the State's appellate prosecutor who was sitting with us for just such occasions, argued against letting in the test. He pointed out that it was the experimental nature of the test which was objectionable, not how much the machine cost, or the hearing ability of the machine. The question was: Did Recruit Campbell hear it, or what did Campbell hear at 3:00 a.m. on May 22, 1981. Drolet cited the legal precepts that for evidence of experiments to be admissible, there must be substantial similarity as to the essential and material facts affecting the comparison; if the comparison be predicated upon substantially different facts, the evidence will not only be irrelevant but will tend to confuse the jury.

Mr. Binder re-argued saying that "we've got to *presume* that Bob Campbell has normal hearing." Had they 'presumed' that I had 'normal hearing' they would have been badly mistaken!

After carefully considering the issue, Judge Cooper ruled out the tape recording being played but allowed the witness to testify as to the results of the test. (The same end results, but judges at times will do that).

The jury was then called back into court whereupon it was necessary to go through the same testimony for benefit of the jury. Binder proceeded with direct examination before the jury.

Binder took the witness through the background and tests performed by the witness with the speed of the car being measured by a stopwatch. The decibels (A) and the ambient sound levels were registered by the sound level meter.

Test No. one clocked the speed of the car at 4.3 miles per hour while the sound level of the expansion joint as the car moved over it was 49 D.B. (A) and the background level was 45 D.B.(A), which shows an overall increase of 4 D.B. (A) over the ambient when the car ran over the expansion joint.

Another test at 6.8 miles an hour recorded the decibel reading as 60 D.B. (A), a tremendous increase over the background ambient level at that time of 41 D.B. (A); another test at 17 miles recorded that the expansion joint noise went up to 68 D.B. (A); at 22.7 miles an hour the reading was at 71 D.B. (A); and at 27.3, it went up to 78 D.B. (A).

The witness testified that a person with normal hearing could hear the expansion joint sound and that in the field of human perception and human hearing, to be able to discriminate between a softer and a louder tone is very difficult for a person to hear a change of zero to one decibel.

The witness said he was standing underneath the bridge to one side next to the bridge piling that was directly underneath the expansion joint, and that he had normal hearing.

Binder: "… Could you hear the expansion joint when the white station wagon went over that expansion joint at three to four miles an hour?"

Witness: "Yes, I could hear the expansion joint when the car went over at that speed."

I then took the witness on cross-examination and asked if he could hear the expansion joint at 4.3 miles an hour, when would he *not be able to hear it?*

Witness: "That is a very difficult point to talk about, and it's something that we are not really too sure because it has been proven in tests by the U.S. Department of the Interior when they were looking at use of recreational vehicles in parks and things like that that a person is able to hear a sound when it is below the ambient sound level. When you're looking at a sound meter and you're looking at a noise source, if the noise source is actually quieter than the ambient sound, it is still possible for a human being to hear that sound."

"In other words, there's a variance between the human ear and that machine that recorded that, isn't there?" I asked.

"Correct."

"You really don't know when the human ear will hear that sound?"

"We can make some fairly close approximations."

"Now, these conditions, the changing conditions, if I understand your testimony, while some of those changes are slight, is it not true that when you take all of those different changing conditions from May of last year to February of this year that it could make several decibels change because of the change in conditions?"

"It could, but I wouldn't have any firm data on that."

For the benefit of the jury, I again went over all the conditions which could affect the recorded sound: the foliage, animal noise, water conditions, flow and level of the river, recent rains, temperature, and condition of the expansion joint, all making some variation in the decibels recorded.

"Yes, it would."

I asked him if the (nearby) Plant McDonough was operating on the morning when he made the test, to which he replied: "It appeared to be operating."

I then asked:

"Do you know if it was operating in May of last year?"

"No, I do not." [All of these things are why the test shouldn't come in].

"Isn't it true that while the machine will pick up what it hears on a continuous basis there that the human ear is different?"

"Yes and no. No ... Well, the machine and the human ear have one thing in common and one thing in difference is that the machine has an on-off switch. The human ear does not have an on-off switch. Like your sense of touch, your sense of hearing and your sense of smell are

24-hour-a-day, seven-day-a-week senses. You do not turn them off or on. But psychologically, you can ignore sound."

I asked: "Isn't it true you can be riding along in your automobile with the radio on and you can miss everything that's said, wouldn't even realize the radio was on; in other words turn it off?"

"Turn it off mentally to yourself, yes. But your ears are still hearing it."

"Yes Sir. But you don't know it, though, do you?"

"Not if you don't want to."

"Yes Sir. You hear what you want to?"

"Correct."

"You don't know what his (Bob Campbell's) hearing ability was?"

"I do not know his hearing ability. No."

I went over his and the machine's location under the bridge.

"Does it make a difference which way you're facing, the area that you're trying to record as far the sound?"

"Yes, it does."

"So if ... so the location of the person that's recording is very important?"

"Yes."

"What about distance? Naturally, the closer you are to the place where you're recording the noise, obviously the easier it is to pick it up?"

"Right! And in open environments, there is a way that you can figure how much the sound level has been reduced." "For every doubling of the distance from where the noise source is, you get a 3 D.B. reduction in the overall sound level."

"... How far away were you from the piling (of the bridge)?"

"6 to 10 feet," he replied. [Now I had him committed].

"And you wouldn't have been standing where Bob Campbell was situated, then, on the morning of May 22, about 40 feet away?" I asked.

"We situated the meter, the meter location, where the defense team told us that they had testimony showing that a person was standing there."

"Oh. Where you were standing making your test, could you see through the rail of the bridge?"

"No, I could not."

Then I showed the witness State's Exhibit 362 (photograph) indicating a piling for the bridge and an expansion joint, and asked him whether or not he was next to that piling. He affirmed he was.

I then showed the witness State's Exhibit 352 where Bob Campbell was situated on the bank, and asked:

"You were not there, were you?"

"We were not that close – not that far away, we were closer to the bridge than that."

"In fact, you can't even see the bridge in there (indicating), can you..?"

"Down here in the corner, right."

In an effort to rehabilitate the witness, Mr. Binder went back on re-direct examination.

Binder: "Tell the jury, isn't it a fact that the machine and the tripod was approximately where Mr. Bailey (another defense attorney) told you Mr. Campbell was?"

"The machine and the tripod is where Mr. Bailey indicated that I should place it."

"And you didn't sit right there all the time, did you?" Binder asked.

"Yes, we did. We have to stay next to the machine to be able to read the numbers that it is giving us." [Wow, I won't object to leading questions by Defense Counsel as long as we have an honest defense witness. The cross-examiner may lead the witness, but the party presenting the witness cannot – if objected to].

On further cross-examination, I thought I would try another question:

"If a person was asleep, it would take a big splash in that river to wake him up, wouldn't it?"

"Well, perhaps. There's been studies performed as to exactly how much sound is needed to wake a person up. And it takes a very great sound level to wake a person up."

The witness leaves the stand. Now, what did all that mean, and what did it prove? If the Defense is trying to support Williams' version of events that he crossed the bridge, as he claims, without stopping and that Recruit Campbell should have heard the noise of the bridge joint – thus, he must have been asleep; then it flies in the face of four officers' testimony. In fact, as I saw the testimony, it just reinforced our case by proving that the recruit under the bridge didn't hear the noise (as he testified) because Williams had entered the bridge slowing to a stop (under 4.3 miles an hour) on the bridge nearer to the Cobb County side. Campbell had always said he never heard the car stop on the bridge, only start up after hearing the splash and seeing the lights.

Mr. Thomas Jones was called as a defense witness by Ms. Welcome in an attempt to get him to say that he saw men in Schlitz jerseys playing basketball at the Ben Hill Recreation Center, but the witness could not confirm any such event. [An FBI agent had testified that Williams claimed he played basketball at the center with a Schlitz- sponsored team]. This seemed to irritate defense counsel when the witness did not testify to what Ms. Welcome seemed to expect from him.

Next, **Officer A. E. Alderman** was called by Mr. Binder. I objected to this officer's testimony on legal grounds – hearsay. The Defense wanted the officer to testify to what was reported by another person, which was inadmissible.

It was noon on Friday. The Judge told the jury that he was going to recess until Monday morning due to the illness of "one of the participants in the trial" and that "this person has put in a key role in this trial, and it would be unfair to go forward in light of this person's illness." The Judge had been trying to put in a full week, going sometimes on Saturday, in an effort to move the case to an orderly completion due to the jury being sequestered. The Judge did not tell the jury that it was Ms. Welcome who became sick apparently after setbacks in her effort to get in evidence which was clearly inadmissible.

It didn't get any better for Ms. Welcome on Monday morning. She proffered what she expected the next witness, an officer, to testify, asking if I would agree to it. I would not and objected to the testimony in whole as being 'hearsay, irrelevant, and immaterial.' Ms. Welcome proffered testimony that she claims would show "the difference in the treatment of suspects," that another suspect's "house was not searched. He was not surveilled. He was not questioned in the same manner that Wayne Williams was. It's for that purpose" – "unequal law enforcement." After Mr. Drolet cited legal precedent on the issue, the Court asked Ms. Welcome if she had any citation of legal authority to which she said: "Your Honor, I'm citing the law which states that the defendant has a right to have an adequate defense and to raise relevant issues." The Court sustained my objection, stating "this is clearly irrelevant."

The Defense called **Randall Bresee,** an assistant professor of textile science from Kansas State University, as their fiber expert. Binder went through his expert's lengthy educational background, and what he deemed to be his qualifications to testify as an expert witness in fiber analysis. The Defense had been granted access by the State to examine the fiber evidence in all 12 cases presented by the State. He admitted that all the 'slides' were made available to him for testing at the crime laboratory. He was at the State's Laboratory for five hours and used 3.75 hours examining the fiber evidence on the evening before his being called to testify by the defense. [At the defense's request, the Judge had ordered the fiber exhibits returned to the Laboratory from the Court for access by the defense expert]. Bresee came into the case after the trial began and after the first defense expert, **Charles Morton,** a California fiber expert, had visited the state crime laboratory several times before trial but was not called to testify for the Defense. No reason was given by the Defense for not having called him at trial – it can only be surmised that the Defense did not like what he would testify to, even perhaps agreeing with the State's experts.

Prosecutor Miller objected to Bresee's being admitted as an expert and questioned him at length on his expertise.

Bresee said he did not own a comparison microscope and had worked on only one criminal case in five years. He had never been employed by a crime laboratory and had never testified in a court of law. He admitted his techniques have not been applied in the forensic area or confirmed by scientific literature.

Miller: "And in order for somebody else to make a determination as to whether or not your experimental techniques work, they would have to test it to see if it worked, wouldn't they"?

Bresee: "I would if I were them."

Miller: "Have you ever used a microspectrophotometer"? [A sophisticated instrument used by the FBI and State experts in their analysis].

Bresee: "No, I haven't."

Defense Attorney Binder argued that Bresee's education qualified him to testify. The Court permitted the testimony on the basis that everything would go to the *weight and credibility* of the testimony – which is customary in such instances.

Bresee did a pillow case experiment in the river for about 30 minutes. He placed a pillow case in the Chattahoochee River; upon removal he found many different types and colors of fibers but none like the Williams' carpet. Not having prepared a written report of his work, he was vague about what he saw or did.

Bresee also examined fibers from Mary Welcome's office hallway at the Bank of the South Building but didn't have equipment so he didn't do a 'lot of tests' – he used a pocket magnifying glass to view the fibers.

He said those fibers looked like the Williams' carpet fibers.

But when asked by Miller if he had done any of the many tests performed by the State experts, his reply:

"No, sure didn't. Like I said, I just did a visual evaluation."

Bresee admitted he never heard of the Wellman 181b carpet fiber in Williams' home except for this case. He didn't look at the carpet from Williams' station wagon. He didn't know the techniques used by the State's experts – Deadman, Peterson and Gaudette – but he was still critical of the conclusions reached by them. However, he did agree with the methods used for fiber comparison which had been described by Deadman. He admitted that multiple fiber associations may be proof of contact!

When asked by Miller:

"Would it be accurate to say that at least since sometime in August of last year that you have wanted to get involved in this case"?

Bresee: "Oh sure. This is a big case. It's an interesting case. "

[In fact, Larry Peterson from the State's Crime Laboratory recently told me that Bresee had initially contacted him and offered his help to the State but was turned down because of his lack of forensic experience. Subsequently, he ended up during trial working for the Defense].

Homer Williams, the defendant's father, was called by the Defense. This was not unexpected, and I was ready for cross-examination. Homer and Faye Williams, I knew, would be essential witnesses for the Defense since they were a close family unit and would be expected to 'save' their only son from a conviction – a son who they had protected and 'doted' on all his life. They had conducted themselves to the point of violating a 'gag' order after repeated warnings from the Judge and were cited for contempt of court. They had used their savings in bailing Wayne out of financial difficulties and in supporting his many ventures, all eventually failing, including the operation of a hobby radio station out of the family home while he was a teenager. As a result the parents were forced into personal bankruptcy. Wayne's interests later led to doing news film and photographs of fires, wrecks, and crime scenes as a free-lancer. The state's investigation was never able to find any sources of income or significant monies collected by Wayne for any of his work. All indications were that Wayne's automobiles, equipment, and expenses were funded by the parents.

The Defense knew, as did we, that the strongest charge was the murder of Cater (the last victim to be recovered) because it centered on an eyewitness seeing Cater with Williams only hours before the 'splash' at the river. Thus, they had to try to 'alibi' Williams for the time he was seen with Cater the evening of May 21, 1981.

Homer testified that he (Homer) was using the family car (station wagon) on May 21, 1981 until about 11:30 p.m. He claimed he was at a Kiwanis Club meeting early in the afternoon, and that he was doing some photography work at a garden club meeting; he returned home about 11:30 p.m. finding Wayne in bed. He testified that Wayne got up and wanted to use the car to go to the Sans Souci nightclub to retrieve a tape recorder he had loaned the manager. He further testified that his son returned home about 4:30 – 5:00 a.m. the same night, telling his parents he had been stopped at the Chattahoochee Bridge and was questioned by the FBI for 2-3 hours.

Homer Williams, on cross-examination, said he believed it was a garden club assignment which kept him out late, but in referring to his assignment log, it indicated only that he had taken a picture of some foreigners from a certain part of Africa at the State Capitol *around lunchtime*. When I pressed him on cross as to his 'nighttime assignment' not being logged, he said:

If it's not in here, it must have been canceled. [So much for the alibi].

Defense Counsel Jim Kitchens led Homer Williams through a litany of the actions of Wayne and of the police searches of the home. Homer testified that he had access to all parts of the house and that Wayne had only been away from home for about two days in the past when he took a trip to California. He said that, when Wayne was a boy, they gave him an electric train set, a tricycle, a bicycle, and a double-barreled combination rifle and shotgun (over and under), and that he took his son hunting and fishing – but that Wayne didn't kill very much, so he gave that up. Homer said he taught his son photography and supported Wayne's low-powered neighborhood radio station which operated out of the home. When Wayne wanted to move the radio station to another location, the parents executed financing documents for equipment. This led to the station closing in 1976 when the parents declared bankruptcy. Homer testified he did not consider Wayne to be a failure but that he had made progress.

But on cross-examination, I outlined Wayne's endeavors, which all failed. He still lived at home, his radio station was a failure, he couldn't support himself, his free-lance photography and talent scout work had not paid off, and he failed at college. I asked him:

Isn't it true that Wayne, despite the fact that everybody expected him to succeed, failed in everything he attempted?

No, sir, Williams responded. The witness had pointed out that Wayne entered Georgia State University in 1977 as a sophomore and ended his college career in the same year – he said Wayne could go to any college he chose. Of course, I never expected Homer to agree with me, but my question was for the jury – the answer he gave didn't matter; the jury would agree with me based upon the evidence before them. .

I read Wayne's grades from his time at Georgia State University in 1977 showing that his grades were primarily below average, and that he withdrew from several classes; he never made an A in anything and made a D in Physics and a C in general psychology.

Defense counsel had Homer tell the jury about his wife's surgery, a radical mastectomy in 1980, follow-up chemotherapy treatments, and their ownership and rental of many automobiles over the past few years.

Homer testified about the two police searches by some 15 law officers who went through the house dusting with black power and tearing up carpet. Defense Counsel Kitchens asked Homer Williams if he knew about the 'slapjack' that police testified they found in the ceiling. The witness responded:

"If they found it in the ceiling, they put it there."

Homer said he took it from a student he was teaching in 1962 and put it in his closet.

On cross-examination, I suggested to the witness that if the FBI had planted the slapjack, they would have planted it in Wayne's bedroom (not the ceiling). [A slapjack is a combative hand-weapon with a pouch containing lead or other hard material covered with leather or cloth material with an extension for a handle, commonly used to 'slap' another up side of the head and sometimes compared or confused with a "blackjack"].

When I questioned Homer on blood found on the carpet in the Williams' bedroom which was soaked through to the pad, he denied the blood was there; but when Kitchens on re-direct examination asked him about it, he explained that a rat fell through a hole in the ceiling above Wayne's face and that they had killed the rat with a broom handle. [It was animal blood].

I queried Homer about the high mileage on the 1979 LTD which had accumulated almost 4,000 miles per month; he said he noticed the high mileage but blamed it on a faulty odometer. I then went to the 1970 white Chevrolet station wagon showing more than 4,000 miles per month during each of the six months they had the car; Homer insisted he drove most of the time (contrary to the State's evidence and Wayne's admission that he had routinely driven that car).

I asked Homer about the burned pictures in the outside barbeque pit which were found during the search. Homer claimed he burned unused photographs of his clients. When asked why he did not shred them, he said that burning them was faster.

On direct examination, defense counsel Jim Kitchens asked Homer about the carpet. Now would be their big attack upon the fiber evidence presented by the State. If the Defense could show the source of the carpet in the Williams' bedroom was **not** the unique Wellman 181b tri-lobal fiber which the State's experts contend matches fibers removed from the victims, then the Prosecution has a major problem. After all, the Wellman fiber made into carpet manufactured by West Point-Pepperell Inc. of West Point, Georgia, was for a limited amount during the year 1970 - 1971.

Homer testified he and his wife actually purchased the carpet in their home in December 1968 (three years before the State contends the Wellman carpet was manufactured). He identified a copy of an advertisement dated December 7, 1968, by Carpet Discount Outlet Inc. of Atlanta in the Atlanta newspaper magazine, which caused the family to make the purchase. Williams said they had not saved the advertisement from the purchase, but testified that during the trial they had gone through archived microfilm files at the Atlanta Public Library and found the advertisement – it read wall to wall carpeting, 3 rooms, $149 – but he said they purchased more expensive carpet. He testified he remembered it because his wife said you've been complaining about having to shellac the floors, and there's an advertisement for cheap carpet here. He said they purchased the carpet to be installed before Christmastime (1968). Homer further testified the installers left the carpet during a lunch break, and when they returned the Williams' German shepherd puppy, Sheba, had eaten a piece of the carpet. He produced Sheba's Kennel Club registration showing she was born in 1968.

Homer identified a commercial photographic slide dated December 1970 which was admitted without objection by me. The slide showed the dog, Sheba, on what Williams said was their *green carpeting* which the witness claimed that, due to filtration, 'not all the green in it comes out.' Of one slide, Williams said: "That's the brown. The filtration makes it look like that." Another slide he claimed was green, but it appeared to be brown. [They wanted the brown carpet in the Williams' home to be green and installed in 1968 rather than in the year the prosecution experts claimed it was manufactured (1970 - 1971)].

Homer Williams claimed that the carpet installer, Wayne Gano, recently visited the Williams' home and verified that he remembered the carpet. But, the Defense would never call Gano as a witness. Our people outside the courtroom learned that Wayne Gano had been subpoenaed by the Defense and had been outside the courtroom all day, but he was not called. In fact, the State had located this witness during the trial and would later call him in rebuttal following the defense's case. Also, we learned that Manny Gladstone, the owner of Discount Carpet Outlet, had been subpoenaed to court by the Defense but was never called as a witness. Our people talked to him, and we knew why – his testimony would not have been helpful to Williams. When counsel for a party does not call a person to testify after interviewing him, the only reasonable inference is that the person interviewed will not testify to the party's interest.

On cross-examination, to get the jury back on track about the truth of the carpet sale, I asked Homer if the name Southern Prudential Home Improvement Corporation meant anything to him. "It don't mean anything to me," he replied. Well, it would mean something before I would be through. I showed him the exhibit: A financing document in the amount of $1,973.88 between Homer and Faye Williams and Southern Prudential Corporation signed December 7, 1971, showing Wayne Gano is listed as a witness to the contract and was filed with the Fulton County deed records. The loan was in 36 monthly installments of $54.83 beginning in February, 1972. The Williams' home was listed as collateral.

The Southern Prudential Corporation had placed an ad in the Atlanta Constitution on December 4, 1971, (consistent with the State's evidence of the carpet purchase) which read in part Carpet Sale, Guaranteed Installation for Christmas, 3 Full Rooms, Wall to Wall, 100% Nylon Broadloom Carpet, $149. It was similar to the ad found by the Williamses dated three years before which suited the defense's needs. If the Defense fails in its effort to prove the Wellman carpet was installed in 1968 as they claim, so does any attempt to convey credibility and trust to the jury.

Now for the last part of my cross-examination of Homer Williams! In my outline, I would reserve certain questions toward the end of cross-examination which I knew the witness would deny, and for which I could prove in rebuttal through witnesses:

Whether Homer and Wayne had any arguments and fights …?

When Wayne came home on May 22, 1981, after having been stopped at the bridge, did he tell you he threw garbage in the river? Have you told anyone that he did (tell you that)?

I knew the witness, who had been shielding and protecting his only son from the beginning, would deny each question.

On direct examination by Defense Counsel, the witness denied any violence on the part of Wayne. I asked him:

"Isn't it true your son assaulted you in the spring of 1981 for your refusal to rent another vehicle for a friend of his, Willie Hunter?"

Homer responded "No, sir."

"Isn't it true he assaulted you in your own home and choked you over your refusal to write another check, after which you grabbed your shotgun and threatened to shoot him?" I asked.

Likewise, he answered in the negative as expected.

The evidence is more effective when proven through testimony of witnesses at the end of the trial nearer to jury deliberation in rebuttal of a denial of the other party. Violence on the part of the defendant is probative in light of the Defense's strategy to spread his good character in evidence, claiming he couldn't and wouldn't hurt a fly much less a human being. When a defendant puts all his good deeds and his good character of a lifetime before the jury, he can hardly complain when the Prosecution reveals his bad deeds.

Faye Williams, the mother of Wayne B. Williams, was called by defense counsel Al Binder, who led her through Wayne's life history. She was a typical mother called to defend her son before the jury, and the Prosecution would give great deference to her testimony without objection if possible. Ms. Williams testified she had retired in 1980 as a public school teacher after 32 years. She came across as the typical middle-class homemaker, wife, and mother who devoted her life to her only child.

Ms. Williams said she was 41 when Wayne was born and that he was a "miracle child" – he was a "fun-loving 100 percent all-American child." She said he leaned toward adult interests because he was with her and Homer so much. She said they had no problems with him, he had a normal temper – there were no violent acts whatsoever – denying she had ever witnessed any "type violent act whatsoever."

She discussed the radio station Wayne built in the house as a young-ster while still in high school. She testified "we had had many V.I.P.'s to come in, and many did their campaigning for their political office right there in my utility room." She named (former) Mayor Sam Massell, Benjamin Hooks, the head of the N.A.A.C.P.; State Representative

Tyrone Brooks; and Mayor Andrew Young – saying all did their broadcasting through Wayne's radio station.

Ms. Williams complained that when the station was moved to Campbellton Road, the financial conditions caused them to go bankrupt rather than let the "flim-flammers" take the station. Rather than allow it, she said "we decided to close and go bankrupt." Following this, the witness said that Wayne did "stringer work," that is "when the regular T.V. man goes off about 12:00 o'clock when his day's work is done, stringers get out and get the hard news and turn it in to the T.V. station." This didn't last long explains Ms. Williams because Wayne's "interests was changing again ...to the music profession." Then he went to college for a brief time. She explained that Wayne would set his mind on a goal and worked toward that goal.

Ms. Williams further testified she was not happy about Wayne leaving Georgia State University, but it wasn't his interest – he wanted to work with young people.

She said the blood on the bedroom carpet came from the rat dropping on the bed. However, I questioned Ms. Williams on cross as to her testimony to the Grand Jury which indicted Wayne on July 10, 1981. At that time, District Attorney Slaton had asked her about the blood in Wayne's bedroom floor for which she replied: "I don't know of any blood being in there."

She had an answer for the slapjack the FBI found in the ceiling – saying that Homer put it in their front bedroom closet. As to the scratches seen on Wayne's arms, she said Wayne had fallen on the back step and "skinned his arm some, scraped it."

As did Homer, Ms. Williams testified to the purchase of the carpet in the house in 1968. She said that they purchased air conditioning in 1971, not the carpet. She related the event to her niece's debutante ball in 1968. She had no documentary evidence of the carpet purchase, but she claimed she went to the library and went through the microfilms for ten minutes and found the "ad" in the paper "just before Christmas" of 1968 which caused them to purchase a more expensive grade of the carpet.

Ms. Williams testified as to the defense film exhibit from a debutante's ball showing the carpet looking brown, not green, explaining that 'they didn't use the correct filter and it doesn't bring the color out."

Previously at her Grand Jury appearance, Ms. Williams had testified when asked by the District Attorney about the carpet: "We had the
whole house wall-to-wall carpeted when we was quite young." When
asked "Who did you do business with there?" She replied "I don't remember, because that's been for years and years. We looked for that
contract, that they had contracted, because it was paid through First
National Bank; but we did not find it because that had been such a long
time." She went on to say that Wayne must have been around five or
six years old because they were looking at some pictures with him on
the floor playing on this same carpet. (Wayne was born on May 27,
1958).

[Obviously, the defense film shows the old brownish carpet in 1968
in the house before the green Wellman fiber carpet was installed in
1971].

Ms. Williams testified that she took the call on May 20, 1981, from a
young lady by the name of Cheryl Johnson, who left her phone number
and who called in response to Wayne's flyer for an audition. She placed
the message on Wayne's message spinner.

On May 21, Ms. Williams said Wayne was home cleaning up, packing things in boxes. He had an upset stomach. Homer went to the
Kiwanis and Garden Club and was home about 11:30 p.m. She said that
Wayne talked to Cheryl that day; and Wayne said he didn't feel good
but had to pick up his tape recorder and try to locate Cheryl's address.
Wayne left about 12:00 (midnight) or later. He returned home hours
later and told them what happened – that he had been stopped by the
police at the river.

I questioned her on cross about her Grand Jury testimony wherein
she gave a varying story, saying that after giving Wayne the message, he
(Wayne) attempted to call Cheryl and didn't get an answer; he then set
his clock to alarm at 1:00 o'clock so he could pick up his tape recorder
at the Sans Souci club. He later told her he went by the club but it was
a very busy night so he didn't go in to ask about the recorder. Then he
decided to look for the address Cheryl had left so he would know where
to go and have an interview with the young lady the next day.

Ms. Williams also told the Grand Jury about the surveillance following the bridge incident, saying it wasn't a secret. When the car left, it
was like a funeral procession with reporters and police following.

Ms. Williams explained the report of a neighbor having seen Wayne taking a box from the house about May 22, saying that Wayne and Homer boxed up this stuff and they took it away.

Ms. Williams described the family dog, Sheba, as being old and feeble with heart-worms – not able to walk much, that she drags around.

The witness admitted that Wayne paid no room and board, and said that he wasn't trying to make money from the talent scout business.

[At the Grand Jury, the witness had previously said that Wayne's income for the past two to three years was from the parents in trying to promote a project that he was working on with young talent and that his biggest interest was music. She had also explained the layout of the house, three bedrooms with Wayne's bedroom in the rear with an office in the back. She agreed that Wayne could drive his car around to the rear and enter from the rear without going through the front of the house. She said that Wayne would bring children home from the group he was working with, and that they did rehearsing in the living-room. For auditions he would rent a place. She agreed that Wayne could bring someone into the house from the rear, saying 'but usually, he lets me know whose (sic) in the house.' She confirms that 'because of his type of work' he keeps late hours. She described the various vehicles Wayne had access to over the past several years, including the station wagon].

In an effort to counter my cross-examination of Homer Williams as to whether there was any violence between him and Wayne, Defense Counsel asked Ms. Williams:

"Do you know of any knock-down drag-out fight Wayne ever had with his daddy?"

"No."

"Have you ever heard of your husband threatening your son?"

"No, I haven't. That's hearsay, again."

Binder elicited from the witness that Wayne couldn't see without his glasses and did not possess "any unusual strength about his body."

Upon cross, I went over many small details verifying that her blood type was "O" (to exclude her of contributing the blood found in the station wagon); Wayne's failing grades' in college; his wanting to work with "young people;" the fact that he had never made a living (financially) at anything (but had been supported by the parents in all his endeavors); his falling (by her version) on the back steps receiving scratches to *the top of his arm* in an effort to explain the scratches down the arms described by four witnesses.

I questioned Ms. Williams extensively about her recollections of May 20-21, 1981, regarding the mysterious Cheryl Johnson.

Ms. Williams testified that she took the call from Cheryl Johnson on May 20; Cheryl claimed she worked, and she had picked up one of Wayne's circulars about finding talent and wanted to get an interview. Ms. Williams wrote down the name, phone number, and message, leaving it for Wayne.

To test her recollection, I would move around to other topics and then return for further questioning.

"You're certain it's not any other date, May –"

"It was the twentieth because Wayne finally talked with her on the twenty-first"

"You say Wayne talked to her on the twenty-first?"

"Yes. Wayne talked with her and set up an appointment."

Ms. Williams went on to reiterate that Wayne told her he talked with Cheryl on the twenty-first of May and set up the appointment.

Some time later, I returned to the topic.

"Do you remember testifying at the Grand Jury, Ms. Williams, that after getting the message that he – meaning Wayne – attempted to call her, and he didn't get an answer?"

"The first time he tried to call her (nods head affirmatively)."

"All right. You remember that now?"

"I remember that."

"Do you also remember testifying at the Grand Jury that Cheryl Johnson was never located?"

"I remember testifying that."

". . . Now, my question now is do you remember testifying earlier at the Grand Jury last year that there was no such number?"

"We couldn't locate her at that number because I understand she had talked with him from some other place."

I asked her: "Are you saying that he located her some other way?"

"They contacted him some other way."

"Who did?"

"A cousin or something."

"A cousin of hers contacted him?" I asked.

"He talked with a cousin of hers."

"And then he would have that number, I suppose?"

"I don't know whether he would now, because there are no numbers in my house now." [This is the first mention that someone other than Cheryl contacted Wayne – not even Wayne ever said this].

I again asked her about a conversation she had with the Grand Jury.

"He tried to call?"

"He tried to call her at home."

"And the number?"

"There's no such number."

Ms. Williams confirmed the testimony with the Grand Jury.

Later, I re-visited the Grand Jury testimony of Ms. Williams.

Question: And do you remember the next question:

"And to the best of your knowledge, he (Wayne) never did make contact with her (Cheryl)?"

Your answer: "He never made – he never made contact with her."

Ms. Williams: "I remember saying that."

I questioned Ms. Williams about her and Homer's denial of any violence between Wayne and Homer.

" … You've never witnessed any fights between your husband and Wayne?"

"I have not."

"You don't recall an incident where Wayne choked your husband in your own home there, do you?"

"I do not recall that. Hearsay," she replies.

"Do you deny that that happened?"

"I deny, and I say its hearsay." [Interesting that the witness thinks its hearsay].

"Do you recall when your husband got the shotgun to him (Wayne)?"

"I never have seen that."

"Were you with your husband and Wayne and another subject on another occasion when Wayne assaulted your husband, Homer?"

"I don't remember that." [She doesn't deny it happened].

Of course, I expected she might deny the incidents between Wayne and Homer; but now, independent testimony may be brought in by the State to prove the incidents did occur.

I zeroed in on Ms. Williams' testimony regarding the bedroom carpet. I showed her several photographs of the carpet, taken during the search on June 22 (1981), asking her:

"And that shows up that green carpet very visibly, doesn't it?"

"Yes," she replied.

"That looks nothing like that brown carpet that was shown on the screen (debutante ball video filmed in 1968)) earlier does it?"

"May I ask, Mr. Mallard, you know, you use different types of filters. If you don't have the right filter, you aren't going to get your right color."

"Have you ever heard of a filter used on a Polaroid camera?"

"I'd have to ask my husband."

I asked Ms. Williams to tell me if that appeared to be the wall-to-wall carpet she purchased in December 1968, which is reflected by the slide (previously identified by the Defense). Ms. Williams insisted on having the slide in her hands. I asked her if she was looking for the date, but she responded:

"I'm looking for my identifying writing."

"Yes, Ma'am. You're looking for the date, aren't you?"

"I'm looking to identify my writing where I have A-22 on it."

"Which carpet is that?"

"That's the carpet in question, the green carpet."

"Did you notice the date – is that the carpet you bought December 68?"

"It appears to be."

"You notice the date on it is January 68. Do you notice that?"

"May I say this: The slide could have been taken in December and processed in January."

"Yes, Ma'am. That would be a year before you say you purchased that carpet."

"When did I purchase the carpet?"

"Well, do you say you purchased it in December of 68?"

"And this is January 68?"

"Yes, Ma'am."

"Well, this is the wrong slide, then."

"It would be 11 months earlier, wouldn't it?" "That's the old carpet, Ms. Williams, isn't it?"

"I really can't identify it. But it should be a newer one than that."

Ms. Williams testified she and Homer got to looking for the "ad" in relation to the age of the dog, and that it was in a "Sunday magazine section ... before the Christmas holidays."

"Now, so you went down to the Library and you looked through until you found an ad at about the time that you wanted it to be; did you not?"

"Incorrect. I was gone from the courthouse less than ten minutes."

I then showed Ms. Williams *State's* Exhibit number 746, an "ad" for three full rooms, wall-to-wall carpet for $149.00 from the Atlanta Constitution, December 4, 1971, similar to the "ad" (Defense Exhibit number 98) except for the dates (hers being dated December 7, 1968).

"Isn't it true, Mrs. Williams that it was this ad, State's Exhibit 746, that you responded to dated December 4, 1971, rather than 1968?"

"No."

"All right." "Does the name Southern Prudential mean anything to you?"

"I don't remember the name Southern Prudential. I just know we answered an ad, and the agent came to the house."

"You don't recall the name Southern Prudential, then?"

"No."

"Aren't they the ones that put the carpet in your home?"

"I don't recall the name."

"Mrs. Williams, isn't it true that you bought the carpet, and it was installed through Southern Prudential and not Carpet Discount Outlet?"

"I don't know who installed it. We were working ..."

"And isn't it true that Mr. Gano installed it?"

"I told you earlier, I do not know a Mr. Gano."

"Was the information you gave us earlier with regard to the loan number and the amount, you had it on some piece of paper, I believe ..."

"Yes."

She went on to explain that she had written down the loan number, North American Acceptance Corporation, paid out July 1972, but that they had destroyed the original paperwork.

"I see. This doesn't indicate what loan it was, though?"

"Well, at that time I didn't have – couldn't have had but two things. It had to be the carpet or the air conditioning. And it wasn't the air conditioning, so it had to be the carpet. So we assumed —"

"Where was it financed?"

"I don't know who financed that thing."

"I show you what's marked State's Exhibit 751, Mrs. Williams. It's a certified copy of a document in the office of the Clerk of the Superior Court in this County. I ask you if you recognize it and see if your name is not on it."

"My name appears on this and I have been down to the Clerk's office, also, and I understand there is some forgery in this."

"What is the forgery?"

"Well, I'd rather let them explain that."

"Is your name forged on there?"

"That's my signature on it, copied."

"Yes Ma'am. And your husband's signature, also?"

"Is copied on there (nods head affirmatively)."

"I'm sorry?"

"I said copied." … But I understand there is some forgery in there. I'm not a lawyer and I don't know what that meant, but my lawyer has a copy of it." [No lawyer or others to my knowledge ever contended the certified court document was a forgery – the defense attorneys never claimed such].

"You understood we gave your lawyer a copy of it the other day?"

"I don't know who gave it. But I think my lawyer went to the place himself. That is my signature." (She admits it's her signature).   I had the witness to further identify her and her husband's signatures on the document.

"And isn't it true that this represented a Deed to Secure Debt on your property to Southern Prudential Corporation?"

"I'm not sure what it was for."

"And Southern Prudential Corporation is the same one that put your carpet in, isn't it, from that ad dated December 4, 1971?"

"No. They did not put my carpet in. Those are not the people that carpeted my house."

"Now, I believe you said that you remembered this "ad" because it was in the Sunday Constitution magazine section?"

"Correct."

"Will you look at your defense exhibit 98 and tell me if that's not a Saturday paper?"

"It's supposed to have been a Sunday paper."

"Yes Ma'am."

"That's what I asked for when I went to the Library and told them what I was looking for."

I pointed out: "But it's a Saturday paper, isn't it? Atlanta Journal, Saturday, December 7, 1968?"

By now, the point was hammered in. [Later in rebuttal, the State would call the owner of Southern Prudential, as well as the installer of the carpet, to identify the Deed to Secure Debt for carpet installed in the Williams home in 1971].

I always assume that a defendant will testify and prepare accordingly – though defense attorneys generally encourage them to stay off the stand rather than expose themselves to cross-examination. Most defendants heed that advice since the jury cannot, by court instruction, use the fact they do not testify against them in any manner.

Jurors want to hear from the defendant. They want him to take the stand and be able to explain away any incriminating evidence; however, most juries will bend over backward to follow a judge's instruction on the law, substantially as follows:

"The defendant is under no duty to present evidence or to take the stand and testify. If a defendant elects not to testify, <u>no inference hurtful, harmful, or adverse to the defendant shall be drawn by the jury, nor shall such fact be held against the defendant in any way.</u>" [Emphasis added].

[In an interview with Trisha Renaud of the Fulton Daily Report years later on February 27, 2002, Co-counsel Jim Kitchens reportedly said that he and Al Binder did not try to talk Wayne out of testifying but did explain the risks involved. Williams chose to testify – a move some believe sealed his fate. Kitchens also reportedly recounted spending hours and hours at the jail with Williams discussing leads and witnesses and concluded that Williams was not particularly likeable – Williams was rude to his parents, Kitchens related, adding: "I didn't like that. I'm from the old school." This is consistent with other sources and information we had that indicated that Williams was demanding and mean to his parents. Rebuttal testimony by the State would support this].

Cross-examination of a defendant is an important event not to take lightly; a jury is expecting him to testify and be believable if he is innocent. Therefore, I start with preparing a file for that event, when I first get involved in a case and add to it as I go along. Careful planning by compiling all his quotes, statements, and other information is helpful in planning an outline for cross. Then I formulate a plan for attack by organizing the cross in segments to enable me to control the interview. [This applies to any witness]. I might move around with the cross to keep the defendant from realizing where I am going until he is boxed in; I like to put the defendant in a position of having to either agree with my strong witnesses or dispute their testimony – the jury then has to believe the accused (who has everything to gain by testifying falsely) or my impartial, unbiased witnesses who have nothing to gain from testifying. No doubt but that Williams would claim all the witnesses who disagreed with him were liars. Usually, defendants will testify in opposition to all the witnesses for the prosecution who say anything which is incriminating against such defendant – thus, jurors will weigh the credibility of the defendant against the State's witnesses, and the jury's task becomes easier.

I was prepared in the event Williams chose to testify. I had a stack of materials, transcripts, books, and files, assuming I would be the one to do the cross. District Attorney Slaton, of course, would do so if he chose.

A couple of days before Williams was expected to follow the parents to the stand (if he chose to do so), District Attorney Slaton told me he would take Williams on cross. I handed the file I had for the cross (expandable folders bulging with documents and transcripts highlighted and with reference to questions and points to be made) along with my outline. I had Williams' five page bio, most of which was false.

I was relieved! I really did not care one way or the other. I didn't need any more pressure, and the added pressure of being told the case may be decided by Williams' testimony didn't help matters. I was there only because the case justified the best effort possible by the prosecution team for a just and true verdict. The public, victims, and families deserved the very best we could do as a prosecution team. I would have been happy to be home with Jo, who was doing well under the circumstances. The next morning, Slaton returned the file to me saying "you can do the cross!"

I knew the approach to a successful cross-examination is different for all defendants. I try to learn all I can about the defendant as a person and to decide what I want from him or her and how best to get it. Are there vulnerable points, criminal history, personal and business information such that you know the person intuitively? Can you lay the foundation for impeachment by subsequent witnesses and evidence which will disprove his/her testimony? Jurors don't like defendants, or anyone, caught testifying falsely. Jurors in such instance will likely discount anything they say.

A different approach and tactic would be required for Williams than for other defendants, like, for instance, Ninaking Anderson. With Williams it would be an 'in your face' aggressive, demanding, lengthy, and detailed approach. He had much he could not explain satisfactorily where Ninaking Anderson, whom I had prosecuted in 1975, was a likable person (though she knifed her husband to death), and I needed to learn something she knew and I didn't.

The prosecution of Ninaking Anderson was another of those cases where Slaton needed some special attention given in a case which was sensitive from a political view and one where we needed to be 'firm but fair.' Defense attorneys and some defense witnesses were friends of the office and personal friends of District Attorney Slaton. Thus, we must see justice is done to the extent possible without there appearing any favoritism for the defendant. Slaton could have recused the office, but he always believed we could execute our sworn duties without passing the mantle to a 'special prosecutor.'

While some observers perceive a trial as a 'battle of the lawyers,' the prosecutor is held to higher standards of conduct so as not to pervert the law or strike illegal blows; however, he is not required to forget he is an adversary in a legal system in a contest as to the righteousness of his cause. His strategy is his own! His discretion in granting mercy is his own! His discretion in granting mercy in one case and not in another (as he sees it) is his own! His eye for the truth is his goal!

While the prosecutor must stay with truth and justice as his goal, when satisfied he is right, he is not required to 'stand down' when the going gets tough. He may in the words of *Stonewall Jackson:*

> **"When war does come, my advice is to draw the sword and throw away the scabbard."**
> *(Paraphrased from Stonewall Jackson's speech to the Cadets at the Virginia Military Institute, March, 1861).*

Thus, Slaton sent me into court against the 'dream team' of attorneys representing Ninaking Anderson – all by myself. After all, it was only three against one, or was it 'even' since I had *truth* and *justice* on my side and as my goal. Should that sound 'corny,' let me add that in truth and reality I would rather be on the virtuous side of an issue in a Court of Law than to be assisted by great legal minds.

[The State vs. Ninaking Anderson[14]]
(A Reflection)

One of the high profile cases in Atlanta to have received a great deal of media attention came with Ninaking Calhoun Anderson, the daughter of Atlanta City Councilman John Calhoun, being charged with the murder of her husband, Quincy Anderson, by stabbing him to death in their home in April 1975. The case was a 'hot potato' since Councilman Calhoun and others supporting his daughter, including Reverend Martin Luther King Sr., were well-respected members of the community and friends of District Attorney Slaton. Ms. Anderson had hired the top three (3) defense attorneys available at that time: City Councilman Marvin Arrington (later to become – and remains so at this time – Superior Court Judge), former State Senator Leroy Johnson, both prominent political figures, and well-known attorney Edward Garland – all formidable and respected members of the State Bar (they would be considered the 'dream team'). I considered them friends as well as respecting their ability in the courtroom. Senator Johnson initially got his start in the Fulton District Attorney's Office in the early 1960s as I began my career as an Investigator. He became the first African American state

---

14   The decision of the Georgia Court of Appeals affirming the conviction is found at 138 Ga. App. 871 (1976).

lawmaker elected since Reconstruction and took office at the State Capitol in January 1963.[15]

District Attorney Slaton was the consummate politician. Slaton had been appointed District Attorney in 1965 and served with distinction for 31 years until he retired, without ever having opposition for the office. He did it by having a reputation of honesty and integrity in the office and by having the support of the public in general and that of the African-American community in particular. He was a great administrator, but he did not personally prosecute cases except for three cases of which I recall [one of those being the prosecution of **Marcus Wayne Chennault in 1974 for the murders of Mrs. Martin (Alberta) Luther King, Sr. and Deacon Edward Boykin, and the wounding of Mrs. Jimmie Mitchell. The shootings occurred in the Ebenezer Baptist Church during Sunday services with a church full of eye-witnesses.** [16]] His not personally prosecuting cases was not unusual in large offices (Atlanta housed the largest prosecutor's office in the state) because of his responsibilities as an elected official in supervising many employees, lawyers and non-lawyers.

The Defense was authorized twice the number of peremptory excusals of jurors as the state (the law was changed only in recent years providing for equal jury strikes between the state and defendant), thus giving the Defense the opportunity to select a jury of their liking – women – who would identify with the defendant, they believed. A jury of 10 women and two men was chosen. I saw it coming; they would present a defense that "he had it coming" – that this was a "good riddance" killing. But I had no idea who would testify. Since the Prosecution had no discovery from the Defense, they could wait until the State put up its case and then call their witnesses, prohibiting me from knowing who they would be until they took the stand. Thus I had no way of investigating or learning anything about the defense witnesses in advance.

15   Recently, an article in the Atlanta Journal Constitution on May 12, 2008, by Jim Galloway, chronicled Senator Johnson's quiet desegregation of facilities at the State Capital after taking office in January 1963 with the help of Governor Carl Sanders without incident – a tribute to both!

16   See Chenault v. The State, 234 Ga. 216; 215 SE2d 223 (1975). Chenault opened fire upon the church congregation on Sunday morning, killing Mrs. King, Sr. and Deacon Boykin, and wounding Mrs. Mitchell. A jury imposed death for the murders and a term of years on the related charges after Chenault presented a defense of insanity. His death sentence was later changed to life, and he died in prison in 1995 at age 44 after suffering a stroke.

[The Defense had limited discovery, including a list of state's witnesses]. The defendant could, of course, sit in the courtroom, listen to all the state's witnesses and then take the stand and weave her testimony to fit the defense theory about the case.

My case was simple: Mrs. Anderson had called police to the home after she stabbed her husband in the kitchen. She explained that he had attacked and choked her as she prepared him lunch; and she must have blacked out. [Lunch items and a bloody steak knife were present on the floor]. He was lying on the floor with stab wounds to the body and face. The husband's bloody T-shirt was lying by his body. She was arrested and charged with murder; the body was removed for autopsy.

Now the defense began: They presented witnesses from all around the country – East coast to West coast – including Air Force personnel who knew the couple during the past 20 years of marriage and who testified to Mrs. Anderson's good character. The deceased was a retired Air Force officer, and Mrs. Anderson, his supportive wife. The defense witnesses – including her father, Council Calhoun, and many other witnesses – testified and described the deceased as a "brutal, profane man" when he was drinking. Over the years he had attacked his wife when he would be drinking; on one occasion he was seen choking his wife, but she got loose and ran from the house and spent the night in the carport.

Character witnesses for Mrs. Anderson included the Reverend Martin Luther King, Sr., and former candidate for lieutenant governor, John Savage.

I sat through day after day of similar testimonies of witnesses labeling the husband as an 'abuser' while her reputation in the community was good. And, I knew the Judge would instruct the jury on good character as a defense, and counsel's closing argument would be justifiable homicide. After all, I've heard that argument before – that 'what good is a life-time of good character if it won't come to your aid in a time of need.'

Sitting alone at counsel table, I began to think that everyone in the courtroom, including the jury, was looking to me as the bad guy, thinking that I should dismiss the case and apologize for putting her on trial. Her three 'dream-team' lawyers were having a 'field day' with this female jury, who was identifying with the defendant; some of the female jurors were glaring at me. I knew I had to find a way to get at the truth; the deceased husband did not deserve to be killed except under legal justification. The prosecutor is almost always looked upon as the 'good guy' – doing the right thing – and here I was looked upon as perhaps the 'bad guy' in prosecuting the case.

The Medical Examiner had testified that the deceased had been stabbed a total of seven (7) times: Twice in the chest and once in the back, with other punctures to the head, face, and arm. I wondered about the sequence of injuries!

Would the defense put the defendant on the stand?

There were unanswered questions in my mind about the wounds and about his T-shirt which was recovered with the body – answers which only she could reveal. Earlier, I nonchalantly had the officer identify the bloody T-shirt as having been seized with the body and submitted into evidence without any reference to its potential importance.

The Defense called Mrs. Anderson to testify – and did she testify! She had the female jurors crying with her when she related the 20 years of suffering at the hands of this brute who would mistreat and abuse her when he was drinking. She claimed that this was just another incident when she was fixing him lunch in the kitchen (she had the knife in her hand) when he came in and started choking her. She said:

"When he put his hands around my neck and started strangling me, I thought it would be my last moment. He had a look on his face I had never seen before." He said, "You make me sick. I hate you. I'm going to kill you, bitch."

Further she testified:

"He had already slapped me twice against the head so hard that my ears were ringing – I don't remember lashing out at him. ... I just blanked. After I saw the blood, I couldn't believe... Then I looked at the knife in my hand and there was blood on it – I knew I must've done it."

She testified about blanking out before in such altercations and had locked herself in the bathroom ... that he had kicked the door down ... and strangled her until she blanked out ... waking up on the bathroom floor.

Despite that he was charming when not drinking, and she loved him.

But, I wanted to know about the T-shirt.

Then she was turned over to me for cross-examination!

I gave her a moment to recover and did my best not to ask her any-thing that would cause her to start crying again. I had to be careful but diligent in the cross-examination because the jury loved her. Abusive or harsh cross-examination wouldn't work. I had to get her to give me details … lead her down the primrose path I wanted her to go.

I softly had her go back through her testimony from beginning to end hoping not to alert the Defense of the point of my interest. I must be delicate with the questioning.

She testified about his choking her … and then what happened, I would ask. After you came to from the blackout, you saw your husband standing?

Describe the blood, the wounds …, and then what happened?

"He walked out of the kitchen."

Where did he go? [Not asked on direct examination]. "He went into the living room … then he returned to the kitchen."

Did he have his T-shirt on when he left and came back? "Yes"

What happened then? "He removed his T-shirt."

Did you see him remove it? "Yes."

What happened I asked? She responded that he dropped to the floor and lay there until police arrived.

I had what I needed!

This was the first time I had ever prosecuted a case where the Defense's evidence lasted longer than the State's case. After all, the burden of proof is upon the state to prove the defendant guilty beyond a reasonable doubt; there is no burden on the defendant to prove anything – or for the defendant to testify at all. At most trials, defense counsel will keep their clients off the stand or try to do so.

Evidence was closed, and closing arguments would be next. But first, a recess was ordered so counsel could get ready.

One of the 'dream-team,' Ed Garland, meandered over to the clerk's table where the evidence was lying and picked up the bag with the bloody T-shirt. I froze! What if he examined it learning what I now knew?

Ha Ha (laugh), Ed – you'll get your hands dirty, I called out to him. [Bloody clothing in a closed bag for months becomes very nasty and smelly]. Garland looked over to me, smiled and immediately dropped the shirt back on the table and walked away.

I had prosecuted several cases against Garland before and considered him one of the best defense attorneys I knew. He has an infectious smile on his 'baby-face' which women love, and a quick mind in the courtroom.

Had Garland examined the shirt, he could not have changed anything – but he might have realized what I may argue in my closing. The advantage of having a great point to make in closing is that, if it gets by the other side without their opportunity to *put their spin on it*, (assuming you have the last word with the jury as I would have in this case) your argument on the point goes un-rebutted. This is pure strategy!

Judge Jack Etheridge called the court to order and asked the Defense to proceed with its closing argument. Both Ed Garland and Senator Johnson argued, as expected, that the State had not proven a case, reminding the jurors of the harsh history of bad acts by the deceased and of Ms. Anderson's good character.

"The subconscious will to survive took over and she survived," said Garland shaking his fists at the jurors. "This man created his own death; caused it over the years. If she'd had a gun, she would have had the right to shoot him right between the eyes, because to kill another to save oneself is the law."

[I was concerned about the principle of 'Jury Nullification.' That is when the jury may see fit to acquit the defendant, disregarding the evidence, because they liked the defendant (especially in light of the tons of "Good Character" testimony), and they disliked the deceased – thus the doctrine of jury nullification].

Senator Johnson described the deceased as a Dr. Jekyll – Mr. Hyde, who beat and kicked his wife many times, evoking tears running down the cheeks of some jurors who shook their heads in concurrence.

He sat down, and the Judge looked at me.

I rose to make my summation to the jury. I walked to the front of the jury box as I had done hundreds of times before; usually the jurors are smiling, friendly, and receptive to the prosecutor. After all, the prosecutor is here to do justice – he wears the white hat. Some of the female jurors wouldn't look at me. I hesitated without saying a word. Then

I walked back along the rail – some of the women were looking at the floor.

The beginning of the summation is very important. You must get the attention of jurors and make strong points about your case – points they will take into the jury room when they retire for deliberation. After all, a human mind will retain only a portion of what is heard. Thus, the first few minutes with the jury is important to 'frame a picture' in their minds about the case or an event, so don't waste the beginning with minutiae.

How will I gain their attention? Suddenly, without warning,

I struck the handrail directly in front of the jurors with my open hand as hard as I could, causing a loud explosion-type sound and some jurors to jump back.

"You folks think you're going to turn her loose, don't you, - Well, you're not" – I said – quickly pointing out because "she's guilty and I will show you why you're going to convict. "

I then saw 24 eyes looking my way – I had their attention. Now I had to produce!

I pulled the poster display in front of the jurors and reminded them of the Medical Examiner's testimony and drawings of the front and back of a human body and his diagramming the injuries to the body of deceased – front and back. The Medical Examiner had diagrammed the seven wounds to the face and body. Except for the wounds to the face and arm, there was one stab wound to the back and two wounds to the chest. I then brought the deceased's bloody T-shirt over to the jury and told them that this shirt would tell the jurors how he was killed – that you can't change the facts or disregard physical evidence. I then pointed out what was obvious after stretching out a wadded-up bloody shirt from the bag: There was only one knife hole in the front of the shirt as well as one hole in the back of the shirt.

How could this be, I questioned – one hole in the front of the shirt but two holes in his chest?

I told the jury I didn't know how it happened until the defendant took the stand, and I learned on cross-examination when she told them the sequence of events in the kitchen: She stabbed her husband; then he walked into the other room, returned – then he removed his own T-shirt, afterward falling to the floor.

Thus, he received the second stab wound to the heart after he had removed his shirt and had fallen to the floor, I said.

The Medical Examiner had testified that either of the three wounds to the torso could have caused death!

I also illustrated with the T-shirt that there was no other way it could have happened, that a man's undershirt has a front and back, and further that the holes in the shirt would not match up with injuries any other way. Thus this leaves the second hole to his chest not matching any holes in the shirt. I then concluded:

"When were the two wounds inflicted to the chest? One before he took the T-shirt off and one afterwards, as he lay there on the kitchen floor gasping for breath. She took that knife and plugged him through the heart. While he was down she decided to go ahead and finish him off. That's the only way."

The jury was all at attention!

There comes a time in any trial when lawyers know they've been 'had.' Garland then knew I 'had his lunch' when I had earlier warned him about getting his hands dirty when he had picked up the shirt during the recess. Though he couldn't have changed anything, he could have given his own explanation. So he now did the only think he could think of to interrupt my presentation to the jury, because he knew he needed to break the momentum – I was on a roll with the jury. So he objected strenuously, claiming I…deliberately waited until the Defense would have no chance for rebuttal to introduce this speculation about the T-shirt, claiming it violated his client's constitutional rights to due process.

Judge Jack Etheridge was reading my mind when he asked Garland without asking me to respond: Mr. Garland, are you suggesting that Mr. Mallard has to tell you of his conclusions…?

Garland acquiesced, Well, Judge, I had to do something …

I went on to summarize the case from a consideration of the evidence that I had elicited of defense witnesses on cross-examination such as: "Just another weekend, a little drinking, fussing, and some one ending up dead."

I had shown from the witnesses on cross-examination that the twenty years of marriage existed with Mrs. Anderson never having filed for divorce or reporting any bad acts by the deceased to any police agency.

The deceased had retired as an Air Force jet pilot. The United States Air Force Command must have thought he was not as bad as the Defense was characterizing him; otherwise, would he have been entrusted with a multi-million dollar jet plane at his fingertips.

I told the jury finally:

"Quincy is speaking to you through this T-shirt, – this little piece of physical evidence is going to convict her ... and that the so-called 'black-out' she claims was so she wouldn't have to explain seven stab wounds."

And then I decided to address the one concern about the jury with ten women: "Women by their very nature are sympathetic and kind-hearted, but, the defendant is faceless to justice, and she has had a fair trial. All she is entitled to is mercy and justice – not acquittal."

While awaiting the jury verdict, Ed Garland acknowledged to me that I did a job on him by warning him away from the 'dirty' T-shirt.

The grand jury had charged murder in the indictment for which she was on trial. Murder is defined by Georgia law (OCGA 16-5-1) as:

(a) A person commits the offense of Murder when he unlawfully and with malice aforethought, either express or implied, causes the death of another human being.

(b) Express malice is that deliberate intention unlawfully to take the life of another human being which is manifested by external circumstances capable of proof. Malice shall be implied where no considerable provocation appears and where all the circumstances of the killing show an abandoned and malignant heart.

Contrary to what most people believe, there are no degrees of murder in Georgia. A lesser degree of homicide which would be applicable to the facts as shown by the evidence in this case and which would be instructed by the Court would be Voluntary Manslaughter, which is defined (Official Code of Georgia 16-5-2) as follows:

> **(a) A person commits the offense of voluntary manslaughter when he causes the death of another human being under circumstances which would otherwise be murder and if he acts solely as the result of a sudden, violent, and irresistible passion resulting from serious provocation sufficient to excite such passion in a reasonable person; however, if there should have been an interval between the provocation and the killing sufficient for the voice of reason and humanity to be heard, of which the jury in all cases shall be the judge, the killing shall be attributed to deliberate revenge and be punished as murder.**
>
> **(b) A person who commits the offense of voluntary manslaughter, upon conviction thereof, shall be punished by imprisonment for not less than one nor more than 20 years.**

It is common in homicides to charge the highest offense that under any theory of the case or evaluation of the evidence the crime could be found to be, since once a trial starts there is no backing up and re-charging to a higher crime. Had the prosecution formally charged Manslaughter – a lesser included offense of murder – and during the trial the evidence evolved that would have justified a consideration by the jury of Murder, there would have been no way to increase the charge; but the judge or jury can always reduce the offense from Murder to a lesser offense (Manslaughter) if the judge gives the jury that option after all the evidence is completed, and there could be found the lesser offense from a consideration of the evidence presented at trial. *The jury can reduce the offense but not increase it.*

The Defense claimed and argued that Mrs. Anderson was completely justified in the killing and should have been acquitted. The defense of "Use of Force" is defined in pertinent part in Official Code of Georgia 16-3-21:

> **(a) A person is justified in threatening or using force against another when and to the extent that he or she reasonably believes that such threat or force is necessary to defend himself or herself or a third person against such other's imminent use of unlawful force; however, except as provided in Code Section 16-3-23, a person is justified in using force which is intended or likely to cause death or great bodily harm only if he or she reasonably believes that such force is necessary to prevent death or great bodily injury to himself or herself or a third person or to prevent the commission of a forcible felony.**

Therefore, the Defense was trying to convince the jury that the defendant was acting in self-defense at the time of the killing, that she believed her life was threatened, and that deadly force was necessary to prevent death or great bodily injury to herself.

On September 7, 1975, the jury returned with a verdict – guilty of Voluntary Manslaughter. It was what I expected after hearing the defendant testify to facts leading up to the stabbing, which warranted a finding that the killing resulted from serious provocation by the deceased against the defendant and in what we call the "heat of passion."

There was obviously provocation, and the killing resulted therefrom – making it a typical voluntary manslaughter – an intentional killing but without malice aforethought. The jury felt the killing was not justified and returned the appropriate verdict.

She could have received from one to twenty years, either in prison or on probation. I recommended a prison term of five years. I could just as easily have said fifteen or twenty years; but she had no prior problems and she was supported by the community and good character witnesses. However, probation was not justified in a homicide under these facts. A human life is too precious to be snuffed out except in cases of absolute 'necessity to prevent death to yourself or another person.'

All cases on the facts are different, and all defendants are different. That is why the law gives the Court such a wide range of sentence, from probation to twenty years in prison. Some defendants are bad people, incorrigible with prior convictions, and would never be rehabilitated while others, like this defendant had led an exemplary life (so far as we knew). Some people will tell you that everyone convicted of a particular crime should receive the same sentence. However, that would not take into account the *person* or the *circumstances of the crime – which are different in every case.* Some defendants have a criminal background while others have an unblemished record, and some crimes (of the same species) are more aggravated than others.

I felt: Except for this one act, she's not a bad person; she just did a bad thing.

This is the Criminal Justice System at work in the interest of justice. Had my recommended sentence not been in line with what the Judge felt was appropriate under the facts of the case, he could have imposed any sentence within the limits of the law which he felt appropriate.

The Judge agreed with my assessment and imposed a five-year prison sentence as recommended, with five additional years to follow and suspended. The following year, the Appellate Court denied a new trial, upholding the Court's rulings, and the defendant had to surrender to serve her sentence.

Justice was done!

The pressure had been building day by day! Would Williams testify? People were predicting that the outcome of the case may hinge on how Williams does on the stand. From the White House, the Justice Department, and the FBI, to the Governor, the Mayor of Atlanta, and Atlanta Police Officials, all were watching and waiting for the madness of the past two years to end with a conviction so Atlanta's young people could get back to their daily affairs without fear of being outside the home.

I never doubted that Williams would testify based on his actions of being in charge from the first day he became known (others doubted it), but I did not go with the flow in believing that the case depended on his testimony as a witness, and how I would do in his cross-examination. I considered the case to be a formidable case which would withstand all the attacks the Defense could muster – there were just too many witnesses, pieces of evidence, and exhibits to explain away.

I had consulted the profiler from the FBI Behavioral Science Unit, Dr. John Douglas, who had been assigned to assist the Task Force in the investigation and who was present during the trial. He had done an analysis and profile of the serial killer, which fit Williams and was available to give testimony if it became relevant. Affirmatively, there was no issue raised by Williams as to a mental defect. We learned, however, that the Defense had an expert psychologist in town during the trial who would possibly testify in Williams' defense in some manner. As a strategy, we advised defense counsel Al Binder of possibly using profiler Douglas and shared the work his unit had done on Williams. We let it be known that Douglas was available for possible rebuttal testimony. We learned the next day that the defense expert was sent packing by the Defense. He was not called. It was a face-off!

Dr. Douglas was helpful in understanding how a serial killer thinks and acts, and he suggested that I keep Williams on the stand as long as possible (something I always do). Douglas suggested that if things didn't go his way Williams may make a feeble attempt at suicide or feign illness or lose his cool and display a personality change. Williams did get sick one day, requiring a recess; other times, he was hurried out of the courtroom with an upset stomach. The second day on cross-examination he would display his temper.

The daily newspapers carried a 'gavel to gavel' recitation of Williams' testimony (as they had pretty much done of the entire trial). Reporters were interviewing people to assess what was going on, and in doing so many friends and acquaintances were overly generous with the praise of my handling the cross. I recite these comments only to show that the atmosphere of those days and pressures upon all of us was highly charged, indicative of the importance of this part of the trial and the expectations concerning what I was about to do.

Williams Testifies –

The accused killer, Wayne Bertram Williams, took the stand in his defense. Who was more prepared, he or I? After three days from now and almost 400 legal pages of testimony, that question may be answered.

Al Binder, his chief defense counsel, would lead him through the mine fields, eliciting responses which he hoped would convince the jurors he was a quiet, respectable member of the community who would never harm anyone. By Binder:

"Tell this jury your name."

"Wayne Bertram Williams."

"Are you the defendant in this case?"

"Yes."

"Now, Wayne, you don't mind me calling you Wayne, do you?"

"No."

"We've become friends over the last few months, haven't we?"

"That's right."

I think it's a mistake for defense counsel becoming personally involved or personal friends with a defendant he is representing, especially in a case of this magnitude. I have observed over the years when that happens, the attorney may have problems with being objective in evaluating the case or strategy at times because of his personal feelings toward the accused. He may tend to look at the case 'with blinders' – only from his client's viewpoint. After a conviction, the attorney many times will take it too personal – he believes only what his client tells him – and will be unable to accept the fact that his client was 'in fact guilty.'

First, Binder asked if Williams knew either of the two men (victims Payne and Cater). His answer was 'no.' Binder then went right into Wayne's background starting with his formative years – kindergarten, nursery school, grade school, associations with other children, etc.

In the sixth grade, Williams related that he and two friends built the radio station as a result of a Youth Experimental Opera Workshop at Douglas High that summer. It started in the utility room at the house. "We did it for fun," he said. Williams went on to relate the rise and fall of the station as testified by the parents. Then Williams testified to his work part-time as researcher in the news business, which followed with his doing 'news stringer work' (free-lancing news – getting the stories at night).

Binder said "there's been a lot of talk here about something called Karate" and asked Williams to step down and stand in front of the jury. He then told him to hold his hands out in front of the jury. Binder then asked if any juror wished to touch his (Williams) hands to see if he had calluses on them. One juror did, and Binder asked if anybody else wished to touch his hands. [Several witnesses testified that Williams said he knew karate, one of them being a defense witness and friend of Williams].

Binder asked him about his weight (162 he said) and about the testimony of Bobby Tolin at the Ambulance Company. Williams said they had "some horseplay," but most of the time, he (Williams) was on the ground. [Williams must have thought well of himself physically to even engage in physical activity with someone six foot two inches and weighing almost 300 pounds].

Williams talked about his dogs. He got Sheba in 1968. He said he would give the dog only a few months to live – she had heartworms.

Williams related that he got started in the music business in 1976 when a female friend who had a group wanted him to manage her. He started into the business full time in 1978, putting out his flyers. He explained: "The problem was in the auditions, we were dealing with people who were from the street with no experience. The flyer was an outline telling them how long it would take, what we wanted to do with them to prepare them to become professionals." He indicated that [we] finally ended up putting the Gemini group together shortly before being arrested.

He discussed the vehicles he had over the years and said they got rid of the Maroon LTD when it broke down before August; the 1976 blue LTD was totaled out in 1977. He further said that the police cars he bought had two way radios and scanners in them – he tried to hide the antennas to keep them from being so obvious. Two vehicles had sirens. They also had amber emergency lights. He responded to fires for news stories, he claimed.

After a brief recess, the Court permitted Binder to bring the dog, Sheba, into the courtroom for a view by the jury. DA Slaton objected saying: "We understand the dog is on its last legs" (laughter). The Court instructed everyone to be absolutely quiet during this demonstration. The dog was walked down the aisle and paraded before the jury, as the Court announced that "the jury has had an opportunity to observe the dog to determine whether or not the dog is frisky or not."

Photo of dog

Williams denied ever making derogatory comments about people of his race, although he said he had used the "N" word. He said it wasn't derogatory when blacks use it to each other although it was if a white person used it. He admitted using derogatory words about white people. He denied having any bad feelings toward poor people or harming anyone.

When asked by Binder if he bore any grudges against Mr. Slaton or the prosecution staff, he responded: "Well, I talked with Mr. Slaton out at the jail one time, and I don't have any malice against him or any of them because I'm saying I understand it wasn't their decision that they got this mess. I don't have any grudge against him. But then again, I wouldn't invite him home for dinner. But I don't have no grudge against him."

Williams discussed the carpet in the house. The original carpet was brown before the wall-to-wall green carpet was installed; he suggested it must have been installed before Christmas of 1969.

Williams said if he was allowed to return to his home, he would continue the work he started with the group. Binder asked: "Did you wake up every morning and want to go to work and do that or did you find it a chore?"

"Well, that is incorrect. One thing, I didn't wake up in the morning. I slept till usually about eleven because I would be up until four, sometimes five in the morning."

Binder asked if he was "homosexual" which he denied. When asked about the boy who testified that Williams put his hand on the boy's penis, Williams responded:

"He's a bare-faced liar." He also denied holding hands with Cater.

Binder elicited that he had spent less than a thousand dollars in 1979 on auditioning fees and $15-20,000 dollars on master recordings – that his parents provided the money.

Williams went on to deny anything the State's witnesses said that may make him look bad. He also described his bio, which I had used about his NASCAR racing and flying a jet plane, as being 'hype,' but he still claimed he had ridden in a jet plane three times – holding the controls once – though he was legally blind according to his eye-doctor's testimony.

He denied the killings. He said that when the FBI stopped him on May 22, 1981, the "nylon cord rope" they claimed was in his vehicle was actually a piece of wire which was laying on the side of the road on I-285. He testified:

"An FBI Agent and Officer Holden noticed it. I told them after I found out why they stopped me, I said, look, you found that thing laying there the same time I did, so don't try to put that thing on me."

Binder asked him: "I want you to tell this jury what in blazes you were doing on the Jackson Parkway Bridge on the night of May 21 . . . ?"

Williams: "To be honest with you, trying to get to the other side of the bridge so I could get home."

Williams denied stopping on the bridge, saying that he was going 20 – 35 miles per hour – he didn't know.

Binder took Williams through the events of May 20-21. Williams testified that on the night of May 19 he did some "pictures" for a Joe Graham and had to re-do them on the morning of May 20. He was up until 10:00 a.m., was tired and hadn't eaten anything, he said. He went to Ben Hill that p.m. to get his car worked on, but he couldn't find Thomas Jones. He went home. On May 21, he was "pretty sick" in bed most of the afternoon; his parents had gone somewhere. He woke up to the telephone ringing. "Some young lady named Cheryl Johnson called me. I did not call her. She called me."

Binder: "Do you remember what that lady said to you, if anything."

Williams: "Yes, she stated that she had called the previous day, which had been May the 20th, and left a message with a lady . . . and she said that she was interested in trying to set up an interview for Friday morning, May the 22nd, and that was what the gist of our conversation was about."

"What was she wanting from you, Wayne?"

"She wanted me to interview her because she had found one of the fliers at a store. And she wanted to get an interview because we were having auditions that Saturday, May the 23rd , and she wanted to attend."

"And what did you tell her, if anything?"

"Well, I asked her some questions about her background. And she mentioned she had a sister or cousin – I don't remember which one – named Barbara that wanted to come. So we talked a little bit about her background and **she set an appointment up for me to see her on the 22nd before 8:30 in the morning.**"

"All right. Now, did she tell you where she lived?"

"**Well, she was vague on that. She mentioned that she was visiting Atlanta and staying with a friend, and she said she wasn't sure of the address. She thought it was Spanish Trace Apartments.**"

After the conversation, Williams testified, he went back to sleep, later to be awakened by his father at 10:00 p.m. He made several telephone calls. He then tells the story of his leaving home about 1:00 a.m., May 22 to pick up his tape recorder from "Gino" at the club. He went to the Sans Souci, walked into the club, and asked 'some girl' at the door if Gino was there.

Being told "Gino was busy," Williams testified he then left. He went toward the Smyrna area to find Cheryl's address for an appointment he claims was for ". . . eight or eight-thirty, something like that" and ". . . it's right behind Dobbins Air Force Base up there." He said:

"I tried to find some apartments that had a C-4, I believe it was."

"Did you find one?"

"I found some, but they were not Spanish Trace."

He then left the area for home, crossing Jackson Parkway Bridge. He testified to the events at the river giving varying accounts of many previous discussions on the events of that night. When asked by Binder if he ever turned his station wagon around after crossing the bridge, he replied:

"I did not turn around at that liquor store, the one at the Jackson Parkway Bridge."

He testified he continued down the road to the Starvin Marvin's (1/4- 1/2 mile down the road) and used the telephone; he then went to a dumpster where he retrieved two boxes and then went back across the bridge. No one stopped him until he was pulled over at I-285. He was then questioned and released.

"... Now, Wayne, there's been a lot of talk in this courtroom about throwing garbage from the bridge. Tell this jury whether or not you threw anything off that bridge."

"I did not throw anything off that bridge."

Binder took Williams through the events leading to his arrest, the interviews, and searches. He testified that after having been interviewed by the FBI he went home to a "... whole army of people in the front yard."

Williams denied being at Terry Pue's funeral, being with Jo Jo Bell or telling anyone he knew karate, as well as other statements attributed to other state witnesses of his being with various victims. As to the testimony of Mrs. Sharon Blakely, Williams said she was not a stable person; later adding that she has always been a very confused person. She doesn't make sense all the time.

"Did you say anything to her whatsoever about throwing any garbage across, over the bridge or anything?"

"She asked me did I throw any garbage off the bridge. She said, and I quote her here, well, the FBI told me you threw some garbage off. I told her I didn't tell them any such thing." [Interesting, he admits a reference to garbage. The FBI did not use that word – they used "body]."

When asked if he led Eustis Blakely to believe he could fly an F-4 (jet fighter plane), Williams responded: "I only told him I had taken a courtesy demonstration ride in an F-4." Williams denied referring to poor black children as "street gruncheons."

Lastly, Binder asked Williams:

"Wayne, you've already told this jury that you are innocent of what you are charged with. Before I turn you over to the prosecution for cross-examination, is there any other thing that I haven't asked you that you want to say to this jury?"

"It's just I know I haven't done anything wrong. That's all."

With that, Williams has, under oath, contradicted or denied the incriminating testimony of most of the witnesses the State has put on the stand. The jury should hopefully be able to easily decide the truth of the matter. I will help the jury in this respect.

The Cross-Examination of Williams -

I asked him what "Gemini," the name of his group, meant to him. He replied it simply meant that each member of the group had two different talents. He volunteered "it had nothing to do with the astrological sign."

I asked if it meant dual or twins or two, for example, as in dual personalities, "good and bad," "Jekyll and Hyde" which he denied (but to which a couple of women on the jury nodded affirmatively).

I questioned him about his telling people that he flew F-4 jet fighters and was a semi-pro race car driver with a NASCAR track rating; was it merely "hype" or "an out and out lie?" He again put his spin on it, though the events were clearly referenced in his lengthy bio. I went back over some of the strong state witnesses who testified about his knowing karate, including his own witness and friend, Mr. Knox; but he still denied any knowledge of karate. I asked him whether he became more independent from grade school to high school and more assertive. He replied he had been assertive all his life. He admitted that he and his parents began to have "minor disagreements" and arguments over the car.

"Did your relationship with your father get much worse during that period?"

"No, it didn't, he replied.

"Do you remember an interview with "US" Magazine while you were out there in the jail?"

"Vaguely, I do."

"Do you remember making the statement to a reporter with "Us" Magazine which later was published, quote, my father and I had disagreements over how much trust he put in me. We had plenty of arguments over the car. I don't drink, but one weekend, I got plenty wasted, plenty, drunk, and my relationship with my father got much worse?"

Williams denied I was quoting correctly, but when given the article, he read it into the record exactly as I had – word for word. I pushed him into admitting that his parents were pressing him to get an education. Williams had also made the statement in the interview that "one thing I've learned is to change with the situation."

Regarding his talent scout business, I elicited that he got his fliers out soliciting young people, after which he did a phone screening. If he decides it's worth his time, he will have the person come to the studio for an audition. He explained it cost from $40 to $200 an hour to do a demo but then said that only those in his group or artists he was working with got to do a demo. I had him identify his signature on the letter. We sparred over a period of time about the contents of his flyer and the representations he made wherein he referred to his company as a "management directional guidance firm for professional entertainers" which he said were members of his group, Gemini. He testified he produced a tune and co-wrote it by the name of "Ain't it a Shame," for which he received money and royalties, but he could produce no evidence of such monies received. I referred him to his letter where he claims to have been involved in album production for a major record label, with one of the producers being Wade Marcus. Although Wade Marcus had denied any such involvement, Williams still claimed that they had a verbal agreement to co-produce the group. I then quoted the letter as saying "Our function is to take the raw talent and develop it into a polished professional unit. We train the youngsters in vocal, instrumental techniques, stage presence, business practices, and character personality improvement." I then asked him who was trained in vocal and instrumental techniques to which he named some members of his group.

"Are you a music teacher?"

"No."

"Who has taught them?"

"I have." [Williams had no training or talent for music].

"Then you go on to indicate to the parents and students, there is no cost to the student or parent at any time, even if they are selected to fill a position, and all items and instructions are provided to properly prepare the person." Is that correct?"

"Yes, it is."

"You foot the bill on everything?"

"Yes."

"All right. Now, would it surprise you to know that Wade Marcus has failed to corroborate your statement that he has any business dealings or any guarantees or any verbal contracts whatever with you?"

"It wouldn't surprise me, no."

"Is that another one of your hypes?"

"No sir."

"Who paid for your costs of transportation, your automobile, your gasoline, your automobile upkeep, and all of your living expenses during this period that you were involved in the talent business?"

"Well, I did, along with my family."

"Did you ever receive any reimbursement from any of the people that you dealt with in the business, any reimbursement by virtue of money that they paid to you or that you received as a result of training them?"

"For the auditions, no."

From other short-term temporary work, he claimed he received a few hundred dollars from several sources for which he had no proof.

The Court recessed the examination of this witness on Tuesday, February 23, 1982, day two of his testimony, for lunch. We continued after lunch.

I questioned Williams about his pamphlet soliciting youngsters between 11 and 21 years old; yet he claims he was going to interview the mysterious Cheryl after he had talked to her on the phone and had determined from the conversation that she was in her late twenties or thirties – yet he still wanted to talk to her?

"Yes, because I had not determined her age from the phone."

"But in your own mind, you determined her to be in her late twenties or thirties?"

"That's correct."

"And it would have been simple to ask her, how old are you, on the phone, wouldn't it?"

"It would have been."

I kept after him on details about his testimony and events for which he always had an answer, ever changing, but seeming to adjust his answers as he went along with prior statements he had made.

I referred him to his testimony about the morning of May 22, 1981, wherein he said that after he left the bridge that a helicopter was flying 'up and down the river.'

"And yet in your testimony you say that it was foggy and dark?"

"It was."

"Well, what was he doing, trying to commit suicide?"

"You'd have to ask him. I don't know."

"Do you know Willie Lee Perryman, Jr.?"

"I sure do."

"You know, don't you, that Willie Lee Perryman lives on Winthrop Drive in Decatur?"

"I've never been to his house."

"That is right across the street from where William Barrett's body was found; you know that, don't you?"

"I'm not familiar with that location."

"You know Jimmy Howard, as I said earlier, lived on Niskey Lake Road?"

"Uh-Huh (positive)."

"Where Alfred Evans' body was found; do you know that?"

"I didn't make the association, no."

I questioned Williams about the many fires at which he appeared and took pictures.

"And did you ever see a fireman carry someone out or carry someone who was injured?"

"It's been so many fires, I could have. I can't say for sure."

"Then you, I gather, you know what a fireman's carry is, do you not?"

He denied knowing, but the jury would understand that injured or dead bodies are often carried by firemen, police, and especially by soldiers.

"You chew bubble gum?"

"Very seldom."

"Swell? How about Swell?"

"Sure, I think I've had some Swell."

[The search of his home revealed a bunch of Swell bubble gum wrappers in the garbage can].

"You've heard the testimony involved where two of the victims in these cases had bubble gum in their bodies, have you not?" [Payne had gum in his teeth, and Middlebrooks had gum in his stomach].

"Sure, I have."

[It may not appear to be significant, but when two of twelve victims had gum in their bodies at autopsy (a high percentage of dead bodies – killed while chewing gum) it gives you something to think about].

"...people thought you were the police on occasion, didn't they?"

"I'm sure people think a lot of things."

"Yes sir. Even Gino Jordan, he's a friend of yours, isn't he?"

"Yes, he is."

"He testified he thought you were in police work, didn't he?"

"Yeah, I heard him say that."

"And you know Willie Hunter lives three blocks from where Larry Rogers' body was found, don't you?"

"Sir, that thought has not crossed my mind until you mentioned it."

"Is that right? Now, you carried a street guide in your car, you indicated earlier, when you were out in Cobb County?"

"Yes."

"The thought never struck your mind to try to look up this address that you were out in the middle of the morning looking for, did it?"

"I had looked up the address before I left home."

"And did you find it?"

"I found a 2300 Benson Pool and apartment C-4. . . Centerview Apartments." [Earlier, he said Spanish Trace apartments].

"Well, did you go to those apartments?"

"I did."

"Did you find Cheryl at those apartments?"

"No, and I wasn't looking for her to be honest with you."

"The fact of the matter is, if you'd just talked to the woman on the phone, you would have found out all you wanted to know, wouldn't you?"

"Wrong."

"The fact of the matter is you never talked to her, did you?"

"Wrong."

[I know he will continue to stick to his story; but when I go over it, he confirms what everybody now knows – it's a concocted reason for his being where he was].

"You indicated earlier you had flown in an F-4. When was that?"

"Gosh, March? I don't remember the exact date of '77."

"March of '77?"

"That's correct."

"Where?"

"It was on a demonstration ride."

"Where?"

"It crossed several states, Georgia, Alabama, and Tennessee."

"And where did you get in the F-4?"

"Dobbins." [Dobbins Air Force Base].

"Who was in there with you?"

"Sir, I'm not going to state that because – I'll tell you why. A particular person is a Captain in the Air Force. He's black. What he did, it was against regulations. You may do what you wish, but I am not going to get him in trouble."

"Who was the pilot?"

"I'm not going to say."

"There was no pilot?"

He still refused to answer; and after considering asking the Court to hold him in contempt, I decided to move on since it would be of no consequence. [No pilot in his right mind would take a chance of losing his pilot's license and being disciplined for such a violation as allowing someone like Williams in a jet fighter plane. The jury would know this].

"You've never been in the Air Force, have you?"

"No sir."

We continued to spar over whether he would have been able to get into an F-4 two-seater jet fighter plane, since he could not meet the strict requirements including testing in a high altitude chamber.

"How much money did you make in the last year or two from your group? I believe you said earlier you haven't made anything from Gemini; is that right?"

"That's correct."

I then referred him to his sworn testimony at his bond hearing on July 14, 1981, where he testified, regarding the Gemini project, saying that he had made "maybe about ten to twelve thousand in the past year or year and a half, has come from that" (meaning the Gemini project).

"And then you were asked, what is the Gemini Project? Your answer: It's a project that we presented to Motown and Capitol Records."

"That's correct."

"They know nothing about it, Mr. Williams."

Again, I returned to his being in Cobb County in the wee hours looking for an address which didn't exist.

"Where did you go when you got up there? Who did you see if anybody?"

"I didn't go looking for anybody. I went to find an address."

"You didn't stop and inquire of anybody, did you?"

"Me being in Cobb County at that time of morning? No."

"Why?" I inquired.

"Sir, they got Ku Klux Klan up there."

"Well, if you are so afraid of the Ku Klux Klan, why did you go up there at three o'clock in the morning?"

"I didn't say I was horrified. What I meant was I wasn't about to get out of that car." [But, he had an appointment – supposedly – to return in the daytime to do an interview].

I continued to do battle with Williams on his different versions of his calling the telephone number he claims Cheryl gave him at different locations, when in fact the number was a recording.

After crossing the bridge he insists he went to Starvin Marvin's store. He again tried calling the number when he got a 'disconnected,' and another 'somebody' answered the phone and said, 'she ain't here; or, there is nobody here, or something,' and slammed down the phone. He now says he made three calls from this location.

Williams takes issue with the statements by the FBI agents and witnesses testifying about his activities at the bridge earlier that night and the day before. He claimed other cars were on the bridge when he was. He admitted his German shepherd dog rode in the station wagon.

"What about the gloves and the flashlight on the front seat in the car? Were those yours?"

"There was a flashlight. I think the gloves were in the glove compartment." [Fibers from the glove (seized at the time of the vehicle search days later) matched fibers on some of the victims].

"What about the nylon cord, twenty-four inches, that was found on the hump in the rear floor?"

"There was a nylon cord at the scene found, but it was not found in my automobile," Williams testified.

"Now, I'm not referring to the wire on the side of the road. I'm referring to the testimony about the nylon cord in your car."

Williams: "The only nylon cord was against the wire on the side of the road. There was none in the car."

[Williams has again changed his testimony. Obviously, he did not remember what he said earlier in his testimony on direct when Binder asked him about the FBI testimony that there was a nylon cord on the rear floor of his car. He told Binder that the cord was actually a wire he first noticed on the roadway, and he said he told the FBI 'not to try to put that on him. Now, he's saying both the wire and cord existed].

I returned to his trying to find Cheryl's address in Cobb County. Williams, when asked why he didn't knock on the door of the apartment number he had been given, explained that he wouldn't want to wake people up at 3:00 a.m.; but when asked if calling her as he claimed he did several times from the bridge area would not wake her up, he testified: "So I figured if I called her about 3:00 to get it straight and if the appointment was as important as she claimed it was to her, she would have wanted to take that phone call."

". . . If it was as important as it was made to you to appear, she would have given you the right number, wouldn't she?"

"Not necessarily."

"And address?"

"Not necessarily."

"Well, according to your version, she called your mother first ,and then she called you again, she made two telephone calls; right?"

"There are people who call more than that and given (sic) false information."

"And it must have been important to her, then?"

"I can't say what was in her mind."

[He's slick as an eel to pin down; but his answers are not necessarily as important as the questions, and how he contradicts himself. The jury is listening and watching him].

After Williams was questioned at the river, he testified he noticed a helicopter following him as he returned to the Sans Souci club and then home.

"Even though you'd been questioned about the murders, you still didn't go straight home, and even though you were scared as you put it?"

"Well, I wasn't questioned about the murders. To be honest with you, I just thought that at the time they thought that I was a suspect or something and they just did that. . . ."

"Well, they emphatically accused you of throwing a body in the river, didn't they?"

"One person did. . . ."

"Yes sir. Wasn't that serious to you at that point?"

"Yeah, it was serious. But I didn't throw no body in the river, so it didn't bother me."

"Didn't you consider this a challenge, really; as your mother put it, you love a challenge?"

Hours passed with Williams still challenging me with questions of his own at times.

". . . Did you tell them (FBI) that you were a student at Georgia State University as a sophomore?"

"No."

"Enrolled in psychology?"

"No. They asked had I taken a psychology course. I told them yes."

"Did you tell him that it wasn't unusual to schedule an appointment at 7:00 a.m. with young girls?"

"I told him a number of things in regard to the polygraph examination." [Williams brought up the polygraph, not the State – so there was no objection].

The cross-examination was beginning to take its toll on Williams, who had stood up well on the first day but was now beginning to be argumentative and antsy with having me come back over matters which I had touched on before – but had not completed. Binder at times would come to his aid by objecting, but he would be reminded by the judge that opposing counsel has the right to a thorough and sifting cross-examination. My further examination would steer away from prior questions but would be an extension of the former examination. If he was testifying from memory as to truthful events, he should have no problem in reciting the truth from time to time – but lies will trip you up.

I referred Williams to his press conference before arrest wherein he talked about going out to Cobb County to find the young lady. At that time he indicated he had never talked to Cheryl; he had called the number several times but got no answer – and that one of his workers had taken the call. When I asked him who was his worker taking the call, he said "my mother."

In his news conference, Williams had said "the appointment was set for Friday morning. Her audition was set for 3:00 o'clock Saturday afternoon."

"And let me ask you this, Mr. Williams. If you had never interviewed the lady, (as he claimed in his news conference) you were trying to find her to interview her, why was there an audition already set for 3:00 Saturday afternoon?" [I wondered how he would get out of this one].

Williams: "Again, if she had to work a twelve-hour shift, common sense would dictate that I would not have another chance to get back in contact with her. So set the audition time while you have the opportunity, just in case you did make the interview."

Mallard: "In other words, you are saying in your news conference that you had an appointment Friday morning and also you had already set an audition for Saturday p.m., 3:00?"

"Yes."

"Without ever having seen her?"

"I think I testified earlier that with some of the people, some of the interviews were not in person, they were done over the phone."

"And it's your testimony without having even a correct phone number, that you already set an audition for Saturday?"

"Yes. I've done that on many occasions."

[I like to shift gears suddenly].

"Do you remember the youngster that testified you picked him up on promises of work, gave him money and fondled him?"

"I remember the testimony."

"And do you deny that?"

"Yes, I do."

"Did you ask him if he played an instrument?"

"Sir, I have never seen him before. What he came in here and said in Court was a lie."

"And Andrew Hayes, the other youngster who testified you used to pick him up at the Game Room in West End along with Tim Hill ... and rode around; did you or didn't you?"

"No."

"And did you take him to the Omni, the Rialto, the Baronet and the Coronet theaters?"

"Sir, I just told you I don't know Andrew Hayes."

I questioned Williams about the reference by Mrs. Blakely to throwing trash off the bridge, which he denied saying on direct.

"Did she ask you what you were doing on the bridge?"

"No, she asked me was I on the bridge."

"Did you tell her that you threw some trash off the bridge, words to that effect?"

"I told her no such thing."

"Did you also tell your daddy when you got home that morning that you threw trash off the bridge?"

"I did not." [We will put up a rebuttal witness to this denial].

"You remember Paris Goodson, do you not?"

"I know Paris."

". . . Wasn't he a lead singer or something in Nationwide (Band)?"

"I just heard from somebody else. I don't know firsthand."

I inquired if he tried to entice him away from the band and if he called Peter Butts with Nationwide about doing just that.

"No. I think Peter called me when I was at a friend's house, Ricky Carter, and we had a brief conversation, and I told Peter what I thought about him."

"What did you think about him?"

"I told him he was a drop shot."

"A drop shot? What is a drop shot?"

"A drop shot to me is a word that can fit anybody. It's just a person who is a drop shot." "I mean, it's not, you know, anything putting somebody down. It's just like you tell somebody, you know, oh, shut up, you stupid or something. It's just a word you use in conversation."

"Well, isn't it putting somebody down?"

"It may be to you, but it wasn't to me."

[He's evading the true import of the term, but I don't know what it means – but maybe I'll try again later]

"Did you ever threaten your father?"

"No."

"Did you ever warn him not to come home tonight?"

"No."

"You never assaulted him, choked him?"

"As big as my daddy is? No."

"You indicated you talked to Wade Marcus, the producer out on the West Coast. When was the last time you talked to him?"

"Oh, goodness, May of '81, I think."

"Do you recall him discussing with you the idea of him sending money to the Missing and Murdered Children Fund?"

"He didn't say he was going to send money. He simply asked me what was that all about, and we had a brief discussion about it."

"I ask you, Mr. Williams, if it's not true that you told Wade Marcus in so many words, don't bother, they're nothing but street prostitutes?"

Williams denied saying that, but said he told Marcus that "some of the killings look like they may be connected, some of them may not be connected, and some of them may just be street crimes. And that is what I told him."

"Do you know where the South River is in DeKalb County?"

"No."

"And I ask you whether or not you were on the South River Bridge North of Waldrop Road in early March, 1981, looking down into the water?"

"I don't know where the South River is, and I don't even think I know where Waldrop Road is."

"Would you tell us what "twinkie" means?"

"A twinkie to me is a sissy."

"How did you get the scratches, Mr. Williams?"

"Which scratches now? There are a couple of different sets of scratches and scrapes."

"Now, you heard about four witnesses testify that you had scratches on either both arms, on one arm, or arm and face."

"My face has never had any scratches on it."

"How did you get them?"

"I got one when I was cooking in the kitchen and got some grease burns, and some I got when I fell when I was trying to get to the telephone."

"Are you saying grease burns give you scratches?"

"Sir, I have a scratch on me that was made two days ago and it's still here. I have very sensitive skin, and it will stay on me. A grease burn gives me a spot, and some of these are spots on my arm."

". . . You heard these witnesses testify it looks like scratches down your arms, the top of your arms. Did you have those type scratches or not?"

"No, and I challenge you to find them with the jury."

". . . My question is did any of those victims scratch you as you were choking the life out of them?"

"Absolutely not."

I now was in his face – up close – looking him directly in the eyes, not giving him time to think of an answer, and as I invaded his territory:

"Isn't it true that while you were choking them to death, with the last breath, they were scratching your arms and face?"

"No."

"Did you experience any panic at any point there?"

"During what?"

"At any point during the time that you were killing these victims?"

"Sir, I haven't killed anybody."

"Isn't it true that you killed them?"

"Sir, I'm about as guilty as you are. Now, if you killed them that would make me guilty. So if you didn't kill them, that means I'm not guilty."

". . . You lived in Atlanta during all of this time of the missing and murdered children, have you not?"

"Yes, I have."

"And no doubt you've thought about it?"

"Sure."

"And you've wondered what kind of person would do such a thing, haven't you?"

"Sure."

"And you agree with me that there are certain things you'd have to look at to determine what kind of person would do such a thing?"

"Maybe to a degree."

"Wouldn't you agree that the person who was doing all these killings would have — would more than likely be a literate person?"

"Not necessarily."

"Well, would you agree that it would be a person who was media conscious?"

"I don't know." [Again, his answers are not as important as the questions. The jury understands].

Al Binder makes his objection to getting into this area. Due to the lateness of the hour, the Judge recesses the trial for the day. **This completes the second day of Williams on the stand.**

Williams had begun to be angry and surly at times – no doubt he was happy the day was ending; perhaps he believed this to be the last part of my cross examination. He would not have a good night at the jail.

Williams vs. Mallard: A test of endurance –

Atlanta Journal staff writers David Hilder and Hyde Post by-lined it as **Williams vs. Mallard: A test of endurance,** as ". . . the battle between the two had spectators and reporters jockeying all afternoon for better seats" and noting that "jurors took notes furiously at the outset and then all but stopped, caught up in watching the exchanges."

The Atlanta Constitution by staff writer Kevin Sack observed that "Mallard sparred with Williams for more than three hours, brushing the defendant with short jabs before landing his strongest punches near day's end." Sack's observation was as I had intended: "Mallard planted a crucial seed in the jurors' minds. They will have to choose – in some matters, at least – between believing a single individual, Williams, or a string of other witnesses who testified against him" and "like most experienced trial lawyers, Mallard showed Tuesday that he often can make a more powerful point with a question than with an answer." Sack evaluated my style as "Mallard's questioning took on a cyclical rhythm. He seemed to lull Williams and the spectators with lengthy, often repetitive exchanges about fine details, then would suddenly splash the courtroom

with antagonistic accusations." Sack quoted one of my associates as
saying that I was "pulling the hammer back. And eventually, it's going
to fall." Attorney Scott Childress is further quoted as saying that "he's
a prosecutor who will seize upon the right moment to take advantage
of (the testimony); he has an innate ability to judge the jury and know
what's important to them."

A Carnival-Like Atmosphere –

The trial of the century had been drawing crowds from the beginning with people lining up at the courthouse early to get a seat in a
courtroom limited to a capacity of about 85. The Atlanta Constitution
by Bob Dart noted that this was the biggest crowd since the trial started
with Williams testifying. It was reported that 400 or so people were in
line for admission to the elevator inside; some waited in line all morning
for a seat that afternoon.

Crowds were increasing in and around the courthouse with Williams
on the stand. It was observed that people were lining up as early as 4:00
a.m. on the courthouse steps and down the street. I recall huge lines
as I would arrive at the courthouse around 7:00 a.m. with TV cameras
and reporters all over the place. I had to push through the gauntlet to
reach the elevators. Some 'victim mothers' were questioned about their
views by the press. Some believed Williams was guilty, and others had
aligned themselves with the Williams' family and lawyers and believed
he was innocent.

*With armed deputies on the roof of the courthouse and with throngs
of people trying to push themselves inside with cameras everywhere, the
scene was chaotic.*

Reporter Bob Dart's by-line *"Circus of Humanity Surrounded
Williams Trial"* reported on March 1, 1982 pretty much told the
story. Reportedly, one woman arrived from St. Petersburg, Florida by
Trailways Bus saying God had guided her on the 12-hour ride, saying
"I'm on a mission. . . This is what the Lord chose me to do" and that
"I came up here last year to tell the people that adults were going to
start getting killed after the children. Now I'm warning: Watch out
for the girls." And another, a defense private detective working without pay from Seattle who specializes in cult killings and a "born-again

Christian," had talked to the Prophetess and responded that she may be onto something. Dart identified "private eyes and prophetesses, cops and commies, suburban housewives and big-time journalists, the curious and the curiosites – they all found their way to the fourth floor of the Fulton County Courthouse during the nine-week-long murder trial … It was a circus of humanity." A young woman was seen selling the communist newspaper, Revolutionary Worker, outside the building; she said the trial had provided her a "helluva market". . . "I already sold a dozen copies," it was reported.

Dart further reported that down the hall from the courtroom was the press viewing room, where the proceedings were watched by the overflow crowd of reporters and technicians, and that during a conference at the bench by attorneys and the judge, an attractive young woman attorney assisting the Court climbed onto the witness chair to listen as one pressroom TV screen was suddenly filled with a close-up of her shapely posterior. "For the next several minutes – unbeknown to her – every twitch by the lady lawyer drew applause from appreciative reporters in the TV room." Dart reported that in Another TV room there was much activity, including the order of green "T-shirts" that said **"Woven With Fibers From The Wayne Williams Trial."**

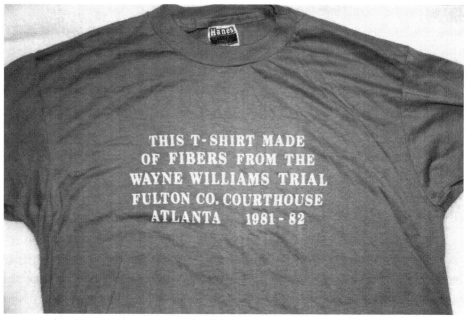

T-shirt photo

Dart further observed that deputies and detectives were everywhere; they were seen conversing on two-way radios and receiving messages through a single earplug and 'sending' over transmitters on their wrists. Private eyes working for the Defense, to show their technological sleuthing superiority, went to Radio Shack and bought earplugs connecting them to their empty shirt pockets; they were seen talking through their wristwatches to imaginary cohorts as they paraded by law officers whispering up their sleeves.

Cross-Examination resumes on Wednesday morning, February 24, 1982.

I immediately started testing Williams' memory about details of his calling for Slaton to visit him at the jail, but he claimed a fuzzy memory. I reminded him that yesterday he seemed to have a memory for details going back years ago. Did he decide overnight to use a different strategy in responding to my questions?

"Did you ever tell him (Slaton) in that whole interview that you talked to Cheryl Johnson, yes or no?"

"That cannot be answered yes or no."

"You did not, did you?"

"I just said it couldn't be answered yes or no."

"You also denied to Special Agent Rackleff of the FBI, when he talked to you on June 3 at the FBI headquarters, that you ever talked to Cheryl Johnson, did you not?"

"That's a lie."

". . . If you wanted to take the I-285/I-20 route home, why not after using the telephone at the Racetrac right at 285, why not get on 285 there rather than coming South toward the bridge?"

"Man, look, what in the world has that got to do with killing somebody?"

The Court: "Mr. Williams, answer the question."

The witness: "Sir, I can't answer the question. I explained to this gentleman all day yesterday, we've been over this question time and time again. Now, I've been through a lot and I'm tired and I'm trying to do the best I can to answer this question. He keeps asking the same thing." The question is did I kill anybody, and I done told this man I haven't.'"

[Now we know what we later learned – that Williams did have a bad night at the jail, and that Binder had visited him last night. Williams started off the morning like a 'bull out of the chute;' he was on the attack].

Judge Cooper called for Binder and me to approach the bench, where the Judge suggested that Binder needed to confer with his client; however, I pressed the judge that my cross-examination should not be interrupted – that it just gives Williams a chance to recover. Binder briefly consoled Williams to get him under control, and we continued.

The profiler, John Douglas, was right in saying Williams would eventually lose his cool. By now, Williams was combative, argumentative, and he clearly indicated a different side of Wayne Williams.

I continued to pepper Williams with contradictions. He was now getting personal with me by suggesting that I probably programmed witnesses.

"And have you done any programming since June of last year," I inquired.

"Tried my best not to."

"I see. All of this testimony on direct by you just came out spontaneously," I asked.

"What has that got to do with what you're asking me?" Williams asked.

"I'm asking you if you were programmed?"

"No. You want the real Wayne Williams? You got him right here."

[Yes. I believe the jury understands it also. I can wind up the cross real soon].

I asked Williams if he had used the 'slapjack' the FBI recovered from his home to "whop somebody up back of the head?" He denied it. [Just another opportunity to remind the jury of the weapon found in the attic].

". . . Mr. Williams, isn't it true that you read something in the news-papers about a false report of a body being dumped on Sigman Road in Rockdale County a day or two before Pue's body was actually left there by you?"

". . . No is the answer to that."

". . . Did you again respond to some publicity in DeKalb County that they hadn't had any bodies dumped out there and dropped Baltazar's body at Corporate Square. Yes or No?"

"Sir, I told you in the beginning, I've not known any of these vic-tims, and that is all there is to it."

"And isn't it true that you did read about that prominent evidence (fibers and hair) in the newspapers of this county, and as a result, started stripping the bodies and throwing them in the rivers?"

"No huh-uh."

"Well, if you are not concerned about the evidence from the bod-ies (as he claimed), did you have an occasion to examine some dog hairs?"

"Later on I did."

"Where was that?"

"That was after June the 3rd, I think in the presence of my Attorney, Ms. Welcome."

"And where did that take place?"

"I think it took place in my house where we had a microscope."

"What hair did you compare?"

"I compared my dog hair with some other dog hair that was from neighbor's dogs next door."

"And you commented on that in your interview with Us magazine?"

"I sure did."

When asked about the FBI interview, Williams claimed they used a deceptive manner. I then pointed out that all his prior testimony, news conference, and waivers of counsel were to the contrary. Williams then pointed out two agents in the courtroom, saying "I signed it for them, and I'm saying both of these two gentlemen right there was two of the main 'goons' down there pushing it" (as he pointed to two FBI agents behind me).

I challenged Williams that he was getting the attention of a lifetime, referring him to the time he was at FBI headquarters and to his many interviews including when he summoned the District Attorney to come to the jail to see him.

"Isn't it a challenge with you?"

"Man, this ain't no challenge right here."

"Isn't it true that every chance you've got to talk, you've done it?"

"Wrong."

"Every agent that wanted to talk to you, you were willing, weren't you?"

"No."

"And to the extent of calling a press conference after you got home?"

I would continue this theme by referring him to the many contacts he and his family had with the media for interviews.

". . . And you've had all kinds of conference hookups through your family with the news media and other people, have you not, while in jail?"

"So what?"

"Well, sir, I'm under the impression you didn't want to talk to the news people about it."

"I only talked to one person in the media in that news conference thing, and that was Ron Sailor."

"The fact of the matter is you've been eating up all the publicity, worldwide publicity, haven't you?"

"No, I haven't. . . . ."

"You feel you received a great deal of attention and recognition through your achievement in grade school?"

"Some."

"Now since graduating from high school, do you feel you've failed to receive that type of recognition that you earlier had in life?"

"I wouldn't say I had any recognition. . . ."

I went on to question him as to whether he felt he was destined for great things. . . after the radio station, and whether he needed the attention and publicity, which he denied.

"Isn't it true that you have been gaining publicity from the first day you became a suspect?"

"Yes, it's true, but I didn't want it."

"Then why did you hold a press conference on June 4?"

"Sir, I have answered that question previously."

". . . And isn't it true that you've had all kinds of interviews and you contacted the press yourself on several occasions?"

"That's a bare face lie."   [The evidence was otherwise].

". . . Mr. Williams: Did you tell Dennis Bentley when the police were tailing you – according to his testimony – he was with you after you were under surveillance in your car, and that you stated, they couldn't catch you, that you wrote the book on it. Did you say that?"

"No, I didn't say nothing like that."

I pointed out that he had 'readily and voluntarily' talked to officers on May 22 at the bridge, again at his home the same morning, later at FBI headquarters, to which he agreed.

Referring him to his presence at FBI headquarters, I questioned him about watching himself on TV while still in the FBI office before leaving the building.

"Isn't it true that this was your center stage, that this was your challenge of your lifetime?"

"You must be a fool."

"Isn't it true that you considered this whole thing a contest between you and the police?"

"No."

"What is your attitude toward the police and law enforcement about it?"

"Today?"

"Well, let's say then?"

"It's basically the same as it is today."

"Isn't it true, a fact that you think and thought then that you could outwit all of your interrogators, the police officers, the FBI, the District Attorney, and everybody?"

"No not at all. I wasn't trying to outwit anybody."

"And as you've stated before in your interview, isn't it true that you felt that it was important for you to be in control of the situation?"

"Sir, you need to read that whole statement in context. . . ."

"Isn't it true that you felt that it was important for you to be in control of the situation?"

"I've just answered that question."

"Isn't it true you also called Inspector Hamrick of the GBI from the jail?"

"Man, what has that got to do with what we're here for?"

"Did you want to challenge him, too?"

"Why don't you answer one of my questions for once?"

"While under surveillance before your arrest, Mr. Williams, did you not drive to Commissioner Brown's house and park in front, blowing your horn?"

"I most definitely did."

"And isn't it a fact that that was done also with Mayor Jackson's house, that you also went by his house?"

"I don't remember going by his house, no."

I then reminded him of his testimony to that effect from his bond hearing before trial.

Now, I would finish it up with a suggestion that Williams' activities as time went by during this two years leading up to his arrest pointed to another on-going motive.

"Mr. Williams, were you playing cat and mouse with the police?"

"I don't have any intention of playing cat and mouse with anybody. It's just that these people have harassed me, you've harassed my parents, friends, and everybody else, trying to put your little two bits worth of mess together, and I'm saying that like anybody else, I got tired of it."

"Can you identify a police car that is not marked?"

"Some."

"Now, when you were put under surveillance, you made them in the first hour or two, didn't you?"

"Sure did."

"And, in fact, in your news conference you bragged about it didn't you?"

"No. I just answered the question. The point was it was the sloppiest surveillance there ever was. Even a two-year-old child could have made them."

"You were proud of that, weren't you?"

"No, I wasn't proud. As a matter of fact, it makes you all look stupid, not me."

"Did you go on to say: Yeah, there were FBI agents that's correct, and I mean, the tail was not obvious?"

"No, the tail was obvious."

"Well, were you proud that you made the FBI in an hour or two?"

"That's even worse than the Atlanta Police if they can't tail somebody."

"Didn't you feel that you were outdoing the police?"

"No, I didn't, because I was not engaged in any type of contest or anything with them. I can't help it because they did a sorry job."

"Well, have you not been comparing yourself with the police, and you do ... feel you outdid them?"

"No. That's something you said. I didn't say that."

I pulled out my shiny copy of the October 13, 1981, "Us" magazine to box him in.

"Well, let me ask you this. In your "Us" magazine interview, do you remember the question asked you: 'You tend to laugh when you talk about the Police.' Do you remember that?"

"I sure did laugh at them, and I called them Keystone Cops because that's just what they acted like."

"Didn't you reply: It doesn't do any good to sit here and cry over it. I would say, if I had to make comparisons, I would compare the FBI to the Keystone Cops, and the Atlanta Police to Car 54, Where Are You."

[The "Keystone Cops" reference is to silent film comedies of the early 1900s featuring bungling incompetent policemen, while "Car 54,

Where Are You" was an American sitcom which ran on NBC during the early 1960s depicting the New York Police as 'falling over themselves,' lost and blundering around].

"And in that interview with. . . Us Magazine you were laughing at the police, weren't you."

A reasonable person could draw the inference that Williams considered himself smarter than the police, FBI, and high officials and put himself in a contest with them as in *Catch Me if you Can.*

I concluded the Cross-examination. Binder got up for re-direct examination. He wanted to leave his client's testimony with the jury by going over some testimony previously covered in a somber, calming manner.

When Binder finished, I got up and went into further cross-examination.

"Have you not been quoted in the New York Times as saying, "I'm a Gemini. By the nature of the very sign I'm born under, I'm no conformist. I'm a very strong-minded person?"

"uh-huh (positive)."

"Do you know Ken Kimbro?"

"Sure do."

"And is it not true that you called Ken Kimbro and his friend Drop Shots?"

"No. I called Kenny Kimbro a Drop Shot."

"And isn't it true that he said that was a derogatory term for kids who live in housing projects?"

"No."

"Isn't that the term that you use it for?"

"No sir. A drop shot can apply to anybody. And to be honest with you, you are a Drop Shot."

[In summary, Williams has called me a "drop-shot" and a "fool" and two FBI agents "goons"].

[Yesterday, he testified that a drop shot was a term he used in conversations to tell someone to 'shut up' and now he's calling me one. However, the only definition I could find in the dictionary was as in racquet games where the ball drops quickly after crossing the net].

"And you consider, do you not, all of the street kids that you referred to and the ones you referred to in your June 4 News Conference, Drop Shots?"

"No. . . ."

I completed my re-cross at this point. Chief Defense Counsel Al Binder announced that the Defense was resting its case at 10:49 a.m., February 24, 1982.

I still believed Williams got his use of the term "Drop Shot" from somewhere – but where, I often wondered. None of us had ever heard the term used.

I would learn the answer a few years later after I was a prosecutor in the adjoining County of Cobb. One of the Assistant Prosecutors there, Chuck Clay, who is a history buff, was reading **The Story of Georgia and The Georgia People [1732 to 1860] by George Gillman Smith, D.D., 2nd ed.,** *Genealogical Publishing Company,* Baltimore, 1968 [originally published circa 1901]. Chuck inquired if Williams had not called me a "Drop Shot." He then showed me a reference to the term at page 350:

> **A large plantation was a little kingdom. The overseer was in charge, a black driver was under him, there were hoe-hands, plowmen, quartermasters, cooks, gardeners, blacksmiths, carpenters, shoe-makers, a midwife, nurses, dairy maids, spinners, weavers, seamstresses, chicken-and turkey-raisers, and even a gang of little negroes, called the 'drop-shot gang,' who carried water and food to the hands in the field."**

Clearly, "drop-shots" in early Georgia history during the slave and plantation days portray "little negroes" in a negative light even in relation to other slaves – on the bottom rung in the hierarchy and as only worthy of carrying water to other slaves in the field – a lower class of slaves.

Much evidence was introduced at trial that Williams considered 'poor street kids' as a lower class than he. The District Attorney in final summation compared Williams to others as "Doing away with inferiors," which was a reasonable inference and valid argument though on a smaller scale than Attila the Hun.

At this point in the trial, since the Defense has rested its case, the State gets the opportunity to present 'rebuttal' evidence to the Defense's case – if we have any. Had the Defense put up no evidence, there would be no rebuttal involved.

PART FIVE

The State's Rebuttal

Atlanta Police Sergeant Troy Daily, who was assigned to employment background investigations, was called to the stand by the State.

Prosecutor Speed had the witness go through the process of investigating applicants for employment. The witness explained that the application asks for an applicant to give their full employment history, starting with their last first, then going back to list each employment they've ever had.

The witness was asked about the file of Kenneth Lawson (the police recruit who resigned under threat of termination and went over to the defense side and testified). Sgt. Daily testified he received information that Lawson had been employed by four (4) other police agencies but was not forthcoming in his (Lawson's) application for the Atlanta Police job. At this point, Binder objected as to hearsay.

A lengthy argument was heard by the Court out of the presence of the jury as to whether the testimony of the officer should come in under an exception to the hearsay rule to explain the conduct of the officer under a cited provision of law. Lawson had written a letter requesting reinstatement, and the follow-up investigation was the result of such action. Speed and Binder finally agreed to a stipulation that the substance of Sgt. Daily's testimony would be read to the jury, in lieu of his in-person testimony as follows:

That if Sergeant Troy Daily of the Atlanta Police Department were to continue testifying in the case, that he would testify that based on information that he had received, he completed a memorandum to be made a permanent part of former officer Lawson's personnel file, that the basis of that action was information that Sergeant Daily received stating the following:

That Officer Lawson had omitted certain information from his application, that information being that he was employed by the Galveston County Sheriff's Office during the period June 17 through October 30, 1979, from which he was terminated; additionally, that he was employed by the Texas City Police Department, Texas, during the period December 31, 1979, through January 30, 1980, from which he was terminated; that, in addition, he had been employed by the Douglasville, Georgia, Police Department during the period November 3, 1976, through March 11, 1977, from which he had been terminated; that he was also employed at the Douglas County, Georgia, Sheriff's Office for one day on May 13, 1977, from which he resigned. The above said information was not a part of his application to the Atlanta Police Department.

Additionally, Sergeant Daily would testify that included within former Recruit Lawson's personnel file are two incident reports from the East Point Georgia Police Department concerning separate domestic disturbances, one report dated June 13, 1981, and the second report dated June 14, 1981."

With that stipulation read to the jury to consider as sworn testimony of Sgt. Daily, the jury will no doubt remember how helpful Lawson was trying to be to the Defense in attacking the state's witnesses. Lawson's prior employment at four different departments for very short periods of time and terminations at three and resignation at one – not counting the Atlanta Police – should be enough for the jury to disregard anything he said on the stand.

Atlanta Police Officer Marion Lee Brooks was next called by Prosecutor Speed. Brooks had been employed for over eight years with the Atlanta Police with two years at the Academy as an instructor. He knew Kenneth Lawson as a recruit of Class 99.

Brooks testified that Recruit Lawson departed the academy on June 17, 1981, and never volunteered any information regarding the incident reported in the East Point Police incident on June 13-14, 1981.

Atlanta Police Officer Carlos Banda next testified. Banda had been with the department for nine years, and his primary function at the Task Force was all incoming communications, whether walk-in visitors, telephone calls, police reports, or letters. He also supervised the recruits who would take the calls and do the reports.

The witness explained that all incoming calls resulted in a 'tip sheet' being filed; any incoming visitor would be interviewed. All information was reviewed by an investigator if relevant – others were put in a basket and reviewed by the witness and another officer. All information was entered into the computer system with a copy to the file.

Officer Banda testified that he checked all the files and records including tip sheets at the Task Force, and that Ms. Nellie Trammell had never contacted the Task Force and had never "hung around the Task Force Office;" the only record was where an officer had gone out and found the witness in late June or July.

Banda was asked if he ever met Ms. Trammell:

"The first contact which I had with Ms. Trammell was here at the trial of Wayne Williams."

"What was the nature of your contact with her at that time?"

"After Miss Trammell testified, as was the procedure, I helped to escort her down to a waiting car which I helped to take her home."

". . . Had you, to your knowledge, ever seen Miss Trammell before that time that you described here in the courthouse, the time of her testimony?"

"No, Sir. The first day I saw Miss Trammell was when we met her at the courthouse."

The witness was then shown State's Exhibit 727, a photograph (No. three) of a woman who had been identified by the defense witness (former recruit Lawson) as the mysterious Nellie Trammell who he claimed frequented the Task Force office. Officer Banda was asked:

"I'm going to ask you to look through there and see if you recognize anyone" (presenting the exhibit with photographs).

"Yes sir."

"And which photograph . . . are you talking about?"

"It's photograph No. 3."

"And how did you happen to recognize that photograph or the person in the photograph?"

"That is Investigator Trimble's mother."

"Sergeant Banda, how do you happen to know Officer Trimble's mother?"

"Investigator Trimble's mother would usually accompany Investigator Trimble home most of the nights. She would come to the Task Force usually between the hours of 3:30 and 6:00 in order to go home with Investigator Trimble."

"Is that the same or a different person from Nellie Trammell?"

"They are two different people."

"Now, Officer Banda, did you know . . . Recruit Ken Lawson?"

"Yes Sir. Ken Lawson worked under me at the Task Force. He worked on the evening watch between 3:00 and 11:00 o'clock."

"All right. Do you recall ever discussing either with Recruit Lawson or in his presence anything about a reward?"

"Yes sir. Mr. Lawson was explained that no person working for the Bureau of Police Services could accept any type of reward in dealing with the Wayne Williams case. That was explained not only to him but every recruit that worked at the Task Force." [This should complete the impeachment of Kenneth Lawson].

Atlanta Police Investigator J.J. Trimble was next called to the stand. She testified she worked at the Task Force office in reviewing the tip sheets. She verified that she had reviewed the tip sheets, and that Nellie Trammell had never made contact with the Task Force office as claimed by Kenneth Lawson.

She further identified the picture which Lawson had identified as Nellie Trammell was actually her (the witness') mother. The witness' mother, Juanita Laster, did come to the Task Force office some evenings to ride home with her from November 1980 through July of 1981. Her mother at the time was attending school at Atlanta Area Tech taking sewing classes; she would bring her sewing basket with her. This occurred

3-4 times a week usually from 3:40 to 3:45 p.m. [Clearly, defense witness Lawson had mis-identified state's witness Nellie Trammell for
Officer Trimble's mother].

On cross-examination, Binder asked:

" . . . And your mother didn't have any visions while she was down
there and report them to any police officers, did she?"

"No."

"And you don't know of anybody that she ever reported visions to,
do you?"

"No."

"Now, how many tip sheets did you go through when you looked for
tip sheets on Nellie Trammell?"

"We have about 9,785 tip sheets."

"And when did you go through them?"

"I went through them this week."

Larry Peterson, the State's expert from the Crime Laboratory, was
recalled in rebuttal.

[Defense fiber expert, Dr. Bresee, earlier testified regarding his comparison of fibers from Mary Welcome's office on the fourteenth floor of
the Bank of the South building to fibers from Williams' home . . . that
they "looked the same." Afterwards, State's expert Peterson obtained a
sample of the fibers from Ms. Welcome's office and did his own comparison, utilizing the same instrumentation he had used for the victim
case examinations.]

"Mr. Peterson, did you have an occasion to examine fibers from the
carpet on the fourteenth floor of the Bank of the South Building in this
City?"

"Yes sir."

"And did you have occasion to compare those fibers with the fibers
from the carpets located in the Williams home on Penelope Road in this
City?"

"Yes sir."

The witness then identified enlargements of photographs of the carpet fibers from each location.

"Mr. Peterson, did you have occasion to make a color comparison between the Williams' carpet and the carpet from Welcome's office...?"

"Yes, I did."

". . . I show you what has been marked as state's exhibit 758 for identification and ask you if you can identify that, sir?"

"Yes sir. This is a curve from a run of the Microspectrophotometer at the Georgia State Crime Laboratory comparing the carpet fibers" (from the Williams home and Welcome's office).

The witness was then brought down before the jury where he showed the jury from exhibit 758 —

"This is a curve representing ten curves which I ran on the microspectrophotometer at the Crime Laboratory. There is five curves of red, five curves in black. The red curves represent five random fibers which I ran on the Microspectrophotometer representing the fibers of Wayne Williams' home. The five curves in black represent five random fibers of the carpet fibers from the fourteenth floor of the Bank of the South Building (indicating)." [The red curve represents the Williams' home fibers; the black curve represents the fibers from Welcome's office/Bank building].

"Now, Mr. Peterson, both of those carpets are the same color, are they not?"

"They are both green. I would not say the same color, no."

"Since they're both green, would you expect there to be some similarity in the sort of curves that the Microspectrophotometer would register for those carpets?"

"Yes. I would say green fibers generally give a fairly similar general curve."

". . . And can you tell us, why it appears that the black curves go higher than the red curves at the end?"

"Well, the way the curves are produced, they reflect the absorption or transmittance of that particular color which is made up of that particular fiber. So the differences in the curves at the end or any other portion of the curve could reflect different dyes that would be present in the fiber."

". . . And based upon the examination you did that's reflected on State's Exhibit 758, what did you conclude as to the comparison of the colors of the carpet in the Williams home with the color of the carpet in the Bank of the South Building?"

"They are, in fact, different colors."

The witness was then asked about a physical comparison of the shapes of the two carpets:

"Mr. Peterson, did you have occasion to compare the cross-sectional shapes of the Williams' carpet and those of the carpet on the Fourteenth Floor of the Bank of the South Building?"

"Yes sir, I did."

Peterson identified state's exhibit 759 and 760 as two photographs which he took reflecting the cross-sectional shapes of the carpeting at the two aforementioned locations. He was then asked to explain any differences he found between the cross-sectional shapes of the two carpets:

"The primary cross-sectional shape present in the Williams' carpeting is that of a single-short-leg fiber. That is, tri-lobal nylon containing two long legs and one short leg." "That composed on the fourteenth floor of the Bank of the South Building that is two short legs and one long leg, that is, two small lobes in the fiber and one long."

The witness was again brought down before the jury box to illustrate the photographs, showing the difference in the cross-sectional shape of the legs (lobes) of the two carpets: Two long and one short legs versus one long and two short legs.

To show there were efforts to find other sources for the trace evidence from the bodies:

"Mr. Peterson, in the course of your investigation, did you have occasion to make any elimination examinations from carpet and fiber samples from the environment of the victims and from public places in Atlanta, such as the Omni and Theaters in the City?"

"Yes, to a great extent, I did."

"Could you tell, please, how many of those you made?"

"I would say approximately 500 fiber samples throughout the course of the investigation, approximately 300 of which were carpet type samples."

". . . And out of that 500 approximately examinations, did you find any items which matched the items from the Williams' environment?"

"None of which I've made associations in this case, no."

The witness was asked to explain the type instruments used in these examinations:

"Well, I would consider them highly sophisticated microscopic equipment. Basically a comparison microscope would cost in the neighborhood of $20,000, a Polarizing Microscope in the neighborhood of $15,000, and the Microspectrophotometer would cost "in the neighborhood of $200,000."

[The defense witness earlier testified he used no such equipment; for his analysis, he used his pocket magnifying glass and only a few minutes of time].

Peterson testified he used such instrumentation because the human eye may not be able to distinguish between certain colors.

Binder on cross-examination:

". . . You know, you're up here to contradict and rebut Doctor Bresee's testimony from Kansas, aren't you?"

"I believe I'm being recalled on an examination of fibers which he had examined, yes."

Binder then asked if Bresee's testimony had been given to him and whether he had read it – he had.

Binder: "You just told this jury that the reason those black lines and those red lines from here to here are all interspersed and mixed up together, just like when you bake a cake, you know, you have to put a little rising in it to make the cake go up. They're all mixed up and that's because – Mr. Miller said that's because of the color; right?"

"The curves reflect the color, yes."

"Now, then he says those black lines went up a little bit and that means now that there's a difference in color, so says Doctor Peterson; right?"

"There are other differences in the curves besides the very end of the curves."

"You didn't answer my question. I said Doctor Peterson says that they're all mixed up and they're all one here, and that's because - - you answered Mr. Miller that's because of color; right?"

"No. I said that the general shape of the curves are very similar because both samples were a green. The curves, in fact, do not match before they get to the very end of the curves."

"But fellow, you look at that and be as honest as you can. That's pretty close, isn't it?"

"In my opinion no, sir."

"They got dissimilar when this little ditty got out of the machine because Doctor Bresee said they were similar, didn't he, and they had to get dissimilar through your mouth, didn't they?"

"No sir. In the comparison on a comparison microscope, the colors are not similar at that point. That is an instrumental readout, if you will, of the colors involved in the two fibers."

Re-Direct by Miller:

"When Professor Bresee was out at the Crime Lab, did he ask to use the Microspectrophotometer to make his color comparison?"

"No sir."

"So he made it with the naked eye, didn't he?"

"I don't know. I would assume so."

Jerry Huth, from the American Plasma Corporation (blood bank), was then called by me to re-enforce the testimony of his co-worker, Ms. Vickie Snipes, who had testified earlier in the trial. The Defense had attacked Ms. Snipes testimony suggesting that Cater perhaps was not there on May 21. Mr. Huth testified he knew Nathaniel Cater as a "plasma donor." He identified the original record for the donor and indicated he was acquainted with Cater. There was a photograph of Cater in the file.

I asked the witness to tell us about the last time Cater was at the blood bank. From the record, he testified on Thursday, May 21, 1981, at which time the witness performed a urinalysis for Cater. The witness said a result of the urinalysis was a "one-plus protein in his urine," meaning he had an excess protein being excreted from his body and was unable to donate on that visit. Cater had last donated on January 30, 1981.

I elicited that Cater had been there on other prior dates and donated. On the last visit, Cater did not sign anything, and on May 19 there was an "x" on the sheet.

Binder accused the witness of misrepresenting and misleading the defense that Cater was in the blood bank on May 21, 1981, comparing a copy of the record furnished to him against the original.

"And that's what you wanted us to believe didn't you?"

"That's a fact that he was there."

"You don't know if Nathaniel Cater was there, you don't have his signature on your piece of paper."

"I know he was there."

Binder: "And the signature on the bottom of this piece of paper wasn't even Nathaniel's name, either, was it? It was one of you folks down there, wasn't it?"

"Yes sir."

"And that's the truth of it, isn't it?"

"(No response)."

On further re-direct by me [with helpful leading questions without objection]:

"Mr. Huth, you were subpoenaed down here, was it a week before last or last week by the Defense?"

"Week before last, I believe."

"With the original file which you have now?"

"Yes sir."

"And that was presented to them (the Defense), was it not?"

"Yes sir."

"And they (the Defense) didn't call you to the stand, did they?"

"No sir."

"They excused you to go home, didn't they?"

"Yes sir."

"And you explained that, what happened then, didn't you?"

"Yes sir."

"Now, take that file back down here (to the jury) and show the jury how you copied the file for the Defense."

"What I did is when they originally came in and asked for the record, I simply folded this over, copied it as such (indicating), giving them a copy of the urinalysis and this block showing the 21st."

"And this block, the urinalysis, relate to that, the 21st?"

"yes."

"And does that indicate the last time he was in there?"

"Yes sir."

"And is that what shows up on this sheet that was presented to them?"

"Yes sir."

"Now, with regard to signing the name, is this name at the bottom of the sheet, is that at the bottom of every sheet?"

"It's not on the bottom of every sheet, but these were new forms that we had just started using that require the name at the bottom."

"Now, could that have been typed down just as well?"

"Yes."

"When does the donor sign the sheet?"

"When he's called up to the screening area and asked these questions." "… [A]nd he'll sign it again when he's paid.…"

"In other words, where it shows donor signature?"

"Yes sir."

Floyd J. Fowler, Jr., employee of the West End News, was called to the stand.

I asked the witness about the type of items they sold: Many things, including magazines, books, and so forth. He said that Wayne Williams frequented the shop and had purchased things, mostly *karate,* electronics, and male nudes magazines. He then identified Williams in the courtroom.

Binder cross-examined the witness extensively as to the number of people he might see – about 200 a day at times; three people worked on a 16-hour shift – the store was open for 16 hours – with the witness and others working single shifts.

Binder attacked the identification of Williams when an officer came to the store, displaying a photo spread and questioning whether the witness could identify anyone.

"How do you know Wayne Williams?"

"From seeing him and him being pointed out by the ownership of the establishment that I was working in."

"Why would they point him out to you?"

"Because he was suspected of shoplifting." [You can't complain when you ask such a general question].

"Really? Did you all arrest him?"

"No sir. But I was told to watch him."

"Did you watch him close?"

"Yes sir."

Wayne Gano who was in the retail carpet business under the company name of Floormaster was called by Prosecutor Speed to the stand. Gano had been in the carpet business a total of about 18 years. The witness identified Southern Prudential Corporation as a carpet business, the owner of which was Lou Speert, for whom the witness had worked.

Gano testified he had been out to the Williams' home recently after Homer Williams had called and asked him to come out and testify that it was our carpets in the Williams' home. He identified Homer Williams (sitting in the courtroom) as the person he met at the Williams' home on Penelope Street "approximately three weeks ago." Gano said his mother accompanied him to the Williams' home where he also saw defense counsel Jim Kitchens. The witness said:

"They asked me to come out and see if it was my carpeting that I put in there."

Question: "Do you recall whether or not you installed the carpet in the Williams' home?"

"Yes, sir, I did."

Without seeing any records, the witness did not know when he installed the carpet but remembers a complaint on the job. The witness was *not* familiar with "Carpet Discount Outlet," the company Mr. and Mrs. Williams claimed had installed the carpet. The witness had never installed any carpet for that business; during that period, he installed for Mr. Speert. The witness testified he was subpoenaed to court by the defense, but he was not called by them.

The cross-examination was conducted by Defense Counsel Jim Kitchens. The witness was reminded that the meeting at the Williams' home was on February 2 and that, when he walked into the home, he had said that he had installed tons of it in Atlanta, some in various banks in the area. Kitchens then showed the witness State's exhibit 751 (Deed to Secure Debt, dated December 7, 1971):

"And it's got the names Homer C. and Faye G. Williams on the front of it?"

"Yes, sir, it does."

"And it also has up above all these x's here, Southern Prudential Corporation?"

"Yes sir."

Kitchens then refers the witness to two signatures written in cursive handwriting:

"Mr. Gano, tell this jury if that's your signature?"

"Well, sir, at first I didn't think it was until it came on T.V. the other night, and my secretary and my mother both says it sure looks like it.

And awhile ago, I signed one for him, and we put it together. I did not think it was at first, Sir."

"What do you think now?"

"I think it is."

"All right, sir. Now, You've changed your mind, then, since I last talked to you, haven't you?"

"Well, it was because it came on T.V. and I saw it."

The witness identified part of the writing in the document, and said he had authorized his boss, Mr. Speert, to sign his name if he wanted to.

On re-direct examination, Speed had the witness sign his name in the presence of the jury and offered the signature for the jury to decide for themselves. There was no objection, and the document (signature) was attached to the Deed to Secure Debt.

Lou Speert, owner of Southern Prudential Corporation, testified that his business was not formed until 1971 and identified its incorporation documents showing November 9, 1971. He said during that time the business was mostly carpeting and floor covering. He went on to identify State's exhibit 746 as an ad he took in the paper for December 4, 1971.

Speert testified that Wayne Gano was doing his carpet installation and identified the "Deed to Secure Debt" showing his (Speert's) signature as president and the signatures of Homer C. Williams and Faye G. Williams, parties to the transaction dated December 7, 1971. The note was later sold to North American Acceptance on December 21, 1971. He testified his company did not install or finance or do anything regarding "air conditioning" which Williams' parents claimed the Deed to Secure Debt in 1971 was for.

On cross-examination, he testified that back in 1968 he worked for another company and did mostly siding. He affirmed that Gano had told him it would be all right to sign his (Gano's) name on contracts, but he had never done so.

The witness testified that Gano had installed the carpet for him in the Williams' home. [This completely removes any doubt about the carpet and when it was installed].

Mr. Vincent Giovannelli, an employee of Delta Air Lines who lived in Decatur, took the stand. I asked him:

"Do you know where the South River is?"

"Yes sir."

". . . Did you have an occasion to be going home on March 2, 1981, in the evening hours?"

"Yes sir".

"About what time do you go home?"

"I was going home from the bank. It was around 4:00 in the afternoon."

". . . Where do you live in relation to the South River and — is it Waldrop Road?"

"I live about two hundred yards - - from Waldrop Road and about two hundred yards from the South River."

"Does the South River go under the road that you pass over?"

"Yes sir."

"Did you have an occasion to see anybody on the bridge at the South River when you were going home?"

"Yes sir."

"And did you get a good look at the person?"

"Yes, I did."

"Was it daylight?"

"Yes sir."

"What was the person doing?"

"Standing up on the curb looking in the river."

". . . Did you a few months later see that person on television?"

"Yes sir."

"And who did you learn that person to be?"

"Mr. Williams (indicating)."

"You're referring to Wayne Williams, the defendant?"

"Yes sir."

I inquired if, when Williams was looking in the river, he had any fishing equipment of any kind, to which the witness said "no." I turned the witness over for cross-examination.

Binder asked for a 'bench conference' with Judge Cooper where he objected to this testimony as there being nothing in the pattern ..., whereupon I pointed out the "Jo Jo Bell" case (pulled from the South River), and the fact that Williams had denied he knew where the South River was. Binder withdrew the objection.

Binder went back over the same testimony, adding that the witness was driving 15 or 20 miles an hour, that he did not see anyone throwing a body in the water, and that he did not recall what he wore that day.

The witness did add that . . . "We were questioned after they found a body in the river, asking if ... did we see anything strange, and that's when the strange person on the bridge came back to me. A person that didn't belong in that area particularly came back to me."

"There's nothing strange about that, is it? Why would you use the word strange?"

"We were asked if we'd seen anything strange in the area that didn't fit, you know, prior to their finding a boy's body downstream from where we live."

"Now, if the fellow was looking in the water and you was driving your car by, how did you see his face?"

"He kind of glanced up when he heard my car coming, I guess. He looked over his shoulder."

"Did the police show you a spread of pictures or just his picture?"

"A spread."

Angelo Fuster, Director of Communications for the Office of the Mayor of Atlanta, was called by me in rebuttal of denials by Homer and Wayne Williams that he (Wayne) returned home after being stopped at the river and told his father that he had "thrown trash in the river." Fuster testified he worked for Mayor Jackson on June 3, 1981, when Wayne Williams was questioned at FBI headquarters:

Mallard: "Mr. Fuster, were you down at FBI Headquarters on that date that I mentioned, June 3, 1981?"

"Yes, I was."

"And to your knowledge, was Wayne Williams in FBI Headquarters?"

"Yes."

"And was also Homer Williams, his father, there?"

"Yes."

". . . Did you know Homer Williams?"

"I recognized him when I saw him, yes."

". . . Did you have a conversation with Homer Williams?"

"Yes, I did."

"Did you have a conversation with him regarding Wayne and what Wayne told him?"

"Yes."

"Now, state whether or not Homer Williams told you whether or not his son, Wayne, was on the bridge."

"Yes. He told me that his son had told him a few nights before that he'd been on the bridge when he was stopped." [Few nights before June 3].

". . . What did he tell you that he did?"

"He said he had stopped to get rid of some trash, kept on going; on his way back, he was stopped by the Police there."

"Now, Homer Williams told you that he stopped to do what? I didn't understand you."   [I wanted it made clear].

"Get rid of some trash." ...

"Did he say where he got his information?"

"His son had told him."

Ms. Welcome took the witness on cross-examination:

"Mr. Fuster, how are you?"

"Fine, thank you."

"We have met before; is that correct?"

"That is correct."

"We used to be at the City together"? [Ms. Welcome was City Prosecutor = City Solicitor].

"That is correct."

"Were you working with the City during the past two or three years that we've had the tragedies in Atlanta?"

"Yes."

"So you're very familiar with the City's role and what the community was feeling during the time that these tragedies were going on?"

"Yes."

"And you also are familiar with the fact that it took several deaths before the city recognized that there was a problem. They denied that there was a problem; isn't that correct?" [I would give her this, though objectionable].

"That is the way that some people look at it, yes."

"Well, that's the way it was. And you also know that Camille Bell and a lot of the mothers had to come down and almost park at the City Hall before the city would recognize — .""

I objected that it was not relevant . . . , when Ms. Welcome inter-
jected "I think it's about time for the Court to tell them to sit down. The
Court is always telling the Defense to sit down." At that point, the Court
had counsel come to the bench, where the Judge sustained my objection,
and told Ms. Welcome to confine it to any relevant questions.

"Mr. Fuster, just prior to May 22, had anyone in City Hall ever
heard of Wayne Williams in connection to the missing and murdered
children?"

[I could have objected to this inasmuch as the witness couldn't speak
for "anyone in City Hall," but sometimes it's faster to move along].

"I hadn't. I cannot speak for anyone else."

"And after May 24, did you or were you familiar with the fact that
there was a lot of pressure brought about to bring someone to justice,
anyone? Are you familiar with that?"

I objected as the Court had ruled before trial that "politics" would not
be injected into the trial. The Court had counsel approach the bench and
instructed the Defense not to inject politics into the trial. Ms. Welcome
asked a few further innocuous questions.

Sheldon Eugene Kemp, age 17, took the stand. I led him through
his acquaintance of Wayne Williams and later in 1978 his becoming a
member of the Gemini Group.

I asked Kemp whether he was over at the Williams' home on
Penelope Street around the summer of 1979; he was.

Mallard: "Will you tell us, if anything, what happened between
Wayne Williams and his mother and father there at their home?"

Kemp: "Yeah. Well, me and my brother, we was sitting in his living room watching television. And Wayne asked his dad to write him a
check, you know, for something, you know. And Wayne didn't – I mean
his dad wouldn't sign the check. So Wayne, you know, started cursing
him and stuff and started trying to, you know, get him and pushing him
and stuff. And when his mom was trying to keep him away from his
dad."

"Mrs. Williams?"

"When she was trying, you know, to keep him away from his dad, he
pushed her out of the way and slapped her, you know."

"He slapped her, his mother?"

"Yeah. And they went on back in some room, you know, in this room. I think it was his dad's room, you know. And he jumped on top of his dad, you know, was sitting on top of his stomach or something, choking him, you know. And his mom was saying that he had some kind of a heart condition or something and she was trying to tell him, you know, to stop messing with him."

"Where did he have his father when they were back in the room, how did he have his father? You said he jumped on him?"

"Yeah. His dad was laying on the bed, you know, and he was sitting on top of him with his hand at his throat (indicating)."

"Both hands as you were indicating there?"

"Yeah, both hands."

"Let me stop you right there. How did his daddy get up?"

"His mom was still trying, you know, to get Wayne off top of him, pulling him off. And he finally got up and that's when his dad went for his shotgun and came back in there and started cursing and said, you know ..."

"Who started cursing?"

"Wayne."

"... What did his daddy do?"

"His daddy, you know, was pointing the gun at him and said he'd shoot his head off." "And after that, I think he got him to sign a check or something, you know, because he went ahead on and took us home after that happened, you know."

". . . Now, you've been with Wayne Williams a lot of times?"

"Yeah. Almost the whole summer of 79 before my mom told me to stop singing with him."

"Have you ridden with him in a car which had a siren?"

"Yeah."

"Was there anything about it, does it have any equipment in it or something?"

"Yeah. It had a Motorola with the mike, you know the kind. And it had a Scanner in there with lights beeping, you know, and had a yellow light in the front and had a blue light...."

"Have you ever seen him use that siren?"

"Yeah. He turned it on on the freeway to show me and my little brother."

Binder took the witness on cross-examination. He attacked right away!

"Now, tell the jury a little bit about yourself. Are you the same Sheldon Kemp that took a knife and stabbed somebody?" Is that you?"

I immediately objected that a witness cannot be impeached by his own testimony in such manner, that it requires a certified copy of the conviction – if one exists. [Frankly, I did not know if the witness had such a record; but if so, it would be easy for them to go downstairs to the Clerk of Court's office and get the record – it only takes a few minutes].

The Judge sustained my objection, as the Defense had tried the same tactic before with a witness. Sometimes, an attempt will be made in such manner where the person was only arrested with the charge being dismissed.

Binder continued:

"Who brought you here to this courtroom today?"

"(No Response.)"

"Have you lost your mind or something? Don't you know?"

THE COURT: Give him a chance, Mr. Binder.

THE WITNESS: I did.

At times, I won't come to the aid of the witness though I think the witness is being mistreated (when I believe the witness can handle it), allowing counsel to overplay his hand with the jury. The jury will not like 'overbearing' counsel intimidating an uneducated youngster.

"No. No man brought you in here. Who was that man?"

"No man brought me in here."

"Sure he did."

"I brought myself."

"Your juvenile officer brought you here, didn't he?"

"No."

"How did you get here today?"

"I drove."

"Drove what?"

"A car."

"What kind of car?"

"I wouldn't like to answer that question."

"You wouldn't? Why, is it a secret what kind of car you drove here?"

"No."

"You tell the jury what kind of car it was."

"I just wouldn't like to answer that question."

"You wouldn't? You know you didn't drive no car here, don't you. You just lied."

"No, I didn't lie."

"You just told this jury a lie. A police car brought you here, son. Now, tell the jury, isn't that the truth? You didn't drive no car here, did you?"

"Yes."

"You look at that jury and tell them the truth. Who brought you here today?"

"I brought myself."

"A police car brought you here, didn't they?"

"MR. MALLARD: YOUR HONOR, I OBJECT TO COUNSEL BADGERING THE WITNESS."

"THE COURT: YOU'VE ASKED SEVERAL TIMES."

"Binder: All right. I'll get onto something else."

"Now, how are you feeling? Are you feeling pretty good?"

"A little nervous."

"Are you upset?"

"No."

"You told the jury any lies today?"

"None that I can think of."

Binder goes on to press the witness as to when he was over to the Williams' home when the alleged incident occurred and as to the past relationships with Williams and why they ended. There were several questions to which the witness never responded. Binder questioned whether Williams kicked the witness out of the group and whether Kemp tried to get a mini-bike out of Mr. and Mrs. Williams.

"And didn't you tell Mr. and Mrs. Williams that you did all this singing and you wasn't paid for it and you wanted that mini-bike?"

"No. My mother was telling me that she wanted me to, you know, show something for all the time that I was taking out, you know, singing."

"Now, you said you was in Wayne's house in the living room, and before this ruckus happened, what was you doing?" "You say you was watching T.V.?"

"Yeah. His mom had just gave me and my brother something to eat for a break or something."

Henry Ingram, an attendant at a downtown parking lot on Courtland and Cain streets, testified that he was working a second job when Williams' parents drove in about 5:00 p.m. one day in May. He further testified that two young men approached the Williams' car and one 'snatched' the driver's door open, pulling out Homer Williams. The two men scuffled in the parking lot. The witness warned the men they were on private property and would have to leave.

Ingram said that before the older man (Homer Williams) left, he explained that his son was angry at his refusal to rent a car for the son's friend. Ingram testified that the younger man (son) returned with his companion and stopped at his father's car and said to him: *"Don't come home tonight."* [After this strong witness, the prior youngster's testimony will become even more credible].

Ingram didn't immediately know who the people were, but he recognized Wayne Williams (as the son) when his picture appeared on TV in June.

On cross-examination, Binder attempted to convince the witness that it was just a dispute concerning Mrs. Williams and the son's attempts to get Homer Williams to enter a hospital for tests.

With this witness, the State completed its rebuttal evidence, after which the Defense had an opportunity to present sur-rebuttal, or rebuttal of our rebuttal.

The New York Times, February 25, 1982, reported that the day before, Williams, "his hostility flaring, rested his case at his murder trial today, then saw a parade of prosecution rebuttal witnesses land blow after damaging blow against his defense." Yes, indeed, just as planned – to have and present damaging rebuttal evidence is very effective in a trial. A jury expects both sides in a controversy to be straight-forward and truthful - even a defendant and his witnesses in a criminal trial.

PART SIX

The Defense Presents Sur-Rebuttal

Dick Terschell was called by the Defense to refute testimony that Williams' hands were those of someone into karate.

Glenn Brock, from the West End News, was called to take issue with some of Floyd Fowler's testimony about Williams being pointed out as suspected of shoplifting.

Mrs. Faye Williams was recalled. She denied that the violent attacks at home and at the parking lot downtown between Wayne and Homer ever occurred.

This rebuttal was so weak, it was pathetic. It should have been obvious to the jury that the Defense was grasping for straws.

The defense then rested! All the evidence from both sides was before the jury.

The jury was excused while the Judge and lawyers took up administrative issues, as well as legal issues concerning a motion for a directed verdict of not guilty (which is customary in cases at this point in time). The motion was denied by the Court.

Cheryl Johnson – where are you? The fact that, on the last day of trial, the Defense failed to produce the mysterious caller who allegedly wanted so badly to get a talent interview just validated what I already knew: *She did not exist.* It was a hastily arranged alibi for being on the bridge at 3:00 a.m. for no reason except to dump a body (which he referred to as trash). The multitude of conflicting stories by Williams and between Williams and his parents indicates that [it] was 'made up.' If Cheryl was anything more than a figment of his imagination, the FBI, police, defense investigators (all over the place), and the news media would have found her; *in fact Cheryl would have found them. All the publicity – the most publicized case in Georgia history through electronic and print media – cried out for Cheryl to come forward and free this innocent man.*

PART
SEVEN

Closing Arguments

It was Friday, February 26, 1982. Final (closing) arguments in the case were heard by six attorneys – three for each side. After nine weeks and almost 1,000 exhibits and 250 witnesses (between both sides), it was described in the next day's edition of the *Atlanta Journal/Constitution* by staff writer Celestine Sibley as "High theater, a little low comedy, mental gymnastics with eloquent displays of logic, personal reminiscences, references to God, Galileo and one lawyer's grand-pappy. It was a cross between a camp meeting and Clarence A. Darrow's jury speech in the Scopes monkey trial. It was Portia and The Merchant of Venice."

Closing arguments occur when the attorney attempts to mold his or her argument around the favorable evidence and the legal instructions you know the Court will give to the jury in an effort to convince the jury of the correctness of your position while explaining away the evidence favorable to the other side. Disregarding the unfavorable evidence will not make it go away – the other side will talk about it. The jury will remember it. Explain it away! For the prosecution, that is normally the defendant's testimony and his family and friends, who come to court biased in his favor. Quite often, they are impeached through various methods. There may also be weaknesses in your own case – 'caress and explain it.' Never play down or give excuses for a circumstantial evidence case – explain why it is factually and legally acceptable and at times stronger than direct evidence. I will at times present a closing argument to the jury regarding what circumstantial evidence is like: One recent evening before retiring for the night, I looked out over my front yard and all I could see was a freshly cut lawn; I had a good night's sleep. The next morning as I got my cup of coffee, I again looked outside, and all I could see was a 'blanket of snow' across my yard! I immediately jumped to the conclusion that it had snowed during the night while I was sleeping; no one told me so, neither did I see it, but a reasonable inference was drawn from the circumstances. I knew it snowed the night before!

Knowing the type jurors you are talking to will be helpful. 'Talking down' to the jury will not help your cause, but talking to them at their level will be helpful. Invite them to use their common sense in applying the law as given by the Court to the evidence in evaluating [it].

With six lawyers presenting their arguments to the jury, it would be a day's event, with the State having the opening and concluding arguments with the defense going in between.

In the 'old days' when this case was tried, there was an unwritten gentlemen's code whereby attorneys resisted objecting to the other's argument to the jury (at least in the Atlanta Circuit), unless the argument just got wholly out of line for which one felt the Judge would sustain the objection; after all, you didn't want the jury to think you were 'interrupting' the other's time with the jury and especially where you knew the Judge would not sustain your objection. This might indicate to the jury that the Judge agreed with the other's argument. Furthermore, the attorneys commonly tell the jury that what he/she says is not evidence, and it is routine for the Judge to instruct the jury that **counsel's argument is not evidence and should not be considered as such by the jury.**

From a legal perspective, the law in Georgia provides wide latitude in concluding argument where counsel may give his interpretation of the facts (and inferences) as shown by the evidence through argument in imagery and illustration. I have seldom seen a judge sustain an objection to counsel's argument to a jury. At most, the judge will normally say to the jury: *the jury will remember what the evidence was in the case.* Further, the Court does not want to come down on either side as agreeing with either side's interpretation of the evidence. Figurative speech has always been regarded as a legitimate weapon in forensic warfare, and flights of oratory and false logic do not call for mistrials or rebuke of counsel. *It is the introduction of facts not in evidence, which gives rise to a legitimate objection.*

I led off with the opening argument for the prosecution and was followed by defense counsels Mary Welcome, Jim Kitchens, and Alvin Binder. Prosecutor Gordon Miller and then District Attorney Lewis Slaton ended the arguments.

For about 45 minutes, I summarized the evidence before the jury with an overview of the case and profiling Williams as Atlanta's killer who had been evading the police dragnets through his activities for two years. I reminded the jury, from the medical examiners' testimony that the killings stopped after Williams' arrest in May; there had been no killings since which would have fit the profile of the victims with un-usual trace evidence on the bodies. I characterized Willlliams as literate, media conscious, mobile, knowledgeable of the area, familiar with po-lice work, and charismatic to economically-aspiring young people.

Although he started out as an achiever early in life, I pointed out Williams' failures in life (which caused his parents to bankrupt), his failure in college, and his inability to make a living while living off his parents while he entered his 'dream world' of the music talent scout business. I suggested he had not "made enough money to buy a ham-burger" from his business activities, but these activities allowed him the ability to get away with the killings for two years through his promises of stardom to the underprivileged, and knowledge of the city and police. The profile I offered for the city's child killer fit Williams – someone who could blend into the fabric of the community, someone charismatic but smart in the ways of the police.

In summarizing evidence in twelve cases of murder, I inferred he was a cunning 'mad-dog' killer. I referred to him as a man with a storm raging inside him who showed his calm, polite side on the first day of cross-examination but showed contempt for everyone including me and the police on the second day with his antagonism. I said he was a Jekyll and Hyde, a split personality, derived from his group name, Gemini.

In arguing Williams' contradictory statements, I pointed out that "if you start lying, you won't know what you last said. And if you start lying and keep repeating lies, you won't know what the truth is." Based on the evidence before the jury, I concluded that Williams was a habitual pathological liar.

Defense Counsel Mary Welcome presented her argument, countering my assertion that Williams was in a 'dream world' with her responding that "Martin Luther King was a dreamer." She went on to present Williams in a good light, citing the many witnesses testifying on his behalf and attacking the state's witnesses. Welcome argued for 49 minutes, saying "I (Mary) am biased" ... and, she criticized the pattern claimed by the State and said that every time the court said to the prosecutor "call your next witness, he was saying: Turn the lights on." Ms. Welcome compared the State's evidence with a 'thimbleful of evidence' and dramatized the reference by portraying to the jury a plastic thimble at the end of her presentation.

Defense Counsel Jim Kitchens presented his argument next, ridiculing the State's case of a "house on rocks" to a "house on sand." He used sarcasm describing the state's evidence as harmless, innocuous things. He complained that the witnesses placing Williams with seven of the twelve victims did not appear until they saw Williams' picture in the news, more specifically attacking Ms. Nellie Trammell (since her eyewitness testimony hurt them badly).

For the next hour and eighteen minutes, Defense Counsel Alvin Binder made his closing remarks to the jury, attacking the State's evidence and presenting Williams in a good light. He talked about Williams on the stand; he referred to his client as "this pudgy, fat little boy" in an effort to convince the jury that physically Williams could not have heaved a body over the bridge rail. Binder criticized State's witnesses, calling Mrs. Blakely a "Judas." Binder attacked the fiber evidence, the pattern, and a lack of evidence as to a motive in the case. He argued that a body entering the river on the right side of the river will float on the right, and vice versa for the left side, citing defense witness Dingle. He discussed the sound test by the Defense. Binder even maintained that Nathaniel Cater was dead on May 19 (contrary to all the State's evidence that he was alive on May 21).

Prosecutor Gordon Miller took 25 minutes in presenting the State's fiber charts and in summarizing the evidence. He noted that fibers from a violet and green bedspread seized from Williams' room were found on all 12 victims; the unusual tri-lobal-shaped Wellman fibers from the Williams' carpet were found on 10 victims. Also, other fiber and hair connections were made, all consistently pointing to Williams' habitat. Miller pointed out that the multiple matches made between 700 fibers found on the victims' bodies and 18 objects in Williams' home and car was significant as a signature, as if Williams had signed his name on the death warrants of the victims.

District Attorney Lewis Slaton took the final closing presentation. For almost an hour, he summarized the strong points about the State's case. Slaton characterized Williams as a 'crafty, cool, and cunning' killer who received too much early on from his parents. Slaton attacked the conclusions of defense expert Dingle who floated dummies down the river. Slaton told the jury that Williams was a stupid person in dropping Cater's body from the bridge with the police hidden below, saying "he failed again." Slaton portrayed Williams as 'doing away with inferiors as Attila the Hun, Adolph Hitler, Idi Amin from Uganda, and Wayne Bertram Williams, Master Race, doing away with inferiors.' Slaton concluded his argument at 4:20 pm, Friday, February 26, 1982.

Judge Cooper instructed the jury on the law for the next 32 minutes.

PART
EIGHT

Jury Deliberations, Verdict, and Controversy

At this point in the trial, everyone breathes with a sigh of relief – in every trial! Now the parties and lawyers would be able to sit back and allow the jury system to work; it's in the hands of the jury, and nothing can go wrong, right? The jury has been sequestered at a hotel and monitored by court bailiffs and deputies when they are not in Court. But, things do happen sometimes beyond the ability of those who have close supervision of the jury.

During the trial while sequestered at the hotel after Court one evening, the jurors were exposed to a drawing, which someone had placed on the wall of their dining room, depicting the outline of a man's face with the word "guilty" appearing on it. The next morning, Judge Cooper called all the attorneys into his chambers and brought the incident to our attention. The bailiff was questioned and revealed that she saw one of the jurors tearing the picture off the wall. Judge Cooper informed counsel of the precautions he had taken to insure that the incident did not again occur, and he asked of defense counsel if he wanted "to say anything as relates to that" issue. Defense Counsel Binder responded that he had nothing further to bring up. The Defense (all defense attorneys were present) did not seek a mistrial – as would be the expectant thing to do in such situations. The question is: Why didn't they do so? I recall thinking at the time that the Defense will vigorously argue for a mistrial, after which the Court will deny the motion but give the jury strong cautionary instructions to disregard the incident, while denying a mistrial. After all, jurors will bend over backwards to follow the Court's instructions, especially in such serious matters.

The obvious answer is that defense counsel discussed the matter among themselves and with Williams, and since the trial was near the end after the longest trial in Georgia history, they felt the case was going good for them. They simply did not want to start over with a new jury. *They didn't want a mistrial but a verdict they thought would be in their favor.* By not requesting special instructions from the Judge to inquire of the jurors who, if anyone, had seen the drawing and for them to be told to dismiss the matter from their minds tells me they did not want to make more of an issue of it by bringing it up. [Over the years, this is the tact taken by counsel in most similar situations]. Though *trial* counsel waived any further action be taken by the trial Court, new defense counsel over the years since raised the issue on appeals – which is the norm, with later attorneys attacking the actions of former defense attorneys.

The issue was later reviewed by both the Georgia Supreme Court on direct appeal and habeas corpus, and by further appeal to the United States District Court in Atlanta; relief was denied Williams due to 'waiver' by the Defense and the adoption of the reasonable strategy of not pursuing the issue based on the reasonable conclusion that a motion for mistrial would not be granted. The Appellate Courts reasoned that, had such a motion for mistrial been pressed, it would not have been an abuse of discretion for the Judge to deny the motion.

After closing arguments and the instructions by the Court late Friday, the jury was allowed to begin deliberations. At about 7:30 p.m. their deliberations ceased, and they were transported back to the hotel for the night. They were returned to court for further deliberations Saturday morning at 9:00 a.m.

With the jury now performing their tasks, I found myself ruminating over the past nine weeks. Would the jury understand the technical evidence, the science concerning the fibers and hair testimony, and the legal instructions by the Judge? I looked back over the enormous case presented by both sides. Closing arguments, I pondered, would help remind them of the important points made by both sides. I second-guessed myself and others in what we could have done but didn't. I knew the Prosecution had presented a powerful circumstantial evidence case which, in my view as a long time prosecutor, is better in some cases than eye-witness testimony. An eye-witness to an event may be wrong, but seldom ever is a good circumstantial evidence case wrong. A circumstantial case draws its strength from so many pieces of evidence, witnesses, and exhibits, all consistently pointing in the same direction (to the accused).

I felt secure that we had a conviction! It was just a question of how long the jury would be deliberating. They had eight weeks of trial testimony from over 200 witnesses (66 from the Defense) and 1000 or so exhibits to review if they wanted to do so.

Saturday noon came with the jurors deliberating except for a short break for a lunch of chili dogs from the Varsity (a long-time local favorite near Georgia Tech).

What was the jury doing, I pondered? There had been no feedback from the jury, no questions for the judge which I thought would occur with such a complicated case. Was there animosity, disagreements, verbal fights? This was a varied jury in all respects across racial, ethnic, economic lines, gender, age, etc.

Before a verdict was rendered by the jury, Judge Cooper announced through a spokesman that he was dismissing the contempt-of-court citations (for violation of the gag order) he had filed against defense counsels Al Binder and Mary Welcome, Williams' parents, and the defense expert pathologist from New York. I expected as much!

Saturday, February 27, 1982 – A Verdict: Near 7:00 p.m., after about 11 hours of deliberation, the jury announced there was a verdict. I was at peace with myself! I felt good that the jury was returning so early in light of the length of the trial. It was a good omen; *they would not have acquitted in that short time.*

The Court made the announcement to a packed courtroom with news people filling the rooms provided. It was a peaceful and quieted atmosphere as the jury was brought into the courtroom. As they marched into the jury box, I did as I always do – I looked at the jurors' eyes and studied their faces and their body language. I had seen this procedure so many times I had become pretty accurate in judging what the verdict would be. I had a 'feel' for what a jury would need to convict, considering also whether the jury would 'want' to acquit or convict the 'person' on trial. Did the jury 'like' the defendant? They would not!!! The evidence was too compelling for this jury to turn a deft ear to it. The jury was not favoring Williams with their eyes or smiles – they were stoic, business-like, and serious.

Judge Cooper asked the foreperson of the jury to give the District Attorney the indictment with the two verdicts, whereupon Slaton read the verdicts: "We, the jury find the defendant guilty on count number one. We, the jury find the defendant guilty on count number two."
Williams Guilty!

Co-counsel Mary Welcome began to cry as the verdict was being read. She had become 'too-involved' or close to her client as happens in such cases, and it was a 'personal' defeat for her.

Both defendant Williams and his father, Homer, addressed the Court. Williams told the Judge he still maintained his innocence and hoped that the person or persons who committed the crimes would be brought to justice. Homer Williams said justice had not been done, and he didn't see how anybody could find 'Wayne' guilty.

Williams was immediately sentenced to two life sentences for murdering Nathaniel Cater and Jimmy Ray Payne.

As Homer Williams was about to leave the courtroom, he turned to the prosecutors' table where we were still seated. He accused Slaton of conducting a 'helluva railroad job' and called us (the prosecutors) "sons-of-bitches." I remember his staring at us with hatred in his eyes. He just didn't want to believe his flesh and blood could do such heinous acts.

The next day, February 28, 1982, the *Atlanta Journal/Constitution* carried a front page headline **"Williams Guilty"** by Journal Staff Writer Bill Montgomery. He quoted the Williams' parents as blaming the conviction on a "lazy, uncaring jury, a 'conniving' prosecutor, and an 'Uncle Tom' Judge." Further, that the father called the trial "a helluva railroad job."

On Sunday, February 28, 1982, *The Seattle Times'* headline was **"Atlanta jury convicts Williams."** Headlines around the world followed suit by announcing that a jury with surprising speed convicted Williams.

But, we should consider the essential element of the trial process – the jury! What evidence in the case swayed them? How were they affected by the long period away from family, business, and their lack of social access?

Jurors were returned from Court by the deputies to their motel rooms where they gathered their belongings and were ushered into vehicles to be transported home after eights weeks away from their regular life.

Journal Staff Writer Ron Taylor, with byline **"Tired, anxious jurors finally free of 'imprisonment'"** in the *Atlanta Journal/Constitution,* on February 28, 1982, reported on the guilty verdict and the jurors' interviews. While the deputies were ushering jurors into vehicles to take them home, from the motel, one reminded Taylor that they had been there eight weeks – you can't tell that in two seconds. One juror reached at home, reportedly gave the normal response: "It was very enlightening. I wouldn't want to do it again any time soon." Taylor pointed out the sad results of a criminal justice system which seems to put jurors in a secondary position to that of a criminal defendant on trial in such a high profile case where it is necessary to shroud jurors from being subject to intimidation or exposure to elements which tend to compromise the jury system: The jurors shared Williams' loss of freedom. While Williams was able to read accounts of his trial in his cell, the jury received papers full of holes where articles had been removed; Williams watched TV without censorship, but the jury's programs were monitored by a deputy. The jury could not see anything about the trial or other similar programs on crime and punishment. The jurors did have some special privileges provided by the Court and others: Dinner with up to two cocktails, visits with relatives which were monitored by deputies, trips for the women to a closed beauty salon and for the men to a closed barber shop (under guard of course). Once, the owners of a family amusement center volunteered the game room to the jurors at no cost. Reportedly, the jurors arrived in a large van after the business had closed to regular customers. Two deputies checked the place out before the jurors were allowed inside. The owner reportedly said: "They were like a bunch of kids that had been cooped up – they were screaming and yelling and bouncing all over the place."

Reportedly, to one 34-year-old-juror, her service to the citizens meant nearly two months away from her three-year old son.

Atlanta Journal Staff Writer Laurie Baum interviewed jurors and reported on March 2, 1982. Ms. Baum reported that a foreperson was first elected; that the jury then went over their notes and isolated 15 issues that required their close attention. The jury reportedly zeroed in on the "numerous lies and inconsistencies in Williams' story," and they were particularly mindful of his activities at the bridge in the early hours of May 22 along with the questioned existence of Cheryl Johnson. Another point of discussion was the date of purchase of the carpet in the Williams' home, a key element of the Prosecution's evidence. One juror offered: "We didn't consider the individual fibers, but the grouping of fibers – the chances that someone else (other than Williams) would have had the same fibers were pretty slim."

The jury reportedly focused on the eye-witnesses. With Cater, the discussion went smoothly. With Payne it was a question which divided the jury at first but was answered with the jury noting there was much more fiber evidence on Payne than on Cater, buttressing the Payne case. One juror reported they were more concerned with why Williams was lying than with a motive for the killings; the juror also said they concentrated on the two cases (Cater and Payne) for which Williams was being prosecuted rather than on the similar cases; however, other jurors indicated the pattern cases did help. Jurors related instances of Williams' behavior on the witness stand and his smart-aleck remarks. One juror reported a desire to see Williams' temper; and when the prosecutor badgered him, "he showed his temper of violence and I was glad to see it." The jurors noted there had been no more similar killings since Williams was arrested.

The jury first voted on the Cater case and were unanimous for guilty. Next they discussed the Payne case, but two jurors voted not guilty with four undecided. Further discussion about a yellow blanket that was in Williams' house during the June 3 FBI search but had disappeared before a June 22 search and about the testimony of carpet and blanket fibers on the bodies caused them to reevaluate the discussion in favor of guilt. About three hours after the Cater verdict, all but one juror had agreed Williams was guilty. The lone holdout was not pressured, it was reported. A juror said they simply continued their deliberations with "calm, cool, rational discussion." Another vote was taken about an hour later with a unanimous verdict. [The jurors' evaluation of the evidence validates my initial decision about the charging process].

Reportedly, a juror said: "We were a religious group, and when we got back to the jury room, we held hands and prayed" and "We had a real peace about the decision. Some people cried because they were relieved it was over and because it was a pity for his parents and for Wayne. We hated the loss of freedom just living in a hotel for two months. We imagined how he'd feel living in jail for the rest of his life. The crying part was an emotional release – it had nothing to do with regret," the juror reported.

Following the verdict, police officials, prosecutors, and defense attorneys were in the lobby of the courthouse as we were pressed by dozens of cameras and reporters for interviews and sound-bites. The media circus followed for days without letup because so many public officials and others (including the defense attorneys) were so ready and willing to vent their opinions about the prosecution of Williams. This was especially so following the announcement by Public Safety Commissioner Lee P. Brown on Monday, March 1, following a thorough review of the remaining cases with Task Force members, he was terminating the Task Force after closing twenty-three (23) of the thirty (30) victims' murders attributed to Williams by trace evidence and as a result of the conviction. Brown announced that the remaining seven cases were being returned to local police departments. All twenty-three of the cases closed (which included Cater and Payne and the ten similar pattern cases) resulted from the presence of synthetic textile fibers and/or dog hair found on the bodies and linked to Williams' home and automobiles; those cases not presented at trial were: Yusef Bell, 9; Christopher Richardson, 12; Aaron Wyche, 10; Anthony Carter, 9; Earl Lee Terrell, 10; Clifford Jones, 12; Aaron Jackson, 9; Curtis Walker, 13; Timothy Hill, 13; Eddie Duncan, 21; and Michael McIntosh, 23.

Of the seven remaining cases, two involved female victims. It was never believed by authorities or prosecutors that the two female victims should have been on the 'list' as attributable to the 'serial killer;' there was no trace evidence, witnesses, or anything linking them to Williams. Of the remaining five cases, Darron Glass's body was never found, and the other four: Edward Hope Smith, Milton Harvey, Jeffrey Mathis, and Patrick Rogers, were believed linked to the pattern by their age, race, family background, and circumstances of their disappearance and locations where the bodies were found.

District Attorney Slaton announced that he had no plans to seek indictments on the other cases in light of the two life terms imposed on Williams, and the weight of evidence in the other cases.

In a normal case, this might be the end of the process, with the exception of the appeals which follow for years. But, would it be so here? Normally, everybody goes away happy with the results of a long, hard battle legally fought before an unbiased jury, with the exception of the defendant, his family and lawyers (possibly a few friends).

And in a normal case, the 'mothers' of the victims would be there with us, supporting us in every aspect of the case as well *in our victory*. I don't recall another case where the mother of the deceased victim was not so involved with the prosecution of the case. From the beginning, we knew we could not rely upon some of the mothers to be supportive of our prosecution of Williams; several were publicly outspoken in his favor. Some did testify in the case.

But again, this was not a normal case from the beginning. Once Williams was identified, Williams and his parents were outspoken in the community. Williams' parents were well-respected church members in the community and were directly involved in his defense. They let no opportunity to speak out publicly escape them.

Following the verdict, some of the 'mothers' were again vociferous in their condemnation of the guilty verdict and denial of Williams' guilt. *Constitution* Staff Writer Bob Dart on March 1, 1982, reported that certain mothers said this was not the end of it – that they would not let it drop – and that Williams was just a scapegoat, that (they) don't give a damn about their black children. (The Mayor, Public Safety Commissioner, Police Chief, the Judge, and many of the jury and witnesses were black).

However noteworthy, one of the mothers whose son was on the Task Force list of thirty, but not presented at trial as one of the twelve victims, responded to reporter Dart that she didn't think it would make any difference if Williams was tried in more cases, saying "They could only give him another life sentence, and he only has one life to serve" …

further that "The man's guilty of those two and the rest of them, too" – which was exactly my position on the matter.

At times, prosecutors find themselves in a situation where they (and others) *know someone is guilty* but for legal reasons they find it not a sustainable prosecution.

The outcry should have been foreseeable but apparently was not. Local leaders and individuals, including the 'mothers' group, found themselves at odds with the decision to terminate the Task Force and close the cases. [However, any of the cases could have and no doubt would have been re-opened if additional evidence or leads were discovered. There comes a time in any investigation when the leads dry up, and there is nothing further to investigate].

Journal Staff Writers Ron Taylor and Dallas Lee in the March 7, 1982, by-line "Why doubts remain" did a comprehensive review with interviews of community leaders wherein it appeared that the perception from the quick closing of cases and the Task Force office without consultation with community leaders meant the remaining cases were not a priority to police. Reportedly, the Reverend Joseph Lowery, president of the Southern Christian Leadership Conference, cited several reasons (which did not necessarily apply to him) for the dissatisfaction among many black citizens: (1) The technical trace evidence (fibers and hair) was hard for some to accept in the absence of eye-witnesses; (2) people did not want to believe the killer came from such a family as the Williams' family, that "sympathy flows out to the parents who fought so ferociously in this thing;" (3) historically the criminal justice system has been seen by black people as oppressive, and it was zeroing in on this one little black guy; and (4) "there was a disappointment that a black guy may be guilty of these awful crimes." Reverend Lowery reportedly added that "black people as a group are thoroughly committed to justice" and that "blacks have been victimized by injustice. That's why I trust the eight blacks on that (Williams) jury."

The *Atlanta Journal* reported on August 4, 1982, that the parents of some of the young blacks whose deaths were blamed on Williams were to meet with Attorney General William French Smith in Washington to seek reopening of the closed cases. Reportedly, Representative Mildred Glover (D-Atlanta), organizer of the journey, and her husband accompanied the group after the delegation received funding for the trip from "private sources that we can't disclose." No luck in D.C.! It was a state prosecution.

Many local reporters and others I knew who sat through the trial, would later tell me that as they saw the State's case slowly coming together that Williams was being unmasked day by day as the child killer, though they had initially doubted the sufficiency of the evidence. The March 1, 1982, edition of the *Atlanta Constitution* editorial called it the "Case Of The Century" pointing out that "A jury deliberated a minimum amount of time before pronouncing Williams guilty. Even before the jury was out, a careful review of the evidence by any unbiased person left little room for doubt" and that "As for the prosecution, District Attorney Lewis Slaton and his assistants were relentless in their pursuit of justice. They built a textbook case against Williams."

PART NINE
Post-Trial

Letters, Accolades, and Woes

Following the verdict and sentencing, I went home to Jo and the kids. Other participants did some celebrating. As I arrived home, Jo said we were visiting neighbors (Marvin and Jo Scobie), and to my surprise I walked into their home which was filled with neighbors and a party! Hanging on the wall was a large drawing of my image in court with finger pointing and in large words: "WELCOME" – "DROPSHOT." This was in reference to Williams' having called me a "dropshot" in response to my question of why he had called street children 'dropshots.' This is the thanks any prosecutor lives for – to be respected and appreciated in the community – in return for long hours and little remuneration.

Gordon Miller and I appeared on Good Morning America!

There were days of taking and answering telephone calls. I then started reading stacks of letters, cards, and other communications and articles sent to me before and after the verdict. Many nice letters were received from my fellow lawyers expressing their praise of a case well tried.

Of special praise was a letter personally to me from FBI Director William H. Webster, U. S. Department of Justice, dated March 25, 1982, wherein he commends me for my part in the prosecution as being "responsible for a large portion of the examination of numerous prosecution and defense witnesses and that your effective cross-examination of Williams was one of the vital points in the trial."

One letter was a surprise! Defense Counsel Alvin Binder wrote District Attorney Slaton a letter (copied to each team member) dated March 4, 1982, wherein he thanked Slaton and the team for "all the courtesies extended by (the office) during his stay in Atlanta." He said: "The presentation of your case was magnificent, thorough and to the point. Each of the gentlemen that took part in the trial displayed his peculiar expertise in a most convincing manner. I was honored to have been your opponent and I found all of you fair and most professional." He went on to write: "The pot still boils in Atlanta apparently" (referring to the unhappy mothers), and suggested that perhaps had the "announcement regarding the Task Force and other cases had been deferred for a week or so there would not have been such an up-roar." Mr. Binder still later wrote me that he had Jo and me in his prayers as we dealt with her sickness – wishing us well.

Most of the communications were positive and suggestive with helpful hints for cross-examination, etc. One letter suggested that when my book was made into a movie, that Gene Hackman should play me, with Wes Sarginson playing Gordon Miller, Telly Savalas playing Wallace Speed, and Harmon Wages playing Joe Drolet. He suggested that Cicely Tyson would play Mary Welcome.

Other letters ran the gamut from psychics to 'nut' cases to ordinary people wanting to help through their suggestions in evaluating the case from having followed the case daily through their news outlets.

I also received a most precious letter to me marked "personal" from Laurelton, New York, with an inspirational card and a three-page handwritten letter from a lady who had learned of my wife's illness and was praying for her and my well-being.

There were many short notes from Utica, New York, to Pasadena, California, to Karlsruhe, Germany – one saying that Williams was a liar and was trying to outsmart everybody including Judge Cooper, adding "wake up men of the jury" and signed "disgusted citizen." A repeat writer from Paramus, New Jersey, offered advice that Williams suffered from an obsessive, compulsive psychosis; another from Virginia compared the Williams' case to that of Bruno Hauptmann in the Charles Lindberg case and the execution of Hauptmann in 1936, saying that I should congratulate myself by following Wilentz's footsteps in convicting another perpetrator of a "crime of the century," and that I may have produced another Hauptmann, a victim of our "o'er hasty" judgment.

Others came from Toledo, Ohio, Richmond, Virginia, Alameda California (suggesting I run Williams' astrological specifics); Anniston, Alabama; Waycross, Georgia; Pittsburgh, Pennsylvania (who saw a vision); one from Oklahoma City was 15 pages and handwritten setting out his impressions of the case; another from New York wrote "how much of an idiot can you be, this is unbelievable for a D.A. – Why not try the truth lie-detector or truth serum. What's wrong? Don't they work; use your head, Justice People – they have a thing called truth serum or lie detector."

Many wrote suggesting that their letters, tips, and information had contributed to the verdict. A packet of letters was received from one writer from Ottawa, Illinois, on February 26, 1982, by Express Mail showing postage of $9.35 (1982 dollars).

As promised, I took Jo on a planned Mediterranean cruise. She immensely enjoyed it. Upon returning, her doctor – not having any good prognosis – referred us to the Cancer Research Center in Houston. We were there for two weeks but to no avail. Jo began getting sicker and sicker, and the chemotherapy was not working; she went through all the stages. Through the summer of 1982, it was all doctors, hospitals, and treatments.

I was seldom at the office during this period. When I was, it was hard to concentrate. I certainly didn't feel guilty about it since I had built up more extra work time during my past years than I would be able to take in Jo's remaining lifetime. The children and I suffered along with Jo. She did her best to keep our spirits up, and we did the same for her. Finally, I admitted Jo to Emory Hospital where she could be cared for to the extent possible during her last days. Her main request was that she be kept as free of pain as possible.

The kids and I had Christmas with Jo in her hospital room; we had a small tree on Christmas day. She seemed so happy! Afterwards, she had me usher the kids out of the room. We talked. She then became sick and lapsed into a coma. Two days later, December 27, 1982 – one year after the beginning of the jury selection in the Williams' case – Jo took her last breath and passed. She was buried on December 29, 1982, in the family plot next to where my father and mother would later be buried at the New Hope Freewill Baptist Church Cemetery near Jesup in Southeast Georgia across the road from the Mallard farm where I grew up as a child (and now own). It was Jo's wish!

But for Jo, there would be no book!

Re-opening the DeKalb Cases

Two of Williams' unusual supporters from early on were Louis Graham and Sidney Dorsey. They championed his cause every chance they got before the media, declaring him innocent. Both Graham and Dorsey were long-time detectives with the Atlanta Police; later they became involved and embroiled in the Task Force investigation and still later became high ranking officers. Graham evolved from Atlanta Detective to Assistant Fulton County Police Chief at the time of the Williams' trial, subsequently to Fulton County Police Chief, and then to DeKalb County Police Chief. At the same time Dorsey was moving up from Atlanta detective to Sheriff of DeKalb County. Both had publicly declared that Williams was innocent, claiming that he was a fall guy, a patsy.

About six months after Graham became DeKalb Police Chief (and 23 years after the trial of Williams), he announced on May 6, 2005, that he was re-opening the investigation into the deaths of four (perhaps five) of the Atlanta child-murder cases in his jurisdiction (DeKalb County): Patrick Baltazar, 12; Curtis Walker, 13; Joseph "Jo-Jo" Bell, 16; and William Barrett, age 17 (all but Walker were used in the trial as pattern cases). Asked by Reporter David Simpson of the *Atlanta Journal and Constitution* (AJC) on May 7, 2005, if he thought his action might upset other officials, he reportedly responded: "This is not done to upset anybody. But if it does, so be it. I'm doing this because it's the right thing to do."

Graham stood before a bank of microphones as he made his announcement that he had created a 'cold case squad' *to find the real killer.* One mother reportedly responded to reporter Ernie Suggs of the AJC: "I was so happy that I didn't know what to do with myself," and "I thought all my worries, hurt and pain was just about to end."

By now, Prosecutors Lewis Slaton and Gordon Miller were deceased. Joe Drolet and I responded in kind that we were sure the murderer was behind bars where he should be, and that Graham could investigate all he wished – we felt nothing worthwhile would be forthcoming (as if Graham, more than 20 years later, was going to find something a task force couldn't find during 1979-1981).

I did question whether Graham could objectively investigate the cases, given his pronouncement that Williams was innocent – that he never believed he (Williams) did anything. I further said: "There's no harm in reopening or continuing the investigation of any unsolved murder, that's done every day. It's just interesting to note that he would come out (publicly) and eliminate the only person who has ever been convicted in the murders at the same time he's opening up the cases." I feared this would further bring hope, then despair, to some of the mothers when nothing comes of Graham's actions.

The media from time to time questioned the progress of the 'cold-case' investigation by Graham's squad.

Very interesting was an article in the *Atlanta Magazine*, August 2005, by Luke Dittrick with photographs of Williams with hands clasped under his chin; and just below was another photograph with a smiling Graham – yes, with his hands clasped in a like manner.

One should consider this interview in the light of an experienced law officer of some 40 years. When asked about his (Graham's) visit with Williams at Valdosta State Prison after reopening the cases, Graham responded that he went there to see if prison had softened Williams up for a possible confession and that he spoke with "Wayne" about himself, school, family, and being an aspiring entrepreneur. Finally, Graham said before leaving (prison) he asked Wayne: "Did you have anything to do with the missing and murdered children in Atlanta, and more specifically, the two you were convicted of?" Graham said Williams "looked me right in the eye and he said, 'Chief, I had nothing to do with that. I swear on my mother's grave, I had nothing to do with that'."

Graham reportedly went on to say "it was the most convincing answer I had all day because I knew that he was sincere ... his sincerity and the fact that this young man really had no reason, he had no reason ..."

[A convicted murderer looked him in the eye and denied his crimes, and Graham believed him; and he had no reason to lie to him? What about getting out of prison?]

The reporter asked: "And you're a good judge of whether someone's lying?" Graham indicated he could go back historically in his career, and he had always been a pretty good judge of people. He then indicated "you know my mind was pretty well made up before I visited him, but I thought it was probably not fair for me to assume or believe that this person is innocent without facing him …." (Should not a jury of 12 make that decision?).

When asked: "Speaking of closure, do you think that reopening these cases runs the risk of providing false hope to the families of the victims?" – Graham responded: "No, that doesn't worry me…." Graham indicated he had new leads, but refused to share them.

Early in the interview, Graham reportedly revealed he knew Williams as a young TV entrepreneur and ambulance chaser who came to crime scenes. Yes, and Williams attended the high school where his (Graham's) wife taught, who also knew Williams.

As reported in the June 26, 2007, issue of the *Fulton Daily Report*, reporter Robin McDonald referred to a 2005 interview with Graham where he "dismissed the legitimacy of the carpet fiber evidence and expressed skepticism as to whether any forensic evidence still existed that could be tested for DNA." Ms. McDonald had learned during the newspaper's yearlong investigation into the forensic evidence against Williams that "DeKalb detectives never sought to locate or review the forensic evidence in the case." Graham suddenly resigned on May 3 (after about a year and half of his appointment as Chief and one year after re-opening the cases). Acting Chief Marinelli on June 21, 2006, announced he was dropping the investigation of the Atlanta child murders, saying: "We dredged up what we had, and nothing has panned out …"

Graham's resignation had nothing to do with the Williams' investigation!

Some of the 'Mothers' of the victims expressed surprise and disappointment, as I expected and predicted.

Without looking to the evidence entered in the court during trial or seeking any testing of the evidence including DNA, Graham's glamorous entry ended with a dud with nothing accomplished but a great deal of time wasted – and *mothers devastated.*

AND WHATEVER HAPPENED TO WILLIAMS' SUPPORTER NO. 2: DEKALB COUNTY SHERIFF SIDNEY DORSEY?

To find out, all one has to do is access the Georgia Reports at 279 Ga. 534, Dorsey versus The State (of Georgia). Dorsey can be found in the Georgia State Prison after having been convicted on July 10, 2002, of Malice Murder and related charges for which he was sentenced to life imprisonment plus additional terms for other offenses. His victim in the murder was Derwin Brown, who ran against and defeated Dorsey in a 2000 re-election for Sheriff of DeKalb County. On December 15, 2000, shortly after Brown defeated Dorsey and just before taking office, Brown was gunned down at the front door of his home by accomplices of Dorsey using a Tech 9 millimeter semi-automatic handgun with a homemade silencer.

From an interview by Bill Torpy of the *Atlanta Journal Constitution,* May 29, 2005, at Reidsville State Prison (where Dorsey was serving his sentences), Dorsey (still defending Williams) reportedly said that Williams "was the perfect suspect, the perfect fall guy." Dorsey reportedly compared his own situation to that of Williams: That Williams claimed he was at the bridge trying to find the address of a woman. Dorsey indicated that he also received a similar strange phone call in 2001 at the time he was under investigation for Sheriff-Elect Brown's murder when an insistent woman contacted his (Dorsey's) private business firm and tried to have him meet her at night in Marietta (Cobb County). Dorsey reportedly said: "I didn't go – it was similar to Wayne Williams – they lured him out to Cobb County. But I didn't go."

How interesting! Now, both Dorsey and Williams *reside* in the Georgia State Prison for life – for murder!!!

Motions, Appeals, and the Ku Klux Klan

On June 28, 1982, Wayne B. Williams sent Chief Jailer Brownlee a handwritten, notarized letter (copied to the Prosecution) stating that he was releasing his attorneys of record, Al Binder and Jim Kitchens, and his chief investigator, Durwood Meyers. He also named Lynn H. Whatley to remain as his attorney of record. Decades of appeals would follow.

The First Round

On December 15, 1982, a Motion for New Trial was heard by Judge Cooper. Williams was represented by a team of four lawyers (including local attorney Lynn Whatley and other out-of-state attorneys) who presented their cause for almost five hours. They argued many issues including that the State had *not* proven that Cater and Payne *were in fact murdered.* The defense group had filed a 77-point brief, including claims of 'inadequate representation' by the trial attorneys (which is always a tactic used when everything else fails – you then attack your own attorneys). The State was represented by Joe Drolet who only needed a few minutes to set the record straight.

Judge Cooper had dealt with most of the issues during trial and promptly denied the defense motion for a new trial.

I had left the Atlanta Prosecutors' Office the month before and restarted my career in the adjoining Cobb County Prosecutor's Office as Assistant to District Attorney Thomas Charron, but I kept up with the activities in the Williams' case.

The Second Round

Williams' appealed the ruling by Judge Cooper to the State Supreme Court, which is routine. The State was again represented by Assistant District Attorney Joe Drolet. Ms. Mary Beth Westmoreland from the State Attorney General's Office filed a brief in support of the State. Ms. Westmoreland would continue representation of the State for decades through the State and Federal Courts in follow-up appeals by Williams.

Williams appeal to the Georgia Supreme Court was decided on December 5, 1983, wherein an 81-page decision was issued upholding the verdict of conviction and sentence (251 Ga. 749, 312 SE2d 40 (1983). A petition for rehearing was denied on January 18, 1984.

The Third Round

On November 11, 1985, a 31-page habeas corpus was filed in Butts County (where Williams was housed) signed by counsel:

Lynn Whatley, local counsel; Bobby Lee Cook, nationally known Georgia counsel; William Kunstler, and Ronald L. Kuby, Center for Constitutional Rights, New York; and Alan M. Dershowitz, Cambridge, Massachusetts – all nationally known for their "causes."

Five years later on September 26, 1990, a 184-page Amended Petition for a writ of habeas corpus was filed in Butts County Superior Court signed by the same foregoing attorneys.

Intermittently, the defense group would request the habeas Judge to schedule hearings on their petition and amended petition containing over 200 pages of alleged errors and arguments in the trial of Williams (more than should be itemized in this book). During 12 years of hearings, the defense group would present testimony, depositions, and other evidence before the Judge in an effort to show Williams did not get a fair trial. The defense would continue the hearings for future dates for further evidence to be obtained and presented to the Court – in an ongoing investigation with court hearings at the behest of the defense.

One of the major issues raised in the habeas was that Williams' was denied access to a secret independent investigation of the Ku Klux Klan (KKK) in relation to the Atlanta child murders.

The first time I heard about the secret investigation into Klan activities by the Georgia Bureau of Investigation (GBI) was about 1985 (long after the trial) when it was publicly revealed that pursuant to an open records request, and the pending habeas proceeding, the issue became prominent: There had been a secret investigation by GBI and certain Atlanta officers (but did not involve the Task Force) arising out of the infiltration of the Klan by police through the use of confidential sources. Had we prosecutors known of this independent investigation, we should have, *and would have,* turned the file over to the defense or the Court (as was done with other exculpatory information during the two year investigation). I later spoke to other members of the prosecution team and learned they were likewise in the dark about the KKK probe.[17]

17   It may seem insincere that we prosecutors wouldn't know about the secret investigation. However, in later interviews of GBI officials including Inspector Robbie Hamrick, I learned it was intended that [it] be kept secret to ensure that leaks did not occur. It was kept from trial attorneys and most of the official task force. The head of the GBI at the time, Phil Peters, feared a race riot if the investigation became public. During the height of the investigation, there had

Since the file was not part of the Task Force files and not given to the defense, the habeas Court rightfully heard evidence upon the matter to determine whether such evidence would have been admissible at trial and whether, had the evidence been disclosed to the defense at trial, the result of Williams' trial would have been different. After all, if such information had been known by the defense but held to be inadmissible, the jury would never have seen it. It would have made no difference in the trial of the case – there would be no harm. Evidence must be relevant and legally admissible in a Court of law – rumor, innuendos, hearsay (for the most part), and gossip will not be heard.

Since the defense was not privy to the secret investigation into the Klan activities, and it was being heard for the first time by the habeas judge, I will incorporate the findings by the Court in full beginning on page 41 of the order of the Court, styled –

ENUMERATION VII. ALLEGED BRADY VIOLATION REGARDING POTENTIAL KU KLUX KLAN INVOLVEMENT IN THE MURDERS:

---

been an explosion at a day care center in Atlanta wherein several children were killed which caused great concern of further fueling the tempers of crowds and leading to race riots; the explosion was later proven to have been caused by an accidental boiler explosion.

Petitioner has raised an allegation in the amended petition and has presented evidence regarding a claim that information was withheld from him regarding essentially a potential suspect in this case and a possible connection with the Ku Klux Klan. This Court has heard testimony regarding this particular claim. The testimony, primarily from GBI Agents Joe Jackson and Robert Ingram, showed that in March of 1981, the GBI received information from an Atlanta Police Officer, Aubrey Melton, that he had a confidential informant who advised him that the Ku Klux Klan might be involved in the killing of young black children in Atlanta. (H.T. 561-562). Based on certain information provided, a group of officers from the GBI as well as the Atlanta Police Department engaged in an extensive investigation of these allegations utilizing various investigative techniques including consensual monitoring, wiretaps, visual surveillance, polygraph examinations and interviews. This investigation was separate from the task force set up to investigate the missing and murdered children, and never became a part of that task force, although officials from the GBI and the Atlanta Police Department were aware of the investigation. The investigation was conducted in March and April of 1981.

As a result of that investigation it was determined that there was no evidence which would link any members of the Sanders family or the Ku Klux Klan to the missing and murdered children, and particularly not to any of the individuals with whom Petitioner was charged with killing. In fact, the only victim mentioned during this particular investigation whose case was utilized at trial was that of Lubie Geter. Agent Ingram and Agent Jackson testified that they found absolutely no evidence which would have connected any member of the Sanders family or the Klan with the killing of Lubie Geter or any of the other missing and murdered children. This Court specifically finds that, although there might have been suggestions or suspicions, none of those suspicions proved to be supported by fact or evidence, and

> Petitioner has failed to show any basis upon which he could
> have obtained any admissible evidence had he had access to
> this entire investigation.
>
> The evidence also revealed that dog hairs were obtained
> as well as fiber evidence, and that this evidence did not
> match the evidence in the missing and murdered children
> investigation. (H.T. 408-411). Based upon this investiga-
> tion, the responsible law enforcement officials concluded
> that the investigation should be closed as there was no ev-
> idence linking the individuals in question to the murders.
> This investigation was closed on or about April 24, 1981,
> well prior to the time that the Petitioner became a suspect
> in these cases. The closing of the investigation into pos-
> sible Klan participation in the missing and murdered chil-
> dren cases seems to have nothing to do with the Petitioner
> becoming a suspect in these cases. Petitioner has yet to show
> any evidence that would connect any member of the Sanders
> family or any member of the Klan with any of the murders
> which were utilized at Petitioner's trial, and has not shown
> how this evidence would have been exculpatory and materi-
> al, nor has any evidence been presented to this Court which
> would have been admissible at trial to show that any other
> individuals were responsible for any of the twelve murders
> utilized at trial.
>
> This Court does find that the Petitioner was not provided with
> information about this investigation prior to or during his trial.

Then Agent Robert Ingram, Georgia Bureau of Investigation, now
retired, recently re-affirmed to me that the two-month investigation of
the Klan ended on April 24, 1981 (a month before Williams appeared
on the Jackson Parkway Bridge wherein he became a suspect), and that
the investigation had cleared all of the Sanders family before Williams
appeared on the scene. Ingram maintains that, being a long-time dedicated law officer, he would have loved to have been able to clear the
long series of killings with an arrest – that would have been a feather in
his cap – but in an investigation you sometimes clear a person, as there

had been thousands of other unfounded leads which were investigated without an arrest.

In the Klan probe, Ingram told me they used all investigative techniques, including electronic investigations, wiretaps, physical surveillances, polygraphs, and at times as many as 15 or more undercover officers maintained wiretaps going 24/7 (twenty-four hours, seven days a week). They even used undercover officers in Animal Control Officer 'uniforms' to gain admission to the Sanders' home without blowing their cover to gain access to the Sanders' dog for dog hair for comparison purposes; also, fibers were obtained from the Sanders' automobile. Samples were furnished the crime lab and were eliminated.

During this 12 years of habeas hearings, the Defense subpoenaed the prosecutors in the case to testify in an attempt to show we knew of the Klan investigation, and that Williams did not get a fair trial, i.e. that we knew of certain past histories of some witnesses, discovery issues, and that Williams' trial attorneys were ineffective, etc.

Attorney Bobby Lee Cook called Slaton to the stand and questioned him at length relative to the merits of the defense-raised-issues; Attorney William Kunstler called me and Joe Drolet wherein we likewise were questioned extensively. Other witnesses were called to testify in person; depositions were taken of others and presented to the Court!

Joe Drolet had left the prosecutor's office during the interim but was appointed Special Assistant Attorney General to assist Ms. Westmoreland in representing the State on the habeas appeal.

Finally on July 10, 1998 (13 years after the Petition for Habeas Corpus was filed), the Defense exhausted their efforts and finished with arguments. They failed in their effort. A 60-page order signed by Superior Court Judge Hal Craig, Flint Judicial Circuit, denied the defense petition for a writ of habeas corpus.

The Fourth Round

The order of the habeas judge was appealed to the Georgia Supreme Court where, after a hearing, it was remanded on July 8, 1999, to the lower court for it to address the issue of a waiver of certain claims.

The Fifth Round

Upon further review of the waiver issue on June 9, 2000, the habeas court again denied relief.

The Sixth Round

An out-of-time appeal (filed 187 days after the previous order) was permitted by a majority of the Georgia Supreme Court where the appeal was again denied on December 14, 2001.

The Seventh Round

Williams then turned to the federal courts in 2005-6 to revisit his past state appeals with motions for discovery of information, including juvenile records of a witness during the trial and potential helpful evidence of the involvement of the KKK in any of the killings. A U.S. Magistrate ordered the State to turn over certain items and documents from the files if available. A new attorney from New York was now representing Williams in federal court.

The Eighth Round

Williams filed a federal civil action for habeas corpus relief on constitutional grounds seeking to overturn his murder convictions in the United States District Court for the Northern District of Georgia, Atlanta Division. After painstakingly sifting through all the many claims, the United States District Court Judge in a 251-page order denied Williams' petition for a (federal) writ of habeas corpus on February 8, 2006.

The Ninth Round

After the *Fulton Daily Report* newspaper attempted to get the Superior Court to grant an order for DNA testing on the Williams' evidence, which was denied, Williams' attorneys for the first time filed their own request for testing which was agreed to by District Attorney Paul Howard. The Court granted the request. The lesson to be learned: Be careful of what you ask – you just might get it!!!

The Tenth Round

In an appeal from the ruling in the (federal) District Court to the United States Circuit Court of Appeals for the Eleventh Circuit, Williams' appeal was again denied on November 8, 2007, on procedural grounds.

WILL THIS GO BEYOND A TEN-ROUND MATCH?

Meanwhile – since the Williams' case would not 'go-away' but would arise again every time something happened (such as another motion hearing or appellate decision), the media would again make inquiries. I received calls; others from the Prosecution Team received calls. Some years after the trial, District Attorney Slaton and Prosecutor Gordon Miller passed away; afterwards, Joe Drolet and I received inquiries. I would decline in many instances to respond as I would again be required to relive the case – but we found we were forced to do so since much of the information put forth by Williams' many high-profile attorneys from around the Globe were just plain wrong. We were losing the public relations battle. We found many magazine articles, internet reports, some newspaper articles, and a book and movie which came out shortly after the trial, to be biased, unbalanced, and far from representing the actual evidence in the case.

During this period I was busy in Cobb County since District Attorney Tom Charron and I were prosecuting many major high-profile cases for which it seemed every time we were in the courtroom the media had live cameras. During the 1980s and 1990s Cobb County had a long string of especially heinous and newsworthy trials with unprecedented news coverage of pre-trial proceedings resulting in change of venue for failure to get a local unbiased jury from having watched news of the proceedings before trial.

As a footnote to the Williams' case, I don't think we were ever able to keep live cameras out of the courtroom since that trial. We had to get used to watching our manners, courtroom conduct, and little strange quirks some people have (let your imagination run wild); perhaps the dress code was affected (prosecutors normally wear conservative dark blue suits, white shirt, tie, while some defense attorneys wear loud or mixed colors, even hats, some with pony tails, etc. and known for their 'trademark' appearance).

I noticed two elements not heretofore a problem which was introduced into a trial after the Williams' case by virtue of cameras in the courtroom: More costly jury trials in high profile cases due to the necessity for a change of venue to far places in the State; and [it] being a distraction to participants exposed to a live camera, making them conscious of the ever-watching eye of the camera – hoping you don't smile at the wrong time or thing, unseemly body language, and the definite 'playing to the camera' in isolated cases.

After Jo's death, I remained in the same home with the children; they were comfortable there – in the neighborhood they knew. Both were involved in sports; Jack Jr. played football while Annie Marie was a cheerleader. The year following Jo's death, I was at a football practice. It was a cold day with the wind blowing. Only a few people were in the bleachers. I sat down at the lowest level near the field by myself. I was freezing. Becky Stroud, a mother of one of the players, came down from above and joined me. She shared her coffee thermos and a blanket. It took the chill off. I was comfortable with this. You see, Becky and Jo were friends – our kids and Becky's three boys (Keith, Christopher, and Gregory) were about the same age. I would see Becky at football games; we started having dinner occasionally. You can see where this is going. It was a gradual 'getting used to' relationship. She had become divorced some time in the past, and we both had children in the same school. But as things will happen naturally, we had a great deal in common; we would talk at night – sometimes for hours. It was easy to fall in love with her – which I did, and she with me; but I felt guilty and almost broke it off because I was afraid the kids would be detrimentally affected. Was our love strong enough to make it work? We couldn't think only of ourselves. Were our children OK with it? Gradually, over time, we and our children became closer. We had built our relationship upon a strong belief that it would work if handled correctly. Since by now our children were graduating from High School with the exception of the youngest of each and the following year would graduate those two, we felt the time was right.

We were married in the Roswell United Methodist Church by Pastor Malone Dodson on August 23, 1986. We have now been married over 20 years. Until Becky came along, I never believed I would be provided another wonderful, beautiful person as a soul-mate, but someone was looking out for us. Jack Jr. and Anne Marie are both married, two children each – and live with their families in the same sub-division and near me. Two of Becky's boys live nearby, while the oldest, Keith and his family live in Orlando – they have two children.

Anne Marie, after high-school, showed little interest in College courses until I suggested she look at nursing; she did and instantly became an "A and Bs" student. Today she is an RN at a local major hospital where she has been since she earned her degree. Jack Jr. is a Federal Law Enforcement Agent.

Life is not a 'bed or roses' I have heard; it must mean you have to do things for yourself! Make things work! Push the things aside which don't work, and 'smell the roses.'

Independent Investigation and Testing of Fibers And Hair 25 Years Later

[Revisiting the Fiber Evidence]

A local publication, the *Fulton County Daily Report*, has been proactive in the coverage of the Williams case – as in other precedent setting cases of the State – and has raised their own questions about the strength of the evidence, including fiber and hair evidence in a criminal prosecution. On February 27, 2002, the paper did a "20 Years Later" thorough analysis of the case from interviews of attorneys in the case with a front page by-line **"Biggest Trial in World Not Dimmed by Time"** by Reporter Trisha Renaud.

Twenty-four years after the trial, because the questions about Williams' conviction would not go away, Reporter R. Robin McDonald of the *Fulton County Daily Report* conducted a year-long investigation. With headlines screaming **"The Atlanta Child Murders, WHY DO THEY STILL HAUNT US?"** on June 29, 2006, she re-visited the case through interviews of attorneys, police officials, politicians, and others. It appears many in the African-American community still held lingering doubts about Williams' guilt with some having a distrust of the trace (fiber and hair) evidence.

The day following the foregoing headlines, Reporter McDonald, on June 30, 2006, surprisingly followed with the revelation of an heretofore unheard of extensive independent investigation with the by-line **(Revisiting the evidence) "FIBERLINKS STILL POWERFUL,"** taking a large part of the publication including color photographs and charts of the fibers found on the victims and connected to Williams. One particular fiber, the Wellman 181b nylon carpet fiber was quoted as being "so rare that forensic experts for the Prosecution considered it a 'virtual fingerprint'."

Why did the *Fulton Daily Report* and Reporter McDonald go to such lengths, time, and expense to expose through publication such extensive investigation of a trial held some 25 years before?

I asked McDonald that question recently and she told me in so many words that she became curious about the strength of the evidence in the case after DeKalb Police Chief Louis Graham reopened the DeKalb cases in 2005. She questioned the strength of the fiber and hair evidence since there had been little known about such evidence because cameras had not been allowed in the courtroom during the trial and therefore had not presented publicly through the media the color comparison charts [of known fibers versus questioned fibers] which were admitted during trial; therefore, such evidence was hard for many to accept or understand. Of course, that period was before the CSI and forensics programs of today. Ms. McDonald also wondered if such technology would hold up in court today.

Reporter McDonald began what was to be almost a year-long investigation through numerous public records requests likened to a "scavenger hunt" in finally tracking down the 25-year-old-forensic evidence preserved in a Fulton County Courthouse vault. She sought permission from Judge Doris Downs, Fulton Superior Court, for a visual record and she was permitted to review and take hundreds of photos; she copied over 1,000 pages of trial testimony from prosecution and defense experts.

McDonald then sought the assistance of the National Center for Forensic Science, the American Academy of Forensic Sciences, and the John Jay College of Criminal Justice at City University of New York in identifying the country's top forensic fiber experts. Two experts, neither of whom was involved in the Williams' case, were selected: Max M. Houck and Nicholas Petraco. Houck, a forensic anthropologist, was director of Forensic Science Initiative at West Virginia University and spent seven years as a scientist at the FBI's national crime laboratory trace evidence unit. Petraco had more than 25 years with the New York City Police Department and its crime laboratory and taught forensic science at John Jay College.

The question posed to the experts was: *In light of modern fiber forensic science, was the fiber evidence that led to Williams' conviction valid science, and were the links among Williams and the victims credible?*

After studying the trial evidence for some time, Petraco concluded that the forensic evidence reviewed by the Williams' jury *shows a conclusive connection between Williams and the 12 homicide victims whose slayings were linked to Williams.* Houck described the forensic evidence as both "compelling" and "convincing." Both experts had some skepticism about the "40 million to one" statistical odds that prosecution experts offered at Williams' trial but agreed that the fibers established a clear link between Williams and 12 victims whose deaths prosecutors introduced to the jury. *Petraco validated the methods that prosecution experts used at trial as the same procedures used today.* Houck said "I wouldn't want to come to a conclusion without looking at the actual fibers, but I think the evidence – if all the fibers match – is certainly compelling. It's very strong, very strong evidence." Ms. McDonald told me she was surprised to learn from the independent experts that the same fiber methodology became a standard for use today and the Williams case was a landmark case for [its] use around the country.

Ms. McDonald said she inquired of Chief Louis Graham after he opened the DeKalb cases if he intended seeking DNA testing of the dog hair since animal DNA testing was available whereupon he dismissed such testing as "junk" evidence. *She learned no one had sought DNA testing of the evidence over the years.*

In an effort to pursue every possible lead, including DNA testing of the forensic evidence, Ms. McDonald, for the newspaper in 2006 in conjunction with the Georgia Innocence Project, filed a public records request in the Superior Court seeking testing of the human and animal hair and any blood evidence available. The Court denied the request as the procedure being used (open records request) did not cover independent forensic testing.

[DNA Testing of Hair]

The amazing thing was that Williams and his attorneys had never requested DNA testing, although DNA testing had been in use in Georgia since the Caldwell [18] case in 1990. Since that time, DNA testing has been routine in Georgia and around the country, and is universally accepted within the scientific community as reliable evidence in a criminal trial.

I have often wondered why Williams' defense teams (of which there were many nationally known and local attorneys) had not filed a motion for testing before 2006. Was it because they knew Williams was guilty and therefore had enough confidence in DNA testing that he would be implicated further? Did they advise him, and he decided upon continuing appeals on legal grounds until he could go no further, and then when he had nothing to lose, he would take this approach? Did the *Fulton Daily Report's* action and the refusal of the Federal District Court in Atlanta to give Williams relief, prod Williams to look to this approach – hoping that the evidence was lost after some 24 years in storage?

That's exactly what happened with the blood evidence from Williams' vehicle, which was serologically matched to two of the victims at trial, but years later was apparently lost or discarded by the crime laboratory in a house cleaning. Luckily, the hair evidence was maintained by the Court Reporter and was available for further testing.

Following the failed attempt to obtain DNA testing by the *Fulton Daily Report*, on November 28, 2006, Williams' attorneys did petition the Court to have evidence in the case submitted for DNA testing. The State, by the present District Attorney, Paul Howard, consented and

---

18   Caldwell v. The State, 260 Ga. 278, 393 SE2d 436, decided July 3, 1990, the landmark case in Georgia on admission of DNA in criminal trials of which District Attorney Tom Charron and I prosecuted the case in Cobb County.

agreed to pay for testing of the dog hair to be conducted by a laboratory mutually agreed upon by the Defense and Larry Peterson of the crime laboratory. Williams' attorneys and Peterson selected the University of California at Davis, School of Veterinary Medicine (Veterinary Genetics Laboratory), which is widely recognized as the premier laboratory in animal forensic science. The dog hairs from five of the twelve victims were selected at random to be tested against hair which had been taken from various areas of Williams' dog, Sheba. [It was agreed that only five (5) cases would be randomly selected for testing]. Also, foreign human hair which had been found on victim Baltazar was forwarded, along with a sample of Williams' DNA, to the FBI Laboratory for comparison.

In February 2007 the Court entered the order for the testing with District Attorney Howard concurring. Howard told me he believed that the results of the DNA tests ... will only provide collateral evidence (of his guilt) in the case and will not affect the verdict of Williams, and that he was certain that the jury got it right. Howard had previously consented to the DNA testing. District Attorney Howard, who was an Assistant District Attorney in the office in 1982 when the Williams case was tried, was familiar with the case. He was elected after Slaton retired in 1996.

I had no problem with his decision to concur with testing to be done. I welcomed it!

The report from the California laboratory dated June 22, 2007, by Ms. Elizabeth Wictum, Director of the laboratory, was received with mitochondrial DNA tests having been performed on the following dog hairs removed from five of the victims as compared with hair from Williams' dog, Sheba:

3 animal hairs from Rogers' head;
3 animal hairs from Stephens' pants;
5 animal hairs from Payne's briefs;
5 animal hairs from Cater's head;
3 animal hairs from Baltazar's shirt

Results were as follows:

"*The same mtDNA sequence (haplotype)* was obtained from each of the evidentiary hairs and the reference sample from Sheba. Therefore, Sheba cannot be excluded as the source of those hairs. The

DNA haplotype ... has been observed 12 times in the VGL Forensics database. This gives a frequency estimate of approximately one in 100 dogs."

Thus, the animal hairs removed from the bodies of the five named victims and the hair sample from Williams' dog contained the "same mtDNA sequence (haplotype)." Haplotype is defined as "the combination of several alleles in a gene cluster." *Taber's Cyclopedic Medical Dictionary,* 19th Edition, Davis.

Following the dog hair testing, defense attorneys indicated they were disappointed. They reportedly told Reporter McDonald of the Fulton Daily Report on June 26, 2007, that they were still waiting for "the more important results" of a DNA analysis (from the FBI) of human scalp hairs found on victim Baltazar and that "these results are much more likely to be definitive." One of Williams' attorneys, John R. "Jack" Martin reportedly said that "I admit its bad news for the Defense, but it doesn't end the case. We were very hopeful that this would be the start of reliable DNA evidence showing he's innocent. It's not. So we have to go dig deeper. We are much more hopeful about the human hair testing because ... there's better science ... if it comes back that it's Wayne's hair, that's the end of the story. But today's not the end of the story."

District Attorney Howard announced after years of idle speculation this should drive the final nail in the Wayne Williams' coffin. He added that when we look at the combination of eye-witness testimony, the trace evidence that resulted from a superb police investigation, and now, these dog hairs found on the bodies of victims, there is no doubt that Wayne Williams is unquestionably guilty of these murders.

Now for the *human hair testing* by the FBI laboratory upon which defense counsel put all their remaining hope: Eight (8) human hair fragments from two (2) scalp hairs recovered from the body of Patrick Baltazar were sent to the FBI laboratory for testing against Williams' DNA. The FBI laboratory was selected for the human hair testing as the State laboratory did not do that particular type testing of hair fragments. The FBI laboratory utilized mitochondrial DNA testing procedures and issued a report on July 11, 2007. The results stated that the *human hair fragments from victim Patrick Baltazar were compared to Wayne Williams' DNA and were found to include Wayne Williams with 3.43% of frequency estimates within the African American race. Williams could not be excluded as the contributor of those human hairs found on Baltazar.*

Traditional testing procedures are utilized where nuclear DNA can be found in the hair roots. Where hair shafts with no roots are being tested, laboratories test for mitochondrial DNA which is inherited from a person's mother only. The mother's children, grandchildren, and so forth have the same mitochondria as the mother. While mitochondrial DNA testing is less discriminating than traditional nuclear DNA testing, scientists still agree it is powerful evidence which will identify a person as being *included* or *excluded* as a suspect.

In the Williams' case, mitochondrial DNA testing has consistently *refused to exclude but to the contrary, has in every test by both laboratories included Williams (and his dog) within the small number of both laboratories' databases.*

I can say for sure, if the DNA testing had been available in 1982, it would have been used at trial as it definitely incriminates Williams in those murders.

The Fulton County Daily Report on August 3, 2007, by Reporter McDonald reported that combined with previously released DNA tests of animal hair taken from the bodies of the victims that were compared with hairs from Williams' dog and an independent examination of forensic fiber evidence made last year at the request of the Daily Report, the latest DNA tests strongly suggest that the jury in the Williams case got it right.

The newspaper quoted their expert, Nicholas Petraco, owner of Petraco Forensic Consulting in New York that "*any sane, independently thinking person would ... come up with the same conclusion... Wayne Williams has been given just about every opportunity for it to go the other way. It hasn't gone the other way.*"

All of the attacks upon the State's evidence during trial, and after trial through the independent scientific testing of fibers by the Fulton Daily Report's independent experts, and now the DNA testing by two laboratories have been unable to show that Williams was innocent as he claims. To the contrary it has reinforced the jury's verdict in respect to the fiber evidence and the DNA tests performed on the dog and human hair found on the victims.

How many juries, appeals, hearings before judges, and testing of evidence will it take? How many decades of the criminal justice system will be necessary to dispense justice in this case! And, the sad commentary on the slowness of dispensing justice is that this case is not all that unique in this respect.

The really sad commentary as stated by District Attorney Howard to me recently that, after the DNA testing of the dog hair was reported, he contacted several of the victims' mothers and advised them of the results. Rather than being thrilled to hear the good news, all they wanted to do was 'vent' about how Williams could not have done it. They had been listening to defense counsel and did not want to hear anything to the contrary. Perhaps, they just didn't want to be wrong in their judgment!

As a follow-up, I recently located Dr. Harold (Hal) Deadman (the FBI fiber expert) who retired after 25 years with the FBI in 1996. He is now teaching forensics at George Washington University, lecturing, and writing. I wanted to know if such use of fiber and hair trace evidence has withstood the test of time, scientifically. (I knew from a legal viewpoint it had – and it was being used around the Country and World, as well as being the favorite of CSI enthusiasts). He responded that he "knew of no valid criticisms by anyone" and "there has been no meaningful criticism of the fiber evidence (or for that matter any of the evidence in the Williams' case) that I am aware of." He said: "This case will always be a landmark case for fiber evidence as well as trace evidence in general."

Regarding the DNA testing recently performed of which he was aware, Deadman responded: "The DNA testing is important because if either the dog hair comparisons or the human hair comparisons (with the hairs recovered from Baltazar) that were discussed at the trial were wrong, the mistaken associations would have been discovered by the DNA testing approximately 99 percent of the time. Since the DNA testing didn't exclude Williams' dog or Williams, we can be very confident that mistakes were not made in the microscopical comparisons. The combination of hair microscopy and DNA testing results in a much stronger association than when either procedure is used separately."

PART
TEN

Epilogue

This story cried out to be told! Ever since the trial, there has been a need and desire on my part to set the record straight with *facts* from the trial as portrayed by a nine week trial and the enormity of hearings and appeals. Now that I am in retirement and had the time to do so, I have addressed the issues with law and facts so far as the length and constraints of this book will allow. Sure, as *in any trial* – there will be minor infractions which the Defense will always point out as error and wish for a new trial, but the question is whether they rise to the level of denying Williams a *fair trial. A person is not entitled to a 'perfect trial' – only a 'fair trial' which is all that can be accomplished by humans.*

Let those who continue to exhort others that Williams was railroaded and to give judgments of such opinions through misrepresentations of the law and facts (by falsehoods, half-truths, omissions, and misrepresentations in direct opposition of the evidence at trial) heed the rulings of the courts over the decades since the trial.

Remember, most of the 'stuff' you have read from the internet and cheap publications was from biased sources and *not under oath in a court of law,* but was quoting people without the facts, personal interviews, opinions, innuendos, hearsay, and thus was not subjected to cross-examination or tested by the *legal rules of evidence.*

An example by a (non-lawyer) writer (who assisted Williams' defense team at trial) that Williams was unfairly convicted in Fulton

County of murdering Cater and should have been prosecuted in Cobb County (if at all) because the body was dropped in the river closer to the Cobb County side – thus venue for prosecution in Cobb. Since no issue was ever raised of proper venue by all the defense attorneys over the years or at trial, could it be that the issue was ridiculous?

To even consider such issue under the facts of this case, you would have to assume that I and all the other prosecutors, Judge, and defense attorneys didn't know basic criminal law 101. The simple statutory law of this state does not provide a haven for murderers just because the State *may not* be able to establish the exact place where the murder occurred or where a 'crime scene' is not found. The law, in pertinent part, provides that a homicide will be prosecuted in the county where the cause of death was inflicted *(if known)* . . . or if it cannot be readily determined in what county ... it shall be considered that the cause of death was inflicted in the county in which *the dead body was discovered* (in Fulton County). The law further provides that a crime if committed on water boundaries of two counties ...and it cannot be readily determined in which county the crime was committed, the crime shall be considered as *having been committed in either county.*

The same writer had been interviewed by Task Force officials during the investigation. He later (after trial) wrote that these high ranking officials with decades of experience had bungled his interview. As he put it, he went to the Task Force Office at their request for an interview and where, after waiting in the outer room, they conducted the interview – after which he left without their having given him his *Miranda Rights; and, thus, had he confessed to the killings they could not have used his confession!* **Wrong again!** Miranda rights (warnings) are required for *Custodial Interrogation: Custody + Interrogation.* A non-custodial citizen-interview requires no warnings! Nothing in the writer's circumstances (as written by him) mandated the warnings – there was 'no custody' (not even the functional equivalent) and 'no interrogation' which would trigger the Miranda warnings. The fact that the interview took place at the police station does not change that legal concept. That is not to say that some police and agencies will nevertheless give the warnings (in an overabundance of caution) because they may not be sure of the fine points of law – like the author. But then, the author was constantly critical of the Judge, Jury, Prosecutors, Police, FBI, the Crime Laboratory witnesses, Medical Examiners, Prosecution Experts – and on and on – while at the same time coming to the defense of Williams.

Everything else aside – think of this: *The murders had intensified and increased in the few months before Williams was caught.* Although all the cases were not used at trial, the Task Force investigation established that the last seven (7) bodies on the task force list were recovered from rivers and three (3) on land between March 6, 1981, and May 24, 1981 – *10 bodies in 10 weeks = one body per week. All were linked to Williams by trace evidence and some witnesses.* But, no bodies have been reportedly pulled from the rivers since May 24 when Nathaniel Cater's body was removed from the Chattahoochee River, nor have similar unsolved, dumped bodies been recovered as the others were from land. Does it take a rocket scientist to see, *what I am saying?* –

Date Body Recovered	Victim	Place
03/06/81	Curtis Walker	South River
03/30/81	Timothy Hill	Chattahoochee River
03/31/81	Eddie Duncan	Chattahoochee River
04/09/81	Larry Rogers	Temple Street area
04/12/81	John Porter	Vacant lot, SW Atlanta
04/19/81	Joseph Bell	South River
04/20/81	Michael McIntosh	Chattahoochee River
04/27/81	Jimmy Ray Payne	Chattahoochee River
05/12/81	William Barrett	Winthrop Drive
05/24/81	Nathaniel Cater	Chattahoochee River

Suddenly it stopped as it began; no more bodies were being dumped!
Because of this string of murders and the dumping of bodies in rivers and along roadways, the police finally snagged the killer by setting the trap on the morning hours of May 22, 1981, when no one in the world but Wayne Bertram Williams suddenly appeared out of the mist. The clever, cunning, serial killer who thought he was smarter than police – who thumbed his nose at authorities – was suddenly *unmasked for the world to see*: He was only human!!!

It has now been 28 years and counting, without anyone — from law enforcement, the medical examiners, state crime laboratory, the media, and especially weeping mothers — recounting any specific event or such claim of an unsolved murder victim pulled from the rivers or dumped by the highways (as trash) and fitting the profile and containing such trace evidence as 'hair from Sheba' or those unusual '181b Wellman fibers' or other fibers from Williams' automobiles, home or items therein – nor for that matter any suggestion that the same type killings occur today!

If there had been one such case, we would all have been made aware of such by the ever vigilant media. Sure – as some will say – there are murders on a regular basis in Atlanta, but none of which we observed during the *Task Force days!!!*

 Independently, two separate accounts have Wayne Williams, out of his own mouth, stopped on the bridge dumping *trash*. *Wayne Williams considered these victims to be the dregs of society – yes, 'trash' to be dumped at will – because they dragged down his race.* Now, Williams is where he belongs!

The prosecution of this case and its verdict has stood the test of time. There is no other substitute for determining the guilt or innocence than a jury trial.

I contacted Williams' present attorney, Lynn Whatley, seeking an interview with Williams where he now sits in his lonely steel cell in state prison. His response: He will get back to me!

Wayne: Before you die in prison, why don't you confess your guilt and do something good – set the mothers' free of their anxiety as to whether their son's killer is still loose? Perhaps the confession will come to your aid in the hereafter.

'Mothers' of Atlanta, the City of Atlanta is back to normal to what it was before the silent killer drove unobserved among you. The mysterious slayer who preyed upon your sons has been slowly but methodically unmasked for the world to see!

Let us accept the fact: *Justice was served!!!*

At this writing, Williams is incarcerated at the Hancock State Prison, Sparta, Georgia, for the rest of his life. The law in effect at the time of trial provided for parole consideration after seven years for which

Williams was first reviewed and turned down in 1986. Williams has now been considered and refused parole six times and is currently set for reconsideration in October, 2011. Walt Davis, Director, Clemency Division, State Board of Pardons and Paroles, in citing a change of the law effective in 2006, advises that an offender must serve 30 years prior to being eligible for parole consideration on a life sentence. Once eligible, the Board can grant parole or set a reconsideration date anywhere from one to eight years in the future. The Board looks to all the facts and circumstances in any such consideration. Thus, I anticipate Williams will be a permanent resident of the State penal system – *for his natural life to which he was sentenced!*

Prosecution Team. L-R: Lewis Slaton; Jack Mallard; Joe Drolet; Gordon Miller; Wally Speed – 2/1982

Photo of Prosecutors at table

Acknowledgements

I do recognize that nothing I have done in my personal life or professional career would have been possible except for those persons who gave me life, courage, ability, and foresight to forge my life in the way it revealed itself.

In my personal life, I recognize and acknowledge my late parents and my large family who gave me guidance. I am happy to give credit to my parents who decided I should be one of eight children, four boys and four girls, all of whom I cherish and thank God we are as close as a family can be; they have supported me over the years with their prayers and love.

I likewise am indebted to my own family: My wife Becky of over 20 years has been there for me in support of anything I chose to do, including writing this book. I especially thank my son-in-law, Frank Neubert, for his technical and computer/printer support systems exper- tise in keeping me up and running; likewise, my daughter-in-law, Dawn (Grimm) Mallard, was always there when I needed advice and direction in my writing and technical support, and my step-son, Gregory Stroud, for his assistance with copy support.

In my professional life, I would never have been a successful pros- ecutor without the support of all those elected District Attorneys in Fulton and Cobb Counties between 1965 and 2007 who appointed me to those positions of Trust, as well as the assistance of those associate prosecutors and support personnel. It was always a 'Team Effort.'

More specifically, I acknowledge my team members in the Williams' trial: The (late) District Attorney Lewis R. Slaton, the (late) Gordon Miller, Joe Drolet, and Wally Speed – it was a 'team effort' the magnitude not before seen in such a complex and lengthy, but coordinated trial.

Lastly, there are many fine people who have contributed to this book in one way or another. By naming them, not necessarily in any order, I am acknowledging the time, advice, assistance and verbal support given me during the period it took in writing and publishing this book:

My friend and retired school teacher Billie Anne Burdett, who tirelessly worked on proofing/editing the many errors she found in the first draft; and her husband, Alan Burdett, for the river/bridge drawing.

There are others of whom I sought advice and assistance including:

Fulton County District Attorney Paul Howard and his Deputy, Bettieanne Hart; Cobb District Attorney Pat head, and Investigator Merritt Cowart and Prosecutor Dana Norman of his office; retired Fulton County Prosecutors Tom Jones, Harvey Moskowitz, Wally Speed, and Joe Drolet;

Arline Kerman (attorney and author); Darryl Cohen (Attorney); Lance LoRusso (Attorney); Jaclyn Weldon White (author); Mary Snyder (author); and Ann Rule (author);

Crime Laboratory Scientists Larry Peterson of Atlanta; Harold A. (Hal) Deadman, of the FBI; and law enforcement officers Robbie Hamrick; Bob Ingram; Gene Moss; R. H. (Bob) Buffington; Welcome Harris; and J.J. (Tribble) James;

Dr. Joseph Burton; Dr. Randy Hanzlick and John Cross, Fulton County Medical Examiner's Office; Benjamin Kittle, retired hydrologist, Corps of Engineers; Walt Davis, Georgia State Pardons and Parole Board; Dr. Allen Carter;

Thomas J. Charron, Cobb County Court Administrator (former: Cobb County District Attorney; Director of Education, National Advocacy Center, National District Attorneys Association; and Executive Director, National District Attorneys Association); W. H. Dink NeSmith, Jr., President, Community Newspapers, Inc.; Professor Ronald L. Carlson, University of Georgia School of Law, Fuller E. Callaway Chair of law Emeritus; Dwight J. Davis, Attorney at Law, King & Spalding; Doc Schneider, Attorney at Law, King & Spalding; Hyde Post, former Reporter and Editor, Atlanta Journal-Constitution; James (Jim) Polk, CNN; Mary Galvin, Dean, National College of District Attorneys, National District Attorneys Association.

My thanks go to R. Robin McDonald of the Fulton Daily Report, and the Atlanta Journal-Constitution and their reporters for their contributions.

Photographs used in this book were obtained through the courtesy of the following people: The drawing of the bridge/river intersection was furnished by Alan Burdett; the T-shirt from the Williams' trial was provided by Hyde Post; I provided the prosecution team photograph; and the trial photographs were obtained through the courtesy of Larry Peterson and the Fulton County Superior Court archives.

Disclaimer:
The age of several of the victims may be incorrect due to a conflict between the police files, autopsy reports, and trial testimony.

About The Author

Jack Mallard is a retired Georgia Prosecutor (1967-2007). He received his Law Degree from Woodrow Wilson College of Law. While in the Atlanta District Attorney's office, he took the lead role in constructing and presenting the case against Wayne Bertram Williams in 1982 arising from the Task Force investigation of the *Atlanta Child Murders*, later called *The Case of the Century.* Jack continued his career in the Cobb County prosecutor's office where he was involved in many sensational prosecutions, including the first two DNA prosecutions in the State *(Caldwell; Greenway),* and the *Fred Tokars* and *Lynn Turner* trials. In retirement, Jack lives with his wife, Becky, on Lake Lanier, North of Atlanta.